ORACLE® *Oracle Press*™

Oracle Database 11g PL/SQL Programming Workbook

D1359355

About the Authors

Michael McLaughlin is a professor of Computer Information Technology at Brigham Young University–Idaho. He is also an Oracle ACE. Michael has worked with the Oracle product stack for 20 years as a developer, DBA, and E-Business Suite Applications DBA.

Michael left Oracle as the Senior Upgrade Manager in Release Engineering for the Oracle Applications Division. He worked at Oracle for more than eight years in consulting, support, and development. He is the inventor of the ATOMS transaction architecture (U.S. Patents #7,206,805 and #7,290,056). The patents are assigned to Oracle Corporation.

He is the author of six books on Oracle technology, including *Oracle Database 11g PL/SQL Programming* and *Oracle Database 10g PL/SQL Programming*.

Michael and his wife Lisa have been married for over 20 years and they have nine children. They live in Idaho near Yellowstone National Park.

John Harper lives with his wife of more than 19 years in Northern Utah County, Utah. They have one adopted daughter whom they cherish and thoroughly spoil. He has been working with databases for the past 11 years, specializing in Oracle administration, schema design, PL/SQL, and information quality.

He currently works for the Church of Jesus Christ of Latter-day Saints as the lead and senior information quality engineer. He enjoys working with data warehousing, business intelligence, and database engineers there. His mentors include Michael McLaughlin and Robert Freeman. His wife says that he wants to be like Tom Kyte when he grows up—well, Tom, and Robert, and Mike to mention just a few.

In his spare time, John enjoys martial arts. During his teenage and early adulthood, he learned JuJitsu, Karate, Judo, and Aikido. He loves Aikido and hopes to teach it one day. He would also love to learn Kyudo if he can find any spare time.

About the Technical Editor

Joseph McLaughlin is a student at Brigham Young University-Idaho studying computer information technology and Chinese. He's an avid Objective C programmer on the iPhone. Joseph also devotes a great deal of time to web development standards and methods. He enjoys computers, programming, hiking, biking, and spending time with his family.

ORACLE® *Oracle Press*™

Oracle Database 11g PL/SQL Programming Workbook

Michael McLaughlin
John M. Harper

New York Chicago San Francisco
Lisbon London Madrid Mexico City Milan
New Delhi San Juan Seoul Singapore Sydney Toronto

The McGraw·Hill Companies

Cataloging-in-Publication Data is on file with the Library of Congress

McGraw-Hill books are available at special quantity discounts to use as premiums and sales promotions, or for use in corporate training programs. To contact a representative, please e-mail us at bulksales@mcgraw-hill.com.

Oracle Database 11*g* PL/SQL Programming Workbook

2 3 4 5 6 7 8 9 0   QDB QDB   14 13 12

ISBN   978-0-07-149369-7
MHID   0-07-149369-7

Sponsoring Editor Lisa McClain	**Technical Editor** Joseph McLaughlin	**Composition** Glyph International
Editorial Supervisor Patty Mon	**Copy Editor** Lisa Theobald	**Illustration** Glyph International
Project Manager Ekta Dixit, Glyph International	**Proofreader** Carol Shields	**Art Director, Cover** Jeff Weeks
Acquisitions Coordinator Meghan Riley	**Indexer** Ted Laux	**Cover Designer** Pattie Lee
	Production Supervisor Jean Bodeaux	

To Lisa, my eternal companion, inspiration, wife, and best friend; and to our children, Sarah, Joseph, Elise, Ian, Ariel, Callie, Nathan, Spencer, and Christianne, who supported me like the champions they are throughout the writing process.

—Michael McLaughlin

To my wife and daughter, who exhibited ultimate patience, kindness, and love as I pounded through this project. To my extended family and colleagues, who could practically recite each chapter after reading them so many times.

—John Harper

Contents at a Glance

PART IV
Appendixes

Contents

PART II
PL/SQL Programming

PART III
PL/SQL Advanced Programming

PART IV

Appendixes

Acknowledgments

Mike, John, Joseph, Meghan, Lisa, and all those behind the scenes at McGraw-Hill deserve ultimate credit for the success of this book. It is no small feat to write any book of this caliber, but to do so in three short months is a tribute to the quality of people they are.

Introduction

The purpose of this workbook is to augment Michael McLaughlin's *Oracle 11g PL/SQL Programming* guide. We, in no way, intend to supersede it; however, if you are already familiar with PL/SQL, this book can serve as a quick reference. We've also set up a bulletin board for questions related to Oracle Database 11*g* PL/SQL Programming:

http://plsql11g.net

We'll be looking for a few great people who share our interest to help moderate the bulletin board. If you're interested, use the contact form on Mike's technical blog site to let us know you'd like to volunteer.

We purposefully packed as many realistic examples into this book as we could, with respect to its overall length. In addition, each chapter contains a plethora of best practices and exercises to aid in your learning of PL/SQL. Finally, we strove to keep the tenor of the book casual and easy to understand. We hope that you will have as much fun reading it as we had in its creation.

We outline the book, suggested reading list, how to learn, the lexicon for the book, the conventions adopted in the book, and the ERD models for the book in the following subsections.

Book Outline

Each chapter contains Best Practices throughout the text, and they're also summarized for you at the end of each chapter in the summary. A list of any downloadable code is found immediately before the summary of the chapter. A mastery check, the last item in each summary, contains a series of true/false and multiple choice questions about content in the chapter. You can find the questions, possible answers, solutions, and explanations in Appendix E.

Part I: PL/SQL Fundamentals

- *Chapter 1: Oracle Development Overview* explains the Oracle development architecture and mechanics of connections.

- *Chapter 2: PL/SQL Basics* offers a crash course on the data types, structures, blocks, cursors, and semantics of the language.

- *Chapter 3: Transaction Scope* explains how you manage transactions in an Oracle database.

- *Chapter 4: Error Management* explains how you understand and manage errors in an Oracle database.

Part II: PL/SQL Programming

- *Chapter 5: Functions* explains how you define and use PL/SQL functions.

- *Chapter 6: Procedures* explains how you define and use PL/SQL procedures.

- *Chapter 7: Collections* explains how you define and use SQL and PL/SQL collections in both SQL and PL/SQL contexts.

- *Chapter 8: Packages* explains how you define and use PL/SQL packages.

- *Chapter 9: Triggers* explains how you define and use PL/SQL triggers.

- *Chapter 10: Objects* explains how you define and use objects in PL/SQL. It also shows you how to deploy them as columns in tables.

Part III: PL/SQL Advanced Programming

- *Chapter 11: Dynamic SQL* explains how you use dynamic SQL statements in a real-world application context.

- *Chapter 12: External Files* explains how you use external tables to support OLTP and data warehousing applications.

Part IV: Appendixes

■ *Appendix A: Wrapping PL/SQL* explains how you can wrap PL/SQL-stored programs to protect their logic from prying eyes.

■ *Appendix B: PL/SQL Hierarchical Profiler* explains how the Oracle Database 11*g* hierarchical profiler works and demonstrates how to use it.

■ *Appendix C: PL/Scope* explains how PL/Scope works and provides a quick concept analysis.

■ *Appendix D: PL/SQL Built-in Packages and Types* explains the packages and types provided by Oracle to support your development of database-centric applications.

■ *Appendix E: Mastery Check Answers* provides a restatement of questions from the summary of each chapter with answers and explanations.

Suggested Reading List

Both authors have spent many years in the database industry. They have carefully applied a consistent and frequent learning regime to their daily tasks. They urge you to do the same, as it is crucial to your success as a database professional. Furthermore, they are aware that the following reading list is lengthy; however, even a brief knowledge of the topics and concepts contained therein will make you more suited to make informed database decisions than 90 percent of the so-called experts in the field.

■ Michael McLaughlin, *Oracle Database 11g PL/SQL Programming,* McGraw-Hill/Professional

■ Thomas Kyte, *Effective Oracle by Design,* McGraw-Hill/Professional

■ David Knox, *Effective Oracle Database 10g Security by Design,* McGraw-Hill/Professional

■ Robert Freeman and Arup Nanda, *Oracle Database 11g New Features,* McGraw-Hill/Professional

■ Robert Freeman and Matthew Hart, *Oracle Database 11g RMAN Database,* McGraw-Hill/Professional

- Thomas Kyte, *Expert Oracle Database Architecture: 9*i *and 10*g *Programming Techniques and Solutions*, Apress

- Jonathan Lewis, *Cost-Based Oracle Fundamentals*, Apress

- Richard Strohm, *Oracle Database Concepts 11*g, Oracle Corporation

- Diana Lorentz, *Oracle Database SQL Language Reference 11*g, Oracle Corporation

- Sheila Moore, *Oracle Database PL/SQL Language Reference 11*g, Oracle Corporation

- Dennis Raphaely, *Oracle Database PL/SQL Packages and Types Reference*, Oracle Corporation

- Shelia Moore, *Oracle Database Advanced Application Developer's Guide 11*g, Oracle Corporation

How to Learn

One of life's wonders that continually amazes us is the ability of children to discover, adapt, and learn about the world around them. It does not surprise us that they spend an average of 10 to 12 hours sleeping per night. In addition, two of their greatest attributes are curiosity and the ability to look at life with an open mind. On the topic of learning, Albert Einstein once stated, "The important thing is not to stop questioning. Curiosity has its own reason for existing."

Understanding the various programming methodologies around PL/SQL may be difficult for you, especially if this is your first computer language; however, if you truly believe in yourself and maintain focus and curiosity, there is nothing you cannot learn.

Lexicon

PL/SQL developers have a propensity to typify their objects and variables. Many of them do so because a mentor passed down the practice to them or they learned it through a trusted publication; however, they do not take the time to learn why this practice was created in the first place.

Most PL/SQL typing resembles the *Hungarian* notation introduced by Charles Simonyi, Chief Architect for Microsoft Corporation until 2002. He designed this notation to be language-independent; however, its roots lay in the BCPL language, which was weakly typed. Weakly typed languages do not place strong restrictions on data types and allow for loose, implicit conversion between variables and data structures. For this reason, Simonyi prefixed his objects with symbols representing their data type—*voila*, the origin of typification.

Many industry leaders either snub or praise object typing. For example, Linus Torvalds, founder of the Linux operating system, stated that encoding the data type of a function into the name is "brain damaged (as) the compiler knows types anyway." Contrariwise, Steve McConnell, author of *Code Complete*, stated, "The basic idea of standardizing (naming convention) on terse, precise abbreviations continues to have value."

Whether you choose to type your objects or not, you must develop or adopt coding conventions and stick to them. Following are three of the most important lessons we have learned from years of PL/SQL and database development:

- Code, no matter how simple or hacked-up, can never be considered temporary once you roll it into production.

- What goes around comes around: at some point you will have to maintain the code you write, or you will inherit a nasty bit of code someone else hacked-up.

- Using a clear and standard naming convention saves time and frustration.

For these reasons, we highly suggest an early adoption of lexical and semantic best practices. For example, you can prefix or suffix user-defined objects with characters representing their data type as follows:

```
CREATE TYPE tt_member_id
  AS TABLE OF number INDEX BY binary_integer;
```

Your typification is not intended to help the compiler understand data types; however, its purpose is to communicate to other developers the characteristics of the objects you create. Here's an example:

```
DECLARE
    gd_creation_date        DATE;
    lv_first_name           VARCHAR2(50);
    lv_last_name            VARCHAR2(50);
    . . .
```

Observe that we prefixed each variable with two symbols representing their global or local characteristics and their data type. Contributors at Oracle's wiki (http://wiki.oracle.com) suggest that typification be limited to prefixing. In addition, the prefix must consist of a letter signifying the type of variable as shown in Table 1.

Furthermore, they suggest that the variable data type must follow the g or 1 symbols as dictated in Table 2.

These are merely suggestions, as you are free to develop standards that best match your environment; however, within this book, we adopt these standards to create a consistent look and feel to all of our code blocks.

Scope	Prefix	Example	Comment
Global Private Variable	G	gd_hire_date	d – date
Local Variable	L	lv_first_name	v – varchar
Parameter	i, o, io	pi_employee_id	i – in, o – out, io – in out

TABLE 1.   *Variable Scope Prefix*

Data Type	Prefix	Example	Comment
Boolean	B	`lb_employee_status`	Prefix common variables
Date	D	`ld_hire_date`	
Number	N	`gv_bonus_percentage`	
Varchar2	V	`gv_department`	
Cursor	cur, c	`c_item`	Prefix cursors and records like this
Record	rec, r	`r_employee`	
Type	typ, t	`typ_monthly_sale`	
Associative array	aa	`aa_sales_rank`	Lexicon varies
Varray	va	`va_top_sales_item`	Lexicon varies
Nested table	Nt	`nt_customer_address`	Lexicon varies
Exception	ex, e	`ex_bonus_too_high`	
Table type	Tt	`tt_customer`	Lexicon varies

TABLE 2. *Variable Data Type Prefix*

Additional Conventions

In addition to the conventions listed in Tables 1 and 2, we use the following standards throughout this book to add emphasis and clarity to our text:

Convention	Meaning
Boldface	We use **boldface** type to denote terms that are defined in the glossary or appendixes.
Italic	We use *italic* type to indicate book titles or an emphasis on specific points.
`Monospaced`	All code blocks are `monospaced`.

Convention	Meaning
`UPPERCASE`	We use `UPPERCASE` to denote all elements supplied by the Oracle RDBMS system, including keywords.
`lowercase fixed-width`	We use `lowercase fixed-width` to signify filenames, executable programs, directory names, and user-supplied objects and types.
`lowercase italic fixed-width`	All placeholders for variables are marked as *`lowercase, italic, fixed-width`*.
`[ ]`	Anything enclosed by square brackets is optional.
`{ }`	Curly braces group items.
`|`	A single pipe represents "or" choices.
`. . .`	Ellipses signify continuance or repetition in syntax or semantic code block examples.

Upper and Lowercase

PL/SQL is a case-independent language, unless you specifically set up Oracle to be case-sensitive or explicitly define object names within the `" "` marks. In our careers, we have seen the use of `camelBack`, `all_lower_case`, `crammedupvariablenames`, and `Mixed_Variations`. For clarity, this reference will use the standards outlined in Oracle's wiki—mainly these:

- All keywords and Oracle supplied objects are `UPPERCASE`.

- User-defined variables and objects are `lowercase`.

- There will be no `camelBackScrunchedUpVariablesThatAreDifficultToRead`.

- All words are separated with an underscore (_) symbol.

We also align all long-running code blocks vertically, as follows:

```
SQL> SELECT   contact_id
  2        ,  member_id
  3        ,  first_name
  4        ,  last_name
  5        ,  last_updated_by
  6        ,  last_update_date
  7     FROM  video_store.contact
  8    WHERE  member_id = 1001
  9      AND  contact_type = 1003
 10  /
```

Observe that we right-justify and uppercase the keywords. We place commas on the left-hand side of the columns and all columns and user-defined objects are lowercase. We use SQL-89 in most of our examples, but welcome/encourage your use of SQL-92. Both authors are aware of the benefits of these standards.

SQL Line Numbers

We create all of our sample code with line numbering, as it is listed by default in the SQL*Plus terminal. We do so to draw your attention to specific lines of code. Moreover, we chunk and comment on longer PL/SQL blocks to aid in your comprehension of examples. Bold highlighting is also used in some examples.

Sample Schemas

Within this text, we reference two sample schemas. Our main schema is a representation of a possible video store. We display its conceptual model as shown in Figure 1.

The second schema set we use consists of the Oracle supplied HR and OE schemas, representing the Human Resource and Sales departments of a fictitious computer sales company. We show its entity relationship diagram in Figure 2.

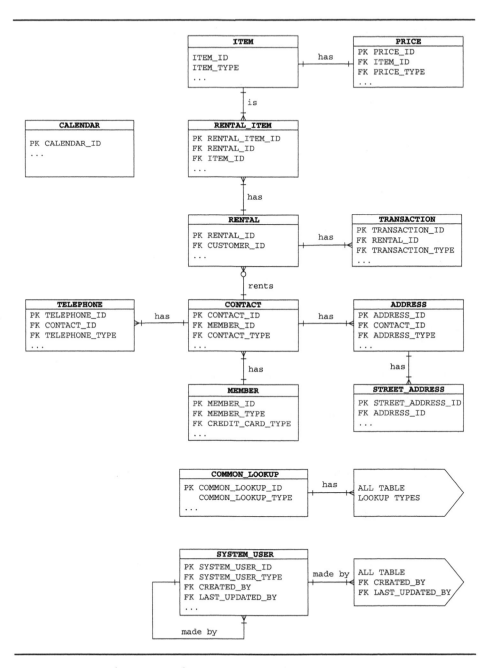

FIGURE 1. *Video store schema*

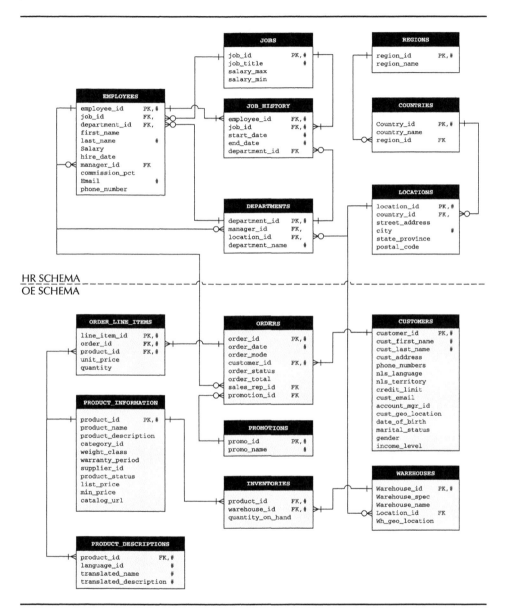

FIGURE 2.   *HR and OE schemas*

PART
I

PL/SQL Fundamentals

CHAPTER
1

Oracle Development
Overview

his chapter introduces you to Oracle PL/SQL development. Because this is a workbook, we want to keep it short and to the point. If you'd like more detail, try reading the companion book, *Oracle Database 11g PL/SQL Programming*.

We'll cover the following in this chapter:

- History and background
- Architecture

Development examples in the book use SQL*Plus because it's the lowest common denominator when it comes to Oracle development. We'd argue that while tools are great, they're also dangerous. Their greatness lies in simplifying tasks and disclosing metadata that might be hidden for months or years without the tool. Their weakness is more subtle. Tools provide opportunities to solve problems when we may not quite understand the problem or solution. Occasionally, the solutions we choose with the tool may be suboptimal or wrong. A solid understanding of Oracle basics lets you use any tool effectively.

History and Background

This is the short version. The idea of relational databases offered a business opportunity, and Larry Ellison saw that opportunity; with a few friends, he formed the Software Development Laboratories (SDL). That company morphed into Relational Software, Inc. (RSI), and subsequently became Oracle Corporation. Oracle then captured the majority of the relational database market.

The concept of a relational database is complex. More or less, the idea of a relational database is to (a) store information about how data is stored or structured, (b) store the data, and (c) access and manage both the structure and data through a common language. SQL, *Structured Query Language,* is that language.

Oracle innovated beyond the limited semantics of SQL and created its dialect. Oracle developers provided an if-then-else semantic through the DECODE statement and hierarchical queries through the CONNECT BY semantic. These concepts set Oracle apart from the competition. ANSI-92 adopted the if-then-else semantic, but implemented it as a case-when-else semantic. Hierarchical queries remain an Oracle dialect standalone.

In the late 1980s, Oracle saw the need for a procedural extension to SQL and created PL/SQL (Procedural Language/Structured Query Language). It was and remains innovative. Perhaps the most important aspect of PL/SQL is that you can call SQL statements from inside it, and you can call PL/SQL from SQL. This feature was maligned for many years by Oracle's competition. People still shy away from PL/SQL to stay *database agnostic*, which is a fancy way to say they want SQL solutions that are easily portable to other platforms. However, major competitors have begun to add stored procedures to their products.

Figure 1-1 shows a timeline that covers the evolution of PL/SQL in the Oracle database. We find it interesting that Oracle has provided 11 major feature upgrades during the 25 year history of the language. You'll note that

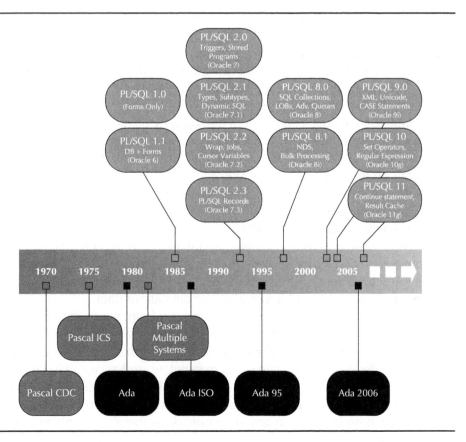

FIGURE 1-1. *PL/SQL language timeline*

Pascal is all but dead and gone, and Ada has only four upgrades in the same space of time. The only other language showing such feature investment is Java.

We conclude from years of experience with the product and other databases, that Oracle made the right call. PL/SQL is an extremely valuable and powerful tool for leveraging the database server. The ability to exploit it is critical to developing dynamic and effective database-centric applications.

Architecture

The architecture of a database has many levels. We'll use a car as an analogy while discussing database architecture. The database administrator (DBA) works with the engine. The database developer sometimes works with the engine and drives the car the rest of the time. In this section, we explain how that happens.

Before we explain how to drive the "Oracle car," we'll give you a quick tour of the factory that produces the car, for two reasons: First, you need to understand some terminology if you're new to the Oracle database. Second, the same SQL that manufactures the database lets you "drive" the database. Likewise, SQL actually runs beneath the wizards that Oracle provides.

An Oracle database is composed of a series of files, processes, and a single database catalog. You create a database by using a tool, such as the Database Configuration Assistant (executable name is dbca in all operating systems). The Database Configuration Assistant is one of the programs that you install on the server tier when you're installing the Oracle product. Collectively, these programs are called a Database Management System (DBMS). The Database Configuration Assistant is a wizard that simplifies how you create an Oracle database.

When you use a wizard to create a database, it creates the necessary files, processes, and database catalog. The catalog is a set of tables that knows everything about the structures and algorithms of the database. You probably have heard it called metadata, or data about data.

Discussing the concept of metadata can overwhelm new users. We don't want to overwhelm you here, but you should know that great power comes with an understanding of metadata! Metadata is nothing more than a bunch of tables that define what you can store, manipulate, and access in a database. An Oracle database is also known as a *database instance*. More or less, the DBMS creates databases like factories create cars. Oracle can create more than one database instance on any server provided there's enough memory and disk space.

The Listener

The Oracle *listener* is a background process that listens for incoming requests to the database. It listens on a single port. The listener routes requests to any database defined in its `listener.ora` configuration file. It knows which database you want based on the network alias you provide. The following shows how you connect to an Oracle Database 11*g* database, assuming you're using the default sample database instance:

```
# sqlplus plsql/plsql@orcl
```

The connection calls the `sqlplus` command line utility with a `PLSQL` user name, `PLSQL` user password (yes, it's trivial), and after the `@` symbol an `orcl` network alias. The network alias maps to a database through the `tnsnames.ora` file, which is part of the client software installed on the server.

The listener configuration file can support multiple databases, unlike MySQL or SQL Server, which require a listener for each database. There's great power in separating the listener from the `oracle` daemon (that's an Oracle service on Windows, and *daemon* is old English for *demon*). Oracle can also link code to one Oracle home and then use a bequeath process to connect to another Oracle home, as is done in the Oracle e-Business Suite.

The easiest analogy for a DBMS would be a word-processing program, such as Word, WordPerfect, or Pages. After installing these programs on your computer, they become factories that let you produce documents. We could probably call them document management systems (DMSs), but they're not quite that capable. They do let you create and manipulate documents. In short, they provide a user interface (UI) that lets you create and edit documents. This is like the steering wheel, accelerator, brakes, and dashboard that let you drive a car.

Oracle also provides a UI, known as SQL*Plus. Oracle actually called its SQL*Plus command line interface the *Advanced Friendly Interface (AFI)*, as still evidenced by the default temporary file buffer, `afiedt.buf`. As experienced users, we can testify that it isn't that advanced by today's standards, nor is it that friendly. At least that's true until you try the command line interfaces of MySQL and SQL Server. After using either, you'd probably conclude as we do that the SQL*Plus UI is both advanced and friendly by comparison.

The command line is the basic UI, but most users adopt tools, such as Quest's Toad (expensive) or Oracle's SQL*Developer (free). They're not that difficult to use once you understand the basics of how connections work, which we cover in this chapter.

The command line is an essential tool when you write production code. Production code must be rerunnable, which means you can run the command when it has already been run before. This means you package a set of related SQL and/or PL/SQL commands into a file, which promotes the file to a script. You run the script file from the command line or from another script that calls scripts. This is why we'll show you how to use the command line in the "Two-Tier Model" section a bit later.

The basic architecture that provides the command line UI also supports graphical user interfaces (GUIs). That architecture is a request and acknowledgment model. You submit a request in the form of a SQL statement or an anonymous PL/SQL block, and you receive a set of data or acknowledgment that your statement or block ran. You may receive a runtime error notification when either fails. You may also receive a "no rows returned" message when no matching data is found by a query. The set of data returned is formally known as an *aggregate table*, a fancy description for a set of records.

There is only one significant difference between the SQL statement and PL/SQL block. An anonymous PL/SQL block doesn't return any data unless you open a door in the SQL*Plus environment. You can do this with the statement

```
SQL> SET SERVEROUTPUT ON SIZE 1000000
```

This opens the buffer door (see Figure 1-2), as seen on the acknowledgment channel from the PL/SQL engine to the SQL*Plus environment. Most GUI tools manage this for you when you run PL/SQL interactively. You need to know how to open that door when you write rerunnable production code, because you may use PL/SQL in the code and may want to output data from PL/SQL to a log file.

Figure 1-2 shows the Oracle processing architecture—or how you operate the car. Notice that all input goes in through the SQL*Plus environment and all results or notifications return through the same environment.

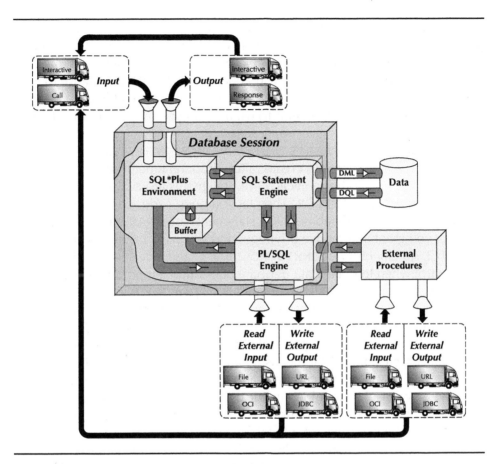

FIGURE 1-2. *Database processing architecture*

The SQL statement engine processes all SQL statements. All means *all*—with no exceptions that we know about. SQL statements fall into categories. SQL statements alone interact with the data, structures, and permissions of databases and control transaction scope. SQL statements are grouped as *Data Definition Language (DDL)*, *Data Manipulation Language (DML)*, *Data Control Language (DCL)*, and *Transaction Control Language (TCL)*. While there are many variations of how you use SQL commands, only 16 basic commands are used—at least you should think of them this way for Oracle certification purposes. An excellent reference on that topic is *OCA Oracle Database 11g: SQL Fundamentals I (Exam 1Z0-051)* by Oracle Press.

Outside of the certification process, a SELECT statement is sometimes placed in a *Data Query Language (DQL)* category. The argument goes that it only queries the data, rather than manipulate it. The problem with the argument, however, is that when you append a FOR UPDATE clause to a SELECT statement, it locks rows in a transactional model, at least in Oracle. That sure seems like manipulation to us, but you've now read both sides of the story.

DDL statements are CREATE, ALTER, DROP, RENAME, TRUNCATE, and COMMENT. They allow you to create, alter, drop, rename, truncate, and comment tables and other objects. DML statements are SELECT, INSERT, UPDATE, DELETE, and MERGE. They let you query, add, change, and remove data from the database. DCL statements are GRANT and REVOKE. They let you grant and revoke privileges and groups of privileges known as *roles*. TCL statements are COMMIT, ROLLBACK, and SAVEPOINT. They let you control when to make data permanent or undo temporary changes.

A SQL statement can call a named PL/SQL program unit, and a PL/SQL block can call a SQL statement. A named PL/SQL program unit is a function or procedure stored in the database catalog. A PL/SQL call to a SQL statement can include only SQL data types and named PL/SQL program units stored in the database catalog. That means it can't call a locally defined function inside a SQL statement. Procedures can't be called inside a SQL statement directly; they must be contained inside a stored function. The reason that you can't call a local function inside a SQL statement is because the SQL engine doesn't have access to a local function.

In the next two sections, we discuss the connection mechanism for Oracle databases. We explain the basics of the *two-tier* computing model and the more complex *three-tier* model. They're essential to your understanding how to use SQL or PL/SQL.

Two-Tier Model

All databases adopt a two-tier model: the engine and the interface. We call these components the *client* and *server*. The client is the interface that lets us issue SQL commands and in Oracle lets you call PL/SQL blocks. The server is the database engine.

A typical installation of the Oracle database installs both the client and server on the database server. That's because the mechanic (or DBA) who maintains the engine uses the same interface to manage many of the parts. Other server-side utilities let the DBA manage part replacement when the server is shut down. This is similar to how you'd replace parts in an engine—you'd shut off the engine before taking it apart to replace something.

Our focus in this workbook is the interface to the running engine. We use the database server copy of the client software when we drive the database from the local server. Sometimes we want to drive the database remotely from a laptop. We have several ways to accomplish that: We can install a copy of the Oracle Client software on a remote machine, or we can use a tool such as SQL*Developer to connect across the network using the Java Database Connectivity (JDBC) or Open Database Connectivity (ODBC) protocols.

We'll cover these communication methods in the following subsections. We begin with a standalone server because it has the fewest parts. The Oracle client separate from the server is next, because it's a natural progression from the standalone server. After laying the groundwork, we'll show you the JDBC and ODBC possibilities in a two-tier model. They come last, because they depend on either the standalone server or a local installation of the Oracle Client software.

Oracle Standalone Communication

The basic communication model requires that a process on the local server acts as the client, and a background process (the Oracle daemon or service) acts as the server. The client process connects to the server process.

You can create a connection like this when you have access to the `sqlplus` executable and a copy of a valid `tnsnames.ora` file. This is true, unless you're the user who installed the Oracle database. That user has special permissions and can connect without going through the Oracle network layer. You find the `sqlplus` executable in the `$ORACLE_HOME/bin` on Linux, Mac OS X, or UNIX. On Windows, you find it in the `%ORACLE_HOME%\bin` directory.

SQL*Plus is an interactive terminal that lets you connect, disconnect, or reconnect to various user accounts. A user account is a database, also known as a *user* or *schema*. Users are therefore scheme, or in some documentation, schemas. Scheme are individual databases in the scope of an Oracle database instance.

As with a terminal shell, you can set environment variables in SQL*Plus. You can see your options by typing the following at a command prompt:

```
SQL> SHOW ALL
```

If you're on the server, you can connect locally without the network. This is important, because occasionally the network layer can get trashed by user configuration errors. A local connection uses an IPC (Internal Process Communication) channel to the Oracle daemon, but you can make that connection only when you're the user who installed the database.

TIP
On Windows, you must be the Administrator account that installed the product, not just a user with Administrator rights, to connect as the local user.

Local connections are there for the privileged user—SYS. However, you can use them to connect to any user when the network is nonoperative or the listener is simply stopped. You connect locally by using the following syntax:

```
# sqlplus system/manager
```

An alternative configuration is available through the Oracle Client component. You access it by leveraging the local `tnsnames.ora` file, or you manually provide the string that a network alias would represent. This type of connection goes through the network layer, which may be as simple as the computer's loopback, or through the DNS server to your local machine. The latter occurs when the `tnsnames.ora` file contains a reference to the hostname or IP address.

TIP
In some networks, outgoing calls are blocked. This means you can connect through the loopback only to a server running on your laptop. You may need to edit your `tnsnames.ora` file manually to make this change.

You connect through the network by using the following syntax:

```
# sqlplus plsql/plsql@orcl
```

Best Practice
Always use network alias and `tnsnames.ora` file resolution of network aliases. Strongly consider setting a `$TNS_ADMIN` or `%TNS_ADMIN%` environment variable to point to your correct `tnsnames.ora` file location.

The connection calls the `sqlplus` command line utility with a `PLSQL` user name, `PLSQL` user password (yes, it's trivial), and after the @ symbol an `orcl` network alias. The network alias maps to a database through the `tnsnames.ora` file, which is part of the client software installed on the server. We recommend that you define the `$TNS_ADMIN` or `%TNS_ADMIN%` environment variable to ensure that you're always pointing to the correct `tnsnames.ora` file. Many developers have chewed up hours trying to figure out why they can't connect because they skipped this step.

The alternative without a `tnsnames.ora` file requires that you provide the complete Oracle Transparent Network Substrate (TNS) string:

```
C:\>sqlplus plsql/plsql@"(DESCRIPTION=(ADDRESS=(PROTOCOL=TCP)(HOST=hostname)
(PORT=1521))(CONNECT_DATA=(SERVER=DEDICATED)(SERVICE_NAME=orcl)))"
```

When you connect to the database with either the network alias or complete string, you form a socket communication between the client and server software. A socket provides state-aware communication, which changes to data during your session and isn't permanent until you commit changes. A failure to commit changes rolls them back. That means they're undone. You'll learn more on the nature of transaction management in Chapter 3.

NOTE
The Oracle TNS resolution can't contain tabs or line returns when you use the TNS string.

You can write the session activity to a relative or local file provided you have the appropriate operating system privileges. A relative file is located in the directory where you call the `sqlplus` program. A local file is written to a fully qualified filename, which means that it includes a directory path from a *logical drive* on Windows or *mount point* on Linux, Mac OS X, or UNIX, and a filename.

You open the file with

```
SQL> SPOOL C:\Data\SomeDirectory\SomeFileName.txt
```

You can run files with the @ symbol before the filename, like this:

```
SQL> @C:\Data\SomeDirectory\SomeScript.sql
```

If you've enabled the SPOOL before the script file runs and the script file enables the SPOOL, the script's log file will cancel your session's log file.

A socket connection is also known as a pessimistic connection because you control the behavior of the server from the client. This type of connection requires a connection that traverses the physical machine's loopback. This means your connection goes from your terminal session to the database daemon via the loopback. As mentioned, it may go through the DNS server when a hostname or IP lookup is required.

This type of communication is like driving your car in the brickyard (Indianapolis Raceway). It's on a predefined track or server.

Oracle Client Communication

The Oracle Client software is a set of libraries that you can install on a Linux, Mac OS X, UNIX, or Windows operating system. Once they're configured, the libraries let you create a socket between your physical (or virtual) machine and a remote server.

The client software lets you create a socket with the server. Sockets between machines typically require software that can exchange messages and maintain a connection. Oracle Client software lets you launch a local client SQL*Plus session. Through the session, you're able to establish a socket with the server and have an interactive session with the database. It provides the same control that you enjoyed from a local connection on the server.

This means you'll need a local copy of the tnsnames.ora file, or the fully qualified string, to connect to the remote database. You can't connect without a network alias in this configuration.

Everything else works exactly as it does in the Oracle standalone communication. The log files, script files, and connection libraries reside on the client, not the server. Client components on the server still mirror those on your client machine. You don't use the remote Oracle Client software; as a result, the Oracle Client software may be a different version than the database version. We'd recommend that you keep the versions as close as possible, and that you use Oracle's certification page for clarity on which ones to deploy in your configuration.

Best Practice
Try to synchronize your Oracle Client software deployment with the Oracle server, and stay in compliance with the certification matrix provided by Oracle Support Services.

Flip back to the "Oracle Standalone Communication" section for connection syntax. As it does in the preceding section, this socket provides state-aware communication. Again, changes to data during your session aren't permanent until you commit them. A failure to commit them rolls the changes back.

This type of communication is like driving your car on designated raceways. It requires preinstallation of software.

JDBC Communication
JDBC changes between releases, so you should ensure that you have the right JDBC files for deployment. JDBC contains a series of class files that let you create a connection with an Oracle database. You need to place those class files inside your class path to make a connection with the database. JDBC connections are two-tier connections, and they're like the prior communication models because they're also pessimistic connections.

You can find the JDBC file in the `$ORACLE_HOME/jdbc/lib` on Linux, Mac OS X, or UNIX. Alternatively, you'll find the executable in the `%ORACLE_HOME%\jdbc\lib` directory on Windows. You generally want to use the version that is consistent with the database. Java 5 and Java 6 are consistent with Oracle 11*g*, but you should use Java 6, which means the `ojdbc6.jar` for Western European solutions or `ojdbc6_g.jar` for globalization solutions. Equivalent files for Java 5 are deployed with Oracle Database 11*g*. You can learn more about configuring the JDBC for Oracle 11*g* in Appendix D of *Oracle Database 11g PL/SQL Programming*.

NOTE
Java's license agreement is something you should read because you must be using a version within one release of the current deployment release.

You put the Oracle JDBC file into your `$CLASSPATH` environment variable on Linux, Mac OS X, or UNIX, like this,

```
# export set CLASSPATH=$ORACLE_HOME/jdbc/lib/ojdbc6.jar:.:$CLASSPATH
```

or into the `%CLASSPATH%` on Windows, like this:

```
C:\> SET CLASSPATH=%ORACLE_HOME%\jdbc\lib\ojdbc6.jar;.;%CLASSPATH%
```

As described in the previous two sections, the JDBC lets you form a socket, which provides state-aware communication. When you make changes through Java, they're not permanent until you commit them. Without a commit, the changes are undone and rolled back. (See Chapter 3.)

This type of communication is like driving on the local roads. You need software to make it work, but it's free, flexible, and easy to deploy.

ODBC Communication

ODBC depends on a shared library that works much like the JDBC library. The library is often language-dependent and always platform-dependent. A Dynamic Link Library (DLL) is required for Windows, and a shared object library is required for Linux, Mac OS X, and UNIX.

The ODBC also forms a socket and all rules that apply about transactions for the previous two-tier methods apply here. You generally must purchase the ODBC driver files. You can build your own from the stubs that Oracle provides, but be warned that it's not that straightforward.

Microsoft Office 2007 ships with an ODBC DLL for the Windows platform, but Microsoft Office 2008 for the Mac OS X platform doesn't ship with a DLL. While we can't make a recommendation (legal risks, and so on), you can find ODBC libraries through Actual Technologies or OpenLink Software that are rumored to work for Mac OS X.

This type of communication is like driving on a toll road. You must have the appropriate software and prepay the fees. However, once you've prepaid you can even do a bit of off-road hot-dogging.

Three-Tier Model

All databases support a three-tier model, because it's really just a middleware solution. The middleware can be a multithreaded JServlet, Apache module, or general software appliance. The middleware generally creates a pool of connections to the Oracle database and shares the connections with requests made by other clients.

Typically in a three-tier model, the client-to-middleware communication doesn't enjoy a state-aware connection. In fact, it's often stateless through the Hypertext Transfer Protocol/Hypertext Transfer Protocol Secure (HTTP/HTTPS) protocols.

This shift in communication semantics means changes are automatic and permanent when they occur. If you submit a data change via an `INSERT`, `UPDATE`, or `DELETE` statement across HTTP/HTTPS and receive acknowledgment of success, that change is permanent. This is known as an optimistic processing model. It alone is a reason for stored procedures that manage transactions across multiple tables in any database.

The exception to an optimistic process occurs when the middleware maintains a lock on the data and manages your transaction scope for you. This type of implementation is done for you by default in Oracle Application Express (APEX), because Oracle APEX maintains a transaction and persistent object state for your activities. The mechanics of how this works would require a chapter of its own. Suffice it to say, this is a possible architecture for your internally developed applications.

Downloadable Code

Because we haven't included any examples in this chapter, there aren't any bundled files.

Summary

This chapter provided a tour of the Oracle development environment for client- and server-side PL/SQL development. You should be positioned to understand, work, and experiment with the examples from the other chapters.

Best Practice Review

■ Always use network alias and `tnsnames.ora` file resolution of network aliases. Strongly consider setting a `$TNS_ADMIN` or `%TNS_ADMIN%` environment variable to point to the correct `tnsnames.ora` file.

■ Try to synchronize your Oracle Client software deployment with the Oracle server, and stay in compliance with the certification matrix provided by Oracle Support Services.

Mastery Check

The mastery check is a series of true or false and multiple choice questions that let you confirm how well you understand the material in the chapter. You may check Appendix E for answers to these questions.

1. ☐ **True** ☐ **False** You use DDL statements to create tables.

2. ☐ **True** ☐ **False** You use DML statements to manipulate data.

3. ☐ **True** ☐ **False** You use DCL statements to grant or revoke privileges.

4. ☐ **True** ☐ **False** You use TCL statements to control timestamps.

5. ☐ **True** ☐ **False** A SELECT statement is a DQL statement, not a DML statement, in all cases.

6. ☐ **True** ☐ **False** The PL/SQL version numbers have always been synchronized with the Oracle Database release numbers.

7. ☐ **True** ☐ **False** You can't connect without a network alias.

8. ☐ **True** ☐ **False** You must have a local copy of a tnsnames.ora file when you use Oracle Client software.

9. ☐ **True** ☐ **False** Oracle, unlike MySQL, includes its listener service as a separate process from its database server-side daemon.

10. ☐ **True** ☐ **False** You can spool individual script files without interfering with a session spool file.

11. Which are valid two-tier communication types?

    A. Oracle standalone communication

    B. Oracle client communication

    C. JDBC communication

    D. All of the above

    E. Only B and C

12. Which of the following is a valid JDBC driver for Oracle 11*g*?

    A. The `ojdbc6_g.jar` file

    B. The `ojdbc6.jar` file

    C. The `ojdbc5.jar` file

    D. All of the above

    E. Only A and B

13. Which of the following does Oracle deploy with each release of the database server?

    A. The Oracle Client software

    B. The JDBC driver files

    C. The ODBC driver files

    D. All of the above

    E. Only A and B

14. Where does the state-aware connection exist in a three-tier model?

    A. Between the JServlet middle-tier and the database

    B. Between the client and the database

    C. Between the Apache server and the database

    D. All of the above

    E. Only B and C

15. Which tier can create pooled connections to share?

    A. The client

    B. The server

    C. The middle-tier

    D. None of the above

    E. Only A and B

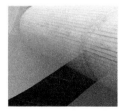

CHAPTER
2

PL/SQL Basics

ou can take many approaches when explaining the basics of any programming language. In the context of a workbook, the briefest is the best. You find more complete treatment in *Oracle Database 11g PL/SQL Programming*. Here we'll focus on the bare bones that you need to code.

You'll learn how to organize your program units, where to put the pieces that make your programs work, what you should and shouldn't do, and what to avoid at all costs. While opinions vary on many aspects of programming, the tips provided here should serve you well, because they've served us well.

You should be able to work through this chapter sequentially or skip to where you need to go for quick insight into a principle, skill, or technique. Here's how this chapter is organized:

- **PL/SQL blocks**   Anonymous and named blocks

- **Variables**   Types, assignments, and operators

- **Control structures**   IF and CASE statements and loops

- **Bulk operations**   Bulk reads and writes to tables

As you read through these sections, you should note that PL/SQL is a *strongly typed* language. Strongly typed languages constrain how you assign or compare values of different data types. PL/SQL borrows its block syntax from the Ada and Pascal programming languages. It's a natural fit with SQL. This is probably why Transact-SQL (T-SQL) and MySQL stored procedures look so much like PL/SQL procedures.

The PL/SQL assignment operator is the := (a colon and equal sign set) and the comparison operator is = (equal sign). This makes parsing SQL statements inside PL/SQL blocks easier. Comparison operators in PL/SQL work like they do in SQL. Oracle's PL/SQL development team has also made sure that other operations are equally straightforward.

PL/SQL Blocks

PL/SQL blocks come in two types: *anonymous*, or unnamed, and *named* blocks. Anonymous block programs have a limited and narrow scope, while named blocks are more extensible and reusable resources.

You can use anonymous block programs in scripts or nested inside other program units. They have scope only in the context of the program unit or script where you put them. You can't call anonymous blocks from other blocks by name, because they haven't got one. All variables are passed to these local blocks by reference, which is the default PL/SQL's scope model. This means an anonymous block program unit can reference any variables in the external or calling scope. The single exception to this rule occurs when you declare a local variable that replaces a calling scope variable.

Since you can't call these program *units*, they don't really have a method access like object-oriented programming languages. They really behave more or less as limited scope lambda functions or subroutine modules.

When you define or declare named block programs, each of the four potential deployment scopes has a distinct behavior and scope.

You can store named block programs directly as functions or procedures in a schema. These functions and procedures are schema-level named programs. Their scope is the most flexible for three reasons: You can call them from the schema where they're defined. Alternatively, you can call them from another schema that's been granted the *execute* privilege on the named program unit. Lastly, you can call schema-level programs across a DB_LINK. DB_LINKs support calls between two database instances across the network. Schema-level named programs present an interesting comparative paradigm because they act as public access methods in the scope of the schema but protected access methods in the scope of the database.

You can store named block programs inside packages in two ways. One way requires that you publish the package function or procedure. You do this by defining the function or procedure specification inside the package specification. This makes them callable from other programs in the same schema or from other programs in scheme where they have the *execute* privilege on the package. These are package functions and procedures. They're closest to static methods with a protected access scope. You can also store functions and procedures exclusively in package bodies. This limits them to internal package access only, and you call these package-level program *units*. They're most like private access methods in object-oriented languages such as Java.

You can store named block programs inside user-defined types (UDTs). Like named block programs inside packages, you can deploy these as published or unpublished methods. You can also make these static or instance methods. Static methods are available without an existing instance, while instance methods require that you first create an instance of the UDT in memory. Static methods act like package functions and procedures, while instance methods act like object type functions and procedures. Chapter 10 covers these types of named block programs.

Finally, you can store named block programs inside the declaration block of anonymous or named block programs. These named block programs are known as *local* named block programs. You can call them only from within the scope of their host program. They can't see other locally named programs unless these other programs are declared before the local programs in the same runtime scope. You can fix this by adopting forward references before declaring local functions. A *forward reference* is a stub for a named block. The stub includes the subroutine name, parameter list, and any return type. Local named blocks are like package-level program units or private access methods in object-oriented languages such as Java. You can find more on this in Chapter 5.

This chapter covers only basics. That means you'll have to wait until Chapter 5 to learn about functions and Chapter 6 to learn about packages. These chapters cover the details about how you develop and deploy named program units.

Prototypes

The basic prototype for an anonymous block PL/SQL program is

```
[DECLARE]
   declaration_statements
BEGIN
   execution_statements
[EXCEPTION]
   exception_handling_statements
END;
/
```

The DECLARE starts the optional declaration block. The BEGIN ends any declaration block and begins the execution block. The optional EXCEPTION may end the execution block. The END ends either the execution or optional exception block.

Best Practice
Always define forward referencing specifications for local named blocks before implementing any of them. This ensures that they can call one another.

Prototypes are great, but they don't show you how to implement the code. You'll now see how to write a simple *Hello World* program in PL/SQL. It'll be an anonymous block program that you can run from a file, the SQL*Plus command line, or SQL*Developer.

NOTE
Tools are great when you understand what they do and dangerous when you don't.

The reality is that most programmers use tools, but sooner or later you'll need to run something from the command line. Since the simplest demonstrations of PL/SQL are from the command line, we've decided to show examples that way throughout the book.

Basic Anonymous Block

Two small details can cause you grief in PL/SQL. The first is that as a strongly blocked language, it requires you to include at least a single statement in each and every block. The second detail is that you'll need to manage output from your PL/SQL programs by enabling a SQL*Plus formatting environment variable SERVEROUTPUT.

For example, the following may look like a complete program, but it isn't. It doesn't have at least one statement in the block to make it work.

```
SQL> BEGIN
  2  END;
  3  /
```

You may wonder why there's a forward slash (/) on the line below the program unit. A forward slash executes the program by sending it to the PL/SQL runtime engine. This program fails with the following error, which basically says it got to the end of the block without finding a single statement:

```
END;
*
ERROR at line 2:
ORA-06550: line 2, column 1:
PLS-00103: Encountered the symbol "END" when expecting one of the following:
begin case declare exit for goto if loop mod null pragma
raise return select update while with <an identifier>
<a double-quoted delimited-identifier> <a bind variable> <<
close current delete fetch lock insert open rollback
savepoint set sql execute commit forall merge pipe
```

The minimal programming unit for an anonymous block includes one statement in the execution block. Conveniently, PL/SQL provides a *null* statement. You can use null statements in blocks to make sure you have basic block control logic correct before you write detailed block logic. Here's the smallest working anonymous block program:

```
SQL> BEGIN
  2    NULL;
  3  END;
  4  /
```

You'll want to remember this, because if you don't, it can cost you many fruitless hours of debugging. The second item was the SQL*Plus environment variable SERVEROUTPUT. You didn't need it when we were testing a basic block because nothing was being output from the program. The *Hello World* program requires you to output a line of text, and that means you must enable SERVEROUTPUT before running your PL/SQL block.

TIP
The effective use of the null statement can help you organize and develop code faster by prototyping your block structure without statements.

If you're in the middle of typing a SQL or PL/SQL statement and fat finger something, you can start over with three keys. Press the ENTER key for a line return, type a period, and then add another line return to abort your active statement. You can find that statement in the afiedt.buf file unless somebody changes the default in the glogin.sql script.

Believe it or not, the filename stands for Advanced Friendly Interface Editor buffer, as mentioned in Chapter 1. If you're laughing, try Microsoft SQL Server 2008's sqlcmd.exe. Afterward, you may realize SQL*Plus is a great tool, albeit imperfect.

Hello World Anonymous Block

The *Hello World* program prints text by calling a stored procedure from a standard package in the Oracle database. The DBMS_OUTPUT.PUT_LINE() call is more or less like echo or print in scripting languages or the

`System.out.println()` static method call in Java. The whole process of running a *Hello World* program looks like this:

```
SQL> SET SERVEROUTPUT ON SIZE 1000000
SQL> BEGIN
  2    dbms_output.put_line('Hello World.');
  3  END;
  4  /
```

It prints this:

```
Hello World.
```

The reserved and keywords in Oracle are case-insensitive. We've chosen to follow the most common use case for capitalization. This should more or less mimic what you'd find in any Generic Syntax Highlighter (GeSHi) editor. String literals in PL/SQL are enclosed by single quotes (apostrophes), as they are in SQL. String literals between the quotes are case-sensitive, and you back-quote a single quote with another single quote.

Quoting Alternative

Beginning with Oracle 10*g* Release 1, the database now lets you replace the familiar single quote with another quoting symbol. This is helpful when you've got a bunch of apostrophes in a string that would individually require back-quoting with another single quote. The old way would be like this:

```
SQL> SELECT 'It''s a bird, no plane, no it can''t be ice cream!' AS phrase
  2  FROM dual;
```

The new way is like this:

```
SQL> SELECT q'(It's a bird, no plane, no it can't be ice cream!)' AS phrase
  2  FROM dual;
```

Both of these produce the following output:

```
PHRASE
-------------------------------------------------
It's a bird, no plane, no it can't be ice cream!
```

This section demonstrates how to handle output, but that's it. The *Hello Somebody* program shows you how to handle both input and output from an anonymous program.

Hello Somebody Anonymous Block

The *Hello Somebody* program prints text by calling the same stored procedure from the *Hello World* program. This section focuses on how input parameters work in PL/SQL anonymous block program units. Input parameters are unknowns before they arrive at any program. This is not a trivial observation but a crucial fact.

You need to plan for both good and bad input parameters. This can be tricky, because a declaration block acts like a header file does in a C or C++ program. Your exception block can't capture runtime errors in the declaration block. The program simply fails with an unhandled exception. You'll learn how to avoid this forever in this section. The trick revolves around your understanding what it means to *define* a variable verses *declare* a variable.

You define a variable by assigning it a name and data type. You declare a variable by defining it and assigning it a value. In some programming languages, assignment is called *initialization*. The rule of thumb on whether you call it one or the other depends on the data type. You typically assign values to scalar variables. Scalar variables hold the value of only one thing and are primitives in Java. On the other hand, you initialize object types. The key object types in Oracle are collections and user-defined object types. Object types are also known as *composite* data types because they can contain multiple things. You'll find more on initializing these composite data types the "Composite Variable Types" section later in this chapter. Chapters 7 and 10 also cover composite variables.

You assign input parameters to anonymous block programs by using substitution variables. SQL*Plus supports the use of substitution variables in the interactive and batch console, which are prefaced by an ampersand (&). Substitution variables are variable-length strings or numbers. You should never assign dynamic values in the declaration block.

The following program defines a variable, assigns it a value, and prints it:

```
SQL> DECLARE
  2    lv_whom VARCHAR2(30);
  3  BEGIN
  4    lv_whom := '&input';
  5    dbms_output.put_line('Hello '|| lv_whom ||'.');
  6  END;
  7  /
```

The Assignment Model and Language

All programming languages assign values to variables. They typically assign a value to the right of the variable. This pattern assigns the right operand to the left operand. You implement it in PL/SQL as follows:

```
left_operand := right_operand;
```

The left operand must always be a variable. The right operand can be a value, variable, or function. Functions must return a variable value when they're right operands and are often called *expressions*. This makes functions return values synonymous with expressions.

The trick here is that only functions returning a SQL data type can be called in SQL statements. Functions returning PL/SQL data types work only inside PL/SQL blocks, and then only in PL/SQL scope.

You might not notice the single quotes around the substitution variable, but they're critical. When the program is run without a valid string value and no quotes, the engine parses over the null value and excludes the right operand in an assignment. The program would throw a PLS-00103 exception because there is no right operand, whereas the engine interprets two single quotes without anything between them as a null string.

It's important to notice there's no example with the assignment being made in the declaration block. That would be *bad* coding practice. By extension, you should avoid assigning actual parameters to local variables in their declaration block. Otherwise, your code may fail at runtime because formal parameters have no size constraints in PL/SQL.

While constants aren't really too useful in anonymous block programs, this is a great place to show you the syntax. The CONSTANT reserved word is placed in between the variable name and the data type. You must declare a constant in your declaration block, which means it is both defined and assigned an *immutable* value.

Best Practice

Always make assignments or initializations in the execution block unless the local variable is a constant or treated as a constant. This eliminates many runtime assignment errors.

The preceding anonymous block is recycled to include a constant on line 2 as follows:

```
SQL> DECLARE
  2    lv_hello CONSTANT VARCHAR2(5) := 'Hello';
  3    lv_whom VARCHAR2(30);
  4  BEGIN
  5    lv_whom := '&input';
  6    dbms_output.put_line(lv_hello ||' '|| lv_whom ||'.');
  7  END;
  8  /
```

An alternative method for processing interactive session-level variables involves what Oracle calls *bind* variables. You preface *bind* variables with a colon (:). You can define bind variables in the scope of a SQL*Plus session. In that scope, only the CHAR, CLOB, NCHAR, NCLOB, NUMBER, NVARCHAR2, REFCURSOR, and VARCHAR2 data types are available. The term "bind variable" also applies to the handling of placeholders in Native Dynamic SQL (NDS) and for read/write hooks into the database Private Global Area (PGA). You also use read/write hooks to manage large objects (LOBs) and read hooks to read reference cursors.

You can create SQL*Plus session variables by using the VARIABLE keyword. Like the example with substitution variables, you should never assign values to bind variables in the declaration block.

Reserved and Keywords

You can't really find a perfect source for reserved and keywords. A careful review of the documentation in Oracle Database 11*g* sources reveals it is imperfect. You can type the following at a SQL*Plus prompt for a fairly accurate list of PL/SQL reserved words:

```
SQL> HELP RESERVED WORDS (PL/SQL)
```

There's no equivalent help command for key words. You can query the V$RESERVED_WORDS view, which appears out-of-date for a partial list. If you leave the parenthetical (PL/SQL) off the `help` command, SQL*Plus will return both SQL and PL/SQL reserved words. Perhaps we'll get clarity on these in a subsequent release of the database.

The following program defines a session-level bind variable. The colon doesn't precede the definition of the variable in the session. You use the colon only inside the PL/SQL program scope. This allows the PL/SQL runtime engine to reach out and access the variable in the SQL*Plus session scope. You use a PL/SQL block to assign a value to the bind variable. Then, you can access the bind variable from any subsequent program for the duration of the connect session.

```
SQL> VARIABLE bv VARCHAR2(30)
SQL> BEGIN
  2    :bv := 'Sam';
  3  END;
  4  /
```

After assigning a value to the session-level bind variable, you can use it as a right operand:

```
SQL> DECLARE
  2    lv_whom VARCHAR2(30);
  3  BEGIN
  4    lv_whom := :bv;
  5    dbms_output.put_line('Hello '|| lv_whom ||'.');
  6  END;
  7  /
```

This prints

```
Hello Sam.
```

You could put any of these anonymous block programs in a file and run them from the SQL*Plus command line. SQL*Plus is both an interactive and batch programming environment. As shown with bind variables, SQL*Plus supports session variables that let you manage and control programs. You run programs interactively from the file system by using the following syntax:

```
SQL> @hello_world.sql
```

This example assumes that you find the script in the relative directory, which is the directory where you started SQL*Plus. You would use the following syntax to run a program from an absolute (canonical) directory in a Windows operating system. The logical drive, C:\, would be replaced by a mount point in Linux or UNIX.

```
SQL> @C:\some_directory_path\hello_world.sql
```

While you now know how to work with anonymous block programs, you should also know that there is a downside to using them. They must be run from the command line or inside other program units. Stored programs provide the same functionality, but you can deploy them into and reuse them from the database.

Hello Somebody Named Block

As with the *Hello Somebody* anonymous block, this program takes an input and produces a result. This section shows you how such a program would work with a procedure and function.

Procedure Blocks

The procedure mimics the anonymous block by printing the result to the console. The subsequent function returns the value and lets the calling program print the result.

A procedure runs inside the scope of another program and performs a task. More often than not, developers call procedures to perform tasks inside an existing transaction scope. Such procedures receive a copy of a variable's value and perform a task, such as inserting or updating a table.

This example procedure simply takes the actual parameter and prints a hello message:

```
SQL> CREATE OR REPLACE PROCEDURE hello_procedure
  2  ( pv_whom VARCHAR2 ) IS
  3  BEGIN
  4    dbms_output.put_line('Hello '||pv_whom||'.');
  5  END;
  6  /
```

You would execute the procedure like this:

```
SQL> EXECUTE hello_procedure('Sam');
```

An equivalent to the EXECUTE command would be enclosing the call in the execution block of an anonymous block, like this:

```
SQL> BEGIN
  2    hello_procedure('Sam');
  3  END;
  4  /
```

Function Blocks

A function runs as an autonomous unit of code. You can call stored functions from inside SQL statements and queries, use them to return a variable value, or perform a task and return a variable value. A number of rules govern when and where you can use functions, and those are qualified in Chapter 5.

The sample function takes an actual parameter and returns a hello message string:

```
CREATE OR REPLACE FUNCTION hello_function
( pv_whom VARCHAR2 ) RETURN VARCHAR2 IS
BEGIN
  RETURN 'Hello '||pv_whom||'.';
END;
/
```

You can't execute a function like you do a procedure, because the EXECUTE command doesn't allow you to manage the return value from the function. At the SQL> prompt, you must use the CALL command to put the value into a session-level *bind* variable.

This demonstrates defining a session level bind variable and calling a function into the bind variable:

```
SQL> VARIABLE result VARCHAR2(20)
SQL> CALL hello_function('Samantha') INTO :result;
```

You can then print the contents of the local variable or return it from a query against the pseudo DUAL table:

```
SQL> PRINT :result
```

The lack of a semicolon or forward slash isn't a typo. Neither is required because the PRINT command is a SQL*Plus command. The slash or semicolon dispatches a SQL statement or a PL/SQL block to their respective engine.

The following queries the bind variable:

```
SQL> SELECT :result FROM dual;
```

As a rule, named blocks are stored in programs because they're more reusable there. Occasionally, you'll find named blocks in complex script files that perform maintenance tasks. You can find out more about functions in Chapter 5, procedures in Chapter 6, and UDT objects in Chapter 10.

Nested Blocks

You can also nest named blocks inside other named blocks or anonymous blocks. The problem with nested named blocks, however, is they're not published blocks. This means that one may call another before the one being called is defined. This type of design problem is known as a *scope error*. The scope of the called program is unknown until after the call is made. It raises a PLS-00313 exception and results in a compile-time error.

```
SQL> DECLARE
  2    PROCEDURE a IS
  3    BEGIN
  4      dbms_output.put_line(b||' World!');
  5    END a;
  6    FUNCTION b RETURN VARCHAR2 IS
  7    BEGIN
  8      RETURN 'Hello';
  9    END b;
 10  BEGIN
 11    a;
 12  END;
 13  /
```

Lines 2 through 5 define a local procedure a. Inside procedure a is a call on line 4 to the function b. The function isn't defined at this point in the anonymous block, and it raises an out-of-scope error:

```
    dbms_output.put_line(b||' World!');
                         *
ERROR at line 4:
ORA-06550: line 4, column 26:
PLS-00313: 'B' not declared in this scope
ORA-06550: line 4, column 5:
PL/SQL: Statement ignored
```

This is a compile-time error because all anonymous block programs are parsed before they're executed. Parsing is a compile-time process. Parsing recognizes identifiers, which are reserved words, predefined identifiers, quoted identifiers, user-defined variables, subroutines, or UDTs. Named blocks are identifiers. Function b isn't recognized as an identifier because PL/SQL reads identifiers into memory from top to bottom. This is a single-pass parsing process. Under a single-pass parser, function b isn't defined before it's called in procedure a.

We can fix this by using *forward references*. A forward reference to a function or procedure requires only the signature of the function or procedure rather than their signature and implementation. These are equivalent to the concept of an *interface* in Java. These prototypes are stubs in PL/SQL. The stub lets the compilation accept the identifier name of a named block before you implement the block.

The following provides forward references for all local functions and procedures. We recommend that you always provide these stubs in your programs when you implement local scope named blocks.

```
SQL> DECLARE
  2      PROCEDURE a;
  3      FUNCTION b RETURN VARCHAR2;
  4      PROCEDURE a IS
  5      BEGIN
  6        dbms_output.put_line(b||' World!');
  7      END a;
  8      FUNCTION b RETURN VARCHAR2 IS
  9      BEGIN
 10        RETURN 'Hello';
 11      END b;
 12  BEGIN
 13    a;
 14  END;
 15  /
```

Lines 2 and 3 provide the stubs to procedure a and function b. This program passes the compile time validation because it's able to resolve all symbols from the top to bottom of the anonymous block. Nested blocks are very useful, but you need to use them correctly.

Variables: Types, Assignments, and Operators

PL/SQL supports many more types than Oracle's SQL dialect supports. These variables can be classified into two main groups: scalar and composite.

A scalar variable contains one and only one thing. In Java, primitives are scalar variables. Characters, integers, and various number data types are scalar variables in most programming languages. Strings are also scalar variables in the context of relational databases.

A composite variable contains more than one scalar or other composite variables in some type of data structure. Structures can be arrays, reference cursors, and user defined types such as arrays, records, or objects.

Some data types are unconstrained but others are constrained. Constrained data types derive specialized behavior from their generalized or unconstrained data type. For example, a user-defined data type of positive integers is a specialization of an integer data type. An unconstrained data type doesn't place artificial limits on the range of a data type.

You'll find a list of scalar variables in Figure 2-1. The illustration groups data types by their four major categories: Boolean, character, dates/ timestamps, and numbers. You can use generic numbers for most business purposes, but you must use the IEE-754 numeric data types for engineering computations.

The chart in Figure 2-1 includes LOBs, but you have three types of LOBs in an Oracle database: Binary Large Object (BLOB), Character Large Object (CLOB), and Binary File (BFILE). The CLOB and BLOB are stored inside the database, while only a reference to the external the BFILE resides in the database.

The following programs demonstrate the assignment of string or numeric literal values to four base data types. Date, timestamp, or interval data types use the TO_CHAR or CAST built-in functions to convert string literal values into valid dates or timestamps. Likewise, you'll need to convert them back to strings to print them with the PRINT_LINE procedure of the DBMS_OUTPUT package. After we show you how to work with the base data types, we'll show you how to work with composite data types.

PL/SQL lets you explicitly or implicitly define data types. Implicit definitions rely on anchoring them to a table or column definition. You anchor data types to catalog objects with pseudo columns or a table. A %TYPE is a pseudo column that lets you anchor a data type to the definition of a column in a table. Alternatively, a %ROWTYPE lets you anchor a record type to the definition of a table or view in the database catalog.

Text Data Types

As you noticed in Figure 2-1, several text data types exist. You probably use variable length strings more frequently than the others because they meet most needs. You can put 4000-byte text into the VARCHAR, VARCHAR2, and NVARCHAR2 data types in SQL, but you can put 32,767 bytes in the same data types PL/SQL. That's typically enough space for most text entries. You should put larger text entries in the CLOB data type.

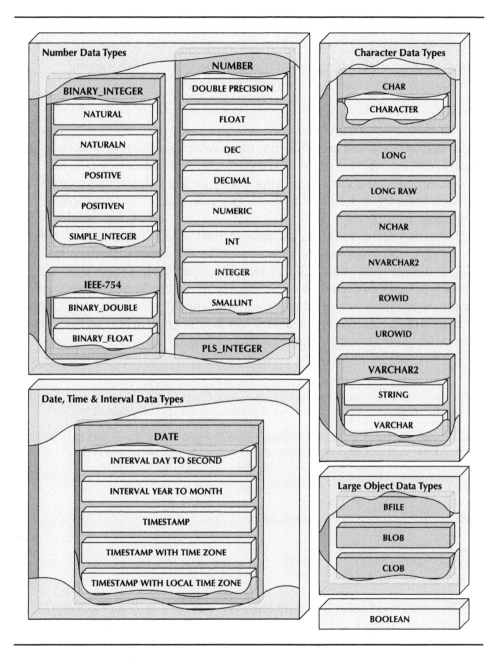

FIGURE 2-1. *Scalar types*

Best Practice

Always use variable-length data types unless there's a compelling business reason to use fixed-length data types.

You have an alternative to variable length data types: the CHAR, NCHAR, and CHARACTER data types. You use them when you want to allocate a fixed-size string. In most cases, you forfeit space for little if any tangible benefit. A perfect use case for a CHAR data type is a column that contains the two-character codes for U.S. states, because it won't allocate space unnecessarily.

You assign literal values to variable or fixed-length data types the same way. In fact, you make assignments to a CLOB the same way when the string could really fit in an ordinary text data type. Those longer than 32,767 bytes are covered in Chapter 8 of *Oracle Database 11g PL/SQL Programming* because they involve external programming languages or the DBMS_LOB package. This sample program shows you the assignment and subsequent space allocation for both variable and fixed-length data types:

```
SQL> DECLARE
  2    lv_fixed     CHAR(40)    := 'Something not quite long.';
  3    lv_variable  VARCHAR(40) := 'Something not quite long.';
  4    lv_clob      CLOB        := 'Something not quite long.';
  5  BEGIN
  6    dbms_output.put_line('Fixed Length   ['||LENGTH(lv_fixed)||']');
  7    dbms_output.put_line('Varying Length ['||LENGTH(lv_variable)||']');
  8    dbms_output.put_line('CLOB Length    ['||LENGTH(lv_clob)||']');
  9  END;
 10  /
```

It prints the space allocation sizes:

```
Fixed Length   [40]
Varying Length [25]
CLOB Length    [25]
```

The LONG and LONG RAW data types are provided *only for backward compatibility.* You should not use them. CLOB data types are the replacements for the *soon to be deprecated* LONG and LONG RAW data types. You can read more about CLOB, BLOB, and BFILE data types in Chapter 8 in *Oracle Database 11g PL/SQL Programming.* The ROWID is provided only for backward compatibility, and its replacement is the *universal row ID*—UROWID. You'll generally touch these only during DBA work, and you generally rely on their implicit conversion to variable-length strings.

Date and Timestamp Types

Dates are always complex in programming languages. The DATE data type is the base type for dates, times, and intervals. Two subtypes are used to manage intervals and three to manage timestamps. The following three subsections show you how to use these date types.

Dates

Two string literal assignments support implicit casting to DATE data types. They are a two-digit day, three-character month, two-digit year; and a two-digit day, three-character month, four-digit year. Any other string literal requires an overriding format mask with the TO_DATE built-in SQL function.

The next program shows you how to assign variables with implicit and explicit casting from conforming and nonconforming strings. Nonconforming strings rely on formatting masks, which you can find in Chapter 5 of the *Oracle Database SQL Language Reference 11*g.

```
SQL> DECLARE
  2    lv_date_1  DATE  := '28-APR-75';
  3    lv_date_2  DATE  := '29-APR-1975';
  4    lv_date_3  DATE  := TO_DATE('19750430','YYYYMMDD');
  5  BEGIN
  6    dbms_output.put_line('Implicit ['||lv_date_1||']');
  7    dbms_output.put_line('Implicit ['||lv_date_2||']');
  8    dbms_output.put_line('Explicit ['||lv_date_3||']');
  9  END;
 10  /
```

It prints the following:

```
Implicit [28-APR-75]
Implicit [29-APR-75]
Explicit [30-APR-75]
```

When you want to see the four-digit year, you use the TO_CHAR built-in function with the appropriate format mask. Dates work differently in Oracle than they do in Microsoft SQL Server and MySQL. You can add a day by simply adding an integer to a date variable, like this:

```
SQL> DECLARE
  2    lv_date   DATE   := '12-MAY-1975';
  3  BEGIN
  4    lv_date := lv_date + 3;
  5    dbms_output.put_line('Date ['||lv_date||']');
  6  END;
  7  /
```

This prints a date three days after the original date:

```
15-May-75
```

You can also work with parts of a day, because dates are really scalar numbers. The integer value sets the date and any fractional value sets the hours, minutes, and seconds. You use the TRUNC built-in function to round down a date to the base date or integer value. This is important when you want to perform interval calculations about the number of elapsed days.

```
SQL> DECLARE
  2    lv_date_1   DATE   := SYSDATE;
  3    lv_date_2   DATE   := lv_date_1;
  4  BEGIN
  5    dbms_output.put_line(TO_CHAR(lv_date_1,'DD-MON-YY HH24:MI:SS'));
  6    dbms_output.put_line(TO_CHAR(TRUNC(lv_date_2),'DD-MON-YY HH24:MI:SS'));
  7  END;
  8  /
```

It prints this:

```
30-APR-09 00:04:13
30-APR-09 00:00:00
```

As you can see from the results, the TRUNC built-in function reduces the scalar date to a whole integer. With the TRUNC command, you are able to calculate the number of days between two dates.

Intervals

The interval subtypes let you represent the interval of a day to seconds, or the interval of a year to months. You can use it, more or less, to capture the interval between dates or timestamps. These are ANSI SQL-1999 specification–compliant data types.

You should know about a quirk regarding intervals: The default values for an INTERVAL DAY TO SECOND data type work when you subtract one DATE from another, provided that you convert them to a TIMESTAMP before the subtraction. That's because the TO_TIMESTAMP function preserves the precision of the DATE, which is less than the TIMESTAMP.

The following program shows that behavior:

```
SQL> DECLARE
  2    lv_interval  INTERVAL DAY TO SECOND;
  3    lv_end_day   DATE := SYSDATE;
  4    lv_start_day DATE := '28-APR-2009';
  5  BEGIN
  6    lv_interval := TO_TIMESTAMP(lv_end_day) - TO_TIMESTAMP(lv_start_day);
  7    dbms_output.put_line(lv_interval);
  8  END;
  9  /
```

The following result prints:

```
+02 20:54:56.000000
```

This works because a DATE data type supports the default precision of *2* for days and *6* for seconds. It would fail with an ORA-01873 when you change the data types to a TIMESTAMP, because a TIMESTAMP requires that you use a precision of *9* for days. The next program shows you the higher precision activity:

```
SQL> DECLARE
  2    lv_interval  INTERVAL DAY(9) TO SECOND;
  3    lv_end_day   TIMESTAMP := SYSTIMESTAMP;
  4    lv_start_day TIMESTAMP := '28-APR-2009';
  5  BEGIN
  6    lv_interval := lv_end_day - lv_start_day;
  7    dbms_output.put_line(lv_interval);
  8  END;
  9  /
```

It prints the interval as a positive number.

```
+000004015 11:54:23.772000
```

The INTERVAL YEAR TO MONTH data type works differently, and the process to obtain the value turns out to be complex. That's probably why it isn't widely used. This example shows you how to use it, because it isn't transparent from the documentation:

```
SQL> DECLARE
  2    lv_interval   INTERVAL YEAR TO MONTH;
  3    lv_end_day    DATE := '30-APR-2009';
  4    lv_start_day DATE := '30-JAN-1976';
  5  BEGIN
  6    lv_interval := TO_CHAR(EXTRACT(YEAR FROM lv_end_day) -
  7                           EXTRACT(YEAR FROM lv_start_day)) ||'-'||
  8                 TO_CHAR(EXTRACT(MONTH FROM lv_end_day) -
  9                         EXTRACT(MONTH FROM lv_start_day)));
 10    dbms_output.put_line(lv_interval);
 11  END;
 12  /
```

The two dates are subtracted by extracting the years and then the months on lines 6 through 9. The TO_CHAR converts the numbers to strings to avoid an ORA-06512 exception, which is a character-to-number conversion error. The concatenation within the expression suppresses implicit casting of the number to a string. The last step implicitly casts a string to an interval through an assignment.

Timestamps

Timestamps, like intervals, are ANSI SQL-1999 components. They offer more precision than the older DATE data type, and Oracle has done a great job of providing built-in functions that move between the two data types. The TIMESTAMP types can be generic or linked to local time zones.

The following demonstrates the difference in precision between the data types. It uses SYSTIMESTAMP as opposed to SYSDATE. The SYSTIMESTAMP captures a more precise time measurement.

```
SQL> DECLARE
  2    lv_date      DATE      := SYSTIMESTAMP;
  3    lv_timestamp TIMESTAMP := SYSTIMESTAMP;
  4  BEGIN
  5    dbms_output.put_line(TO_CHAR(lv_date,'DD-MON-YY H24:MI:SS'));
  6    dbms_output.put_line(lv_timestamp);
  7  END;
  8  /
```

The `TIMESTAMP` provides fractions of seconds beyond hundredths of seconds:

```
30-APR-09 23:15:16
30-APR-09 11.15.16.731000 PM
```

You should use the `TIMESTAMP` data type when you're working with finer grained timing events. That said, many traditional uses of the `DATE` should probably continue to be used.

Number Types

Numbers are straightforward in PL/SQL. You assign integer and complex numbers the same way to all but the new IEEE 754-format data type.

The basic number data type is `NUMBER`. You can define a variable as an unconstrained or constrained `NUMBER` data type by qualifying the precision or scale. Precision constraints prevent the assignment of larger precision numbers to target variables. Scale limitations shave off part of the decimal value, but allow assignment with a loss of value.

The following demonstrates what happens when you assign a larger precision `NUMBER` data type value to a variable with a smaller precision. The first number between the opening parenthesis and comma defines the precision or total number of digits to the left and right of the decimal point. The second number between the comma and the closing parenthesis defines the scale or total number of digits to the right of the decimal point.

```
SQL> DECLARE
  2    lv_number1  NUMBER(6,2);
  3    lv_number2  NUMBER(15,2) := 21533.22;
  4  BEGIN
  5    lv_number1 := lv_number2;
  6    dbms_output.put_line(lv_number1);
  7  END;
  8  /
```

The assignment on line 5 throws the following exception:

```
DECLARE
*
ERROR at line 1:
ORA-06502: PL/SQL: numeric or value error: number precision too large
ORA-06512: at line 5
```

You see the error because the physical digits of the NUMBER(6,2) data type can't hold all the digits from the source variable. To eliminate the error, you need to change the precision value of 6 to 7. That allows the entire number to fit in the data type.

The next example leaves the precision at 6 but changes the decimal scale to 1. As mentioned earlier, this change lets the assignment work. Unfortunately, you lose the precision of the hundredth decimal value by shaving it off.

```
SQL> DECLARE
  2    lv_number1  NUMBER(6,1);
  3    lv_number2  NUMBER(15,2) := 21533.22;
  4  BEGIN
  5    lv_number1 := lv_number2;
  6    dbms_output.put_line(lv_number1);
  7  END;
  8  /
```

Here's how the value in lv_number1 appears after the assignment prints:

```
21533.2
```

You lose the entire decimal value when you assign a NUMBER data type with a decimal to any of the integer data types. Unlike Java and most other procedural programming languages, PL/SQL doesn't require you to acknowledge this loss of precision by making the assignment explicit.

You can see the implicit casting of a NUMBER data type to an INTEGER data type in the following code:

```
SQL> DECLARE
  2    lv_number1  INTEGER;
  3    lv_number2  NUMBER(15,2) := 21533.22;
  4  BEGIN
  5    lv_number1 := lv_number2;
  6    dbms_output.put_line(lv_number1);
  7  END;
  8  /
```

The program would print this:

```
21533
```

Likewise, you could perform the same task on line 5 by using the FLOOR function before making the assignment between two variables (that use the NUMBER data type), like so:

```
5    lv_number1 := FLOOR(lv_number2);
```

The FLOOR function effectively rounds down to the nearest integer value. It shows you explicitly how to *shave off a decimal value*.

You should avoid mixing and matching numeric data types to avoid the loss of mathematical value in your data. When you must mix numeric data types, you can prevent the loss of mathematical value during assignments by disallowing such assignments or qualifying in comments that you don't care about the loss of information. The latter is a valid approach when you're reporting in hundreds, thousands, and millions, provided you do the sum first before discarding the sum's decimal value.

The new IEEE 754-format data types are single-precision and double-precision numbers. Their design supports scientific computing. The BINARY_FLOAT is a *32-bit* floating point number and the BINARY_DOUBLE is a *64-bit* floating point number.

```
SQL> DECLARE
  2    lv_number1  BINARY_FLOAT;
  3    lv_number2  BINARY_DOUBLE := 89015698736543.4028234663852886E+038d;
  4  BEGIN
  5    dbms_output.put_line(lv_number2);
  6    lv_number1 := lv_number2;
  7    dbms_output.put_line(lv_number1);
  8  END;
  9  /
```

It prints the following:

```
8.9015698736543403E+051
Inf
```

Best Practice
Always use the consistent numeric data types to avoid implicit loss of numeric precision. Unconstrained number data types often present the best solution.

Best Practice
Always check the validity of assignments before making them when a type mismatch is possible. This technique avoids assigning infinity when you need a real value.

The output from this program shows you what happens when you assign a value from a `BINARY_DOUBLE` to a `BINARY_FLOAT` variable. The outcome may result in an error, but it most certainly won't manifest itself during the assignment. Your program will probably throw an exception when you attempt to use the new variable.

In this case, the `BINARY_DOUBLE` value is simply too large for a `BINARY_FLOAT` data type. The value assigned to the `BINARY_FLOAT` is infinity because the *64-bit value* represents infinity within the scope of a *32-bit data type*. You should note that no error is raised during the assignment and that the implicit casting could break your program's downstream logic.

Composite Variable Types

Composite variables differ from scalar variables because they hold copies of more than one thing. Composite variables can hold a structure of data, which is more or less like a row of data. Alternatively, composite variables can hold collections of data. Beginning with Oracle Database 9*i*, Release 2, the following variable types can be used:

- **An SQL UDT**   This can hold a structure of data. Two implementations are possible with a UDT: an ordinary structure and an instantiable object type. The latter returns a copy of a class instance and the former returns a set of related data. Chapter 10 covers the instantiable object type, and you'll work through an example of the UDT structure in this section.

- **A PL/SQL record type**   This can hold a structure of data, like its SQL cousin. You can implement it by anchoring the data type of elements to columns in tables and views, or you can explicitly define it. You should consider explicit declarations because nesting these types doesn't work well in some cases that are hard to identify.

- **An SQL collection** This can hold a list of any scalar SQL data type. You have two possibilities with SQL collections: A *varray* behaves virtually like a standard array in any procedure or object-oriented programming language. It has a fixed number of elements in the list when you define it as a UDT. The other, a *nested table*, behaves like a list in standard programming languages. It doesn't have a fixed number of elements at definition and can scale to meet your runtime needs within your Private Global Area (PGA) memory constraints.

- **A PL/SQL collection** This can hold a list of any scalar SQL data type or record type, and it can also hold a list of any PL/SQL record type. Unlike with the other collections, you're not limited to a numeric index value. You can also use a string as the index value. This is aptly named for that duality of character as an *associative* array. Many experienced programmers still call this a PL/SQL table, as established in the Oracle Database 8 documentation.

You see how to implement a PL/SQL-only solution before the more flexible and extensible solution. The best solution returns a SQL collection with a record structure because you don't have to wrap it in a pipelined table function to use it in SQL. You should note what works and doesn't work when making these assignments to these data types.

One of the major downsides of pipelined table functions is that they create system-generated name types in the data catalog. These become tedious to tie back to your application and more expensive to maintain in your code tree.

You can implement a PL/SQL record structure and collection in a simple anonymous block program. This program defines the PL/SQL record structure on lines 2 and 3, and the collection of the record structure on line 4. Line 6 creates a variable of the collection and instantiates a null collection.

```
SQL> DECLARE
  2    TYPE title_structure IS RECORD
  3    ( title VARCHAR2(60), subtitle VARCHAR2(60));
  4    TYPE title_table IS TABLE OF title_structure;
  5    lv_counter        PLS_INTEGER := 1;
  6    lv_title_table    TITLE_TABLE := title_table();
  7    CURSOR c ( cv_search VARCHAR2 ) IS
  8      SELECT  item_title, item_subtitle
  9      FROM    item
```

```
10      WHERE    REGEXP_LIKE(item_title,'^'||cv_search||'*+')
11      AND      item_type = (SELECT common_lookup_id
12                              FROM   common_lookup
13                              WHERE  common_lookup_type = 'DVD_WIDE_SCREEN')
14      ORDER BY item_release_date;
15  BEGIN
16    FOR i IN c ('Harry') LOOP
17      lv_title_table.EXTEND;   -- Extends memory to the collection.
18      lv_title_table(lv_counter) := i;
19      lv_counter := lv_counter + 1;
20    END LOOP;
21    FOR i IN 1..lv_title_table.COUNT LOOP
22      dbms_output.put_line(lv_title_table(i).title);
23    END LOOP;
24  END;
25  /
```

The execution section allocates memory space to the collection and assigns a record structure by using the cursor for loop reference. This type of assignment is possible only in the context of PL/SQL.

TIP
Line 10 of the first composite variable type uses
*' *+ ' in the regular expression but you should*
generally use ' . ', which does the same thing.

The more elegant and effective solution is to define SQL data types for a record structure and collection of record structures. This is tricky, because you would use the same object definitions to create instantiable object types, but these aren't instantiable object types. They are reusable SQL record structures or UDTs. You can find their type definitions in the database catalog.

Creating these models is a three-step process. You define the record structure, then the collection, and finally a function to show how to return the collection from a PL/SQL-to-SQL context. Ultimately, you can simply query the models inside a SQL statement. This makes them reusable in the context of external programming languages such as C#, Java, and Hypertext Preprocessor (PHP).

You create the base SQL UDT like this:

```
SQL> CREATE OR REPLACE TYPE title_structure IS OBJECT
  2  ( title varchar2(60), subtitle varchar2(60));
  3  /
```

> **Best Practice**
>
> Always use SQL data types as return values of your functions. An SQL data type will never require that you write a pipelined table function wrapper to use it in SQL, and the data type is always available for inspection as a named collection and structure in the catalog.

You can create the collection by using a *varray* or *nested table*. The table is always the more flexible and least subject to change. It's generally a good idea always to use a nested table. You create a SQL collection of the object type like this:

```
SQL> CREATE OR REPLACE TYPE title_table IS TABLE OF title_structure;
  2  /
```

A nested table as a collection is advantageous because it doesn't have a fixed size. It allows for more flexible use. Chapter 7 covers collections.

The function is a rather trivial example, but is effective by its readability and small size. Naturally, when you write real logic, it will be a bit more complex, because this could easily be solved as an ordinary query:

```
SQL> CREATE OR REPLACE FUNCTION get_full_titles
  2  ( title_in VARCHAR2 ) RETURN TITLE_TABLE IS
  3    lv_counter       PLS_INTEGER := 1;
  4    lv_title_table     TITLE_TABLE := title_table();
  5    CURSOR c ( cv_search VARCHAR2 ) IS
  6      SELECT   item_title, item_subtitle
  7      FROM     item
  8      WHERE    REGEXP_LIKE(item_title,'^'||cv_search||'.')
  9      AND      item_type = (SELECT common_lookup_id
 10                            FROM   common_lookup
 11                            WHERE  common_lookup_type = 'DVD_WIDE_SCREEN')
 12      ORDER BY item_release_date;
 13  BEGIN
 14    FOR i IN c (title_in) LOOP
 15      lv_title_table.EXTEND;  -- Extends memory to the collection.
 16      lv_title_table(lv_counter) := title_structure(i.item_title
 17                                                   ,i.item_subtitle);
 18      lv_counter := lv_counter + 1;
 19    END LOOP;
 20    RETURN lv_title_table;
 21  END;
 22  /
```

Best Practice
Always use a table collection over a varray because it isn't constrained by a fixed limit. Varrays invariably require limit changes, and those cost time and money.

Line 4 declares the collection variable by instantiating it as a null value collection. Inside the *for* loop, line 15 extends memory space for a new element in the collection. Line 16 assign an instance of the title structure to an indexed element of the collection. It is critical that you note that the assignment requires that you explicitly construct an instance of the structure by passing actual parameters of equal type.

You can then query the result as follows:

```
SQL> SELECT title FROM TABLE(get_full_titles('Harry'));
```

The column name is no longer that of the table, but is that of the element in the SQL record structure. It returns the set of Harry Potter movies available in the video store as of this writing:

```
TITLE
--------------------------------------------
Harry Potter and the Sorcerer's Stone
Harry Potter and the Chamber of Secrets
Harry Potter and the Prisoner of Azkaban
Harry Potter and the Goblet of Fire
Harry Potter and the Order of the Phoenix
```

Composite variables are tremendously valuable assets in the PL/SQL and SQL programming environment. They let you define complex logic in named blocks that you can then simple query in C#, Java or PHP programs. You should take advantage of them where possible.

Control Structures

Control structures do two things: They check logical conditions and branch program execution, or they repeat (iterate) over a condition until it is met or they're instructed to exit. The *if*, *elsif*, *else*, and *case* statements are conditional structures, while loops allow you to repeat behaviors and are known as iterative structures.

IF Statement

The *if* or *elsif* statements work on a concept of Boolean logic. A Boolean variable or an expression, like a comparison of values, is the only criterion for an *if* or *elsif* statement. While this seems simple, it isn't, because truth or untruth has a third case in an Oracle database. A Boolean variable or expression can be true, false, or null. This is called *three-valued logic*.

You can manage three-valued logic by using the NVL built-in function. It allows you to impose an embedded check for a null and return the opposite of the logical condition you attempted to validate.

The following illustrates checking for truth of a Boolean and truth of an expression, ultimately printing the message that neither condition is true:

```
SQL> DECLARE
  2    lv_boolean BOOLEAN;
  3    lv_number  NUMBER;
  4  BEGIN
  5    IF NVL(lv_boolean,FALSE) THEN
  6      dbms_output.put_line('Prints when the variable is true.');
  7    ELSIF NVL((lv_number < 10),FALSE) THEN
  8      dbms_output.put_line('Prints when the expression is true.');
  9    ELSE
 10      dbms_output.put_line('Prints because both variables are null values.');
 11    END IF;
 12  END;
 13  /
```

This prints

```
Prints because both variables are null values.
```

Three-Valued Logic

Three-valued logic means basically that if you find something is true when you look for truth, it is true. By the same token, when you check whether something is false and it is, then it is false. The opposite case isn't proved. That means when something isn't true, you can't assume it is false, and vice versa.

The third case is that if something isn't true, it can be false or null. Likewise, if something isn't false, it can be true or null. Something is null when a Boolean variable is defined but not declared or when an expression compares something against another variable that is null.

Best Practice
Always use the NVL built-in function to reduce three-valued logic to two-valued logic because it increases the stability and readability of your code.

This always prints the *else* statement because the variables are only defined, not declared. PL/SQL undeclared variables are always null values.

The NVL built-in function lets you create programs that guarantee behavior, which is most likely the most important thing you can do as a developer. The guarantee becomes possible because you're changing the rules and making natural three-valued logic behave as two-valued logic. Sometimes, that's not possible, but oddly enough, when it isn't possible, there's a use case that will compel you to provide code for the null condition.

Case Statement

The *case* statement appears very similar to a switch structure in many programming languages, but it doesn't perform that way because it doesn't support fall-through. Fall-through is the behavior of finding the first true case and then performing all remaining cases. The *case* statement in PL/SQL performs like an *if-elsif-else* statement.

There are two types of *case* statements: One is the simple case and the other is the searched case. You can use a CHAR, NCHAR, or VARCHAR2 data type in simple *case* statements, and any Boolean *expression* in searched *case* statements.

The following program shows you how to write a simple *case* statement. The selector variable is a VARCHAR2 variable assigned a value through a substitution variable.

```
SQL> DECLARE
  2    lv_selector VARCHAR2(20);
  3  BEGIN
  4    lv_selector := '&input';
  5    CASE lv_selector
  6      WHEN 'Apple' THEN
  7        dbms_output.put_line('Is it a red delicious apple?');
  8      WHEN 'Orange' THEN
  9        dbms_output.put_line('Is it a navel orange?');
```

```
10     ELSE
11        dbms_output.put_line('It''s a ['||lv_selector||']?');
12   END CASE;
13 END;
14 /
```

The WHEN clauses validate their values against the CASE selector on line 5. When one WHEN clause matches the selector, the program runs the instructions in that WHEN clause and exits the CASE block. The *break* statement found in languages such as C, C++, C#, and Java is implicitly present.

A searched *case* statement works differently than a simple case because it doesn't limit itself to an equality match of values. You can use a searched case to validate whether a number is in a range or in a set. The selector for a searched case is implicitly true and may be excluded unless you want to check for untruth. You provide a false selector value on line 2 if the WHEN clauses validate against a false condition. The following program validates against truth:

```
SQL> BEGIN
  2     CASE
  3       WHEN (1 <> 1) THEN
  4         dbms_output.put_line('Impossible!');
  5       WHEN (3 > 2) THEN
  6         dbms_output.put_line('A valid range comparison.');
  7       ELSE
  8         dbms_output.put_line('Never reached.');
  9     END CASE;
 10 END;
 11 /
```

The range validation on line 5 is met and it prints this:

```
A valid range comparison.
```

Unlike the *if* and *elsif* statements, you don't need to reduce the natural three-valued logic to two-valued logic. If a searched *case* statement's WHEN clause isn't met, it continues until one is met or the *else* statement is reached.

Iterative Structures

Iterative statements are blocks that let you repeat a statement or set of statements. They come in two varieties: a guard on entry and guard on exit loop. Figure 2-2 shows the execution logic for these two types of loops.

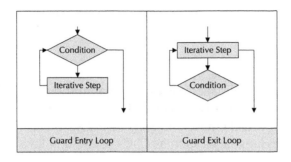

FIGURE 2-2. *Iterative statement logic flows*

Three loop structures in PL/SQL let you implement iteration. They are the *for, while,* and *simple* loop structures. You can use them either with or without a cursor. A *cursor* is a PL/SQL structure that lets you access the result of a query row-by-row or as a bulk operation.

For Loop Statements

You can implement the *for* loop as a *range* or *cursor* loop. A *range* loop moves through a set of sequential numbers, but you need to know the beginning and ending values. It is a guard-on-exit looping structure. You can navigate through a *for* loop forward or backward by using an ascending integer range.

```
SQL> BEGIN
  2    FOR i IN 0..9 LOOP
  3      dbms_output.put_line('['||i||'] ['||TO_CHAR(i+1)||']');
  4    END LOOP;
  5  END;
  6  /
```

The value of the *iterator*, i, is equal to the numbers in the inclusive range values. The iterator has a PLS_INTEGER data type. This program prints this:

```
[0] [1]
[1] [2]
[2] [3]
 . . .
[7] [8]
[8] [9]
[9] [10]
```

Best Practice
Range *for* loops should start with a 1 to ensure they synchronize with the 1-based index numbers of arrays and cursors.

Range *for* loops typically start with *1* and move to a higher number, but you can use a *0* (zero) as the low value in the range. A zero is rarely used as a starting point because arrays and cursors use 1-based numbering. The example shows you how to do it, but we want you to know that you *shouldn't do it*.

The next range loop moves through the sequence from the highest to the lowest number, and it uses a 1-based number model. You should notice that the only evidence of decrementing behavior is the REVERSE reserved word.

```
SQL> BEGIN
  2    FOR i IN REVERSE 1..9 LOOP
  3      dbms_output.put_line('['||i||'] ['||TO_CHAR(i+1)||']');
  4    END LOOP;
  5  END;
  6  /
```

Cursor *for* loops work with data sets returned by queries. You have two possible static patterns. You also have an implicit dynamic cursor and a parameterized dynamic cursor. The first example shows you how to write a static cursor without a declaration block. You should write this type of code only when you're doing a quick test program or standalone script.

```
SQL> BEGIN
  2    FOR i IN (SELECT item_title FROM item) LOOP
  3      dbms_output.put_line(i.item_title);
  4    END LOOP;
  5  END;
  6  /
```

Line 2 contains the static cursor inside parentheses. At runtime, the query becomes an implicit cursor. Implicit cursors like these should *always be static queries*. You should put queries into formal cursors, and then call them in the execution block, like this:

```
SQL> DECLARE
  2    CURSOR c IS
  3      SELECT item_title FROM item;
```

```
4  BEGIN
5    FOR i IN c LOOP
6      dbms_output.put_line(i.item_title);
7    END LOOP;
8  END;
9  /
```

The program declares a formal static cursor on lines 2 and 3. The *for* loop implicitly opens and fetches records from the cursor on line 5. This type or program is more readable than the previous example. It is also adaptable if your requirements evolve from a static to dynamic cursor. Whether or not you define cursors with formal parameters, you can include variables in a formal cursor declaration.

The following shows you how to implement a cursor with a formal parameter. The alternative would be to switch the cursor parameter with a substitution variable on line 6.

```
SQL> DECLARE
  2    lv_search_string VARCHAR2(60);
  3    CURSOR c (cv_search VARCHAR2) IS
  4      SELECT   item_title
  5      FROM     item
  6      WHERE    REGEXP_LIKE(item_title,'^'||cv_search||'*+');
  7  BEGIN
  8    FOR i IN c ('&input') LOOP
  9      dbms_output.put_line(i.item_title);
 10    END LOOP;
 11  END;
 12  /
```

The lines of interest are 3, 6, and 8. Line 3 declares the formal parameter for a dynamic cursor. Line 6 shows the use of the formal parameter in the cursor. Line 8 shows the actual parameter calling the cursor. The call parameter is a substitution variable because the anonymous block then becomes dynamic. You can replace the formal parameter on line 6 with a substitution variable, but that's a very poor coding practice. As a rule, you should always define formal parameters for dynamic cursors.

Best Practice
Dynamic cursors should always have formal parameter signatures.

This concludes the basics of a *for* loop. A twist on the *for* loop involves the WHERE CURRENT OF clause, which is discussed in the next section.

WHERE CURRENT OF Clause   A big to do about nothing would be the WHERE CURRENT OF clause. In our opinion, bulk operations are generally the better solution. It's important to show an example in a workbook like this, so we've got two.

The first shows you how to lock a row with the cursor and then update the same table in a *for* loop, as follows:

```
SQL> DECLARE
  2    CURSOR c IS
  3      SELECT * FROM item
  4      WHERE  item_id BETWEEN 1031 AND 1040
  5      FOR UPDATE;
  6  BEGIN
  7    FOR I IN c LOOP
  8      UPDATE item SET last_updated_by = 3
  9      WHERE CURRENT OF c;
 10    END LOOP;
 11  END;
 12  /
```

Line 5 locks the rows with the FOR UPDATE clause. Line 9 correlates the update to a row returned by the cursor.

The next example demonstrates how to use the WHERE CURRENT OF in a bulk operation. It's an unavoidable forward reference to material covered later in this chapter.

```
SQL> DECLARE
  2    TYPE update_record IS RECORD
  3    ( last_updated_by  NUMBER
  4    , last_update_date DATE );
  5    TYPE update_table IS TABLE OF UPDATE_RECORD;
  6    updates UPDATE_TABLE;
  7    CURSOR c IS
  8      SELECT last_updated_by, last_update_date
  9      FROM item
 10      WHERE  item_id BETWEEN 1031 AND 1040
 11      FOR UPDATE;
 12  BEGIN
 13    OPEN c;
```

```
14    LOOP
15      FETCH c BULK COLLECT INTO updates LIMIT 5;
16      EXIT WHEN updates.COUNT = 0;
17      FORALL i IN updates.FIRST..updates.LAST
18        UPDATE item
19        SET    last_updated_by = updates(i).last_updated_by
20        ,      last_update_date = updates(i).last_update_date
21        WHERE CURRENT OF c;
22    END;
23    /
```

Like the row-by-row example, the FOR UPDATE clause on line 9 locks the rows. The WHERE CURRENT OF clause on line 21 correlates the update to the rows returned by the bulk collected cursor.

Now that we've shown you how to do it, why would you want to? The same thing can be accomplished by a correlated UPDATE statement, like this:

```
SQL> UPDATE item i1
  2  SET    last_updated_by = 3
  3  ,      last_update_date = TRUNC(SYSDATE)
  4  WHERE  EXISTS (SELECT NULL FROM item i2
  5                 WHERE  item_id BETWEEN 1031 AND 1040
  6                 AND    i1.ROWID = i2.ROWID);
```

In fact, Oracle's documentation indicates that it recommends correlated update and delete statements over the use of the WHERE CURRENT OF clause. *We have to recommend native SQL solutions when they're available.*

The range and cursor *for* loops are powerful iterative structures. Their beauty lies in their simplicity and their curse lies in their implicit opening and closing of cursor resources. You should use these structures when access to the data is straightforward and row-by-row auditing isn't required. When you need to perform row-by-row auditing, you should use a *while* or simple loop because they give you more control.

While Loop Statements

A *while* loop is a guard on entry loop. You need to manage both the entry and exit criteria of a *while* loop. Unlike the *for* loop, with the *while* loop you don't need an index value because you can use other criteria to meet

the control entrance and exit. If you use an index, the Oracle 11*g*
CONTINUE statement can make control more complex because it allows
you to abort an iteration and return to the top of the loop:

```
SQL> DECLARE
  2    lv_counter NUMBER := 1;
  3  BEGIN
  4    WHILE (lv_counter < 5) LOOP
  5      dbms_output.put('Index at top ['||lv_counter||']');
  6      IF lv_counter >= 1 THEN
  7        IF MOD(lv_counter,2) = 0 THEN
  8          dbms_output.new_line();
  9          lv_counter := lv_counter + 1;
 10          CONTINUE;
 11        END IF;
 12        dbms_output.put_line('['||lv_counter||']');
 13      END IF;
 14      lv_counter := lv_counter + 1;
 15    END LOOP;
 16  END;
 17  /
```

This prints the following:

```
Index at top [1][1]
Index at top [2]
Index at top [3][3]
Index at top [4]
```

Only odd number counter values make it to the bottom of the loop, as
illustrated by the second printing of the counter value. That's because the
CONTINUE statement prints a line return and returns control to the top of
the loop. You could also do the same thing with the GOTO statement and
label. You enclose labels inside *guillemets*, also known as angle brackets.
They're available in releases prior to Oracle 11*g*, and while it pains us to tell
you about them, here's an example:

```
SQL> DECLARE
  2    lv_counter NUMBER := 1;
  3  BEGIN
  4    WHILE (lv_counter < 5) LOOP
  5      dbms_output.put('Index at top ['||lv_counter||']');
  6      IF lv_counter >= 1 THEN
  7        IF MOD(lv_counter,2) = 0 THEN
  8          dbms_output.new_line();
```

```
9             GOTO skippy;
10         END IF;
11         dbms_output.put_line('['||lv_counter||']');
12       END IF;
13       << skippy >>
14       lv_counter := lv_counter + 1;
15     END LOOP;
16   END;
17   /
```

The GOTO statement on line 9 skips to the incrementing instruction for the control variable on line 13. It is actually a bit cleaner than the CONTINUE statement shown earlier.

The GOTO statement should be avoided whenever possible. The CONTINUE should be used minimally and carefully. The *while* loop is powerful, but can be tricky if you're not careful when using a CONTINUE statement. A poorly coded *while* loop that contains a CONTINUE statement can cause an infinite loop.

Simple Loop Statements

The *simple loop statement* is anything but simple. You use it when you want to control everything that surrounds access to an explicit cursor. Some of these controls are provided through four built-in cursor attributes. Table 2-1 lists these cursor attributes.

Attribute	Definition
%FOUND	This attribute returns TRUE only when a DML statement has changed a row.
%ISOPEN	This attribute always returns FALSE for any implicit cursor.
%NOTFOUND	This attribute returns TRUE when a DML statement fails to change a row.
%ROWCOUNT	This attribute returns the number of rows changed by a DML statement or the number of rows returned by a SELECT INTO statement.

TABLE 2-1. *Cursor Attributes*

These attributes work with cursors or ordinary SQL statements. For example, the following anonymous block uses cursor attributes to manage printing log statements to the console:

```
SQL> BEGIN
  2    UPDATE    system_user
  3    SET       last_update_date = SYSDATE;
  4    IF SQL%FOUND THEN
  5      dbms_output.put_line('Updated ['||SQL%ROWCOUNT||']');
  6    ELSE
  7      dbms_output.put_line('Nothing updated!');
  8    END IF;
  9  END;
 10  /
```

The SQL%FOUND on line 4 checks whether a SQL statement was processed. SQL is a reserved word that links to an anonymous cursor, which is any SQL QUERY, INSERT, UPDATE, or DELETE statement run in the execution block. If SQL%FOUND returns TRUE, then line 5 prints the number of rows updated in the table.

A typical simple loop opens a cursor, fetches rows from a cursor, processes rows from a cursor, and closes a cursor. The following program demonstrates those steps and illustrates an anchored data type:

```
SQL> DECLARE
  2    lv_id    item.item_id%TYPE;   -- This is an anchored type.
  3    lv_title VARCHAR2(60);
  4    CURSOR c IS
  5      SELECT   item_id, item_title
  6      FROM     item;
  7  BEGIN
  8    OPEN c;
  9    LOOP
 10      FETCH c INTO lv_id, lv_title;
 11      EXIT WHEN c%NOTFOUND;
 12      dbms_output.put_line('Title ['||lv_title||']');
 13    END LOOP;
 14    CLOSE c;
 15  END;
 16  /
```

This program defines one variable by anchoring the data type to the definition of the ITEM_ID column in the item table. When the definition of the table changes, you don't have to change your program because it will adjust automatically. The first statement after you start a simple loop fetches a row of data, and the second, line 11, checks to make sure a row was fetched. Line 11 also exits the loop when no record is found, which is typically after all rows have been read or no rows were found.

You can extend the preceding model by creating a user-defined record structure and returning the row into a single record structure. Record structures are composite variables. The following example uses a %ROWTYPE pseudo column to anchor a catalog table definition to a local variable:

```
SQL> DECLARE
  2    lv_item_record item%ROWTYPE;    -- This is an anchored type.
  3    CURSOR c IS
  4      SELECT   *
  5      FROM     item;
  6  BEGIN
  7    OPEN c;
  8    LOOP
  9      FETCH c INTO lv_item_record;
 10      EXIT WHEN c%NOTFOUND;
 11      dbms_output.put_line('Title ['||lv_item_record.item_title||']');
 12    END LOOP;
 13    CLOSE c;
 14  END;
 15  /
```

On line 11, the LV_ITEM_RECORD.ITEM_TITLE statement returns the value of a field in the row of data. The dot between the local variable and column name is the *component selector*. You actually read this reference from right to left. It means the ITEM_TITLE is selected from the LV_ITEM_RECORD component, which is a local variable.

You could also create a record type explicitly. This is done when you want only a subset of the columns in a table and you don't want to create a view. A local record set variable would be like the following:

```
TYPE item_record IS RECORD
( id     NUMBER
, title VARCHAR2(60));
```

There are some glitches down the road with local types like these because they're limited exclusively to a PL/SQL context. The "Composite Variable Types" section earlier in this chapter shows the better alternative.

Bulk Operations

Oracle 10*g* and 11*g* (supported releases at the time of writing) provide bulk processing capabilities. They differ somewhat from the structures we've presented, but they follow the general look and feel. Where possible, bulk processing should be the default in your batch processing and high-volume processing of data.

The following program shows you how to select groups of rows into array structures. You do this with the BULK COLLECT clause. We've chosen a limit of 20 simply to make it simple with the sample data. Real-world solutions may be hundreds or thousands of records at a time, but *we would recommend a range of 250 to 500.*

```
SQL> DECLARE
  2    TYPE title_record IS RECORD
  3    ( title     VARCHAR2(60)
  4    , subtitle VARCHAR2(60));
  5    TYPE title_collection IS TABLE OF TITLE_RECORD;
  6    lv_title_collection TITLE_COLLECTION;
  7    CURSOR c IS
  8      SELECT   item_title, item_subtitle
  9      FROM     item;
 10  BEGIN
 11    OPEN c;
 12    LOOP
 13      FETCH c BULK COLLECT INTO lv_title_collection LIMIT 20;
 14      EXIT WHEN lv_title_collection.COUNT = 0;
 15      FOR i IN 1..lv_title_collection.COUNT LOOP
 16        dbms_output.put_line('Title ['||lv_title_collection(i).title||']');
 17      END LOOP;
 18    END LOOP;
 19    CLOSE c;
 20  END;
 21  /
```

This program is more complex than earlier examples and forward references the concept of collections. After creating a record structure, you create another local collection data type. You then create a variable of the collection type. Line 13 BULK COLLECTs the collection of a record structure into a single variable. The range FOR loop on lines 15 through 17 reads the collection and prints only one column value from the each record.

Best Practice

The LIMIT statement should generally be in the range of 250 to 500 for online transactional processing.

After you've selected the data, you should be able to insert or update target tables in the same bulk-processing units. You can do so with the FORALL statement. The following lets you perform a bulk update:

```
SQL> DECLARE
  2    TYPE title_record IS RECORD
  3    ( id        NUMBER
  4    , title     VARCHAR2(60)
  5    , subtitle VARCHAR2(60));
  6    TYPE title_collection IS TABLE OF TITLE_RECORD;
  7    lv_title_collection TITLE_COLLECTION;
  8    CURSOR c IS
  9      SELECT    item_id, item_title, item_subtitle
 10      FROM      item;
 11  BEGIN
 12    OPEN c;
 13    LOOP
 14      FETCH c BULK COLLECT INTO lv_title_collection LIMIT 20;
 15      EXIT WHEN lv_title_collection.COUNT = 0;
 16       FORALL i IN lv_title_collection.FIRST..lv_title_collection.LAST
 17          UPDATE    item_temp
 18          SET       item_title = lv_title_collection(i).title
 19          ,         item_subtitle = lv_title_collection(i).subtitle
 20          WHERE     item_id = lv_title_collection(i).id;
 21    END LOOP;
 22  END;
 23  /
```

The FORALL statement on lines 16 through 20 updates 20 rows at a time, but it could easily be more. Bulk processing reduces the context switches in the database and improves online transaction processing application throughput.

Downloadable Code

The examples in this chapter are so small that they weren't bundled into files.

Summary

This chapter has covered the basics of the PL/SQL programming language. You should be able to use this information as a foundation for other chapters of this book.

You should also check the introduction for references to further your study of these topics.

Best Practice Review

- Always define forward referencing specifications for local named blocks before implementing any of them. This ensures that they can call one another.

- Always make assignments or initializations in the execution block unless the local variable is a constant or treated as a constant. This eliminates many runtime assignment errors.

- Always use variable-length data types unless there's a compelling business reason that requires fixed-length data types.

- Always use the consistent numeric data types to avoid implicit loss of numeric precision. Unconstrained number data types often present the best solution.

- Always check the validity of assignments before making them when there's a possibility of a type mismatch. This technique avoids assigning infinity when you need a real value.

- Always use SQL data types as return values of your functions. They'll never require you to write a pipelined table function wrapper to use it in SQL, and the data type is always available for inspection as a named collection and structure in the catalog.

- Always use a nested table collection over a varray because it isn't constrained by a fixed limit. Varrays invariably require limit changes and those cost time and money.

- Always use the NVL built-in to reduce three-valued logic to two-valued logic because it increases the stability and readability of your code.

- Range *for* loops should start with a *1* to ensure they synchronize with the 1-based index numbers of arrays and cursors.

- Dynamic cursors should always have formal parameter signatures.

- The LIMIT statement should generally be in the range of 250 to 500 for online transactional processing.

Mastery Check

The mastery check is a series of true or false and multiple choice questions that let you confirm how well you understand the material in the chapter. You may check Appendix E for answers to these questions.

1. ☐ **True** ☐ **False** You can define a block without a statement in it.

2. ☐ **True** ☐ **False** You can use the ELSE IF block in an IF block.

3. ☐ **True** ☐ **False** You can define and use a RECORD structure in PL/SQL.

4. ☐ **True** ☐ **False** You can define an OBJECT type in SQL or PL/SQL.

5. ☐ **True** ☐ **False** You can use a *for* loop when you know the exit condition in advanced and you're guarding exit not entrance to the loop.

6. ☐ **True** ☐ **False** A *while* loop guards on entry.

7. ☐ **True** ☐ **False** A simple loop must work with a cursor.

8. ☐ **True** ☐ **False** You use the CONTINUE statement to exit a loop.

9. ☐ **True** ☐ **False** Like Java, PL/SQL makes the GOTO a keyword, but doesn't let you use it.

10. ☐ **True** ☐ **False** The BULK COLLECT INTO lets you select a complete cursor or a range of rows from a cursor into a collection of a record structure.

11. Which are valid PL/SQL data types?

    A. BOOLEAN

    B. PLS_INTEGER

    C. BINARY_DOUBLE

    D. All of the above

    E. Only A and B

12. Which of the following are valid cursor attributes?

    A. `%FOUND`

    B. `%ISOPEN`

    C. `%COUNT`

    D. All of the above

    E. Only A and B

13. Which of the following are label delimiters?

    A. `<>`

    B. `<<>>`

    C. `{}`

    D. All of the above

    E. Only A and B

14. Which is the correct way to descend through a range of numbers in a `FOR` loop?

    A. `FOR i IN 10..1 LOOP`

    B. `FOR i IN 1..10 REVERSE LOOP`

    C. `FOR i IN REVERSE 1..10 LOOP`

    D. All of the above

    E. Only B and C

15. Which syntax ends a `FORALL statement`?

    A. `END FORALL;`

    B. `END LOOP;`

    C. `END FORALL LOOP;`

    D. None of the above

    E. Only A and B

CHAPTER
3

Transaction Scope

T his chapter discusses the intricacies of transaction control and scope. It also demonstrates how to create PL/SQL programs that intelligently handle large volumes of database interactions. Understanding transaction control is vital for developers and DBAs who want to create stable systems that ultimately protect enterprise information from data corruption or loss. We divide this chapter into the following topics:

■ The Database ACID Test

■ Multi Version Concurrency Control (MVCC)

■ Savepoints, commits, and rolling back transactions

■ DML locking

■ Isolation control

■ Invoker and definer rights

The Database Acid Test

Three people deserve the credit for coining the phrase *Database ACID Test.* The first was James Nicholas Gray. Back in 1981, he produced a whitepaper named, *The Transaction Concept: Virtues and Limitations,* for Tandem Computers, Inc. Within this article, he related database transactions to real-world agreements such as marriages and business contracts. He stated that transactions should be legal and binding, and that they must guarantee the following:

■ **Consistency**   Transactions must obey a system of rules or legal protocols.

■ **Atomicity**   Transactions must all succeed or fail together.

■ **Durability**   Transactions must persist.

Finally, Gray roughly defined commit, rollback, undo, and redo logfiles. The article was visionary, and its effect on the modern database system is remarkable.

Theo Haerder and Andreas Reuter wrote a follow-up article for the *Association for Computing Machinery Journal* (ACM) entitled "Principles of Transaction-Oriented Database Recovery." In this paper, they expanded on Gray's ideas, adding the belief that transactions must also be isolated from each other. Here's their new list (providing the acronym *ACID*):

■ Atomicity

■ Consistency

■ Isolation

■ Durability

Atomicity

Atomicity is requisite in all middleware, Enterprise JavaBeans (EJBs), Service Oriented Architecture (SOA), Web Services, and Relational Database Management Systems (RDBMS). No matter which buzzword is used, systems must manage transactions at their most *atomic* level. These systems must adopt strict all-or-nothing methodologies or information chaos reigns.

One of the authors dealt with a customer creation system that regularly produced partial customer records. Business intelligence (BI) reports calculated millions of customers; however, a notable percent of them were not active. It was difficult to determine the validity of inactive accounts. Account removal became the focus of regular data cleansing efforts.

Root-cause analysis revealed that customer creation required data entry into three systems. Two of them depended on Oracle databases, while the other relied on a much older legacy system. Middleware programmers issued *insert* and *commit* statements to each system individually, orphaning records when any of the three transactions failed. As a result, account managers had difficulty knowing which accounts were not real and should not receive periodic mailers, promotions, and catalog delivery.

Financial losses skyrocket in systems like these, even if middleware systems successfully complete customer registration 99 percent of the time. For instance, a small annual investment of $15 multiplied by 1 percent of 10 million customers is $1,500,000.

Consistency

Database transactions must successfully select, insert, update, or delete records in a manner that conforms to system rules and regulations.

Noncompliant transactions must not be committed. Without absolute regulation, durability, otherwise known as data integrity, is not certifiable.

Dirty transactions consist of database activity that violates system rules. This type of interaction can occur when simultaneous users trump each other's processes. For example, consider two users, Jane and Joe. Jane, a customer service representative, attempts to remove a customer order at the same time Joe, a sales manager, attempts to add another line item to that order. His interaction, inserting a record in the ORDER_LINE_ITEM table, is dependent on the parent ORDER_ID record that Jane is attempting to remove. If the system does not provide proper consistency checks, Jane and Joe's activities trump each other. In addition, to guarantee consistency, both transactions should fail (Figure 3-1).

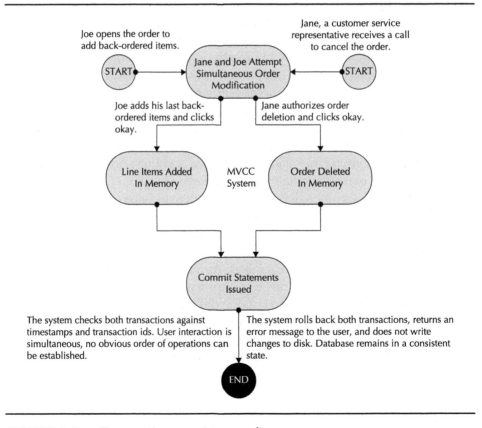

FIGURE 3-1. *Transaction consistency diagram*

Isolation

Isolation means that users cannot see the transactions of other users until those transactions are complete and committed. Recall that Jane and Joe's database activities had a tendency to trump each other. Theo Haerder and Andreas Reuter suggested that their activities must be isolated from each other to prevent dirty transactions. Furthermore, record locking must provide a way to ensure consistent reads and writes.

Durability

Many catastrophic conditions can prevent records from being permanently stored to disk, including power, network, system, and hard drive failures. Data loss is also caused by malicious actions from disgruntled employees and hackers. Unfortunately, durability is not an automated process. One of the primary responsibilities of the DBA is to create and maintain data recoverability strategies.

A DBA cliché states, "DBAs must have two things up-to-date: a good resumé, and a recent backup." DBAs say this because if their recovery (from backup) fails, they will need the resumé. Fortunately, Oracle provides a Recovery Manager (RMAN), Flashback query/database, point-in-time recovery, archive logs, and redo logs to aid the DBA in this quest. The DBA should take advantage of redundant disk arrays and tape storage technologies in addition to these tools.

Best Practice

Always ensure that you have a good backup. It is not good enough merely to activate backup programs such as RMAN. Validate and test your backups on a regular basis to ensure recoverability.

Multiversioned Concurrency Control

MVCC employs the use of database snapshots to provide users with memory-persistent copies of the database. Users interact with data in memory instead of directly manipulating the database. Only a handful of database systems employ MVCC, as it is a complex technology and is costly to develop; however, these systems benefit from the ability to serve many user transactions simultaneously. Moreover, products from vendors that offer MVCC can isolate user transactions from each other, completely protecting the data from dirty transactions.

Oracle MVCC Tidbit

Oracle first offered MVCC in version 7 of its RDBMS nearly 20 years ago. The company continues to improve on this technology with each major release of its database system.

Savepoints, Commits, and Transaction Rollbacks

This section discusses three crucial subjects in PL/SQL application design. It is vital that you carefully study each topic so you can correctly implement systems that comply with the qualities of atomicity, consistency, isolation, and durability.

Savepoints and Rollback

Use the SAVEPOINT command to create named positions in your transactions. Retract data manipulation to a named savepoint by issuing the ROLLBACK command. Issuing the ROLLBACK command without naming savepoints takes back all transactions to the last COMMIT point. The next two examples will demonstrate basic savepoint creation and complexities related to savepoint management.

Example 3-1: Creating a Simple Savepoint in PL/SQL Savepoint creation is quite simple. The only input to the command is its name. This example creates only one SAVEPOINT named ASSIGN_PROMO_ID. It commits if all updates are successful and rolls back transactions if any errors occur:

```
SQL> DECLARE
  2     CURSOR c_sales_promo IS
  3       SELECT   order_id
  4         FROM   oe.orders
  5        WHERE   promotion_id IS NULL
  6          AND   to_char( order_date, 'MMYYYY') = '081999';
  7  BEGIN
  8     SAVEPOINT assign_promo_id;
  9     FOR r_sales_promo IN c_sales_promo LOOP
 10       UPDATE   oe.orders
 11          SET   promotion_id = 2
 12        WHERE   order_id = r_sales_promo.order_id;
 13     END LOOP;
 14     COMMIT;
 15  EXCEPTION
 16     WHEN OTHERS THEN
 17       ROLLBACK TO assign_promo_id;
 18  END;
 19  /
```

This example is fairly simple and straightforward; however, typical rollback logic is much more complicated.

Example 3-2: Complex Savepoint and Rollback Logic We created the following program to illustrate the possibility of logical errors in savepoint management. The example is lengthy but represents a more realistic point of view. For clarity purposes, we segment and annotate it. The first block creates a table in the HR schema named SALES_COMPENSATION:

```
SQL> CREATE TABLE hr.sales_compensation
  2  ( sales_rep_id          NUMBER
  3  , qtr_sales_period      VARCHAR2(5)
  4  , qtr_order_total       NUMBER
  5  , qtr_gross_profit      NUMBER
```

```
 6   , qtr_salary_amount      NUMBER
 7   , qtr_bonus_paid         NUMBER
 8   , qtr_probation_flag     CHAR
 9   , update_timestamp       TIMESTAMP
10   );
```

Our program inserts quarterly sales information, including bonuses paid, into this table:

```
SQL> DECLARE
  2     ln_sales_bonus          NUMBER;
  3     lb_sales_probation      BOOLEAN;
  4     CURSOR c_sales IS
       ... omitted for brevity ...
 22   BEGIN
 23     SAVEPOINT a;
 24     FOR r_sales IN c_sales LOOP
 25       IF    r_sales.qtr_gross_profit -
 26            ( r_sales.qtr_salary_amount +
 27              r_sales.qtr_gross_profit *
 28              r_sales.commission_pct ) > 1000
 29       THEN
 30         ln_sales_bonus := r_sales.qtr_salary_amount +
 31                            r_sales.qtr_gross_profit *
 32                            r_sales.commission_pct;
 33       INSERT
 34         INTO   hr.sales_compensation
 35         VALUES ( r_sales.sales_rep_id
 36                , r_sales.qtr_sales_period
 37                , r_sales.qtr_order_total
 38                , r_sales.qtr_gross_profit
 39                , r_sales.qtr_salary_amount
 40                , ln_sales_bonus
 41                , 'N'
 42                , systimestamp
 43                );
 44       END IF;
 45     END LOOP;
```

Notice that we created a SAVEPOINT named a. Also observe that we created a variable named LB_SALES_PROBATION. It is of BOOLEAN data type, meaning that it accepts TRUE and FALSE values. Its default value is set to FALSE. The program toggles this value when a salesperson does not produce $500 in net profit per quarter. We set the value automatically to FALSE because pessimistic programming is preferred and reduces the amount of programming needed. Also note that the LN_SALES_BONUS variable is set only if the salesperson's net profit is greater than $1000. This kind of logic is typical in real-world examples.

> **Best Practice**
> Never assume that user input or program logic will create the results you are looking for. A pessimistic approach reduces and simplifies program logic.

In the following section, salespersons do not receive quarterly bonuses because their net profit is less than $1,000. Additionally, the LB_PROBATION_FLAG remains FALSE. Finally, we create SAVEPOINT b:

```
46    SAVEPOINT b;
47    FOR r_sales IN c_sales LOOP
48      IF    r_sales.qtr_gross_profit -
49          ( r_sales.qtr_salary_amount +
50            r_sales.qtr_gross_profit *
51            r_sales.commission_pct ) < 1000
52      AND   r_sales.qtr_gross_profit -
53          ( r_sales.qtr_salary_amount +
54            r_sales.qtr_gross_profit *
55            r_sales.commission_pct ) > 500
56      THEN
57        INSERT
58          INTO   hr.sales_compensation
59        VALUES  ( r_sales.sales_rep_id
60                , r_sales.qtr_sales_period
61                , r_sales.qtr_order_total
62                , r_sales.qtr_gross_profit
63                , r_sales.qtr_salary_amount
64                , 0
65                , 'N'
66                , systimestamp
67                );
68      END IF;
69    END LOOP;
```

The following block creates a SAVEPOINT named c. If the salesperson nets less than $500 profit per quarter, a record is inserted into the

HR.SALES_COMPENSATION table with no bonus. Additionally, the
QTR_PROBATION_FLAG column is set to 'Y':

```
 70     SAVEPOINT c;
 71     FOR r_sales IN c_sales LOOP
 72       IF      r_sales.qtr_gross_profit -
 73          ( r_sales.qtr_salary_amount +
 74            r_sales.qtr_gross_profit *
 75            r_sales.commission_pct ) < 500
 76       THEN
 77         INSERT
 78           INTO  hr.sales_compensation
 79         VALUES  ( r_sales.sales_rep_id
 80                 , r_sales.qtr_sales_period
 81                 , r_sales.qtr_order_total
 82                 , r_sales.qtr_gross_profit
 83                 , r_sales.qtr_salary_amount
 84                 , 0
 85                 , 'Y'
 86                 , systimestamp
 87                 );
 88         lb_sales_probation := TRUE;
 89       END IF;
 90     END LOOP;
 91     -- Logic is purposefully set to throw SAVEPOINT. Rolling back to A
 92     -- retracts all updates.
 93     IF lb_sales_probation = TRUE THEN
 94       ROLLBACK TO SAVEPOINT a;
 95     END IF;
 96     COMMIT;
 97   EXCEPTION
 98     WHEN OTHERS THEN
 99       DBMS_OUTPUT.PUT_LINE ( SQLERRM );
100       ROLLBACK TO SAVEPOINT a;
101   END;
102   /
```

Observe that we leave the variable LB_SALES_PROBATION set to
false unless the salesperson nets a quarterly profit less than $500. This
allows the if-then block on line 93 to execute, which rolls back our
changes to savepoint a. There are three problems with this logic:

■ The LB_SALES_PROBATION variable remains TRUE in subsequent
   loops.

■ The IF-THEN block on line 93 rolls back all prior transactions,
   including those we want to keep.

■ SAVEPOINT complexity is compounded due to ambiguous labeling.

Best Practice

Label savepoints in a succinct but descriptive manner. Double-check your logic and make sure you roll back to the correct point in time.

Example 3-3: Savepoint Destruction   In our final example on rollback and savepoint commands, we illustrate how savepoints are destroyed when rollback commands are issued.

It is possible to wipe out savepoints. Here's an example:

```
SQL> BEGIN
  2     SAVEPOINT create_job;
  3     INSERT
  4       INTO  hr.jobs
  5     VALUES ( 'GrandPumba'
  6            , 'The grand owner of the business.'
  7            , 20000
  8            , 99999
  9            );
 10
 11     SAVEPOINT create_employee;
 12     INSERT
 13       INTO  hr.employees
 14     VALUES ( 999
 15            , 'Jane'
 16            , 'Doe'
 17            , 'doeja@oracle.com'
 18            , '+1 (123) 456-7890'
 19            , trunc ( sysdate )
 20            , 'GrandPumba'
 21            , 9999
 22            , .5
 23            , null
 24            , 90
 25            );
 26
 27     SAVEPOINT add_job_history;
 28     INSERT
 29       INTO  hr.job_history
```

```
30     VALUES  ( 999
31             , trunc ( sysdate )
32             , trunc ( sysdate + 2000 )
33             , 'GrandPumba'
34             , 90
35             );
36
```

Our next block will roll back to the savepoint named CREATE_JOB. This action destroys the savepoints CREATE_EMPLOYEE and ADD_JOB_HISTORY.

```
37     ROLLBACK TO SAVEPOINT create_job;
38     ROLLBACK TO SAVEPOINT add_job_history;
39   EXCEPTION
40     WHEN OTHERS THEN
41       DBMS_OUTPUT.PUT_LINE ( sqlerrm );
42   END;
43   /
ORA-01086: savepoint 'ADD_JOB_HISTORY' never established
```

Notice the ORA-01086 error message. The second ROLLBACK command, issued on line 38, fails because we issued a rollback to a prior savepoint on line 37.

Commit

The COMMIT statement tells Oracle to make your data manipulation statements permanent. When you issue this command, log-writers write your changes to archive and redo log files. Log-writers do not write directly to datafiles. Instead, database-writers make your changes permanent during time-outs or when threshold values are reached. You need to know the following options and caveats associated with COMMIT statements:

- Data dictionary manipulation *forces implied commits.*

- Comments in the COMMIT command write to the DBA_PC2_PENDING dictionary view.

- You must have the FORCE TRANSACTION or FORCE ANY TRANSACTION system privilege to force a commit.

- The NOWAIT option does not validate writing to redo and archive log files.

■ The WORK option is persistent across all COMMIT statements. It was added to provide compliance with ANSI SQL.

Because the list of options is small, we demonstrate all five options to the COMMIT command in the next three examples.

Example 3-3: Issuing a Standard Commit   We first issue a standard commit to illustrate its most basic form:

```
UPDATE   employees
   SET   salary = salary * 1.03
 WHERE   department_id in (20,30,40);

COMMIT;
```

The preceding query is the same as this:

```
UPDATE   employees
   SET   salary = salary * 1.03
 WHERE   department_id in (20,30,40);

COMMIT WORK WRITE IMMEDIATE WAIT;
```

Example 3-4: Issuing a Commit with the Nowait and Batch Options   The use of NOWAIT *does not* validate the writing of changes to redo and archive log files. In this case, you can get yourself into a lot of trouble by overriding Oracle defaults:

```
INSERT
   INTO   oe.orders
          ( order_id, order_date, customer_id, order_status
          , order_total, sales_rep_id, promotion_id
          , gross_profit )
 VALUES   ( 2459, systimestamp, 981, 10, 15395.12, 163, 1, 7697.56 )

COMMIT WRITE BATCH NOWAIT;
```

Best Practice
Avoid overriding the Oracle commit wait process. Doing so may place your transaction(s) at risk.

Example 3-5: Forcing Commit Statements and Writing Comments   In few cases, you need to force a COMMIT statement to write changes to archive and redo logs. Use this method in those instances:

```
INSERT
  INTO  hr.job_history
VALUES  ( 100, '01-Jan-2000', trunc( sysdate ), 'AD_PRES', 90 );

COMMIT
  COMMENT 'In-doubt transaction forced by process xyz on date 123;

COMMIT FORCE '2.33.192';
```

An account with DBA privileges is required to issue the COMMIT FORCE command. The information inside the single quotation (' ') marks represent an in-doubt transaction ID. This value is found in the DBA_2PC_PENDING dictionary view. Additionally, you can commit a single corrupt transaction or all of them using the CORRUPT_XID and CORRUPT_XID_ALL options, respectively. These values can be found by querying the V$CORRUPT_XID_LIST dictionary view.

Best Practice
Forcing in-doubt transactions requires an intimate knowledge of Oracle System Change Numbers (SCNs) and the data dictionary. Use COMMIT FORCE only when transactions can't be tried again.

DML Locking and Isolation Control

Back in 1916, the U.S. government formed an over-arching standards organization named the *American National Standards Institute* (ANSI). It replaced many smaller engineering communities that were sprouting up at the time. We owe many of our modern methods and thoughts to that organization. Today we use standards defined by both ANSI and the *International Standards Organization* (ISO).

The ANSI-SQL92 and ISO/IEC 9075 code define SQL. Although it is a very informative read, we suggest you read it only if you need a quick fix for insomnia or you want something to do on a very long flight. However, knowing the gist of these standards helps you understand why database vendors create isolation levels the way that they do. A quick look into the

Isolation Level	Dirty Read	Unrepeatable Read	Phantom Read
Read committed	Possible	Possible	Possible
Read uncommitted	Not Possible	Possible	Possible
Repeatable read	Not Possible	Not Possible	Possible
Serializable	Not Possible	Not Possible	Not Possible

TABLE 3-1. *ANSI-92 Isolation Levels*

*Oracle Database Advanced Application Developer's Guide 11*g reveals some very interesting information about ANSI-92 isolation levels (see Table 3-1).

Notice that dirty database reads are possible in the ANSI read committed level. Remember that in database terms, a dirty read is the anomaly when

ANSI-92 Tidbit

In July 1992, Digital Equipment Corporation created a major update of the ANSI-89 standard called ANSI-92. Many topics were introduced, including current ANSI SQL joins. For example, the following query is ANSI-89–compliant:

```
SELECT   e.employee_id
     ,   e.first_name
     ,   e.last_name
     ,   e.salary
     ,   j.min_salary
     ,   j.max_salary
  FROM   hr.employees e
     ,   hr.jobs j
 WHERE   e.job_id = j.job_id;
```

This query represents the newer ANSI-92 method of the query:

```
SELECT   e.employee_id
     ,   e.first_name
     ,   e.last_name
     ,   e.salary
     ,   j.min_salary
     ,   j.max_salary
  FROM   hr.employees e INNER JOIN hr.jobs j
    ON   e.job_id = j.job_id;
```

Operation	Read Committed	Serializable
Dirty write	Not Possible	Not Possible
Dirty read	Not Possible	Not Possible
Unrepeatable read	Possible	Not Possible
Phantoms	Possible	Not Possible
Row-level locking	Yes	Yes
Reads Block Writes	No	No
Writes Block Reads	No	No
Row Level Blocking Writers	Yes	Yes

TABLE 3-2. *Oracle Read-Committed vs. Serializable Transactions*

parallel sessions occasionally see changed data from another session; and, as stated previously in our MVCC discussion, only a handful of vendors truly provide isolation. Some vendors skimp on isolation to provide more throughputs. In our mind, this practice is not acceptable, as you can forfeit data integrity completely when allowing dirty reads.

Oracle does not allow dirty database reads or writes. The only transactional faux pas possible are unrepeatable and phantom reads. Unrepeatable reads happen in large systems where update or delete statements change the data between a user's first and subsequent selects. Phantom database reads are very similar but differ in the fact that new data is introduced. Another glance into the *Oracle Database Advanced Application Developer's Guide 11*g reveals the information shown in Table 3-2.

Concurrency

Oracle shields users from dirty transactions via its MVCC feature and row/table locking. All user–data interaction occurs in memory, not on disk; however, it is possible for users to trump each other by issuing nonsimultaneous transactions. In the following scenario, users Jane and Joe issue transactions that illustrate this possibility.

Notice that Jane's update is not visible until she issues a commit. This is due to Oracle's MVCC feature. In addition, her changes are kept in memory

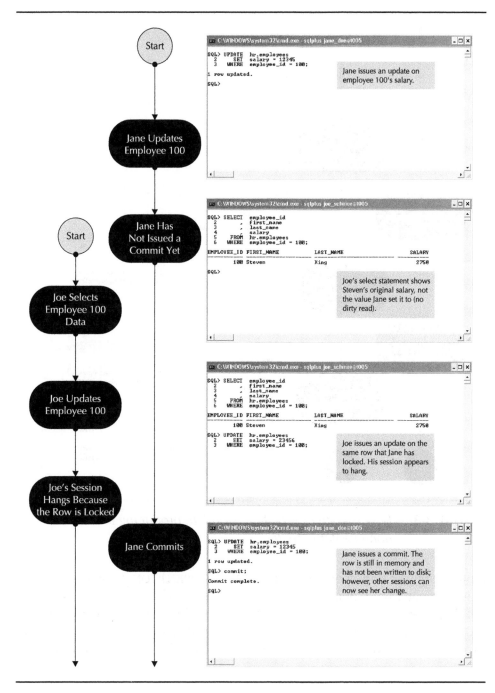

FIGURE 3-2.   *Jane and Joe attempt parallel updates.*

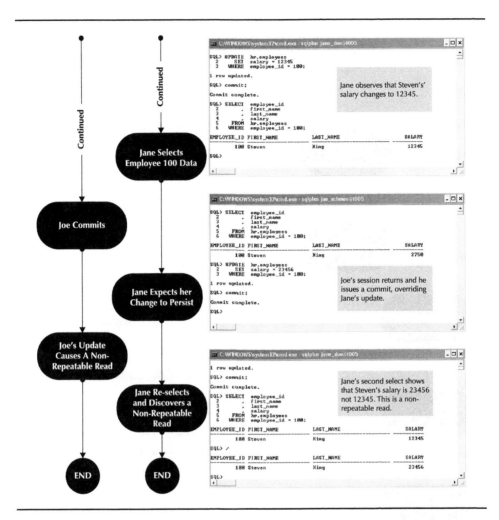

FIGURE 3-3. *Joe's update trumps Jane's update producing a nonrepeatable read.*

for the length of time specified by the UNDO_RETENTION parameter. This parameter has a default value of 900 seconds. If Joe issues a long-running query that lasts longer than the allotted time, he will receive an ORA-01555: SNAPSHOT TOO OLD ERROR. Be sure to set this parameter to a larger value in systems that require more than 5 minutes per query.

Transaction-Level Read Consistency

How do you prevent nonrepeatable or phantom reads? In some systems, this behavior is not acceptable and consistent reads are required. Observe in Table 3-2 that phantom and nonrepeatable reads are not possible when the database is set to the serializable mode. If your application requires read consistency, you must issue the SET TRANSACTION READ ONLY command. This must be the first statement you issue or you will get an ORA-01453: SET TRANSACTION must be first statement of transaction error.

It is very helpful to name your set transaction statement, especially when tracing distributed transactions. An example follows.

Example 3-6: Setting Transaction Level to Read Consistency

```
SQL> SET TRANSACTION READ ONLY NAME 'Distributed to NYC';
Transaction set.

SQL> SELECT  product_id
  2       ,  warehouse_id
  3       ,  quantity_on_hand
  4    FROM  oe.inventories@nyc_001
  5   WHERE  product_id = 3246;

PRODUCT_ID WAREHOUSE_ID QUANTITY_ON_HAND
---------- ------------ ----------------
      3246            6              161
      3246            7              148
      3246            8              136
      3246            2              225
      3246            5              175

SQL> commit;
Commit complete.
```

The 'Distributed to NYC' comment added to this set transaction statement is stored in the DBA_2PC_PENDING view. Information will remain in the view until the transaction is completed.

Best Practice

Name distributed transactions with the SET TRANSACTION NAME parameter.

Locking

In Figure 3-2, you saw the results of Oracle automatic table locking. This is the default mode and represents a balance between maximum concurrency and serialization. This is the preferred method; however, as with commit and set transaction statements, Oracle provides an override for locking tables. The following statements lock tables within transactions:

- SELECT FOR UPDATE

- SET TRANSACTION READ ONLY

- SET TRANSACTION ISOLATION LEVEL SERIALIZABLE

- LOCK TABLE

We demonstrate how to set a transaction in Example 3-6 but have not illustrated how to issue the LOCK TABLE and the FOR UPDATE clause within cursors. Here we show both methods because they are short.

Example 3-7: Using FOR UPDATE Within Cursors

```
SQL> DECLARE
  2     CURSOR c_employees IS
  3       SELECT  *
  4         FROM  hr.employees
  5       FOR UPDATE WAIT 10;
  6  BEGIN
  7    FOR r_employees IN c_employees LOOP
  8      UPDATE  hr.employees
  9         SET  salary = salary * 1.025
 10       WHERE  CURRENT OF C_employees;
 11    END LOOP;
 12  END;
 13  /
```

Rights Needed to Lock Tables

You automatically have rights to lock all tables that you own. If you need to lock tables in another schema, you must have the LOCK ANY TABLE system privilege.

Notice the FOR UPDATE WAIT 10 phrase on line 5. This phrase instructs Oracle to lock the rows referenced in the C_EMPLOYEE cursor. The WAIT 10 keywords tell Oracle to wait 10 seconds if a lock already exists on the rows referenced in your cursor. Your update will abort if the prior lock continues for more than 10 seconds. The following options are viable:

- WAIT [N], where N is the number of seconds you want to wait

- NOWAIT

If your transaction needs to persist, you should omit the numeric argument. The NOWAIT keyword instructs Oracle to return your transaction immediately if a lock is already acquired. The WHERE CURRENT OF phrase references the latest row in your cursor. Finally, be aware that your lock will persist until you issue a COMMIT/ROLLBACK.

Example 3-8: Issuing a Lock Table Statement

```
SQL> LOCK TABLE hr.employees IN EXCLUSIVE MODE NOWAIT;
Table(s) Locked.

SQL> UPDATE  hr.employees
  2    SET  salary = salary * 1.025
  3    WHERE  department_id = 10;
1 row updated.

SQL> COMMIT;
Commit complete.
```

Unlike the FOR UPDATE clause, the LOCK TABLE command locks every row in the table. In addition, the phrase IN EXCLUSIVE MODE completely locks out all activity but select statements. Valid lock-modes include the following:

- **ROW EXCLUSIVE**   The least restrictive lock level allows for row sharing and prevents users from locking the entire table or in ROW SHARE mode.

- **ROW SHARE**   Identical to ROW EXCLUSIVE without the exclusive share restriction; also known as SHARE UPDATE mode.

- **SHARE**   Allows selects but prohibits other updates.

- **SHARE ROW EXCLUSIVE**   Identical to SHARE mode with the additional restriction of preventing users from locking in SHARE mode.

- **EXCLUSIVE**   The most restrictive level prevents all DML activities but selecting.

Improving Transactional Performance

Oracle strives to improve its performance with each new release. However, your actions can both impede and take advantage of these features. One method of increasing performance is to bump up memory and CPU capability. While this is necessary at times, if your programs are not written for performance and scalability, you will always be adding hardware with very little gain. This method is expensive and not very rewarding.

A much better approach is to design your applications/programs for performance. Think ahead and create code that takes maximum advantage of Oracle features. One of the authors was asked to work with PeopleSoft for a job that took 7 hours to complete. The job was vital to business operation, and it constantly frustrated business users because it took so long to finish.

After a quick analysis, the author suggested that the developers rewrite their "serially designed" code to take advantage of bulk DML operations. The results were astonishing, as new completion times were under a minute. The best practices outlined here will greatly improve your transaction throughput and enable maximum use of Oracle-supplied performance features.

Database Agnosticism

It continually amazes us that developers regularly write *bloat-ware*, in the name of database agnosticism. It makes little sense that they sacrifice overall system performance for their desire to write less code. Yet, on the same whim, they prefer to manage complex constraint logic within their programs, which greatly increases total lines of code.

Invoker and Definer Rights

We briefly cover the topic of invoker and definer rights in this section. It is an advanced topic related to function, procedure, and package design, which we will discuss, in detail, in Part Two of this book.

Oracle created two methods of executing PL/SQL code for security purposes; in both cases, execution rights are associated to a user. In the first instance, the owner or definer of a PL/SQL program retains all rights for program execution. You carry out this option by issuing the AUTHID DEFINER keywords in the header of your named program.

Any user who receives rights to run a PL/SQL program compiled in this manner runs it as the owner. This option is extremely handy when you do not want, or cannot manage, hundreds or thousands of rights to the program or its associated objects. It is also exceedingly dangerous when the owner has elevated privileges. For example, a user who does not have enough rights to modify employee salary may misuse a program that maintains employee information when the program owner has rights to do so. We urge you to be careful in creating programs with definer rights.

In the second case, you issue the AUTHID CURRENT_USER keywords in the header of your program. This instructs Oracle to execute the program with the rights of its invoker. In this scenario, you can grant rights more liberally because the user never inherits the rights of the program owner. Here's an example.

Example 3-9: Issuing Definer Rights   In the following pseudo code, we create a function named QUARTERLY_SALES. When executed, it runs as the owner. All users who are granted the EXECUTE privilege to this function will run it as the HR user.

```
CREATE OR REPLACE FUNCTION hr.quarterly_sales
( pi_employee_id in number
, pi_quarter     in date
)
AUTHID DEFINER
AS
... declarative code goes here ...
BEGIN
... do something here and return ...
EXCEPTION
... handle the exception here and return ...
END;
/
```

Example 3-10: Issuing Invoker Rights   In the following pseudo code, we create a procedure called GIVE_RAISE. When executed, it runs as the user who invoked it. All users who are granted the EXECUTE privilege to this procedure will run it as themselves.

```
CREATE OR REPLACE PROCEDURE hr.give_rasie
( pi_employee_id in number )
AUTHID CURRENT_USER
AS
... declarative code goes here ...
BEGIN
... do something here ...
EXCEPTION
... handle the exception here ...
END;
/
```

Downloadable Code

The examples in this chapter are organized into six exercise files:

- ex03-01.sql demonstrates how to create a SAVEPOINT.

- ex03-02.sql demonstrates how to manipulate more than one SAVEPOINT.

- ex03-03.sql demonstrates how you can destroy SAVEPOINTs.

- ex03-04.sql demonstrates commit methods for Exercises 4–7.

- ex03-05.sql demonstrates how to lock with wait.

- ex03-06.sql demonstrates how to lock with no wait.

These programs should let you see the code in action. We think a download is friendlier then a cumbersome disk because the code doesn't take a great deal of space.

Summary

In this chapter, we discussed transaction control in moderate detail. We strongly encourage your continued study on this topic, as it will aid you in creating robust applications that provide maximum protection to the data held therein. A comprehensive collection on this topic is found in the following books:

- *Oracle 11g PL/SQL Programming Guide*, McGraw-Hill/Professional
- *Oracle Database Concepts 11g*, Oracle Corporation
- *Oracle Database Advanced Application Developer's Guide 11g*, Oracle Corporation

Best Practice Review

- Always ensure you have a good backup. It is not good enough just to activate backup programs such as RMAN. Validate and test your backups on a regular basis to ensure recoverability.

- Never assume that user input or program logic will create the results you are looking for. A pessimistic approach reduces and simplifies program logic.

- Label savepoints in a succinct but descriptive manner. Double-check your logic and make sure you roll back to the correct point in time.

- Avoid overriding the Oracle commit wait process. Doing so may place your transaction(s) at risk.

- Forcing in-doubt transactions requires an intimate knowledge of Oracle System Change Numbers (SCNs) and the data dictionary. Use `COMMIT FORCE` only when transactions can't be tried again.

- Name distributed transactions with the `SET TRANSACTION NAME` parameter.

- Keep your schema objects analyzed to take advantage of Oracle optimization.

- Use appropriate cost-based optimizer hints.

- Use bind variables and caching to perform less SQL parsing and disk IO.

- Consider bulk operations when you need to modify large data sets.

- Use the USE ROLLBACK SEGMENT CLAUSE of the SET TRANSACTION command if you do not use automatic undo management.

- Use the DBMS_APPLICATION_INFO.SET_ACTION procedure to preface your code. This enables you to measure performance of specific program modules.

- Know and understand the need to set locking levels and serializability. As serializability increases, overall concurrency decreases.

- Reuse cursors and reduce the overall time spent parsing by increasing the MAX_OPEN_CURSORS parameter.

Mastery Check

The mastery check is a series of true or false and multiple choice questions that let you confirm how well you understand the material in the chapter. You may check Appendix E for answers to these questions.

1. ☐ **True** ☐ **False** The acronym ACID represents a standard for transaction processing in relational databases.

2. ☐ **True** ☐ **False** Atomicity means all or no part of a transaction is written to permanent storage.

3. ☐ **True** ☐ **False** Consistency means that all transactions in a concurrent, multi-user system are granted even amounts of time to the servers CPU and memory.

4. ☐ **True** ☐ **False** Isolation means that no part of a transaction can be seen until all of it is completed and committed to the database.

5. ☐ **True** ☐ **False** Durability means that transactions are written to redundant disk arrays after the transaction is complete.

6. ☐ **True** ☐ **False** A SAVEPOINT lets you set a marker that lets you undo transactions that occur after the SAVEPOINT without undoing the transactions before the SAVEPOINT.

7. ☐ **True** ☐ **False** A rollback lets you undo everything in the session since you signed on, and can ignore SAVEPOINT markers that you've set.

8. ☐ **True** ☐ **False** A rollback lets you undo everything in the session since you set a SAVEPOINT.

9. ☐ **True** ☐ **False** A COMMIT is always automatic with each DML statement.

10. ☐ **True** ☐ **False** The NOWAIT option of a COMMIT ensures that you validate all writes to the redo and archive log files.

11. Which are valid sequencing patterns for a transaction?

  A. A SAVEPOINT, COMMIT, and ROLLBACK

  B. A SAVEPOINT, ROLLBACK, and COMMIT

  C. A SAVEPOINT and COMMIT

  D. All of the above

  E. Only B and C

12. Which of the following is not part of the ACID acronym?

  A. Acid

  B. Concurrency

  C. Insulation

  D. Durability

  E. None of the above

13. The acronym MVCC represents Oracle's attempt to achieve what?

  A. A multiuser voice communication concurrency protocol

  B. A multiversioned concurrency control for database consistency

  C. A multidatabase virtual community concurrency protocol

  D. All of the above

  E. None of the above

14. Which of these parameters let you extend or shorten how long the database retains transaction history?

   A. An UNDO_WAIT parameter

   B. An UNDO_LOCK parameter

   C. An UNDO_RETENTION parameter

   D. All of the above

   E. Only A and B

15. Which of these are valid lock modes in an Oracle database?

   A. A ROW SHARE parameter

   B. A SHARE parameter

   C. A ROW EXCLUSIVE parameter

   D. All of the above

   E. Only A and C

CHAPTER
4

Error Management

his chapter introduces the topic of error management. It references Chapter 5 of *Oracle Database 11g PL/SQL Programming Guide*. Careful study of this chapter will prove very helpful to you.

After reviewing thousands of PL/SQL programs throughout our professional careers, we've concluded that the lack of error management and proper instrumentation are the most common deficiencies found. Too often, many developers and DBAs leave out error management because of project time constraints or because they don't deem it necessary.

Unfortunately, such actions lead to inconsistent data and/or security vulnerabilities within the database. For example, hackers typically begin their database attacks by sending random bits of data into functions, packages, and procedures. They do so in an attempt to discover whether programs are susceptible to SQL injection. This method of attack is known as *fuzzing*. Database professionals protect their systems from attacks like these when they properly handle input and error conditions.

DBMS_ASSERT and Bind Variables

Two methods of database hardening include the use of bind variables and the DBMS_ASSERT package. DBMS_ASSERT is used to validate that input parameters are formed correctly and that schema and object names actually exist. Bind variables prevent the nesting of anonymous PL/SQL blocks. *Oracle Database 11g PL/SQL Programming Guide* illustrates how this is done.

This chapter also illustrates best practices in error management. It shows that properly managed exceptions are preferred and vital in creating robust and secure Oracle database systems. It is divided into the following topics:

- Error types
- Built-in exceptions
- User-defined exceptions
- Management and format of exceptions
- PL/SQL instrumentation

Error Types

PL/SQL errors are separated into two main categories. The first group handles syntax inaccuracies within your code. These types of errors are easy to spot because the PL/SQL compiler prints an ORA error message to your screen for each problem found.

Runtime or semantic errors are much more difficult to notice. They are caused by logical faults within your PL/SQL code. The results of logical mistakes can be disastrous. For example, mathematical errors may incorrectly compensate employees, or they may give customers discounts that are too large for a given sales campaign. While the first scenario may be easier to remediate, it would be extremely difficult and embarrassing to ask your customer for more money because of a program error.

Compilation Errors

In the following three examples, we discuss a few of the possible syntax error messages, also known as *error stacks*. Our purpose is to show you how to understand them, not to illustrate the thousands of possible error conditions. The first example demonstrates what the compiler will do with the lack of an ending semicolon.

Example 4-1: Missing Semicolon

```
SQL> BEGIN
  2    DBMS_OUTPUT.PUT_LINE ( 'Hello World!' )
  3    END;
  4    /
END;
*
ERROR at line 3:
ORA-06550: line 3, column 1:
PLS-00103: Encountered the symbol "END" when expecting one of the following:
:= . ( % ;The symbol ";" was substituted for "END" to continue.
```

See that the PL/SQL compiler printed the line number, errant block, ORA, and PLS messages to the screen. In this example, line 3 is referenced along with a message stating that the END symbol was reached when the compiler expected a semicolon after the DBMS_OUTPUT.PUT_LINE command. This example is fairly simple. It is easy to observe the exact location of our typo. This is not the case in real-world scenarios, however. For example, PL/SQL blocks often span hundreds of lines, which increase the likelihood of

Best Practice
Keep an electronic copy of *Oracle Databases Error Messages 11g Guide* handy to aid you in debugging. We always do.

syntactical errors. Additionally, the complexity of PL/SQL error stacks grows very fast when multiple errors are discovered.

Also note that the PLS-00103 error states our problem in an easy to understand manner. You may encounter times when ORA or PLS messages are not readily understood. In these circumstances, refer to *Oracle Databases Error Messages 11g Guide* to discover their true meaning.

A quick look into *Oracle Databases Error Messages 11g Guide* gives you information about ORA-06550 and PLS-00103 error messages, as shown in Table 4-1.

Combining error messages and stack output reveals exactly where the compiler found the typo and what it expected.

In our next example, we demonstrate another common error: the transposition of the equal and assignment operators. In PL/SQL the equal sign (=) is used for comparison. The assignment operator (:=) is used to allocate values to variables. Novice coders often mix them up, creating all

Error Message	Description
ORA-06550:	Line string, column string: string.
Cause:	Usually a PL/SQL compilation error.
Action:	None
PLS-00103:	String
cause:	This error message is from the parser. It found a token (language element) that is inappropriate in this context.
action:	Check previous tokens as well as the one given in the error message. The line and column numbers given in the error message refer to the error.

TABLE 4-1. *ORA-06550 and PLS-00103 Errors*

kinds of syntax errors at compilation. We're lucky because the compiler also prints some extraneous information about the semicolon on line 9.

Example 4-2: Multiple Error Stack

```
SQL> DECLARE
  2     lv_full_name VARCHAR2(50);
  3
  4     CURSOR c_emp IS
  5       SELECT  *
  6         FROM  hr.employees;
  7  BEGIN
  8     FOR r_emp IN c_emp LOOP
  9       lv_full_name = r_emp.first_name||' '||r_emp.last_name;
 10
 11       IF r_emp.department_id := 50 THEN
 12         DBMS_OUTPUT.PUT_LINE ( lv_full_name );
 13       END IF;
 14     END LOOP;
 15  END;
 16  /
     lv_full_name = r_emp.first_name||' '||r_emp.last_name;
                  *
ERROR at line 9:
ORA-06550: line 9, column 18:
PLS-00103: Encountered the symbol "=" when expecting one of thefollowing::= . (@
% ;
ORA-06550: line 9, column 58:
PLS-00103: Encountered the symbol ";" when expecting one of the
following:. ( ) , * @ % & - + / at mod remainder rem <an exponent (**)> and or ||
ORA-06550: line 11, column 28:
PLS-00103: Encountered the symbol "=" when expecting one of the
following:. ( * @ % & = - + < / > at in is mod remainder not rem then
<an exponent (**)> <> or != or ~= >= <= <> and or like like2 like4 likec between
|| multiset
```

Observe that the error message codes are the same two we saw in Example 4-1. This is because the PL/SQL compiler uses ORA-06550 and PLS-00103 in all cases when it discovers wayward tokens.

Both stack messages related to the equal operator make sense; however, the message about the semicolon seems superfluous. You may see this kind of behavior as you debug PL/SQL code. To become efficient at debugging, you must be able to identify pertinent information in the error stack.

Our final example on syntax errors demonstrates what the PL/SQL compiler will do when errantly referencing the C_EMP cursor within the R_EMP for loop.

Example 4-3: Referenced Cursor Object Is Out of Scope

```
SQL> DECLARE
  2    CURSOR c_emp IS
  3      SELECT  *
  4        FROM  hr.employees;
  5  BEGIN
  6    FOR r_emp IN c_emp LOOP
  7      DBMS_OUTPUT.PUT_LINE ( c_emp.first_name );
  8    END LOOP;
  9  END;
 10  /
     DBMS_OUTPUT.PUT_LINE ( c_emp.first_name );
                                    *
ERROR at line 7:
ORA-06550: line 7, column 34:
PLS-00225: subprogram or cursor 'C_EMP' reference is out of scope
ORA-06550: line 7, column 5:
PL/SQL: Statement ignored
```

Notice that the PLS message has changed. In this case, the PL/SQL compiler correctly identifies that we have inadvertently introduced the phrase C_EMP.FIRST_NAME instead of R_EMP.FIRST_NAME. To gain a better understanding of why this error occurred, we must reference *Oracle Databases Error Messages 11*g *Guide* once again for information shown in Table 4-2.

Error Message	Description
PLS-00225:	Subprogram or cursor '*string*' reference is out of scope.
Cause:	The prefix in a qualified name was a subprogram or cursor that was not in an enclosing scope—i.e., a subprogram or cursor name is being used as a scope qualifier for a reference to an entity (within that subprogram or cursor) that is not in scope.
Action:	a) If the intention was to refer to a local variable of a non-enclosing function, this is not allowed; remove the reference b). If this is a parameterless function, and the intention was to access a field of the result of a call to this function, then use empty parentheses in the call.

TABLE 4-2. *PLS-00225 Error*

It is tempting, even for advanced PL/SQL programmers, to write large blocks of code without stopping to perform occasional compilations. We rarely see programmers who can do this without creating errors. Debugging many errors at once can be time-consuming to say the least, especially if unnecessary information is printed in the error stack, as shown in Example 4-2.

A more efficient method of programming would be to create each program block in logical groups, compiling after functional units are finished. For example, a reasonable start might include the creation of variables, initial cursors, and loops, as follows:

Example 4-4: An Iterative Coding Approach Prevents Unnecessary Debugging

```
SQL> DECLARE
  2    ln_year                 NUMBER := 2000;
  3    ln_total_salary         NUMBER;
  4
  5    CURSOR c_orders IS
  6      with sales_by_quarter as
  7      (   SELECT o.sales_rep_id
  8               , TO_CHAR ( o.order_date, '"Q-"Q" "YYYY' ) sales_quarter
  9               , SUM ( o.gross_profit ) gross_profit
 10          FROM oe.orders o
 11         WHERE TO_CHAR ( o.order_date, 'YYYY' ) = ln_year
 12      GROUP BY o.sales_rep_id
 13             , TO_CHAR ( o.order_date, '"Q-"Q" "YYYY' )
 14      )
 15      SELECT e.first_name||' '||e.last_name full_name
 16           , e.salary
 17           , e.commission_pct
 18           , sbq.*
 19        FROM hr.employees e
 20           , sales_by_quarter sbq
 21       WHERE e.employee_id = sbq.sales_rep_id
 22         AND rownum <= 3;
 23  BEGIN
 24    FOR r_orders IN c_orders LOOP
 25      dbms_output.put_line  ( r_orders.full_name||' '||
 26                               r_orders.sales_quarter||' '||
 27                               r_orders.gross_profit
 28                            );
 29    END LOOP;
 30  END;
 31  /
```

Observe that we limited the cursor to three rows and called the `DBMS_OUTPUT.PUT_LINE` command to display the results. It is prudent to limit program output during these initial phases of coding, especially if tables defined within your cursors have thousands or millions of rows. Once you are happy with your current block, begin coding the next logical section:

```
SQL> DECLARE
  2    ln_year                 NUMBER := 1999;
  3    ln_total_salary         NUMBER;
  4    lv_bonus_achieved       CHAR := 'N';
      ... omitted for brevity ...
 26      ln_total_salary :=  r_orders.salary +
 27                          r_orders.gross_profit *
 28                          r_orders.commission_pct;
 29
 30      IF r_orders.gross_profit >= 10000
 31      THEN
 32        ln_total_salary   := ln_total_salary + r_orders.gross_profit * .05;
 33        lv_bonus_achieved := 'Y';
 34      END IF;
 35
 36      DBMS_OUTPUT.PUT_LINE ( r_orders.full_name||' '||
 37                             r_orders.sales_quarter||' '||
 38                             r_orders.gross_profit||' '||
 39                             r_orders.salary||' '||
 40                             r_orders.commission_pct||' '||
 41                             ln_total_salary||' '||
 42                             ( r_orders.gross_profit - ln_total_salary )||' '||
 43                             lv_bonus_achieved
 44                           );
 45
 46      lv_bonus_achieved := 'N';
 47    END LOOP;
 48  END;
 49  /
```

This program prints the following to screen:

```
DBMS_OUTPUT:
------------
Lindsey Smith Q-4 1999 31922.55 8240 .05 11432.255 20490.295 Y
Nanette Cambrault Q-2 1999 24 7725 .02 7725.48 -7701.48 N
Oliver Tuvault Q-3 1999 38863.6 7210 .02 9930.452 28933.148 Y
```

In this iteration we did the following:

- Added the variable `LV_BONUS_ACHIEVED`

- Assigned the `LV_TOTAL_SALARY` variable a value of `SALARY + GROSS_PROFIT * COMMISSION_PCT`

- Gave an extra 5 percent bonus to each salesperson based on total gross profit

- Printed these results to the screen

Iterative coding allows you to wrap your mind around what you're doing. It also empowers you to think in a consistent and logical manner. Finally, this method saves you countless hours poring over large blocks of code in an attempt to discover your mistakes.

> ### Best Practice
> Perform occasional compiles based on logical code units.

Semantics Errors

Semantics errors are logical mistakes that are made within your programs. For example, in our preceding illustration we paid each salesperson their salary plus commission. We tested the results for all orders and discovered that some salespeople were getting compensation greater than their gross profit. Running the block for the year 1999 returned the following:

```
DBMS_OUTPUT:
- - - - - - - - - - -
Lindsey Smith Q-4 1999 31,922.55 8,240 .05 11,432.255 20,490.295 Y
Nanette Cambrault Q-2 1999 24 7,725 .02 7,725.48 -7,701.48 N
Oliver Tuvault Q-3 1999 38,863.6 7,210 .02 9,930.452 28,933.148 Y
```

Observe that Nanette Cambrault made $7725.48 in the second quarter of 1999. Her sales brought in a whopping total of $24 in gross profit. This scenario caught our interest, so we ran our program against all the sales records. Our mistake totaled $39,767.14. Mind you, this number isn't nearly as big as it could be. The HR and OE sample schemas hold limited amounts of data. For instance, the OE.ORDERS table has only 105 records. Most thriving companies will have similar tables that hold millions of records. If you multiply $39,767.14 by a factor of 1000 or more, you will begin to see the magnitude of this error.

Oracle-Supplied Error Conditions

Oracle provides more than 2300 pages of predefined error conditions. In addition, they have already given you a condition and message for anything you can dream up. Still, it is common to see PL/SQL developers spending numerous hours coding their own variations on the same themes. When asked why they spent so much time creating custom error handling, developers often state that they "didn't know Oracle did that." Table 4-3 represents a short list of Oracle-supplied error conditions.

Prefix	Message Type	Pages
AMD-	Catalog Metadata Error Messages	7
AUD-	InterMedia Audio Error Messages	3
DBV-	DBVERIFY Data Integrity Error Messages	1
DRG-	Oracle Text Error Messages	65
EXP-	Export System Error Messages	12
IMG-	InterMedia Image Error Messages	20
IMP-	Import System Error Messages	12
KUP-	External Table System Error Messages	17
LCD/LRM-	Parameter Error Messages	6
LFI-	BFILE Error Messages	9
LPX-	XML Parser Error Messages	33
NCR-	Remote DB Error Messages	8
NID-	DBNEWID Database ID and Name Utility Error Messages	11
NMP-	SNMP Error Messages	2
NNC-	Names Client Error Messages	7
NNL-	Names Control Utility Error Messages	35
NNO-	Names Server Error Messages	23
NPL-	Names Server Network Presentation Layer Error Messages	4

TABLE 4-3. *A Short List of Oracle Error Messages*

Prefix	Message Type	Pages
NZE-	Network Security System Error Messages	2
O2F-	Oracle Type Translator File Error Messages	11
O2I-	Oracle Type Translator Interface Error Message	11
O2U-	Oracle Type Translator Utility Error Message	11
ORA-	General Oracle Error Messages	1273
PCB-	Pro*Cobol Error Messages	20
PCC-	Pro*C Error Messages	23
PGA-	Program Global Area Error Messages	22
PLS-	PL/SQL Error Messages	75
PLW-	PL/SQL Logical Errors Related to Dead/Unused Lines of Code	5
QSM-	Performance Summary Advisor Messages	51
RMAN-	Recovery Manager Messages	127

TABLE 4-3. *A Short List of Oracle Error Messages (continued)*

Oracle SQLCODE and SQLERRM

Every error in *Oracle Databases Error Messages 11g Guide* has a unique number and message. The numeric value associated to error conditions is called the SQLCODE. You can associate your own variables to SQLCODE numbers via the PRAGMA EXCEPTION_INIT keywords. This is especially helpful when you wish to perform specific tasks when Oracle errors are raised. Example 4-5 shows how to use PRAGMA EXCEPTION_INIT to catch errors.

Example 4-5: Using PRAGMA EXCEPTION_INIT to Catch System Errors

```
CREATE TABLE hr.emergency_contact
  ( employee_id    NUMBER
  , full_name      VARCHAR2(50)
  , phone_home     VARCHAR2(15)
  , phone_cell     VARCHAR2(15)
  , phone_pager    VARCHAR2(15)
  );
```

This creates a table that we use to demonstrate error handling with the `PRAGMA EXCEPTION_INIT` phrase:

```
ALTER TABLE hr.emergency_contact
   ADD ( CONSTRAINT ec_employee_id_unk
         UNIQUE ( employee_id, full_name ));
```

The `ALTER TABLE` command creates a unique constraint of the aggregated `EMPLOYEE_ID` and `FULL_NAME` columns. The following PL/SQL program contains no exception block and attempts to violate the database constraint:

```
SQL> BEGIN
  2     INSERT
  3        INTO hr.emergency_contact
  4     VALUES ( 1
  5            , 'Jane Doe'
  6            , '+1.123.456.7890'
  7            , NULL
  8            , '+1.123.567.8901'
  9            );
 10   END;
 11   /
```

Observe that we throw the `ORA-00001` unique constraint error when we rerun our PL/SQL block:

```
SQL> /
DECLARE
*
ERROR at line 1:
ORA-00001: unique constraint (HR.EC_EMPLOYEE_ID_PKY) violated
ORA-06512: at line 4
```

If you need to catch this error and perform additional tasks against it, you can do the following:

```
SQL> DECLARE
  2     unique_constraint exception;
  3     pragma exception_init (unique_constraint, -00001);
  4   BEGIN
  5     INSERT
  6        INTO hr.emergency_contact
  7     VALUES ( 1
  8            , 'Jane Doe'
```

```
 9              , '+1.123.456.7890'
10              , NULL
11              , '+1.123.567.8901'
12              );
13   EXCEPTION
14     WHEN unique_constraint THEN
15       DBMS_OUTPUT.PUT_LINE ( 'Oops! You threw the unique_constraint error');
16   END;
17   /
Oops! You threw the unique_constraint error
```

Notice that we create a UNIQUE_CONSTRAINT exception variable. Then we associate the variable to the SQLCODE with the PRAGMA EXCEPTION_INIT keywords. When our program encounters the ORA-00001 error, it allows us to DBMS_OUTPUT.PUT_LINE instead of immediately breaking out of the program.

Exception Scope

Continuance of PL/SQL blocks is maintained by encasing potential errant code within anonymous sub-blocks. Sub-block nesting can continue for nearly 100 levels before the compiler can no longer parse your code. Typical parent-child nests are no deeper than 5–10 levels. The next four examples show the following encasing techniques:

- Standard sub-block encasement

- Loop sub-block encasement

- Save point redirection

- GOTO branching

Our first example demonstrates basic sub-block encasement.

Example 4-6: Encasing Sub-blocks

```
SQL> DECLARE
  2     ln_parent          NUMBER;
  3     ln_child_level1    NUMBER;
  4     ln_child_level2    NUMBER;
  5     ln_random_0_1      NUMBER;
  6   BEGIN
  7     BEGIN
  8       DBMS_OUTPUT.PUT_LINE ( 'Made it past Parent.' );
```

```
 9        ln_random_0_1 := ROUND ( DBMS_RANDOM.VALUE ( 0, 1 ));
10        ln_parent := 1 / ln_random_0_1;
11        BEGIN
12          DBMS_OUTPUT.PUT_LINE ( 'Made it past Child Level 1.' );
13          ln_random_0_1 := ROUND ( DBMS_RANDOM.VALUE ( 0, 1 ));
14          ln_child_level1 := 1 / ln_random_0_1;
15          BEGIN
16            DBMS_OUTPUT.PUT_LINE ( 'Made it past Child Level 2.' );
17            ln_random_0_1 := ROUND ( DBMS_RANDOM.VALUE ( 0, 1 ));
18            ln_child_level2 := 1 / ln_random_0_1;
19          END;
20        END;
21      END;
22    EXCEPTION
23      WHEN OTHERS THEN
24        DBMS_OUTPUT.PUT_LINE ( SQLERRM );
25    END;
26    /
```

The output of the script shows:

```
Made it past Parent.
ORA-01476: divisor is equal to zero
```

A second run of the script tells us that we made it farther:

```
Made it past Parent.
Made it past Child Level 1.
ORA-01476: divisor is equal to zero
```

In this scenario, we use the Oracle random number package, DBMS_RANDOM, to provide 1 and 0 values. It lets us simulate a DIVIDE_BY_ZERO condition. Notice that the first and second executions succeed at differing levels. This illustrates the ability of sub-blocks to catch the errors immediately related to their level. Sub-blocks can handle only the errors related to themselves and raised errors within child blocks.

Our second example encases an error-prone block within a FOR loop. When our expected error is triggered, we print the error and continue.

Example 4-7: Encasing Within Loops

```
SQL> DECLARE
  2      ln_employee_id          NUMBER;
  3      ln_order_total          NUMBER;
  4
```

```
 5    CURSOR c_employee IS
 6      SELECT *
 7        FROM hr.employees;
 8  BEGIN
 9    FOR r_employee IN c_employee LOOP
10      ln_employee_id := r_employee.employee_id;
11
12      DECLARE
13        no_salesman_found    exception;
14      BEGIN
15        SELECT SUM ( order_total )
16          INTO ln_order_total
17          FROM oe.orders
18         WHERE sales_rep_id = ln_employee_id;
19
20        IF ln_order_total IS NOT NULL THEN
21          DBMS_OUTPUT.PUT_LINE ( ln_order_total );
22        ELSE
23          RAISE no_salesman_found;
24        END IF;
25      EXCEPTION
26        WHEN no_salesman_found THEN
27          DBMS_OUTPUT.PUT_LINE ( 'Caught NO_SALESMAN_FOUND' );
28      END;
29    END LOOP;
30  EXCEPTION
31    WHEN OTHERS THEN
32      DBMS_OUTPUT.PUT_LINE ( SQLERRM );
33  END;
34  /
```

The exception is triggered and the following message is printed to screen:

```
Caught NO_SALESMAN_FOUND
```

Best Practice

Allow error messages to be propagated up to their calling application instead of using the WHEN OTHERS phrase.

Our third example nests an anonymous block within a FOR loop. Only 35 records in the HR.EMPLOYEES table will correctly trigger the SUM(ORDER_TOTAL) assignment of the LN_ORDER_TOTAL variable. The rest will throw a NO_DATA_FOUND error.

Example 4-8: Savepoint Exception Retry

```
SQL> DECLARE
  2    ln_employee_id          NUMBER := 1;
  3    unique_constraint       EXCEPTION;
  4
  5    PRAGMA EXCEPTION_INIT ( unique_constraint, -00001 );
  6  BEGIN
  7    FOR i IN 1..10 LOOP    -- insert 10 rows
  8      FOR j IN 1..15 LOOP -- try 10x before giving up.
  9        BEGIN
 10          SAVEPOINT my_savepoint;
 11            INSERT
 12            INTO hr.emergency_contact
 13            VALUES
 14            ( ln_employee_id
 15            , 'Jane Doe'
 16            , '+1.123.456.7890'
 17            , NULL
 18            , '+1.123.567.8901'
 19            );
 20          EXIT; -- exit block if successful... otherwise we would get a
 21                -- possible 10x10 inserts.
 22        EXCEPTION
 23          WHEN unique_constraint THEN
 24            ROLLBACK TO my_savepoint;
 25            ln_employee_id := ln_employee_id + 1;
 26        END;
 27      END LOOP j;
 28    END LOOP i;
 29  END;
 30  /
```

Note that we roll back all transactions to the named SAVEPOINT, and then we increment the LN_EMPLOYEE_ID variable by 1 and try again with the inner loop.

Best Practice
Use savepoints to roll back partial transactions. This prevents orphaned data, thereby maintaining data integrity.

In the Example 4-9, we create a basic loop structure with the TRY_AGAIN label and GOTO statement. This method is also known as *branching*. We want to caution you in the use of this method, because manual management of looping structures can sometimes create infinite loops.

Example 4-9: Savepoint Redirection

```
SQL> DECLARE
  2     ln_employee_id          NUMBER;
  3     ln_order_total          NUMBER;
  4
  5     CURSOR c_employee IS
  6       SELECT *
  7       FROM hr.employees
  8       WHERE commission_pct IS NOT NULL;
  9   BEGIN
 10     FOR r_employee IN c_employee LOOP
 11       ln_employee_id := r_employee.employee_id;
 12       <<try_again>>
 13       BEGIN
 14         SELECT SUM ( order_total )
 15         INTO ln_order_total
 16         FROM oe.orders
 17         WHERE sales_rep_id = ln_employee_id;
 18
 19         DBMS_OUTPUT.PUT_LINE ( ln_order_total );
 20       EXCEPTION
 21         WHEN NO_DATA_FOUND THEN
 22           GOTO try_again;
 23       END;
 24     END LOOP;
 25   END;
 26   /
```

A short time ago, one of the authors was asked to help debug a package in a large educational system. The database had been upgraded and engineers were having trouble with a package that made classroom and teacher assignments. The problem was that CPU and memory usage spun

Best Practice
Avoid the GOTO command.

out of control each time the package was called. Additionally, the package occasionally went into limbo.

Upon inspection, the author discovered that the original developer did not understand recursive programming patterns. Instead of looping through class assignments in reverse logical order, the developer built a complex set of labeled sub-blocks. If certain conditions were met, the developer issued a GOTO command to send the program to its appropriate block. This logic worked swimmingly until the data didn't agree with the developer's finite set of conditions.

Our advice is, never use GOTO unless

- You know for certain your finite set of rules will never need to change.

- Your data is constrained to support said rules.

- You have a nuclear-powered shock collar rigged up for anyone even thinking about changing the rules.

- You develop an omniscience that helps you know better.

Defining Custom Error Conditions

To define your own error conditions, you must first create an exception variable. Then you add code within your PL/SQL block to raise that error condition. Finally, you must account for your error within the exception block of your PL/SQL code as follows.

Example 4-10: Creation of User-Defined Error Conditions

```
SQL> DECLARE
  2    ln_order_total    number;
  3    ln_promotion_id   number := 1;
  4    ln_order_count    number;
  5    no_promo_found    exception;
  6  BEGIN
  7    SELECT COUNT(*)
  8      INTO ln_order_count
  9      FROM oe.orders
 10     WHERE promotion_id = ln_promotion_id;
 11
 12    IF ln_order_count > 0 THEN
 13      SELECT SUM ( order_total )
 14        INTO ln_order_total
```

```
15        FROM oe.orders
16       WHERE promotion_id = ln_promotion_id;
17    ELSE
18      raise no_promo_found;
19    END IF;
20  EXCEPTION
21    WHEN no_promo_found THEN
22      DBMS_OUTPUT.PUT_LINE ( 'No Sales found for Promotion: '||ln_promotion_id);
23  END;
24  /
```

This outputs:

```
No Sales found for Promotion: 1
```

In this scenario, we use LN_ORDER_COUNT variable to check for records that match our search criteria. If the count is greater than 0, we add up the ORDER_TOTAL column and assign it to the LN_ORDER_TOTAL variable.

We see developers use this logic all the time. They do this because they know that the COUNT(*) function always returns data, and thus avoids the NULL record dilemma. The problem is that Oracle already handles this scenario with the NO_DATA_FOUND condition. We shorten the prior block by doing the following.

Example 4-11: Shortening Error Code by Using Oracle-Defined Conditions

```
SQL> DECLARE
  2    ln_order_total     number;
  3    ln_promotion_id    number := 1;
  4  BEGIN
  5    SELECT order_total
  6      INTO ln_order_total
  7      FROM oe.orders
  8     WHERE promotion_id = ln_promotion_id;
  9  EXCEPTION
 10    WHEN NO_DATA_FOUND THEN
 11      DBMS_OUTPUT.PUT_LINE ('No Sales found for Promotion: '||ln_promotion_id);
 12  END;
 13  /
```

The output is what we saw earlier:

```
No Sales found for Promotion: 1
```

Observe that we shorten the prior block by 11 lines and do not have to create or manage our own exception condition or variable. We also do not have to document and publish a list of error conditions. This benefit is huge in complex systems where technical documentation rapidly becomes a full-time job.

> ### Best Practice
> Know the built-in errors and leverage them to simplify your code.

You will save countless hours of maintenance if you limit your exception programming to Oracle's built-in error codes and variables. Consult *Oracle Databases Error Messages 11*g *Guide.* You can use the PRAGMA EXCEPTION_INIT keywords to associate predefined error conditions to your exception variables.

The RAISE_APPLICATION_ERROR procedure is part of the DBMS_STANDARD built-in package. It allows you to raise ORA- related messages without first declaring exception variables or using the EXCEPTION_INIT *pragma.*

Example 4-12: Using RAISE_APPLICATION_ERROR to Catch Error Conditions

```
SQL> DECLARE
  2    CURSOR c_rental IS
  3      SELECT  c.member_id
  4            , c.first_name||' '||c.last_name full_name
  5            , t.transaction_amount
  6        FROM  video_store.transaction t
  7            , video_store.rental r
  8            , video_store.contact c
  9       WHERE  r.rental_id = t.rental_id
 10         AND  r.customer_id = c.contact_id;
 11  BEGIN
 12    FOR r_rental IN c_rental LOOP
 13      IF r_rental.transaction_amount > 75 THEN
 14        RAISE_APPLICATION_ERROR ( -20001, 'No transaction may be more than $75', TRUE );
 15      END IF;
 16    END LOOP;
 17  END;
 18  /
DECLARE
*
ERROR at line 1:
ORA-20001: No transaction may be more than $75
ORA-06512: at line 14
```

Notice that we did not have to create an exception variable. In addition, we associated the user-defined 20001 SQLCODE to the error message. The TRUE argument tells the procedure to include the error in the error stack. The default value of the third argument is FALSE, which tells the RAISE_APPLICATION_ERROR procedure to clear the error stack and print only the user-defined error message.

PL/SQL Instrumentation

Many of the PL/SQL applications you write will take longer than a few seconds to execute. We've seen some pretty creative methods of tracking program execution. One of the most common but problematic techniques is to use timestamps with commits. Updated timestamp columns flag which rows have been programmatically affected. The problem is, however, that commits are inherently expensive and throwing them in the middle of your application is a sure fire way to do the following:

- S-L-O-W down your application

- Spike the memory and CPU usage on your Oracle server

- Generate tons of redo log information

What we need is a method of writing application activity without taxing the system. This kind of output is also known as *program instrumentation*. The following two examples demonstrate how this should be done.

In our first example, we show a procedure called PLS_LOGGER that writes application information to screen, table, file, or all three. The output format is similar to other programming instrumentation and contains a timestamp, level of message, the name of the program, and an error message. Running the procedure in its most basic form generates the following results.

Example 4-13: Using the PLS_LOGGER Procedure

```
SQL> BEGIN
  2     FOR i IN 1 .. 5 LOOP
  3        pls_logger  ( pi_program_name   => 'SCREEN_PROGRAM_ERROR'
  4                    , pi_log_level      => 'INFO'
  5                    , pi_write_to       => 'SCREEN'
```

```
6                        , pi_error_message  => 'This execution writes to SCREEN.'
7                        );
8
9      pls_logger    ( pi_program_name   => 'WARN_PROGRAM_ERROR'
10                      , pi_log_level     => 'WARN'
11                      , pi_write_to      => 'TABLE'
12                      , pi_error_message => 'This execution writes to TABLE.'
13                      );
14
15     pls_logger    ( pi_program_name   => 'FATAL_PROGRAM_ERROR'
16                      , pi_log_level     => 'FATAL'
17                      , pi_write_to      => 'ALL'
18                      , pi_error_message => 'This execution writes to ALL.'
19                      , pi_file          => 'my_logfile.txt'
20                      );
21     END LOOP;
22
23     FOR j in 1 .. 5 LOOP
24        pls_logger  ( pi_program_name   => 'FATAL_PROGRAM_ERROR'
25                      , pi_log_level     => 'FATAL'
26                      , pi_write_to      => 'FILE'
27                      , pi_error_message => 'This execution writes to FILE.'
28                      , pi_file          => 'my_logfile.txt'
29                      );
30     END LOOP;
31   END;
32   /
```

This generates the following:

```
08:04:24.74100 APR 25, 2009 [INFO] SCREEN_PROGRAM_ERROR This execution writes to SCREEN.
08:04:24.75700 APR 25, 2009 [FATAL] FATAL_PROGRAM_ERROR This execution writes to ALL.
...
```

It also prints the following to the `my_logfile.txt` file:

```
04:04:13.73614 APR 25, 2009 [FATAL] FATAL_PROGRAM_ERROR This execution writes to ALL.
04:04:13.73719 APR 25, 2009 [FATAL] FATAL_PROGRAM_ERROR This execution writes to ALL.
...
```

DBMS_APPLICATION_INFO

The DBMS_APPLICATION_INFO package is one of many built-in programs that Oracle provides. It is extremely helpful in determining program status during execution. We discuss this package in detail in Appendix D of this book.

Our `PLS_LOGGER` program merely wraps functionality provided by Oracle. We use `DBMS_OUTPUT` to print to screen, a standard `INSERT` to write to the `PROGRAM_LOG` table, and `UTL_FILE` to write to file. Our program takes the input shown in Table 4-4.

Input	Description
`pi_program_name:`	The name of your program.
`pi_directory:`	The name of the directory `PLS_LOGGER` will write to. The file must be created prior to writing.
`pi_file:`	The name of the file `PLS_LOGGER` will write to. The file must be created prior to writing.
`pi_log_level:`	The level of warning you want to write.
`pi_write_to:`	The kind of output you wish to write: `SCREEN`, `TABLE`, `FILE`, `ALL`.
`pi_status:`	Either a 1 or 0. Output with a 0 status is typically informational. Output with a 1 status indicates failure.
`pi_error_message:`	The error message you want to write. This text is limited to 500 characters in our example. You must modify the table properties to increase this amount.

TABLE 4-4. *PLS_LOGGER Input Parameters*

Running the `PLS_LOGGER` in the manner described previously cannot properly demonstrate the power of a program like this. To do so, we must create a more realistic program. In the following example, we do so using the `DBMS_APPLICATION_INFO` built-in package to write to the `V$SESSION_LONGOPS` system view.

Example 4-14: An Instrumented PL/SQL Program   In an effort to provide a realistic sample of program instrumentation, we've create the following program. It's not terribly long or complex; however, it may be a bit challenging for novice PL/SQL programmers. For this reason, we subdivide and comment on each logical block:

```
SQL> DECLARE
  2    ln_nohint        NUMBER := DBMS_APPLICATION_INFO.SET_SESSION_LONGOPS_NOHINT;
  3    ln_rindex        NUMBER := DBMS_APPLICATION_INFO.SET_SESSION_LONGOPS_NOHINT;
  4    ln_slo           NUMBER;
  5    ln_target        NUMBER := 55334;
  6    lv_opname        VARCHAR2(30) := 'Update Customer Credit';
  7    lv_target_desc   VARCHAR2(30) := 'updating row:';
  8    ln_total_work    NUMBER := 0;
  9    ln_sofar         NUMBER := 0;
 10
 11    CURSOR c_cust IS
 12      SELECT   customer_id
 13      FROM   customers
 14      WHERE  nls_territory in ( 'CHINA', 'JAPAN', 'THAILAND' );
```

See that we create several variables in the BEGIN section. These variables become input parameters in the DBMS_APPLICATION_INFO.SET_SESSION_LONGOPS procedure. We also create a cursor that pulls 115,155 rows of data from the CUSTOMERS table.

```
 15    BEGIN
 16      SELECT   count(*)
 17      INTO   ln_total_work
 18      FROM   customers
 19      WHERE  nls_territory in ( 'CHINA', 'JAPAN', 'THAILAND' );
 20
 21      PLS_LOGGER  ( pi_program_name    => 'Update Customer Credit'
 22                  , pi_log_level       => 'INFO'
 23                  , pi_write_to        => 'SCREEN'
 24                  , pi_error_message   => 'Updating '||ln_total_work||' rows.'
 25                  );
```

We set the LN_TOTAL_WORK variable and print to screen a message stating that we will be updating 115,155 rows of data.

```
 26      SAVEPOINT default_credit_limit
 27      FOR r_cust IN c_cust LOOP
 28        ln_sofar := ln_sofar + 1;
 29
 30        UPDATE   customers
 31           SET   credit_limit = credit_limit * .95
 32         WHERE   customer_id = r_cust.customer_id;
 33
 34        DBMS_APPLICATION_INFO.SET_SESSION_LONGOPS
 35        ( rindex   => ln_rindex
 36        , slno     => ln_slo
```

```
37          , op_name => lv_opname
38          , target  => ln_target
39          , target_desc => lv_target_desc
40          , context     => 0
41          , sofar       => ln_sofar
42          , totalwork   => ln_total_work
43          , units       => 'row updates'
44          );
45     END LOOP;
46     COMMIT;
47   EXCEPTION
48     WHEN others THEN
49       ROLLBACK to default_credit_limit -- you must do this first
50       PLS_LOGGER  ( pi_program_name    => 'Update Customer Credit'
51                   , pi_log_level       => 'FATAL'
52                   , pi_write_to        => 'ALL'
53                   , pi_error_message   => SQLERRM
54                   );
55     COMMIT; -- commits the fatal insert.
56   END;
57   /
```

Observe that we use the DBMS_APPLICATION_INFO built-in package to show general program status. This information is available outside the session that executes your code. It also does not require a commit. These attributes are extremely helpful when you want to create applications that scale well. Also, note that we printed to screen only on major program milestones.

Best Practice
Instrument your PL/SQL programs.

Finally, observe that we wrote system-critical errors to table and file. Your application may require similar logic. You can also expand this theme by setting flags that determine verbosity.

Downloadable Code

The examples in this chapter are organized into 14 exercise files:

- ex04-01.sql demonstrates the effect of a missing semicolon.

- ex04-02.sql demonstrates a multiple error stack return.

- `ex04-03.sql` demonstrates the impact of an out-of-scope error.

- `ex04-04.sql` demonstrates how iterative coding prevents unnecessary debugging.

- `ex04-05.sql` demonstrates how using a `PRAGMA EXCEPTION_INIT` catches system errors.

- `ex04-06.sql` demonstrates how you should encase sub-blocks.

- `ex04-07.sql` demonstrates how you should encase within loop structures.

- `ex04-08.sql` demonstrates how to implement a `SAVEPOINT` retry.

- `ex04-09.sql` demonstrates how to implement a `SAVEPOINT` redirection.

- `ex04-10.sql` demonstrates how to create user-defined error conditions.

- `ex04-11.sql` demonstrates how to shorten error code handling by using Oracle defined conditions.

- `ex04-12.sql` demonstrates how to use `RAISE_APPLICATION_ERROR` to catch an error condition.

- `ex04-13.sql` demonstrates how to use the `PLS_LOGGER` procedure.

- `ex04-14.sql` demonstrates how to instrument a PL/SQL program.

These programs should let you see the code in action. We think a download is friendlier then a cumbersome disc because the code doesn't take a great deal of space.

Summary

We have seen many thousands of programs, and few programs qualify as being polished, or for that matter complete. Developers and DBAs are required to spend countless hours babysitting and double-checking program results when PL/SQL programs are created without proper error handling and instrumentation. Additionally, partial transactions require even more time to perform data cleanup. You will inherently save yourself many late nights by *instrumenting* your code and by providing proper error management.

Best Practice Review

- Keep an electronic copy of *Oracle Database Error Messages* handy to aid you in debugging. We always do.

- Perform occasional compiles based on logical code units.

- Allow error messages to be propagated up to their calling application instead of using the WHEN OTHERS phrase.

- Use savepoints to roll back partial transactions. This prevents orphaned data, thereby maintaining data integrity.

- Avoid the GOTO command.

- Know the built-in errors and leverage them to simplify your code.

- Instrument your PL/SQL programs.

Mastery Check

The mastery check is a series of true or false and multiple choice questions that let you confirm how well you understand the material in the chapter. You may check Appendix E for answers to these questions.

1. ☐ **True**   ☐ **False**   Semantic errors occur at compile time.

2. ☐ **True**   ☐ **False**   You should always filter in-bound web parameters with the DBMS_ASSERT package.

3. ☐ **True**   ☐ **False**   Compile-time errors happen when you use improper syntax or keywords.

4. ☐ **True**   ☐ **False**   DRG- errors are related to the DBVERIFY utility.

5. ☐ **True**   ☐ **False**   PLS- errors are related to PL/SQL.

6. ☐ **True**   ☐ **False**   ORA- errors are related to general database errors and SQL.

7. ☐ **True**   ☐ **False**   The LPX- errors are related to InterMedia.

8. ☐ **True** ☐ **False** The RAISE_APPLICATION_ERROR lets you throw a custom exception and is equivalent to the RAISE statement.

9. ☐ **True** ☐ **False** The EXCEPTION_INIT is a PRAGMA that lets you use default exception errors in your PL/SQL block.

10. ☐ **True** ☐ **False** The SQLCODE returns the error code number for a thrown error in your PL/SQL block.

11. Which of the following error code prefixes might you see working with the import utility?

   A. EXP-

   B. IMP-

   C. KUP-

   D. All of the above

   E. Only A and C

12. Which of the following error code prefixes might you see working with the export utility?

   A. IMP-

   B. EXP-

   C. KUP-

   D. All of the above

   E. Only B and C

13. Which of the following error code prefixes might you see working with external tables?

   A. IMP-

   B. EMP-

   C. KUP-

   D. All of the above

   E. None of the above

14. You use a `PRAGMA EXCEPTION_INIT` to do what?

    A. Declare a user-defined exception.

    B. Enable a user-defined exception.

    C. Create an exception name that maps to an Oracle error code number.

    D. All of the above.

    E. Only A and C.

15. What must you do to throw the call `RAISE_APPLICATION_ERROR`?

    A. You first set the `PRAGMA EXCEPTION_INIT` in the program block.

    B. You use a range of error numbers between -20,000 and -20,999.

    C. You must declare a variable of the `EXCEPTION` type.

    D. All of the above.

    E. Only B and C.

PART
II

PL/SQL Programming

CHAPTER
5

Functions

unctions are specialized program units or named blocks in PL/SQL. They can exist as solitary objects in your database schema. Standalone functions like these are also known as *schema-level functions.*

You can also deploy functions inside packages. (Chapter 2 discusses this concept, and Chapter 8 describes how packages work with functions and procedures.) When you define a function in a package specification, it becomes a published function and available for calls from other schema-level program units. If you opt to define functions in the package body, they become package-only functions. This makes them available to other functions and procedures in the package, but makes them inaccessible to external program units. Package scope functions are the closest equivalent to local functions inside anonymous or named-block programs because they have private scope access.

Another alternative for defining functions exists inside user-defined object types. These functions are known as *member* or *static functions.* You can call static functions without creating an instance of a user-defined object type because they're published program units. At least you can call them when they're defined in your schema or you're granted *execute privilege* on them. They also have the capacity of serving as alternatives to class constructor functions. Like packages, object types may have hidden or local-only scope functions.

This chapter focuses on schema-level functions by covering the following:

- Function architecture

- Function development

You'll also get intimately familiar with parameter modes, call syntax, data return types, and limitations of when and where you can do what with functions. There are two patterns of functions, and you'll discover both *pass-by-value* and *pass-by-reference* in this chapter.

Function Architecture

Before you see the details of how you implement and use functions, you should first understand what a function is and how it does work. Functions are *black boxes*, production facilities where you put raw things in and take processed things out.

The Black Box

The *black box* (the term comes from the engineering lexicon) is part of verification and validation. Verification is a process that examines whether you built something right. Validation checks whether you built the right thing. For example, you validate that the manufacturing line is producing iPod nanos, and then you verify that they're making them according to the new specification.

Integration testing validates whether components work as a part. You can't see how the product works. You only know what it should do when you provide input, such as a function that should add two numbers. If one plus one equals two, then the function appears to work against expectations. This is black box testing.

Black box testing is the process of validation. Verification requires peering into the black box to inspect how it behaves. This type of testing is called *white box testing* because you can see how things actually work—step-by-step. Unit testing verifies that your function or procedure builds the thing right. An example would be verifying that you're using the right formula to calculate the future value of money using compounding interest.

The two major function architectures, *pass-by-value* and *pass-by-reference* models, are used in different ways. You chose the former when you want a standalone behavior and the latter when functions act as subroutines inside the transaction scope of another program unit.

Pass-by-Value Functions

A *pass-by-value* function receives values when they're called. They return a single thing upon completion. The tricky parts with this type of function are the data types of the inputs and outputs. Inputs are formal parameters and have only one mode in pass-by-value programs, and that's an IN-only mode. An IN-only mode means that you send a copy of either a variable value or a literal value into the function as a raw input. These copies are actual parameters or call parameters. All raw materials (call parameters) are consumed during the production of the finished goods—or the return value of this type of function. The return type value of the function must be assigned to a variable in a PL/SQL block, but it can also be returned as an expression in a SQL query.

Best Practice
Always provide the parameter mode for all parameters unless all parameters are IN-only mode variables, in which case exclude the mode.

The following illustration depicts how a pass-by-value function works. What's hidden in this context? The hidden element of a stored program in an Oracle database is the back door that lets a function transact against the database. This means a function's black box may contain an insert, update, or delete statement. Actually, it may contain a set of statements. The collection of statements may collectively be a transaction. This back door to a transactional database is available only when you use the function in an *exclusively* PL/SQL scope.

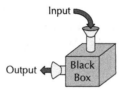

Pass-by-Reference Function

When you call a *pass-by-reference* function, you send at least one or more references to local variables as actual parameters. Formal parameters therefore may have any one of three possible modes: IN, IN OUT, and OUT.

The following list (lifted from a table, with a few changes, from *Oracle Database 11g PL/SQL Programming*) shows subroutine parameter modes:

- **IN** The IN mode, the default mode, means you send a copy as the actual parameter. Any formal parameter defined without an explicit mode of operation is implicitly an IN-only mode parameter. It means a formal parameter is read-only. When you set a formal parameter as read-only, you can't alter it during the execution of the subroutine. You *can* assign a default value to a parameter, making the parameter optional. You use the IN mode for all formal parameters when you want to define a pass-by-value subroutine.

■ **OUT**   The OUT mode means you send a reference, but a *null* as an initial value. A formal parameter is write-only. When you set a formal parameter as write-only, no initial physical size is allocated to the variable. You allocate the physical size and value inside your subroutine. You can't assign a default value, which would make an OUT mode formal parameter optional. If you attempt that, you raise a PLS-00230 error. The error says that an OUT or IN OUT mode variable cannot have a default value. Likewise, you cannot pass a literal as an actual parameter to an OUT mode variable because that would block writing the output variable. If you attempt to send a literal, you'll raise an ORA-06577 error with a call from SQL*Plus, and a PLS-00363 error inside a PL/SQL block. The SQL*Plus error message states the output parameter is not a bind variable, which is a SQL*Plus session variable. The PL/SQL error tells you that the expression (or, more clearly, literal) cannot be an assignment target. You use an OUT mode with one or more formal parameters when you want a write-only pass-by-reference subroutine.

■ **IN OUT**   The IN OUT mode means you send a reference and starting value. A formal parameter is *read-write*. When you set a formal parameter as read-write, the actual parameter provides the physical size of the actual parameter. While you can change the contents of the variable inside the subroutine, you can't change or exceed the actual parameter's allocated size. The IN OUT mode restrictions on default values and literal values mirror those of the OUT mode covered earlier.

While you can call a pass-by-reference function by using session-level variables, that's really not the functions' role. Pass-by-reference functions belong as components in the scope of either pass-by-value programs or stored procedures. The next illustration shows you the generalized format of pass-by-reference functions.

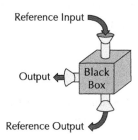

Interestingly, raw materials (call parameters) aren't fully consumed in pass-by-reference functions, as they are in pass-by-value functions. While `IN`-only mode parameters are fully consumed, `IN OUT` mode variables are returned generally in an altered state. `OUT` mode variables are the result of some processing inside the black box that you opt not to return through the function's formal return type.

Function Model Choices

What are the rules of thumb with regard to choosing a pass-by-value or pass-by-reference function? They're quite simple, as you'll see.

You should implement a pass-by-value function when you want to produce a result by consuming the input. You also should implement a pass-by-value function when you want to use the function in a SQL statement. A pass-by-value function is ideal when its transaction scope is autonomous. In object-oriented programming terms, you want to use a pass-by-value function when you want the lowest possible coupling.

When programs are loosely coupled, they're more flexible and reusable in applications. Tightly coupled programs are intrinsically linked to form a processing unit—like root beer and vanilla ice cream are used make a traditional root beer float, so are these programs blended to form a processing unit.

You implement a pass-by-reference function when you need to couple behavior of the calling and called program units. This happens when the function is called in a single threaded execution scope, which is the default in most transactional database applications. Tightly coupled programs such as these let you opt to return values through the `IN OUT` or `OUT` mode formal parameters. When the parameters receive raw and return processed data, the formal return value of the function becomes a signal of success or failure.

PL/SQL functions that use the return type to signal success or failure typically implement either a Boolean or number data type. They use the Boolean when you design them to work exclusively inside PL/SQL blocks and a number when they may need to work in either a SQL or PL/SQL scope.

Best Practice
Use a *pass-by-value* model when you want to use the function inside SQL statements or as an autonomous function.

> **Best Practice**
>
> Use *pass-by-reference* models when you want to verify completion and return results for client-side or web-based program interactions. You should also seriously consider writing these server-side functions as autonomous units.

A pass-by-reference function is ideal when you want to couple client-side interaction with server-side modules. In this context, you should define the function as autonomous. Autonomous functions run in their own transaction scope and are thereby independent of the calling transaction scope. The only way you know whether they succeeded or failed is to capture their return state through the function return type.

A pass-by-reference function is generally a bad idea when you simply want to couple two server-side programs. When the programs are on the same tier and may be called in the same serial transaction scope, you should implement the behavior as a pass-by-reference procedure. A pass-by-reference procedure is a specialized form of a function that returns no value. Procedures are most like C, C++, C#, or Java methods that return a *void* rather than a tangible data type. You can read more about procedures in Chapter 6.

Transaction Scope

Transaction scope defines whether you are doing things serially or concurrently. When you run things serially, when one instruction at a time is issued in a sequence, programs run in the same transaction scope. Concurrent programming is known as *threaded program execution*. Threaded programming poses challenges, because you've got to keep track of different pieces and make sure that they work in unison. That means that either everything happens that should or nothing happens that shouldn't before anything occurs.

Concurrent programs depend on the ACID principle: transactions are atomic, consistent, isolated, and durable. You can see more on that in Chapter 3.

Serial transaction scope uses a SAVEPOINT to set a starting point, a ROLLBACK to undo all changes either from a SAVEPOINT or the beginning of the session. Some prefer to say from the beginning of the connection, but that's really imprecise in an Oracle context. However, if the word *connection* works for you, that's fine. A COMMIT makes permanent any and all changes from the last COMMIT or session start, minus any changes rolled back.

These types of transactions are the bread and butter of transactional databases. They're useful when you want to ensure a series of insert, update, or delete statements are *all* made or *all* undone.

Concurrent activities in databases often involve recording an attempt to change data. Independent activities are called *autonomous* transactions. While these are triggered by a processing event, they are left to run or fail independently of the calling process scope. They exist in their own independent transaction scope.

Call Notation

Three calling notation options are available in an Oracle 11*g* database. One is positional notation, another is named notation, and the last is mixed notation. You use positional notation only when making SQL calls to PL/SQL functions in Oracle 10*g* and the concept of mixed notation doesn't exist. In an exclusively PL/SQL context, you can make named notation calls in Oracle 10*g* databases.

We use a single simple function to examine the three types of call notations available in Oracle 11*g*. The sample function takes three optional parameters, which all have an IN-only mode of operation, and are all number data types. They're also optional because they've all got default values as part of their formal parameter definitions.

The sample function takes the raw values and provides a result. It substitutes 0 or 1 when no value is provided in a definition.

```
SQL> CREATE OR REPLACE FUNCTION three_paddles
  2  ( a NUMBER := 0, b NUMBER := 0, c NUMBER := 1 ) RETURN NUMBER IS
  3  BEGIN
  4    RETURN (a - b) / c;
  5  END;
  6  /
```

The following subsections demonstrate how you call this function with any of the three calling notations.

Positional Notation

This is the easiest method because it works in a straightforward way. The actual call parameters map to the formal parameters in sequence, but you must provide an actual parameter, or call value, for each formal parameter in the list. The parameter list is also known as the *signature* of the function. You enter a *null value* when you want to skip a mandatory or optional parameter in the middle of a signature.

For example, if you provide only two positional call parameters, you'd return the product of the subtraction of the second parameter value from the first parameter value:

```
SQL> BEGIN
  2    dbms_output.put_line(three_paddles(3,4,5));
  3  END;
  4  /
```

The call parameters return -0.2, which is the product of 3 minus 4, divided by 5.

Named Notation

This is often the most intuitive notation to programmers. It is also probably the best syntax to avoid product support throwing working code back over the cubicle wall, because it is readable by many novices to the programming language.

Many folks like named notation because the call says formal parameter *x* receives the value *y*. Actual call parameters don't have to map to the formal parameter sequence when using named notation. However, you must provide call values to all mandatory parameters. You typically pass a null value to mandatory parameters when you want to ignore mandatory parameters. Sometimes this works but most times it doesn't because mandatory parameters typically require values for their program unit to work correctly.

The following example shows you how to reorder and call the parameters. This lets you choose a more meaningful order based on your understanding of the function call.

```
SQL> BEGIN
  2    dbms_output.put_line(three_paddles(c => 4, b => 3, a => 5));
  3  END;
  4  /
```

The call parameters chosen tell us the function subtracts 3 from 5, and then divides the product of the subtraction by 4, and returns 0.5 as a result.

Mixed Notation

Last but not least, in terms of effort, is a mixed notation. This notation has a couple rules that you must know. If you pass positional actual parameters, they must precede any named notation calls. There should be omissions only of optional parameters after the first named call parameter.

```
SQL> BEGIN
  2    dbms_output.put_line(three_paddles(8, c => 4));
  3  END;
  4  /
```

The first parameter is the formal parameter a, so the result is 8 minus 0 divided by 4.

You've now read about the architecture, transaction scope, and call notation methods of functions. The next sections show you how to use the functions in SQL or PL/SQL contexts.

Function Development

One of the more important aspects of PL/SQL functions is how you can call them in select, insert, update, and delete statements. You should know some key restrictions before you begin the design phase. A PL/SQL function *can't contain a Data Manipulation Language (DML) statement* or call another PL/SQL unit that contains a DML statement without raising an ORA-14551 exception. That error means you cannot perform a DML operation inside a query.

PL/SQL functions also may return only a subset of their native data types. Officially, you can return only a BLOB, BFILE, BINARY_DOUBLE, BINARY_FLOAT, BYTE, CHAR, CLOB, NCHAR, NCLOB, NVARCHAR2, REFCURSOR, or VARCHAR2 data type. You can also return collections of scalar variables of those aforementioned data types in a SQL or PL/SQL context. You can return collections of composite variables (often known as object tables) in a SQL context. While you can return aggregate tables defined in PL/SQL in a PL/SQL context, they can also be returned in a SQL context through pipelined functions. You can also return collections of user-defined object types. Chapter 7 shows you how to work with aggregate tables and collections of user-defined object types.

Several types of functions work well when called from SQL. The next sections review four of them: deterministic, parallel enabled, pipelined table, and result cache functions. All of these examples use the pass-by-value model because that's generally the best practice for functions called by SQL statements. This means that the parameter mode will always be `IN-only`.

Before we lead you into these examples, there's an issue to cover. While you can call functions that have no parameter list without the open and closing parentheses inside a SQL statement or PL/SQL blocks, you must use the empty parentheses calling the same program in a `CALL` statement. You're guess is as good as the next person's when it comes to why such a restriction exists, but it does exist, at least through the second release of Oracle 11*g* Database.

Here's an example calling the `three_paddles` function introduced earlier in the "Call Notation" section:

```
SQL> VARIABLE output NUMBER
SQL> CALL three_paddles INTO :output;
```

It generates the following error:

```
CALL three_paddles INTO :output
                   *
ERROR at line 1:
ORA-06576: not a valid function or procedure name
```

If you include the empty parentheses, this works fine:

```
SQL> CALL three_paddles() INTO :output;
SQL> SELECT :output FROM dual;
```

Naturally, you can simplify your life by calling it through SQL, like this:

```
SQL> SELECT three_paddles FROM dual;
```

The parentheses aren't required most of the time, but you should consider using them all of the time. A good habit like that makes sure your code will always work consistently.

Deterministic Clause

A deterministic function guarantees that it always works the same way with any inputs. It also guarantees that the function doesn't read or write data from external sources, such as other stored programs or database tables.

The pv function shows you how to create a simple deterministic function. These are great tools when you need to apply a formula to a set of values.

```
SQL> CREATE OR REPLACE FUNCTION pv
  2  ( future_value    NUMBER
  3  , periods         NUMBER
  4  , interest        NUMBER )
  5  RETURN NUMBER DETERMINISTIC IS
  6  BEGIN
  7    RETURN future_value / ((1 + interest/100)**periods);
  8  END pv;
  9  /
```

You can call this program with the CALL method like this:

```
SQL> VARIABLE result NUMBER
SQL> CALL pv(10000,5,6) INTO :result;
SQL> COLUMN money_today FORMAT 99,999.90
SQL> SELECT :result AS money_today FROM dual;
```

It would print today's value of $10,000 five years in the future at 6% annual interest, barring another financial meltdown, like this:

```
MONEY_TODAY
-----------
   7,472.58
```

Alternatively, you can query data as input values and return values like this:

```
SQL> WITH data_set AS
  2  ( SELECT   235000 AS principal
  3  ,             30 AS years
  4  ,          5.875 AS interest
  5    FROM      dual )
  6  SELECT pv(principal,years,interest) AS money_today
  7  FROM   data_set;
```

It returns this result:

```
MONEY_TODAY
-----------
  42,390.17
```

Note that deterministic clauses are acceptable functions that you can put in materialized views. They're also what Oracle recommends for user-defined functions that you use in SQL statement clauses.

PARALLEL_ENABLE Clause

The merge function shows you how to create a simple function that can be called from either the SQL or PL/SQL context. It takes three strings and concatenates them into one. This type of function removes concatenation from your queries by placing it into a function. It has the benefit of ensuring that format masks are always maintained in a single location.

```
SQL> CREATE OR REPLACE FUNCTION merge
  2  ( last_name      VARCHAR2
  3  , first_name     VARCHAR2
  4  , middle_name VARCHAR2 )
  5  RETURN VARCHAR2 PARALLEL_ENABLE IS
  6  BEGIN
  7    RETURN last_name ||', '||first_name||' '||middle_name;
  8  END;
  9  /
```

The PARALLEL_ENABLE clause on line 5 lets you designate that the function is safe to parallelize during query optimization. While the SQL engine can make these decisions, designating the function as safe does save a few milliseconds. Function-based indexes are often built on functions that are both deterministic and parallel-enabled.

TIP
Deterministic functions should be parallel-enabled when they return more than one row and their result set is dynamic based on queries from the database.

You can call this program like this:

```
SQL> SELECT merge(c.last_name, c.first_name, c.middle_name) AS customer
  2  FROM    contact c;
```

You should parallel-enable PL/SQL wrappers to Java program libraries, because the Oracle 11*g* optimizer never deems that a Java library is thread-safe. Unfortunately, there's no guarantee that the cost optimizer will act on your suggestion.

Pipelined Table Clause

The pipelined table clause is very powerful but if you want to use it, you need to make a couple forward references to Chapter 7. A pipelined table function lets you translate collections of SQL or PL/SQL record data types into SQL-compatible aggregate tables. You access aggregate tables through SQL statements by using the TABLE function.

While you can do this with SQL or PL/SQL records, we recommend that you use SQL data types where possible. As you'll discover in Chapter 11, SQL object types can't be targets for reference cursor assignments. This limitation applies both to structures and collections of structures.

There are only two times when you need to work with PL/SQL data types and pipelined table functions. One is when your design requires you to return the contents of a reference cursor into an aggregate table. The other is when you work with existing code bases that often overuse pipelined table functions.

You create a record structure as the first step in creating a traditional pipelined table function. Record structures are exclusively PL/SQL structures; however, when you create a pipelined table function, Oracle creates implicit catalog entries that let you translate the PL/SQL record to an aggregate table. *Aggregate table* is both a fancy and formal term that describes the results from a query. We use it to make sure you have the vocabulary for other Oracle documentation.

The only way to create a reusable record structure is to put it inside a package specification. The same rule holds true for an exclusively PL/SQL collection type. The package wraps it and defines it where we can't readily see the structure's data type unless we view the package source.

This creates our record structure inside a library package specification:

```
SQL> CREATE OR REPLACE PACKAGE pipelining_library IS
  2    TYPE common_lookup_record IS RECORD
  3    ( common_lookup_id          NUMBER
  4    , common_lookup_type        VARCHAR2(30)
  5    , common_lookup_meaning VARCHAR2(255));
  6  TYPE common_lookup_table IS TABLE OF common_lookup_record;
  7  END pipelining_library;
  8  /
```

Having created the structure, we can now define a pipelined table function in one of two ways: We can create one inside a package body or as a schema-level function. The only difference is that we don't need to reference the

package name when we define the function inside the same
`pipelining_library` package body. We need to reference the
package name when we define the function in another package body
or as a schema-level function. Otherwise, they can't find the base record
structure or collection type.

TIP
*While we're not prepared to say it's a best
practice, you may consider placing structures
in library specifications, and implementing
dependent functions as schema objects. We
prefer to put both in packages and write
schema-level functions as wrappers to the
package functions.*

Here's our sample pipelined table function:

```
SQL> CREATE OR REPLACE FUNCTION get_common_lookup_record_table
  2  ( pv_table_name  VARCHAR2, pv_column_name VARCHAR2 )
  3  RETURN pipelining_library.common_lookup_table
  4  PIPELINED IS
  5
  6    -- Declare a local variables.
  7    lv_counter INTEGER := 1;
  8    lv_table   PIPELINING_LIBRARY.COMMON_LOOKUP_TABLE :=
  9                 pipelining_library.common_lookup_table();
 10
 11    -- Define a dynamic cursor that takes two formal parameters.
 12    CURSOR c (table_name_in VARCHAR2, table_column_name_in VARCHAR2) IS
 13      SELECT   common_lookup_id
 14      ,        common_lookup_type
 15      ,        common_lookup_meaning
 16      FROM     common_lookup
 17      WHERE    common_lookup_table = UPPER(table_name_in)
 18      AND      common_lookup_column = UPPER(table_column_name_in);
 19
 20  BEGIN
 21    FOR i IN c (pv_table_name, pv_column_name) LOOP
 22      lv_table.EXTEND;
 23      lv_table(lv_counter) := i;
 24      PIPE ROW(lv_table(lv_counter));
 25      lv_counter := lv_counter + 1;
 26    END LOOP;
 27  END;
 28  /
```

Line 3 defines the functions dependence on a collection defined in the `pipelining_library` package, which must be in the specification to be available for our definition. Check Chapter 8 for more on packages. Line 4 defines the function as a pipelined table function—or pipelined for the compiler. We declare an empty collection inside the function's declaration block on lines 8 and 9. Chapter 7 has more on constructors if they're new to you.

You can test the function but a bit of formatting makes the output cleaner. These SQL*Plus commands set the display column sizes before you query the collection:

```
SQL> COLUMN common_lookup_id      FORMAT 9999 HEADING "ID"
SQL> COLUMN common_lookup_type    FORMAT A16  HEADING "Lookup Type"
SQL> COLUMN common_lookup_meaning FORMAT A30  HEADING "Lookup Meaning"
SQL> SELECT   *
  2  FROM     TABLE(get_common_lookup_record_table('ITEM','ITEM_TYPE'));
```

A pipelined function inherits the record structure element names from an implicit data type, which is created in the catalog when you compile the pipelined function. It is also removed from the catalog when you drop the pipelined function. The query returns this:

```
   ID Lookup Type       Lookup Meaning
----- ----------------- ------------------
 1013 DVD_FULL_SCREEN   DVD: Full Screen
 1014 DVD_WIDE_SCREEN   DVD: Wide Screen
 1015 GAMECUBE          Nintendo GameCube
 1016 PLAYSTATION2      PlayStation2
 1019 VHS_DOUBLE_TAPE   VHS: Double Tape
 1018 VHS_SINGLE_TAPE   VHS: Single Tape
 1017 XBOX              XBOX
```

A pipelined table function call works only in a SQL context, as in the foregoing example. You can consume the results in a PL/SQL block, provided you do so in a SQL context. The following is a quick example:

```
SQL> DECLARE
  2    CURSOR cv_sample IS
  3      SELECT *
  4      FROM   TABLE(get_common_lookup_record_table('ITEM','ITEM_TYPE'));
  5  BEGIN
  6    FOR i IN cv_sample LOOP
  7      dbms_output.put('['||i.common_lookup_id||']');
  8      dbms_output.put('['||i.common_lookup_type||']');
```

```
 9        dbms_output.put_line('['||i.common_lookup_meaning||']');
10     END LOOP;
11   END;
12   /
```

Just because we *can* do something, doesn't mean we *should* do it. There is a better way than a pipelined table function in this case, and it uses a collection. As mentioned, check Chapter 7 for more on collections.

You should now have the know-how to define pipelined table functions. We'll show you a better way to manage these problems unless one of two caveats applies. Those sticky rules that govern when you must use a pipelined table function are (1) You are returning the value of a reference cursor into a record structure or collection of record structures; and (2) You are dealing with old code that you can't rewrite—ouch, we feel your pain.

We tell you to use SQL data types in new code for two key reasons: First, SQL data types are naturally defined and auditable in the database catalog with meaningful names. Second, they can be found without manually inspecting all package specifications.

You use pipelined table functions when you want to return a collection of records. Record collections can correspond to catalog tables or views, but they're more frequently some subset or superset of catalog objects. The following example assumes a non-catalog record structure.

We'll now show you step-by-step how to implement the equivalent of a pipelined table function that is callable in SQL. The first step requires you to create a SQL record type. It is actually a user-defined object type without a return clause, like this:

```
SQL> CREATE OR REPLACE TYPE common_lookup_object IS OBJECT
  2  ( common_lookup_id        NUMBER
  3  , common_lookup_type      VARCHAR2(30)
  4  , common_lookup_meaning   VARCHAR2(255));
  5  /
```

Best Practice

Define record structures and collections as SQL data types, and use only SQL data types as return data types in lieu of pipelined table functions.

Note that the object type constructor requires both a semicolon to terminate the block and a forward slash to execute the block. Next, you'll create a collection of the SQL object type, which is really a record type.
You create an unbounded list like this:

```
SQL> CREATE OR REPLACE TYPE common_lookup_object_table
  2  IS TABLE OF common_lookup_object;
  3  /
```

Like the object type, the collection type requires both a semicolon to terminate the block and forward slash to run the block. You've now got the data type necessary to define a function returning the SQL collection. This SQL collection of a user-defined object type is known as an object table.
Many developers are familiar with pipelined table functions, but unfamiliar with using SQL data types. They often create PL/SQL data types in package specification, and then work in that exclusively.

```
SQL> CREATE OR REPLACE FUNCTION get_common_lookup_object_table
  2  ( table_name   VARCHAR2
  3  , column_name VARCHAR2 )
  4  RETURN common_lookup_object_table IS
  5
  6    -- Define a dynamic cursor that takes two formal parameters.
  7    CURSOR c (table_name_in VARCHAR2, table_column_name_in VARCHAR2) IS
  8      SELECT   common_lookup_id
  9      ,        common_lookup_type
 10      ,        common_lookup_meaning
 11      FROM     common_lookup
 12      WHERE    common_lookup_table = UPPER(table_name_in)
 13      AND      common_lookup_column = UPPER(table_column_name_in);
 14
 15    -- Declare a counter variable.
 16    lv_counter INTEGER := 1;
 17
 18    -- Declare package collection data type as a SQL scope table return type.
 19    lv_list COMMON_LOOKUP_OBJECT_TABLE := common_lookup_object_table();
 20
 21  BEGIN
 22
 23    -- Assign the cursor return values to a record collection.
 24    FOR i IN c(table_name, column_name) LOOP
 25      lv_list.extend;
 26      lv_ist(counter) := common_lookup_object(i.common_lookup_id
 27                                            ,i.common_lookup_type
 28                                            ,i.common_lookup_meaning);
 29      lv_counter := lv_counter + 1;
 30    END LOOP;
 31
```

```
32    -- Return the record collection.
33    RETURN lv_list;
34  END get_common_lookup_object_table;
35  /
```

Line 4 has the first important item, where we define the function return type as the collection of your user-defined record structure. You construct a zero element collection of the record structure on line 19. Before you can assign a value to the collection, you must first allocate space in memory. Line 25 extends the collection, which means you add space for one new element. The assignment to the collection variable is on lines 26 to 28. You construct an instance of the record structure as the right operand, and then you assign the instance of the record structure as an element in the list.

You can test the function but a bit of formatting makes the output cleaner. These SQL*Plus commands set the display column sizes before you query the collection:

```
SQL> COLUMN common_lookup_id      FORMAT 9999 HEADING "ID"
SQL> COLUMN common_lookup_type    FORMAT A16  HEADING "Lookup Type"
SQL> COLUMN common_lookup_meaning FORMAT A30  HEADING "Lookup Meaning"
SQL> SELECT   *
  2  FROM     TABLE(get_common_lookup_object_table('ITEM','ITEM_TYPE'));
```

The query returns this:

```
   ID Lookup Type       Lookup Meaning
----- ---------------- -------------------
 1013 DVD_FULL_SCREEN   DVD: Full Screen
 1014 DVD_WIDE_SCREEN   DVD: Wide Screen
 1015 GAMECUBE          Nintendo GameCube
 1016 PLAYSTATION2      PlayStation2
 1019 VHS_DOUBLE_TAPE   VHS: Double Tape
 1018 VHS_SINGLE_TAPE   VHS: Single Tape
 1017 XBOX              XBOX
```

Pipelined table functions are probably overused as server-side components, but we suspect that's because they're simple and compatible with how programmers view collections. Our experience teaches us that they are also underutilized in client-side programs because using the TABLE function isn't as widely understood as other approaches. However, we recommend you opt for a function that returns an object table because it works naturally in both a SQL and PL/SQL context.

RESULT_CACHE Clause

The result cache is a new feature of the Oracle 11*g* Database. It allows you to define a function and hold the result sets in a cache for reuse. This is quite an improvement over simply pinning packages in memory to speed execution. You query the result cache rather than the source table or view with the second, third, and so on, queries of the function. This reduces computation cycles and improves throughput.

Result cache functions do have some limitations, however. They can return only scalar or collections of scalar variables.

You can also link the result cache to the source table or tables. When you link a result cache to a table, you ensure that any underlying change to the table flushes the previous result cache. This prevents a dirty read from the cache and compels the function to seek a read-consistent result set.

Like the pipelined table functions, we'll need to forward reference Chapter 7 because result caches work best with collections. You define a collection of a scalar variable length string as follows:

```
SQL> CREATE OR REPLACE TYPE lookup IS TABLE OF VARCHAR2(325);
  2  /
```

We can now define a result cache function. It uses the RELIES_ON clause, which ensures that any change to the underlying data will clear the cache. The function also does something tricky: it concatenates three string elements into a single string by using a | (pipe) as a delimiter. This lets you use a result cache to return a record set.

```
SQL> CREATE OR REPLACE FUNCTION get_common_lookup
  2  ( table_name VARCHAR2, column_name VARCHAR2 ) RETURN LOOKUP
  3  RESULT_CACHE RELIES_ON(common_lookup) IS
  4    -- A local variable of the user-defined scalar collection type.
  5    lookups LOOKUP;
  6
  7    -- A cursor to concatenate the columns into one string with a delimiter.
  8    CURSOR c (table_name_in VARCHAR2, table_column_name_in VARCHAR2) IS
  9      SELECT   common_lookup_id||'|'
 10      ||       common_lookup_type||'|'
 11      ||       common_lookup_meaning
 12      FROM     common_lookup
 13      WHERE    common_lookup_table = UPPER(table_name_in)
 14      AND      common_lookup_column = UPPER(table_column_name_in);
 15  BEGIN
 16    OPEN c(table_name, column_name);
 17    LOOP
 18      FETCH c BULK COLLECT INTO lookups;
 19      EXIT WHEN c%NOTFOUND;
```

```
20   END LOOP;
21     RETURN lookups;
22 END get_common_lookup;
23 /
```

Line 3 contains the definition of a result cache that relies on the current contents of the `common_lookup` table. A bulk fetch on line 18 eliminates the line-by-line approach of the pipelined table function.

Once you've concatenated the data into a string, you need to have a way to extract it. Before you query it, we'll format the output to ensure it doesn't wrap oddly, by using these three SQL*Plus statements:

```
SQL> COLUMN id        FORMAT A4   HEADING "ID"
SQL> COLUMN type      FORMAT A16 HEADING "Lookup Type"
SQL> COLUMN meaning FORMAT A30 HEADING "Lookup Meaning"
```

The following query uses a set of regular expressions to parse the strings:

```
SQL> SELECT
  2    SUBSTR(
  3    REGEXP_SUBSTR(l.column_value,'^([[:alnum:]])+([|])',1,1),1
  4    , LENGTH(
  5      REGEXP_SUBSTR(l.column_value
  6               ,'^([[:alnum:]])+([|])',1,1)) - 1) AS id
  7    ,SUBSTR(
  8    REGEXP_SUBSTR(l.column_value,'([|])([[:alnum:]]|_)+([|])',1,1),2
  9    , LENGTH(
 10      REGEXP_SUBSTR(l.column_value
 11               ,'([|])([[:alnum:]]|_)+([|])',1,1)) - 2) AS type
 12    ,SUBSTR(
 13    REGEXP_SUBSTR(l.column_value,'([|])(([[:alnum:]])|:| )+$',1,1),2
 14    , LENGTH(
 15      REGEXP_SUBSTR(l.column_value
 16               ,'([|])(([[:alnum:]])|:| )+$',1,1)) - 1) AS meaning
 17  FROM   (SELECT column_value
 18           FROM   TABLE(get_common_lookup('ITEM','ITEM_TYPE'))) l;
```

You should notice that the trick to extracting this from the result cache requires an inline view. The `column_value` column name is the default name for all collections of scalar data types. The regular expressions let us parse the first, middle, and last strings.

System Reference Cursors

Systems reference cursors are PL/SQL-only structures. They're very powerful when coupled with external programming languages that support the OCI8 libraries, such as PHP. You can define a strongly or weakly typed system reference cursor. Strongly typed reference cursors are anchored to a table or view, while weakly typed reference cursors can accept any record structure assigned by a query. The SYS_REFCURSOR is the default weakly typed system reference cursor.

You define a strongly typed reference cursor anchored to the item table like this:

```
TYPE some_cursor_name IS REF CURSOR RETURN item%ROWTYPE;
```

You define a weakly typed reference cursor like this:

```
TYPE some_cursor_name IS REF CURSOR;
```

While you can define a weakly typed reference cursor, it doesn't make sense to do so. You should always use the SYS_REFCURSOR when you require a weakly typed reference cursor because it's predefined and universally available.

The following shows you how to write a function that returns a weakly typed, default, system reference cursor:

```
SQL> CREATE OR REPLACE FUNCTION get_full_titles
  2  RETURN SYS_REFCURSOR IS
  3    lv_titles SYS_REFCURSOR;
  4  BEGIN
  5    OPEN lv_titles FOR
  6    SELECT  item_title
  7    ,       item_subtitle
  8    FROM    item;
  9    RETURN lv_titles;
 10  END;
 11  /
```

Line 2 defines the return type as the generic weakly typed system reference cursor, and line 3 defines a variable using the generic system reference cursor. Line 5 shows you how to open the reference cursor.

Best Practice
Use the default weakly typed system reference cursor when you need a weakly typed reference cursor, and define them only when you need to anchor them as strongly typed reference cursors.

The following shows you how to read the contents of the system reference cursor at the SQL prompt:

```
SQL> VARIABLE output REFCURSOR
SQL> CALL get_full_titles() INTO :output;
SQL> SELECT :output FROM dual;
```

It's a bit more complex to manage the output of a weakly typed system reference cursor in a PL/SQL program. First, you must know the structure that it will return, or you can't process it.

The following shows how to read and manage the output from the get_full_titles function:

```
SQL> DECLARE
  2     -- Define a type and declare a variable.
  3     TYPE full_title_record IS RECORD
  4     ( item_title     item.item_title%TYPE
  5     , item_subtitle item.item_subtitle%TYPE);
  6     lv_title FULL_TITLE_RECORD;
  7
  8     -- Declare a system reference cursor variable.
  9     lv_titles SYS_REFCURSOR;
 10  BEGIN
 11     -- Assign the reference cursor function result.
 12     lv_titles := get_full_titles;
 13
 14     -- Print one element of one of the parallel collections.
 15     LOOP
 16       FETCH lv_titles INTO lv_title;
 17       EXIT WHEN titles%NOTFOUND;
 18       dbms_output.put_line('Title ['||lv_title.item_title||']');
 19     END LOOP;
 20  END;
 21  /
```

Note that line 6 defines a variable of a known type, line 9 defines a system reference variable, and line 11 assigns the reference from the system reference cursor to a local variable. You then fetch the records into the local record structure variable and print the contents.

Before you develop a lot of programs that use system reference cursors, you should know that they drive structural coupling of your programs. They're helpful in some situations where you want to serve up content to PHP web pages—but, more or less, that's about it.

Recursive Functions

You can define recursive functions in PL/SQL. They're neat devices when they fit a problem but they can have a high cost in terms of computational cycle when they don't. Recursive functions call themselves until they reach a base case, which is similar to a leaf node in a search tree.

You can use two varieties of recursion: One is called *linear* recursion because it calls only one copy of it self inside each recursion. The other is called *nonlinear* recursion because it calls itself two or more times inside each function when the base case isn't met.

Here is the standard Fibonacci problem, which is a nonlinear recursion example:

```
CREATE OR REPLACE FUNCTION Fibonacci
( n BINARY_DOUBLE ) RETURN BINARY_DOUBLE IS
BEGIN
  IF n <= 2 THEN
    RETURN 1;
  ELSE
    RETURN fibonacci(n - 2) + fibonacci(n - 1);
  END IF;
END fibonacci;
/
```

Our advice on recursion is simple: use it only when you know how it works.

Pass-by-Reference Functions

Pass-by-reference functions can exhibit many of the behaviors we've worked through earlier in the chapter. As discussed, they can have IN, IN OUT, or OUT mode parameters. An IN mode parameter passes in a value that can change but is consumed wholly. An IN OUT mode parameter passes in a reference that can change and be returned in a new state. An OUT mode parameter passes in nothing but can return something.

A simple example of this concept is a program with only one input parameter and one input and output parameter. The input and output parameter increments each time you call the program.

```
SQL> CREATE OR REPLACE FUNCTION adding
  2  ( a IN     NUMBER
  3  , b IN OUT NUMBER ) RETURN NUMBER IS
```

```
4   BEGIN
5     b := b + 1;
6     RETURN a + b;
7   END;
8   /
```

We'll use bind variables to keep this as simple as possible to illustrate the approach. You have to define them in the session, and then assign values to bind variables inside a PL/SQL block, like this:

```
SQL> VARIABLE one NUMBER
SQL> VARIABLE two NUMBER
SQL> BEGIN
  2     :one := 1;
  3     :two := 0;
  4   END;
  5   /
```

We'll also need an output variable, like this one:

```
SQL> VARIABLE output NUMBER
```

Now we can call the pass-by-reference function with the bind variables:

```
SQL> VARIABLE output NUMBER
SQL> CALL adding(:one,:two) INTO :output;
SQL> CALL adding(:one,:two) INTO :output;
```

We can then query the two bind variables, like this:

```
SQL> SELECT :one, :two FROM dual;
```

It prints

```
      :ONE        :TWO
---------- ----------
         1           2
```

After two calls, the input only variable is the same, but the input and output variable has grown by two. That would continue as long as we call it. The most useful way to use pass-by-reference functions is when you want to ensure something happens and return the changed values.

Downloadable Code

The examples in this chapter are organized into five files:

- The `deterministic.sql` script contains the deterministic function example.

- The `parallel.sql` script contains the parallel-enabled function example.

- The `pipelined.sql` script contains the pipelined and alternative to pipelined function examples.

- The `result_cache.sql` script contains the result cache function.

These programs should let you see the code in action. We think a download is friendlier then a cumbersome disc because the code doesn't take up a great deal of space.

Summary

This chapter has covered the basics of the PL/SQL functions. You should be able to use this information as a foundation for working with functions and subsequent examples in this book.

You should also check the introduction for references to further your study of these topics.

Best Practice Review

- Always provide the parameter mode for all parameters unless all parameters are IN-only mode variables, in which case exclude the mode.

- Use a *pass-by-reference* models when you want to verify completion and return results for client-side or web-based program interactions. You should also seriously consider writing these server-side functions as autonomous units.

■ Define record structures and collections as SQL data types, and use only SQL data types as return data types in lieu of pipelined table functions.

■ Use the default weakly typed system reference cursor when you need a weakly typed reference cursor, and define them only when you need to anchor them as strongly typed reference cursors.

Mastery Check

The mastery check is a series of true or false and multiple choice questions that let you confirm how well you understand the material in the chapter. You may check Appendix E for answers to these questions.

1. ☐ **True** ☐ **False** You can use positional call notation when passing only mandatory parameters, provided all optional parameters are at the end of the signature.

2. ☐ **True** ☐ **False** You can use positional references after named references when using a mixed call notation.

3. ☐ **True** ☐ **False** You define a deterministic function when you can guarantee that it works the same way all the time.

4. ☐ **True** ☐ **False** The PARALLEL_ENABLE clause tells the optimizer that a function is safe to parallelize.

5. ☐ **True** ☐ **False** Pipelined table functions are indispensable tools that let you manage collections of object types.

6. ☐ **True** ☐ **False** You can define RESULT_CACHE functions to work with any type of SQL collection data type.

7. ☐ **True** ☐ **False** The RELIES_ON clause creates a dependency between the cached function results and a table, which discards the function results when the table data changes.

8. ☐ **True** ☐ **False** You can put DML statements inside functions that are callable from queries.

9. ☐ **True** ☐ **False** You can define recursive functions in PL/SQL.

10. ☐ **True** ☐ **False** The default mode of formal parameter operation in PL/SQL supports a pass-by-value function type.

11. What are the valid clauses that describe functions in PL/SQL?

    A. A RESULT_CAHCE clause

    B. A RELIES_ON clause

    C. A PIPELINED clause

    D. All of the above

    E. Only A and C

12. What mode(s) of operation supports a pass-by-reference parameter?

    A. The IN mode

    B. The IN OUT mode

    C. The OUT mode

    D. All of the above

    E. Only B and C

13. A pipelined table function typically returns what type of variable?

    A. A SQL collection of an object data type

    B. A PL/SQL collection of a record data type

    C. A PL/SQL record data type

    D. All of the above

    E. Only B and C

14. What type of function would you use in a materialized view?

    A. A deterministic function

    B. A parallel-enabled function

    C. A pipelined table function

    D. All of the above

    E. Only A and B

15. What makes a pipelined function necessary?

    A. Calling the function with a collection data type in the parameter list

    B. Calling the function inside a SQL context

    C. Calling the function inside a PL/SQL context

    D. All of the above

    E. Only B and C

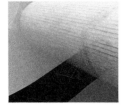

CHAPTER
6

Procedures

rocedures, like functions, are specialized subroutines. When they exist as standalone procedures, you call them schema-level procedures. Like functions, you can use procedures inside anonymous or other named PL/SQL blocks. They can also be defined and implemented inside packages and user-defined object types. There are two differences between procedures and functions: Unlike functions, procedures don't have a formal return data type and can't be used as an expression or right operand; and, unlike functions, you can't call procedures in SQL statements.

Like functions, you can define a function in a package specification. This makes it a published procedure of the package. You can call published procedures from any schema that has *execute* permission on the package. Alternatively, you can define procedures in a package body. Procedures inside a package body are like private access methods in languages such as C, C++, C#, or Java. They can be called only from other program units inside the package. The same is true when you define a procedure inside a named anonymous or named block, because they can be accessed only from that local block. Procedures such as these are hidden inside other program units and have local program scope.

You can also define procedures inside user-defined object types. Inside object types, you can define them as static or instance procedures. You can call static procedures without creating an instance of a user-defined object type because they act as compile-time programs. As compile-time programs, they have no access to instance data. Member procedures in a user-defined object type must be instantiated before you can access their member procedures. You can also hide procedures inside of object types, and they thereby become private procedures.

Since Chapter 8 focuses on packages, this chapter covers schema-level procedures:

- ■ Procedure architecture
- ■ Procedure development

If you didn't master parameter mode in Chapter 5, you should at least review Table 5-1. We will cover how to call procedures, and the limitations of when and where you can do what with procedures. Like functions, two patterns of procedures exist: *pass-by-value* and *pass-by-reference*. This chapter covers both approaches, and you'll better understand these if you understand single transaction scope, discussed in Chapter 3.

Procedure Architecture

A procedure is essentially a function with a void return type. As such, you can't use it as a right operand because it doesn't have a return value. Procedures are black boxes (see Chapter 5), like functions.

Procedures provide a named subroutine that you call within the scope of a PL/SQL block. While the behavior differs slightly whether you pass call parameters by *value* or *reference*, the inputs and outcomes are the only ways to exchange values between the calling block and the procedure.

The nature of the call parameters provides one of two procedure architectures: a *pass-by-value* or a *pass-by-reference* model. A pass-by-value model accepts values to perform a task, while a pass-by-value model accepts values or references to perform a task. Reference variable values may change inside a procedure like this and return altered values to the external variable references. You chose a pass-by-value model when you want a delegation behavior, and you choose a pass-by-reference model when you want a shared or cooperative processing environment.

In a delegation behavior, the inputs are consumed by the subroutine and nothing is returned to the calling scope. Shared or cooperative processing means that a subroutine performs an operation on one or more calling scope variables. Cooperative processing doesn't consume all inputs but refines some of them. It acts like an oil refinery that processes crude oil, additives, and chemicals into fuel.

Pass-by-Value Procedures

A *pass-by-value* procedure receives values when they're called. They return nothing tangible to the calling scope block, but they may interact with the database. Pass-by-value procedures implement a delegation model. Procedures are often used to group and control a series of Data Manipulation Language (DML) statements in the scope of a single transaction.

The mode of all formal parameters is IN-only for pass-by-value procedures. This means they receive a copy of an external variable or a numeric or string literal when you call the procedure. Call parameters can't be changed during the execution of a subroutine. You can transfer the contents from a call parameter to a local variable inside the procedure and then update that calling scope variable.

The following illustration depicts how a pass-by-value procedure works. What's hidden in this context? The hidden element of any stored program is that it can change data in the database. This means a procedure's black box may contain an insert, update, or delete statement. As we've mentioned, a procedure often contains one or more DML statements. These frequently defines a single transaction, which means all or nothing occurs.

Pass-by-Reference Function

You send one or more references to local variables as actual parameters when you call a *pass-by-reference* function. Therefore, formal parameters may have any one of three possible modes: IN (the default), IN OUT, and OUT.

The IN mode means you send a copy as the actual parameter. This is the default behavior. Any formal parameter defined without an explicit mode of operation is automatically an IN-only mode parameter. As mentioned, you can't assign values to call parameters inside a procedure. You can assign call parameter values to local procedure variables.

The IN OUT mode means you send a reference and starting value, while the OUT mode means you send a reference but a *null* as an initial value. You can see more on subroutine parameter modes in Table 5-1.

While you can call pass-by-reference procedures by using session-level variables, that's really not the procedures' role. Pass-by-reference procedures belong as components inside other anonymous or named blocks. The next illustration shows the generalized format of pass-by-reference procedures.

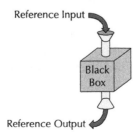

IN OUT call parameters aren't fully consumed by pass-by-reference procedures. While IN-only mode parameters are fully consumed, OUT mode variables don't have a value to consume. IN OUT mode variables are designed to submit a reference with a value and receive a replacement value at the conclusion of a subroutine.

OUT mode variables are the result of some processing inside the black box. They are generally derived by some algorithm that uses other call parameters and constant values inside the procedure. Sometimes OUT mode variables perform similar roles to a function's formal return type.

Transaction Scope

As discussed earlier, transaction scope defines whether you are processing things serially or concurrently. You run one instruction at a time when processing subroutines in a serial context. A single transaction scope is the default processing model, but you can define procedures as autonomous procedures. Autonomous procedures run in their own transaction scope. This means that events inside an autonomous procedure may occur while the calling program scope may fail.

You implement concurrent programming through autonomous procedures. Autonomous procedures are the closest thing that PL/SQL has to threads. Like threads in concurrent programs, autonomous procedures can create challenges because you've got to keep track of discrete pieces and points of synchronization.

Concurrent programs depend on the ACID principle (atomic, consistent, isolated, and durable) just as much as serial programs, but they may allow part to complete while other parts fail. You can read more on ACID transactions in Chapter 3.

While serial transaction scope uses a SAVEPOINT to set a starting point, a ROLLBACK undoes all changes either from a SAVEPOINT or from the beginning of the session. A COMMIT makes permanent any and all changes from the last COMMIT or session start, minus any changes rolled back or processed in an autonomous transaction scope.

These types of transactions are the bread and butter of transactional databases. They're useful when you want to ensure that a series of insert, update, or delete statements are *all* made or *all* undone.

Concurrent activities in databases often involve recording an attempt to change data. These independent activities, or autonomous transactions, don't impact the integrity of the main transaction context. You can therefore

Best Practice

You should design procedures to work inside a calling scope. This means you shouldn't define them as autonomous procedures unless they're writing a message for a critical event trigger, and that trigger's going to terminate the calling transaction scope.

write data without impacting the main transaction context. It is the ideal role for an autonomous procedure.

Call Notation

While we covered call notation for functions in Chapter 5, we'll do a quick review here. You have three call notation options in an Oracle 11*g* database. One is *positional*, another is *named*, and the last is *mixed notation*. You can use positional notation only when making SQL calls inside PL/SQL blocks in Oracle 10*g*. Likewise, the concept of mixed notation doesn't exist there.

NOTE
Chapter 5 provides examples of performing these types of calls.

You've now read about the architecture, transaction scope, and call notation methods of procedures. The next sections show you how to use PL/SQL procedures. You can't call a procedure in a SQL context.

Procedure Development

Procedures are more straightforward than functions because there are fewer options in how you define them. You can define them as pass-by-value or pass-by-reference models

Like functions, you can call procedures interactively at the SQL*Plus command line. Examples in the next two sections show you how to create and call pass-by-value and pass-by-reference procedures.

Bind Variable Scope

Oracle uses the term *bind* variable in several places where they serve different specific purposes but they do more or less a single thing. They let anonymous or named block programs have runtime access to a variable from the calling scope program.

You can use bind variables to call out from the following:

- An anonymous block to the SQL*Plus session, such as a script file

- A database trigger's anonymous block to the firing block

- A Native Dynamic SQL (NDS) statement to the calling scope block

You can't use bind variables where they don't have a known scope and defined relationship. An example would be trying to create a pass-by-value procedure to set a SQL*Plus bind variable, like this:

```
SQL> CREATE OR REPLACE PROCEDURE assign_bind_variable
  2  ( call_parameter VARCHAR2 ) IS
  3  BEGIN
  4    :bv_sample := call_parameter;
  5  END;
  6  /
Warning: Procedure created with compilation errors.
```

You can see the warning message by typing the following:

```
SQL> show errors
Errors for PROCEDURE ASSIGN_BIND_VARIABLE:
LINE/COL ERROR
-------- -----------------------------------------
4/3      PLS-00049: bad bind variable 'BV_SAMPLE'
```

This fails because there's no defined relationship between an unknown calling program unit and the encapsulated bind variable. Defined relationships are a prerequisite for a bind variable's scope.

At least one of the sample programs uses a local bind variable as a call parameter. This is a demonstration case and unlikely something you'd do in production. We should also mention that, procedures can manage bind variables only as call parameters. Any attempt to use a bind variable inside a stored procedure definition raises a `PLS-00049` exception.

Pass-by-Value Procedures

A basic pass-by-value procedure simply takes a call parameter and performs some action with it. That action consumes the copy because at the conclusion of the procedure the values no longer exist. It is possible that they were printed or that they were inserted or updated into database tables. They may also have simply filtered insert, update, or delete statements.

Here's a small example pass-by-value program that works in the same transaction scope as the calling program. It takes only one parameter, which uses the default `IN`-only mode.

```
SQL> CREATE OR REPLACE PROCEDURE print_hello
  2  ( whom VARCHAR2 ) IS
  3  BEGIN
  4      dbms_output.put_line('Hello '||whom||'!');
  5  END;
  8  /
```

You can see the output by setting a SQL*Plus environment variable and printing it:

```
SQL> SET SERVEROUTPUT ON SIZE 1000000
SQL> EXECUTE print_hello('there');
Hello there!
```

We can modify this program slightly and demonstrate the calling scope of variables in a nested block within a named block:

```
SQL> CREATE OR REPLACE PROCEDURE print_hello
  2  ( whom VARCHAR2 ) IS
  3    lv_default CONSTANT VARCHAR2(30) := 'world';
  4    lv_whom             VARCHAR2(30);
  5  BEGIN
  6    BEGIN
  7      IF whom IS NULL THEN
  8        lv_whom := lv_default;
  9      ELSE
```

```
10          lv_whom := whom;
11        END IF;
12      END;
13      dbms_output.put_line('Hello '||lv_whom||'!');
14    END;
15    /
```

This little example teaches a number of principles. Notice that the only value available to print is either a runtime call variable or a local constant. The nested block is the only place where the lv_whom variable is assigned a value. While the lv_whom variable is defined in the external scope, it is available in any nested block regardless of how many levels might separate it from the container's scope. The container in this case is the procedure.

If you call the program without a parameter value, it prints this:

```
SQL> EXECUTE print_hello(null);
Hello world!
```

You must call the procedure with a null because the formal parameter is required or mandatory. Interestingly, passing a null is the way to send nothing. This is consistent with the generalized principle in programming that you signal a loss of precision by explicit casting. You signal your knowledge of sending nothing when you call the procedure with a null value.

An attempt to call the procedure without a value would trigger the following exception:

```
SQL> EXECUTE print_hello;
BEGIN print_hello; END;
      *
ERROR at line 1:
ORA-06550: line 1, column 7:
PLS-00306: wrong number or types of arguments in call to 'PRINT_HELLO'
ORA-06550: line 1, column 7:
PL/SQL: Statement ignored
```

Best Practice

You should never assign a dynamic value to a variable in the declaration block, because any error can't be caught by the local exception handler. The error is tossed back to the calling scope block.

The preceding programs illustrate what pass-by-value programs do and how they work. A more practical example is a procedure that controls a set of DML statements, such as a set of inserts to several tables.

Since the book uses a video store example for the sample database, the example shows how to insert a new member account. The solution involves three components: a collection of strings, which you learn more about in Chapter 7; a stored procedure to add a contact with address and telephone; and a stored procedure to insert into the member table, along with a couple local functions. The procedure that adds a new member calls the procedure that inserts the contact information. As you learn in Chapter 8, these should be in a package with standalone schema-level PL/SQL wrappers.

The collection is a three-element varray:

```
SQL> CREATE OR REPLACE TYPE street_address_table IS VARRAY(3) OF VARCHAR2(30);
  2  /
```

The add_contact procedure controls a single scope transaction to insert all relevant data or no data. It's unfortunately a bit long, but we show it in its entirety because it's a great example of handling parameters and a transaction.

```
SQL> CREATE OR REPLACE PROCEDURE add_contact
  2  ( member_id            NUMBER
  3  , contact_type         NUMBER
  4  , last_name            VARCHAR2
  5  , first_name           VARCHAR2
  6  , middle_name          VARCHAR2 := NULL
  7  , address_type         NUMBER   := NULL
  8  , street_address       STREET_ADDRESS_TABLE := street_address_table()
  9  , city                 VARCHAR2 := NULL
 10  , state_province       VARCHAR2 := NULL
 11  , postal_code          VARCHAR2 := NULL
 12  , country_code         VARCHAR2 := NULL
 13  , telephone_type       NUMBER   := NULL
 14  , area_code            VARCHAR2 := NULL
 15  , telephone_number     VARCHAR2 := NULL
 16  , created_by           NUMBER
 17  , creation_date        DATE     := SYSDATE
 18  , last_updated_by      NUMBER
 19  , last_update_date     DATE     := SYSDATE) IS
 20
 21     -- Define a local variable because an address may not be provided.
 22     lv_address_id        NUMBER;
 23
 24  BEGIN
 25
```

```
26    -- Set savepoint to guarantee all or nothing happens.
27    SAVEPOINT add_contact;
28
29    INSERT INTO contact VALUES
30    ( contact_s1.nextval
31    , member_id
32    , contact_type
33    , first_name
34    , middle_name
35    , last_name
36    , created_by
37    , creation_date
38    , last_updated_by
39    , last_update_date);
40
41    -- Check conditions before inserting an address.
42    IF address_type IS NOT NULL    AND
43       city IS NOT NULL            AND
44       state_province IS NOT NULL AND
45       postal_code IS NOT NULL     THEN
46
47       INSERT INTO address VALUES
48       ( address_s1.nextval
49       , contact_s1.currval
50       , address_type
51       , city
52       , state_province
53       , postal_code
54       , created_by
55       , creation_date
56       , last_updated_by
57       , last_update_date);
58
59       -- Preserve primary key for reuse as a foreign key.
60       lv_address_id := address_s1.currval;
61
62       -- Check conditions before inserting a street address.
63       IF street_address.COUNT > 0 THEN
64         FOR i IN 1..street_address.COUNT LOOP
65
66           INSERT INTO street_address VALUES
67           ( street_address_s1.nextval
68           , lv_address_id
69           , i
70           , street_address(i)
71           , created_by
72           , creation_date
73           , last_updated_by
74           , last_update_date);
75
```

```
76         END LOOP;
77       END IF;
78
79     END IF;
80
81     -- Check conditions before inserting a telephone.
82     IF telephone_type IS NOT NULL AND
83        country_code IS NOT NULL AND
84        area_code IS NOT NULL AND
85        telephone_number IS NOT NULL THEN
86
87       INSERT INTO telephone VALUES
88       ( telephone_s1.nextval
89       , contact_s1.currval
90       , lv_address_id          -- Reuse the foreign key if available.
91       , telephone_type
92       , country_code
93       , area_code
94       , telephone_number
95       , created_by
96       , creation_date
97       , last_updated_by
98       , last_update_date);
99
100      END IF;
101
102      COMMIT;
103
104  EXCEPTION
105
106      WHEN others THEN
107        ROLLBACK TO add_contact;
108        RAISE_APPLICATION_ERROR(-20001,SQLERRM);
109
110  END add_contact;
111  /
```

You should note that the add_contact procedure uses transaction control to ensure everything or nothing happens. It conditionally inserts an address or telephone when the data supports their insertion, and it may insert both. Unfortunately, this procedure has a critical problem. It contains it's own commit. Procedures like this should never contain a commit, because they're called as a subroutine of a larger transaction scope. The calling scope program should issue the commit.

The calling program is actually another standalone procedure. It inserts into the member table and then calls the add_contact procedure. At some future date, you may want to modify this sample to insert more than one contact at a time. You rewrite the formal parameters to take a set of contacts, but a more effective solution would be to convert the insert into the member table into a *merge* statement. A merge statement lets you insert a new record or update an existing record. This type of solution would let you call the same procedure from a web form to insert a first or second contact.

Here's the sample code:

```
SQL> CREATE OR REPLACE PROCEDURE add_member
  2  ( membership_type      VARCHAR2 := 'GROUP'
  3  , account_number       VARCHAR2
  4  , credit_card_number   VARCHAR2
  5  , credit_card_type     VARCHAR2 := 'VISA_CARD'
  6  , contact_type         VARCHAR2 := 'CUSTOMER'
  7  , first_name           VARCHAR2
  8  , middle_name          VARCHAR2
  9  , last_name            VARCHAR2 := NULL
 10  , address_type         VARCHAR2 := 'HOME'
 11  , st_addr1             VARCHAR2 := NULL
 12  , st_addr2             VARCHAR2 := NULL
 13  , st_addr3             VARCHAR2 := NULL
 14  , city                 VARCHAR2 := NULL
 15  , state_province       VARCHAR2 := NULL
 16  , postal_code          VARCHAR2 := NULL
 17  , country_code         VARCHAR2 := NULL
 18  , telephone_type       VARCHAR2 := 'HOME'
 19  , area_code            VARCHAR2 := NULL
 20  , telephone_number     VARCHAR2 := NULL
 21  , created_by           NUMBER
 22  , creation_date        DATE     := SYSDATE
 23  , last_updated_by      NUMBER
 24  , last_update_date     DATE     := SYSDATE) IS
 25
 26    -- Declare surrogate key variables.
 27    lv_member_id NUMBER;
 28
 29    -- Declare local function to get type.
 30    FUNCTION get_type
 31    ( table_name   VARCHAR2
 32    , column_name VARCHAR2
 33    , type_name    VARCHAR2) RETURN NUMBER IS
 34      retval NUMBER;
 35    BEGIN
 36      SELECT    common_lookup_id
 37      INTO      retval
 38      FROM      common_lookup
 39      WHERE     common_lookup_table = table_name
 40      AND       common_lookup_column = column_name
 41      AND       common_lookup_type = type_name;
 42      RETURN retval;
 43    END get_type;
 44
 45  BEGIN
 46
```

```
47    -- Set savepoint to guarantee all or nothing happens.
48    SAVEPOINT add_member;
49
50    INSERT INTO member VALUES
51    ( member_s1.nextval
52    ,(SELECT common_lookup_id
53      FROM   common_lookup
54      WHERE  common_lookup_table = 'MEMBER'
55      AND    common_lookup_column = 'MEMBER_TYPE'
56      AND    common_lookup_type = membership_type)
57    , account_number
58    , credit_card_number
59    ,(SELECT common_lookup_id
60      FROM   common_lookup
61      WHERE  common_lookup_table = 'MEMBER'
62      AND    common_lookup_column = 'CREDIT_CARD_TYPE'
63      AND    common_lookup_type = credit_card_type)
64    , created_by
65    , creation_date
66    , last_updated_by
67    , last_update_date);
68
69    -- Call procedure to insert records in related tables.
70    add_contact(
71      member_id => lv_member_id
72    , contact_type => get_type('CONTACT','CONTACT_TYPE',contact_type)
73    , last_name => last_name
74    , first_name => first_name
75    , address_type => get_type('ADDRESS','ADDRESS_TYPE',address_type)
76    , street_address => street_address_table(st_addr1, st_addr2, st_addr3)
77    , city => city
78    , state_province => state_province
79    , postal_code => postal_code
80    , telephone_type => get_type('TELEPHONE','TELEPHONE_TYPE',telephone_type)
81    , country_code => country_code
82    , area_code => area_code
83    , telephone_number => telephone_number
84    , created_by => created_by
85    , last_updated_by => last_updated_by);
86
87  EXCEPTION
88    WHEN others THEN
89      ROLLBACK TO add_member;
90      RAISE_APPLICATION_ERROR(-20002,SQLERRM);
91  END add_member;
92  /
```

Lines 70 to 85 contain the call to the previously created procedure. With little trouble, you could make a second call for the other party in a group membership.

The biggest problem with this example is actually the local function. The local get_type function is available only in a PL/SQL scope. This is why it's used only in the call to the add_contact procedure and not inside the insert statement. You could fix this problem by defining the get_type function as a schema-level function.

Best Practice
You should generally design functions as schema-level programs when you plan to use them for validation checks. This lets you use them in both SQL and PL/SQL contexts.

Pass-by-Reference Procedures

A basic pass-by-reference procedure takes one or more call parameters by reference. Inside the procedure, the values of the reference variables may change. There, scope is defined by the calling program unit, and to some extent they treat variables much like nested anonymous blocks. The following demonstrates the ability of a nested anonymous block to access a calling scope variable.

```
SQL> DECLARE
  2    lv_outside VARCHAR2(50) := 'Declared in outer block.';
  3  BEGIN
  4    BEGIN
  5      lv_outside := 'Re-assigned a value in the anonymous block.';
  6    END;
  7    dbms_output.put_line('Variable Value ['||lv_outside||']');
  8  END;
  9  /
```

This prints the value assigned inside the nested block, as shown:

```
Variable Value [Re-assigned a value in the anonymous block.]
```

While the preceding example demonstrates that anonymous inner blocks have access to calling block variables, procedures work a bit differently. A procedure has access only to variables it receives at call time, and those variables are actual parameters. You can call a procedure with parameters only when they're defined with formal parameters.

The following demonstrates a pass-by-reference procedure that mimics the behavior of the preceding nested anonymous block program:

```
SQL> CREATE OR REPLACE PROCEDURE change_string
  2  ( cv_string IN OUT VARCHAR2 ) IS
  3  BEGIN
  4    cv_string := 'We''re inside the procedure.';
  5  END;
  6  /
```

The procedure has only one formal parameter and its mode is IN OUT, which means it is passed by reference. Line 4 in the stored procedure performs the same feature as line 5 in the nested anonymous block.

After you declare a local SQL*Plus bind variable, you can call the stored procedure as follows:

```
SQL> VARIABLE no_real_value VARCHAR2(50)
SQL> EXECUTE change_string(:no_real_value);
```

You can see the local results by calling the SQL*Plus PRINT command:

```
SQL> PRINT no_real_value
```

You probably noticed that the no_real_value session variable didn't require a colon like a *good* bind variable. That's because the SQL*Plus PRINT command accesses it in its native session scope and no colon is required.

You can treat it like a bind variable by calling it from a SQL statement, like this:

```
SQL> SELECT :no_real_value AS NO_REAL_VALUE FROM dual;
```

Both print the same results:

```
NO_REAL_VALUE
-----------------------------------------
We're inside the procedure.
```

A similar PL/SQL block program calls a pass-by-reference procedure, such as the following:

```
SQL> DECLARE
  2    lv_outside VARCHAR2(50) := 'Declared in outer block.';
  3  BEGIN
  4    change_string(lv_outside);
  5    dbms_output.put_line('Variable Value ['||lv_outside||']');
  6  END;
  7  /
```

It prints the same value. Line 4 shows you how to call a pass-by-reference variable. It also shows you that the value was changed inside the named block program. More or less, this is the same type of behavior that you find on line 5 of the preceding nested anonymous block.

The uses of pass-by-value procedure like these should be limited to in scope, or more precisely, inside a single transaction scope. That's the default setting, but you can define them to run in their own transaction scope. You declare that type of function with the anonymous precompiler instruction `PRAGMA AUTONOMOUS_TRANSACTION`.

The following shows you how to create an *autonomous* pass-by-reference procedure:

```
SQL> CREATE OR REPLACE PROCEDURE change_string
  2  ( cv_string IN OUT VARCHAR2 ) IS
  3    PRAGMA AUTONOMOUS_TRANSACTION;
  4  BEGIN
  5    cv_string := 'We''re inside the procedure.';
  6  END;
  7  /
```

Line 3 shows the syntax to declare a procedure as independent of the calling program's transaction scope. You really should avoid this unless you've got a compelling business problem that requires such a design.

Downloadable Code

The examples in this chapter are organized into one file:

■ The transaction_procedure.sql script contains the `add_contact` and `add_member` procedures.

These programs should let you see the code in action. We think a download is friendlier then a cumbersome disc because the code doesn't take up a great deal of space.

Summary

This chapter covered the basics of PL/SQL procedures. You should be able to use this information as a foundation for working with procedures and subsequent examples in this book.

You should also check the introduction for references to further your study of these topics.

Best Practice Review

■ You should design procedures to work inside a calling scope. This means you shouldn't define them as autonomous procedures unless they're writing a message for a critical event trigger, and that trigger's going to terminate the calling transaction scope.

■ You should never assign a dynamic value to a variable in the declaration block, because any error can't be caught by the local exception handler. The error is tossed back to the calling scope block.

■ You should generally design functions as schema-level programs when you plan to use them for validation checks. This lets you use them in both SQL and PL/SQL contexts.

Mastery Check

The mastery check is a series of true or false and multiple choice questions that let you confirm how well you understand the material in the chapter. You may check Appendix E for answers to these questions.

1. ☐ **True** ☐ **False** You can use a procedure as a right operand in another PL/SQL block.

2. ☐ **True** ☐ **False** You can use session-level bind variables inside procedure definitions.

3. ☐ **True** ☐ **False** You should declare variables by assigning them static or dynamic call parameter values inside the procedure's declaration block.

4. ☐ **True** ☐ **False** You can call a procedure without a parameter list when all parameters have default values.

5. ☐ **True** ☐ **False** You can exclude open and closed parentheses when no call parameters are included.

6. ☐ **True** ☐ **False** Procedures are best suited to managing a transaction inside another PL/SQL block's execution scope.

7. ☐ **True** ☐ **False** Procedures should always include a COMMIT unless they're called as autonomous program units.

8. ☐ **True** ☐ **False** There are no practical alternatives to procedures that use cursors to check for records before deciding to insert a new row or update an existing role.

9. ☐ **True** ☐ **False** Insert statements inside a procedure can call local functions defined in the procedure.

10. ☐ **True** ☐ **False** Autonomous transaction procedures should always use default IN mode formal parameters.

11. Which are valid clauses in a PL/SQL procedure?

    A. A RESULT_CACHE clause

    B. A RELIES_ON clause

    C. A PIPELINED clause

    D. None of the above

    E. Only A and C

12. What mode(s) of operation supports a pass-by-value parameter?

    A. The IN mode

    B. The IN OUT mode

    C. The OUT mode

    D. All of the above

    E. Only B and C

13. What PRAGMA lets you create an autonomous procedure?

    A. An AUTONOMOUS_FUNCTION

    B. An AUTONOMOUS_PROCEDURE

    C. An AUTONOMOUS_TRANSACTION

    D. All of the above

    E. Only B and C

14. What mode of operation should a pass-by-value procedure use?

   A. An `IN` mode

   B. An `IN OUT` mode

   C. An `OUT` mode

   D. All of the above

   E. Only B and C

15. What is the biggest problem with using pass-by-value procedures in web-based applications?

   A. It is difficult to prepare a JDBC statement with a procedure.

   B. It is difficult to prepare a PHP statement with a procedure.

   C. There is no way to confirm processing without a subsequent query.

   D. All of the above

   E. Only A and B

CHAPTER
7

Collections

ollections are arrays and lists—at least, that's the way we've label them since the advent of Java. A collection in an Oracle database acts like an array when you define it as a *varray*, and it acts like a list when you define it as a *nested table* or an *associative array*. The varray and nested table are SQL data types, and they're indexed initially by sequential integers. This typically means they're densely populated structures because they don't have gaps, which is an exception that we'll discuss in this chapter. Associative arrays differ from nested table because they can have sequential or nonsequential numeric indexes, or string indexes. They're sparsely populated structures because they may have gaps in their index sequence.

You can implement both varray and nested table data types as either SQL or PL/SQL data types. Associative arrays are, however, exclusively a PL/SQL data type. You may know them as PL/SQL tables, index-by tables, or associative arrays. Everybody agrees that the "PL/SQL tables" label is a bad naming convention because it's misleading. These aren't tables, except in the scope of arrays of object or record structures in the System Global Area (SGA) memory.

This chapter focuses on how, when, and where to use collections in Oracle server-side solutions. Rather than cover duplicate generic behaviors that are shared between collections, we'll discuss them by focusing on their base data types.

- Scalar collections

- Object type collections

- Record type collections

If you didn't read or you don't remember Chapter 5, some of these examples may require that you flip back to that chapter for a quick review. These discussions move quickly through examples and point to the best places to use these different techniques. Moreover, you should attempt to deploy SQL data types where possible and limit the use of PL/SQL-only types for a number of reasons.

Some basic concepts aren't repeated from one section to the next here to conserve space. That means you should at least skim through the first part before you focus on an example, or you can flip back through the pages as necessary.

Oracle PL/SQL Tables

The last temporal reference (not a "Star Trek" episode) to *PL/SQL tables* we could find is in the *Oracle Call Interface Programmer's Guide, Release 8.0*. We all should really use "associative array" because it is futile to resist the Oracle collective. (Note to forum afficionados: The label isn't a figment of your imagination. It actually does originate in the official documentation as late as 1998 and in the terminal release of Oracle 8.)

Figure 7-1 offers a high-level view of how you can use collections in PL/SQL programs. The varray and nested tables that you define in SQL are available as aggregate tables. They're implicitly converted for you at runtime, which means the description of these types are in the data catalog. The same can't be said for their PL/SQL equivalents. PL/SQL associate arrays of PL/SQL records have no scope in SQL, and they can't be implicitly converted to work in SQL unless you write a pipelined function. You can find an example of this explicit conversion in Chapter 5.

Aggregate tables come in two flavors: single and multiple dimension types. The USER_TYPES view holds the definition of single dimension collection. A combination of the USER_TYPES and USER_TYPE_ATTRS views hold the definitions of multiple dimension collections.

PL/SQL collections are available only in PL/SQL unless you convert them to aggregate tables through pipelined table functions. When you define

Collection Data Type	Scope	SQL Call Parameter	PL/SQL Call Parameter	SQL Function Return	PL/SQL Function Return
Varray	SQL	Yes	Yes	Yes	Yes
Nested Table	SQL	Yes	Yes	Yes	Yes
Aggregate Table*	SQL			Yes	
Varray	PL/SQL		Yes		Yes
Nested Table	PL/SQL		Yes		Yes
Associative Array	PL/SQL		Yes		Yes

Figure 7-1. *Collection access and return type scopes*

pipelined tables that convert PL/SQL collections, the database writes system-generated type data in the catalog. It is found in the same views as the varray and nested tables.

Scalar collections return with a `COLUMN_VALUE` column name. Composite collections (multidimensional aggregate tables) return with an explicitly described record type. As mentioned, the information to convert these implicitly is in the database catalog for varrays and nested tables. Unfortunately, the same is not true for collections of PL/SQL record types. They don't implicitly convert to a SQL context. You must explicitly convert them through pipelined table functions. Figure 7-1 also shows that PL/SQL return types are limited to an exclusive PL/SQL-only scope.

As you work through the examples, keep in mind one rule: *Just because we can, doesn't mean we should.* If we've learned nothing else from Bryn Llewellyn, the PL/SQL product manager, it's that! More often than not, SQL data types are the best solution. SQL data types have context in the Oracle Call Interface (OCI), Java, SQL, and PL/SQL. They are also named data types in all cases within the Oracle 11*g* Database schema.

> **NOTE**
> *Covering set operations and the collection API didn't fit in the workbook. You'll have to check the Oracle documentation or Chapter 7 of* Oracle Database 11g PL/SQL Programming *for that detail. Where relevant to the examples, we've squeezed in as much as possible.*

Scalar Collections

A *scalar* variable is any data type that holds one thing at a time. A number, integer, date, or timestamp are clear examples of scalar variables because they map across other programming languages. Strings are also scalar variables in databases. This is convenient because we can leverage regular expressions to stuff more than a single thing into a large string. That's what we did in Chapter 5 with the Oracle 11*g* result cache function.

The next three subsections show you how to use varrays, nested tables, and associative arrays of scalar variables. Each section has examples of self-contained PL/SQL block programs, PL/SQL functions returning these collection types, and SQL and PL/SQL parameter passing of collections variables.

Varrays

You can implement varrays as SQL or PL/SQL data types. As illustrated in Figure 7-1, SQL scope data type definitions have wider uses than PL/SQL definitions. This section shows working examples of both.

SQL Scope Varrays of Scalar Variables

The first step requires that we create a schema-level data type. The following command defines a varray collection of three elements with a base element type of a variable-length string with a maximum length of 20 characters.

```
SQL> CREATE OR REPLACE TYPE scalar_varray AS VARRAY(3) OF VARCHAR2(20);
  2  /
```

We can use this in an anonymous or named block program. We'll first demonstrate it in an anonymous block program and then as a return type from a schema-level function.

```
SQL> DECLARE
  2    lv_coll1 SCALAR_VARRAY := scalar_varray('One','Two','Three');
  3    lv_coll2 SCALAR_VARRAY := scalar_varray();
  4  BEGIN
  5    FOR i IN 1..lv_coll1.COUNT LOOP
  6      lv_coll2.EXTEND;                -- Allocates space to the collection.
  7      lv_coll2(i) := lv_coll1(i); -- Assigns a value.
  8    END LOOP;
  9    FOR i IN 1..lv_coll2.count LOOP
 10      dbms_output.put_line('lv_coll2'||'('||i||')'||'['||lv_coll2(i)||']');
 11    END LOOP;
 12  END;
 13  /
```

NOTE
If you're coming to PL/SQL from C, C++, or Java, the biggest change in the example is probably that the index values are enclosed in ordinary parentheses, *not square brackets.*

Lines 2 and 3 show that SQL varrays have a constructor with the same name as the data type. You can construct a collection instance with values or without values. There's no space allocated for elements when you use a null value constructor. This means you'll need to allocate space later, as is done with the EXTEND method.

Line 5 introduces the COUNT function, which is our first demonstration of the Oracle Collection API. The COUNT function tells you how many elements in the array have been allotted memory. It doesn't tell you how many have been assigned a value, unless you mandated that collection elements have a not null value. Before you assign a value to the initialized but empty collection, you must create space for an element. You do that with the EXTEND method on line 6.

An alternative would be to extend all the required space in one command before the loop. This is possible because the EXTEND method is overloaded. Overloading means the method behaves differently when you pass no parameter, one parameter, or two parameters to the method. More detail on this method can be found in Chapter 7 of *Oracle Database 11*g *PL/SQL Programming*. If you yank line 6 and put it before the first loop, it would look like this:

```
lv_coll2.EXTEND(lv_coll1.COUNT);   -- Allocates all space at once.
```

The balance of the program simply prints what you've assigned from one to another scalar varray. However, don't forget to enable SERVEROUTPUT before you run it, or you won't see a thing.

Moving from the basics to a function, here's a function that returns the SQL scalar varray that we created earlier. The function dispenses with the printing because we'll do that when we call the function in a query.

```
SQL> CREATE OR REPLACE FUNCTION get_varray
  2    ( pv_one    VARCHAR2 := NULL
  3    , pv_two    VARCHAR2 := NULL
  4    , pv_three VARCHAR2 := NULL )
  5    RETURN SCALAR_VARRAY IS
  6      lv_coll SCALAR_VARRAY := scalar_varray();
  7    BEGIN
  8      FOR i IN 1..3 LOOP
  9        IF pv_one IS NOT NULL AND i = 1 THEN
 10          lv_coll.EXTEND;
 11          lv_coll(i) := pv_one;
 12        ELSIF pv_two IS NOT NULL AND i <= 2 THEN
 13          lv_coll.EXTEND;
 14          lv_coll(i) := pv_two;
 15        ELSIF pv_three IS NOT NULL THEN
 16          lv_coll.EXTEND;
 17          lv_coll(i) := pv_three;
 18        ELSE
```

```
19         NULL; -- This can't happen but an ELSE says it wasn't forgotten.
20       END IF;
21     END LOOP;
22     RETURN lv_coll;
23   END;
24   /
```

This function takes zero to three elements and returns a scalar varray of those elements. It uses and *if-else-if* block to make sure that it assigns only those call parameters that have non-default values. That means it can return a varray of zero to three elements.

You can use the TABLE function to translate the SQL collection into an aggregate table of scalar values. The column name for all scalar collections is COLUMN_VALUE, but you'll see that's not the case for collections of user-defined object types. Those column values are preserved and mapped in the database catalog.

```
SQL> SELECT column_value FROM TABLE(get_varray('Uno','Due'));
```

It prints this:

```
COLUMN_VALUE
--------------------
Uno
Due
```

The output is exactly what we expect: two rows of variable length string data. You can put the query inside a inline view or subquery factoring clause (that's the WITH statement) if you want to provide an alias for the column name.

An inline view would be done like this:

```
SQL> SELECT sq.italian_numbers
  1  FROM   (SELECT column_value AS italian_numbers
  2          FROM TABLE(get_varray('Uno','Due'))) sq;
```

A subquery factoring clause has advantages because the subquery can be reused in multiple places within a single query. This is not the case with an inline view. You'd write this into a subquery factoring clause like this:

```
SQL> WITH subquery AS
  2    (SELECT column_value AS italian_numbers
  3     FROM TABLE(get_varray('Uno','Due')))
  4  SELECT sq.italian_numbers
  5  FROM   subquery sq;
```

Varray Golden Oldie

The implicit casting from a varray to a nested table is a new feature in Oracle 11*g*. It is one change that we don't seem to find in the documentation.

Oracle 10*g*, Release 1, required that you explicitly cast the varray into a nested table before retrieving it with the TABLE function, like this:

```
SQL> SELECT column_value
  2  FROM    TABLE(CAST(get_varray('Uno','Due') AS SCALAR_TABLE))
  3  /
```

The implicit casting is clearly simpler and easier. We say dispense with the old casting method and enjoy the simpler syntax.

The subquery factoring clause is the recommended solution over an inline view. This is portable to SQL Server but not MySQL. Inline views are generally more portable if that's a major concern during implementation.

The last thing to demonstrate about scalar varrays is how you can use them as formal parameters in functions, and pass the result of other functions as actual parameters. We mix it up a bit in the book by calling actual parameters call parameters but the terms are naturally interchangeable.

We explore call parameters from two perspectives: pass-by-value and pass-by-reference functions. The first function defines a formal parameter of a scalar varray and returns another scalar varray because the formal parameter uses an IN-only mode, which means it is a pass-by-value function. The second function defines and returns the same scalar varray because it uses an IN OUT mode, which makes it a pass-by-reference function. (If these terms are new to you, flip back to Chapter 5 to read about them.)

The pass-by-value function accepts and returns a collection data type:

```
SQL> CREATE OR REPLACE FUNCTION filter_varray
  2  ( pv_scalar_varray SCALAR_VARRAY )
  3  RETURN SCALAR_VARRAY IS
  4    lv_scalar_varray SCALAR_VARRAY := scalar_varray();
  5  BEGIN
  6    lv_scalar_varray := pv_scalar_varray;
  7    lv_scalar_varray.TRIM(1);
```

```
 8     RETURN lv_scalar_varray;
 9   END;
10   /
```

Line 4 declares a local variable and initializes it. Line 6 assigns the contents of the call parameter to the local variable. Line 7 trims the last element from the varray. When the variable is returned by the function, the last element is gone.

You can test this function with the following call:

```
SQL> SELECT    column_value
  2  FROM      TABLE(filter_varray(get_varray('Eine','Zwei','Drei')));
```

It returns:

```
COLUMN_VALUE
-------------------
Eine
Zwei
```

This demonstrates the power of using collections as return types. The example shows you how to do a similar thing with a pass-by-reference function. Pass-by-reference functions don't work inside queries when they return collections because you can't define a session-level (bind) variable with a collection data types. We could change the function to return a number or variable-length string, but it's a better idea to test it as it is with a collection return type in an anonymous block.

NOTE
It is tempting to provide a null constructor as the default value for formal parameters, but this does absolutely nothing. A null call to the parameter raises an ORA-06531: Reference to an uninitialized collection.

The pass-by-reference function definition is shown here:

```
SQL> CREATE OR REPLACE FUNCTION filter_varray
  2  ( pv_scalar_varray IN OUT SCALAR_VARRAY)
  3  RETURN BOOLEAN IS
  4    lv_return BOOLEAN := FALSE;
```

```
 5  BEGIN
 6    pv_scalar_varray.TRIM(1);
 7    lv_return := TRUE;
 8    RETURN lv_return;
 9  END;
10  /
```

We can test this pass-by-reference program with the following anonymous block:

```
SQL> DECLARE
  2    lv_scalar_varray SCALAR_VARRAY := scalar_varray('Eine','Zwei','Drei');
  3  BEGIN
  4    IF filter_varray(lv_scalar_varray) THEN
  5      FOR i IN 1..lv_scalar_varray.LAST LOOP
  6        dbms_output.put_line('varray'||'('||i||')'||':'||lv_scalar_varray(i));
  7      END LOOP;
  8    END IF;
  9  END;
 10  /
```

The program shows that a call to the function with a local collection variable returns a modified copy of the local variable. It trims the last member from the collection inside the function, and what we have left are these:

```
varray(1):Eine
varray(2):Zwei
```

This section has shown you how to use and manipulate SQL schema-level scalar collections. There's really only one major difference between the varray and nested table. That's the physical limit on elements in a varray. While the COUNT and LAST methods return the highest index value inside the variable, the LIMIT returns the maximum number. The LIMIT method works only with varray data types.

You would raise an ORA-06533: Subscript beyond range if you switch the LAST method call with the LIMIT method call on line 5 in the preceding anonymous block. That error is thrown because the loop would

Best Practice
You should use a varray only when you're certain the domain of possibilities won't change; otherwise, your code will require more frequent maintenance.

try to count beyond the populated data to the maximum possible index value. The TRIM method in the function removed the third element in the varray and its index value. That's what would trigger the subscript beyond range error.

As you'll see when you work through the examples in the "Nested Tables" section a bit later, these types are virtually the same. However, you should generally use the nested table; our experience has shown that we seldom know the fixed limit of any domain of values in a database.

PL/SQL Scope Varrays of Scalar Variables

In this section, we work with scalar arrays in an exclusive PL/SQL context. The first example program declares, initializes, assigns, and accesses local scalar collection variables.

```
SQL> DECLARE
  2    TYPE plsql_varray IS VARRAY(3) OF VARCHAR2(20);
  3    lv_coll1 PLSQL_VARRAY := plsql_varray('One','Two','Three');
  4    lv_coll2 PLSQL_VARRAY := plsql_varray();
  5  BEGIN
  6    lv_coll2.EXTEND(lv_coll1.COUNT); -- Allocates space to the collection.
  7    FOR i IN 1..lv_coll1.COUNT LOOP
  8      lv_coll2(i) := lv_coll1(i);    -- Assigns values one at a time.
  9    END LOOP;
 10    FOR i IN 1..lv_coll2.count LOOP
 11      dbms_output.put_line('lv_coll2'||'('||i||')'||':['||lv_coll2(i)||']');
 12    END LOOP;
 13  END;
 14  /
```

On line 2, we define a local scalar collection variable. It is a user-defined type for the duration of the anonymous block program. If there were a SQL data type that used the same name, this type would replace it for the scope of the program. The first variable is defined and assigned a constructed instance with three elements. A null constructor initializes the second scalar collection variable. Space is allocated for all three elements before the assignment loop is started on line 6. The second loop simply prints the values.

Local variable scope in an anonymous block means that a user-defined scalar collection can be called in that same local scope only. This rule also applies to package or object type bodies, where you can access functions defined there only from inside the package or object body.

Functions also require some steps that differ from those of SQL data types. You can't define a function formal parameter or return type until the data type exists in the database catalog. Any attempt to do so raises a compile time failure exception. You can access a PL/SQL scalar collection type in other program units when you define it in a package specification.

The following defines a scalar collection data type in a package specification:

```
SQL> CREATE OR REPLACE PACKAGE coll_utility IS
  2    TYPE plsql_varray IS VARRAY(3) OF VARCHAR2(20);
  3  END;
  4  /
```

Anybody with execute permissions on the package has access to this data type. Unfortunately, you can't describe packages to find data types. You must inspect the code by querying the USER_SOURCE view, like this:

```
SQL> COLUMN line FORMAT 999 HEADING "Line"
SQL> COLUMN text FORMAT A76 HEADING "Source Code"
SQL> SELECT   line, text
  2  FROM     user_source
  3  WHERE    name = 'COLL_UTILITY'
  4  /
```

This produces the following:

```
Line Source Code
---- --------------------------------------------------
   1 PACKAGE coll_utility IS
   2   TYPE plsql_varray IS VARRAY(3) OF VARCHAR2(20);
   3 END;
```

Believe it or not, the type is now known to the catalog. You refer to the data type through the package with a period, which is actually the component selector, between the two.

The following function defines its return data type by referencing the package and data type within the package. We'll reuse a previous example because it will show a better comparison.

```
SQL> CREATE OR REPLACE FUNCTION get_varray
  2  ( pv_one    VARCHAR2 := NULL
  3  , pv_two    VARCHAR2 := NULL
  4  , pv_three  VARCHAR2 := NULL )
```

```
 5  RETURN COLL_UTILITY.PLSQL_VARRAY IS
 6    lv_coll COLL_UTILITY.PLSQL_VARRAY := COLL_UTILITY.PLSQL_VARRAY();
 7  BEGIN
 8    FOR i IN 1..3 LOOP
 9      IF pv_one IS NOT NULL AND i = 1 THEN
10        lv_coll.EXTEND;
11        lv_coll(i) := pv_one;
12      ELSIF pv_two IS NOT NULL AND i <= 2 THEN
13        lv_coll.EXTEND;
14        lv_coll(i) := pv_two;
15      ELSIF pv_three IS NOT NULL THEN
16        lv_coll.EXTEND;
17        lv_coll(i) := pv_three;
18      ELSE
19        NULL; -- Can't ever happen but it wasn't forgotten.
20      END IF;
21    END LOOP;
22    RETURN lv_coll;
23  END;
24  /
```

Lines 5 and 6 basically are the only changes. Instead of referring to a SQL data type, you refer to a PL/SQL package specification data type. We could repeat the balance of the examples, but you'd see only one consistent theme. The code now references a PL/SQL package specification data type every place it references the SQL data type.

The preceding subsections have shown you how to work with varrays. The next sections extend these examples by showing you the differences between varrays and nested tables.

Nested Tables

In a big reference book, we'd repeat the examples in the preceding section because sometimes books don't get read from start to finish. A workbook is a different type of book, and here we're going to point you back to the preceding section for everything but how you define a nested table.

Nested tables and varrays are so closely related that very little changes exist between the examples here and those in the last section. The only real changes are how you define a SQL and PL/SQL nested table data type.

```
SQL> CREATE OR REPLACE TYPE scalar_varray AS TABLE OF VARCHAR2(20);
  2  /
```

Best Practice
You should generally use a nested table data type for collections because it works in both SQL and PL/SQL contexts and it doesn't impose a fixed-size constraint.

The change inside a PL/SQL block is likewise trivial. Here's the required type definition inside a PL/SQL block:

```
DECLARE
    TYPE plsql_varray IS TABLE OF VARCHAR2(20);
    ... some statements ...
BEGIN
    ... some statements ...
END;
/
```

Nested tables don't have a physical maximum size. You should consider using nested tables rather than varrays as a rule because they're simpler to maintain in your code. They have exactly the same behavior minus the physical limitation on the maximum number of elements in a collection.

This concludes the SQL data types. The next section introduces you to single and multiple dimensional PL/SQL arrays, which is another way to describe scalar collections.

Associative Arrays

An associative array is very different from a varray or a nested table. Unlike the other two collections, an associative array is not an object type and doesn't require that you construct an instance of the data type. You also must assign values one-by-one, or through a bulk fetch operation from a cursor. As mentioned, associative arrays are constrained exclusively to a PL/SQL context.

The anonymous block is another twist on the same anonymous block program that we worked with in earlier examples in this chapter:

```
SQL> DECLARE
  2      TYPE plsql_table IS TABLE OF VARCHAR2(20) INDEX BY BINARY_INTEGER;
  3      lv_coll1 PLSQL_TABLE;
  4      lv_coll2 PLSQL_TABLE;
  5  BEGIN
  6      FOR i IN 1..3 LOOP
```

```
 7      lv_coll2(i) := 'This is '||i||'.';      -- Assigns one at a time.
 8    END LOOP;
 9    FOR i IN 1..3 LOOP
10      dbms_output.put_line('lv_coll2'||'('||i||'):['||lv_coll2(i)||']');
11    END LOOP;
12  END;
13  /
```

Line 2 demonstrates that an associative array definition differs from a nested table. You append the `INDEX BY BINARY_INTEGER` clause to the type definition. This subordinate clause qualifies that a collection is a PL/SQL associative array. Line 7 shows the assignment of a value to an element in the collection. The program doesn't have a call to the `EXTEND` method because there's no need to allocate space prior to the assignment of a value.

You can find a bulk fetch example in the "Record Type Collections" section later in this chapter. You can also use parallel associative arrays when you need two or more related elements in a collection, but we think that doing so is unwise. The "Object Type Collections" and "Record Type Collections" sections show you better solution options.

Object Type Collections

An *object type* variable comes in two distinct flavors. One flavor is a real object, which, we believe, means you can instantiate it. Chapter 10 covers instantiable object types. The other flavor is a implicit object; it allows you to create a structure of listed attributes. This type of object lets you create SQL collections of records. In C or C++, these are structures.

Object type collections are more commonly known as composite data types because they comprise elements inside elements, which make them, more or less, two-dimensional arrays. The structure is a named index, while the rows of elements are numeric or name indexed rows. An object type collection uses a numeric index, while the associative array record type collection may use either a numeric or a string index.

There's no sense repeating the content between varray and nested tables in this section. While it's possible that you might want to implement an object type collection as a varray, the likelihood of nested tables seems much stronger. Therefore, we'll focus on their implementation from the context of nested tables.

It is also possible that you could implement associative arrays of object types. This is not what we'd suggest you do, but we can see it as an implementation choice. You'll find an example that supports this direction, too.

You create a noninstantiable object type like this:

```
SQL> CREATE OR REPLACE TYPE common_lookup_object IS OBJECT
  2  ( lookup_id       NUMBER
  3  , lookup_type     VARCHAR2(30)
  4  , lookup_meaning  VARCHAR2(255));
  5  /
```

This creates a record structure that exists at the SQL level. It is called an object type or user-defined type (UDT), but acts like a record structure in PL/SQL. After you create the object type, you define a SQL schema-level collection of the object type, such as the following:

```
SQL> CREATE OR REPLACE TYPE common_lookup_object_table
  2  IS TABLE OF common_lookup_object;
  3  /
```

The object type and collection of an object type are the basis for the examples in the following subsections. They allow us to show you a very powerful feature in a small footprint of code.

SQL Nested Tables

The biggest advantage of a nested table that contains a composite data type is that you can use it either as a SQL or a PL/SQL context. This is not the case with an associative array of PL/SQL record types. The fact that you can use collections of object types virtually supplants the need for associative arrays of record types. It also almost obsoletes pipelined table functions because they're no longer needed to convert associative arrays into a SQL context. The primary use of pipelined table functions should be managing the associative arrays when they're generated from Native Dynamic SQL (NDS) statements. This restriction applies when an NDS statement returns a system reference cursor that can be assigned only to a PL/SQL record structure or associative array. Chapter 11 shows how that's done.

The following demonstrates a function that returns a SQL collection of a composite object type. You can implement it as a standalone schema-level function or inside a package, because the data type is defined at the schema level.

```
SQL> CREATE OR REPLACE FUNCTION get_object_table
  2  ( pv_table_name   VARCHAR2
  3  , pv_column_name VARCHAR2 )
  4  RETURN common_lookup_object_table IS
  5    -- Define a dynamic cursor that takes two formal parameters.
  6    CURSOR c (table_name_in VARCHAR2, table_column_name_in VARCHAR2) IS
  7      SELECT    common_lookup_id AS lookup_id
  8      ,         common_lookup_type AS lookup_type
  9      ,         common_lookup_meaning AS lookup_meaning
 10      FROM      common_lookup
 11      WHERE     common_lookup_table = UPPER(table_name_in)
 12      AND       common_lookup_column = UPPER(table_column_name_in);
 13    -- Declare a counter variable.
 14    lv_counter INTEGER := 1;
 15    -- Declare a collection data type as a SQL scope table return type.
 16    lv_list COMMON_LOOKUP_OBJECT_TABLE := common_lookup_object_table();
 17  BEGIN
 18    -- Assign the cursor return values to a record collection.
 19    FOR i IN c(pv_table_name, pv_column_name) LOOP
 20      lv_list.EXTEND;
 21      lv_list(lv_counter) := common_lookup_object(i.lookup_id
 22                                                 ,i.lookup_type
 23                                                 ,i.lookup_meaning);
 24      lv_counter := lv_counter + 1;
 25    END LOOP;
 26    -- Return the record collection.
 27    RETURN lv_list;
 28  END get_object_table;
 29  /
```

Notice several important things in the example. Line 4 shows the return type of our user-defined composite collection. Line 16 shows that, like the previous examples, we need to construct an empty instance of the collection type. Line 20 shows that we need to allocate space—after all, it's a nested table. The *assignment trick* is on lines 21 through 23. The cursor columns are passed as call parameters to the object type, and the instantiated structure is then assigned to an element in the collection.

You can call and process this function in SQL. The following formats the output for us, thanks to the fact that SQL*Plus still maintains its legacy as a report writer:

```
SQL> COLUMN lookup_id       FORMAT 9999 HEADING "ID"
SQL> COLUMN lookup_type     FORMAT A16  HEADING "Lookup Type"
```

```
SQL> COLUMN lookup_meaning FORMAT A30   HEADING "Lookup Meaning"
SQL> SELECT   *
  2  FROM     TABLE(get_object_table('ITEM','ITEM_TYPE'));
```

The table function allows us to access the rows of the collection as if it were a normal query. Notice that it returns definitions of the object type's element names, like a query would retain the column names from a table or view. This is also true when we call it from a Java or PHP program. This works because object type definitions are stored in the database catalog when they're created.

It prints a list of common lookup values that you could use in a web page or form widget, as shown here:

```
  ID Lookup Type        Lookup Meaning
----- ---------------    ------------------------------
 1013 DVD_FULL_SCREEN    DVD: Full Screen
 1014 DVD_WIDE_SCREEN    DVD: Wide Screen
 1015 GAMECUBE           Nintendo GameCube
 1016 PLAYSTATION2       PlayStation2
 1019 VHS_DOUBLE_TAPE    VHS: Double Tape
 1018 VHS_SINGLE_TAPE    VHS: Single Tape
 1017 XBOX               XBOX
```

Now that you've seen how to access collections from SQL, let's move on to passing the return from the function as a call parameter to another PL/SQL function. (We keep these examples small to make the concepts evident—we know these examples don't do much with the data.)

```
SQL> CREATE OR REPLACE FUNCTION process_collection
  2  ( pv_composite_coll COMMON_LOOKUP_OBJECT_TABLE )
  3  RETURN SYS_REFCURSOR IS
  4    lv_sample_set SYS_REFCURSOR;
```

Best Practice

You should use object types in lieu of record types, because object types are formally defined inside the database catalog with meaningful names. PL/SQL record types and collection sets are qualified only after you implement a pipelined table function, and their names are system-generated gobbledygook.

```
 5  BEGIN
 6    OPEN lv_sample_set FOR
 7      SELECT * FROM TABLE(pv_composite_coll);
 8    RETURN lv_sample_set;
 9  END;
10  /
```

Line 2 has the composite collection type as formal parameter. Line 7 uses a SQL statement to place the results into a reference cursor. You can now select it as a normal query, like this:

```
SQL> SELECT process_collection(get_object_table('ITEM','ITEM_TYPE'))
  2  FROM dual;
```

While this prints the same result set that printed in the preceding example, it demonstrates that you can pass the results in and process them in PL/SQL. Another example in the following sections will show how PL/SQL row-by-row processing works.

PL/SQL Nested Tables

These examples build on the preceding code in this chapter. They demonstrate how you create and use a PL/SQL-only nested table collection type that uses a SQL object type.

The first thing you must do is create a PL/SQL collection type based on the SQL object type. You do that by defining the collection inside a package specification. Packages are covered in Chapter 8; if they're new to you, flip to that chapter for a quick primer.

Here's the required specification:

```
SQL> CREATE OR REPLACE PACKAGE sample IS
  2    TYPE plsql_table IS TABLE OF common_lookup_object;
  3  END sample;
  4  /
```

The next step reuses the basic GET_OBJECT_TABLE function but with a couple changes. Specifically, it is now the GET_PLSQL_TABLE function and it returns a PL/SQL-only nested table. You can tell that the return type is limited to the PL/SQL scope because a package name precedes the collection data type, as qualified on line 4.

```
SQL> CREATE OR REPLACE FUNCTION get_plsql_table
  2  ( pv_table_name  VARCHAR2
  3  , pv_column_name VARCHAR2 )
```

```
 4   RETURN sample.plsql_table IS
 5     -- Define a dynamic cursor that takes two formal parameters.
 6     CURSOR c (table_name_in VARCHAR2, table_column_name_in VARCHAR2) IS
 7       SELECT   common_lookup_id AS lookup_id
 8       ,        common_lookup_type AS lookup_type
 9       ,        common_lookup_meaning AS lookup_meaning
10       FROM     common_lookup
11       WHERE    common_lookup_table = UPPER(table_name_in)
12       AND      common_lookup_column = UPPER(table_column_name_in);
13     -- Declare a counter variable.
14     lv_counter INTEGER := 1;
15     -- Declare a collection data type as a SQL scope table return type.
16     lv_list SAMPLE.PLSQL_TABLE := sample.plsql_table();
17   BEGIN
18     -- Assign the cursor return values to a record collection.
19     FOR i IN c(pv_table_name, pv_column_name) LOOP
20       lv_list.extend;
21       lv_list(lv_counter) := common_lookup_object(i.lookup_id
22                                                  ,i.lookup_type
23                                                  ,i.lookup_meaning);
24       lv_counter := lv_counter + 1;
25     END LOOP;
26     -- Return the record collection.
27     RETURN lv_list;
28   END get_plsql_table;
29   /
```

The instantiation of the collection type on line 16 also references the PL/SQL collection type defined in the SAMPLE package specification. You can't call this function in a SQL context or you'll raise an exception (also shown in Figure 7-1). For example, this call is invalid because it returns an exclusively PL/SQL collection data type:

```
SQL> SELECT *
  2  FROM    TABLE(get_plsql_table('ITEM','ITEM_TYPE'));
```

It would throw the following exception:

```
FROM    TABLE(get_plsql_table('ITEM','ITEM_TYPE'))
              *
ERROR at line 2:
ORA-00902: invalid datatype
```

You can use this as a formal function parameter. When you use it as a formal function parameter, it can be called only inside a PL/SQL scope.

The following uses the exclusive PL/SQL data type as a formal parameter:

```
SQL> CREATE OR REPLACE FUNCTION print_collection
  2  ( pv_composite_coll SAMPLE.PLSQL_TABLE )
  3  RETURN BOOLEAN IS
  4    lv_counter NUMBER := 0;
  5    lv_result  BOOLEAN := FALSE;
  6  BEGIN
  7    WHILE lv_counter < pv_composite_coll.COUNT LOOP
  8      lv_counter := lv_counter + 1;
  9      IF NOT lv_result THEN
 10        lv_result := TRUE;
 11      END IF;
 12      dbms_output.put_line(pv_composite_coll(lv_counter).lookup_meaning);
 13    END LOOP;
 14    RETURN lv_result;
 15  END;
 16  /
```

You can call this program only from inside a PL/SQL block. Like the previous example with a PL/SQL return data type, any SQL call of the PRINT_COLLECTION function would return an ORA-00902 error.

Here's how you'd call the function from inside an anonymous block:

```
BEGIN
  IF NOT print_collection(get_plsql_table('ITEM','ITEM_TYPE')) THEN
    dbms_output.put_line('Not populated!');
  END IF;
END;
/
```

This section has demonstrated how you work with nested tables in both a SQL and PL/SQL context when the base data type is a SQL user-defined object type. These are flexible and powerful tools that help you build robust application code. Just remember where, when, and how they work.

Record Type Collections

A *record type* variable is a PL/SQL data type exclusively. It is the most common collection type in legacy code, like the Oracle eBusiness Suite. Collections of these variables are the PL/SQL tables mentioned at the beginning of this chapter. They became available in Oracle 7.3. Before then, you had to write parallel arrays of scalar variables.

A PL/SQL record type defines a data structure, which is more or less like a row in a database table. The difference is that these exist only in memory. You can't return a PL/SQL record structure data type or collection of data types natively in SQL. However, you can convert them from a PL/SQL collection into a SQL aggregate table by using a pipelined table function.

This section shows you how to use associative arrays of PL/SQL record types. It leverages the same general code concepts used in preceding sections.

The first thing you need to do is rebuild your package specification to include both a PL/SQL record type and the collection record type. It would look like this:

```
SQL> CREATE OR REPLACE PACKAGE sample IS
  2    TYPE common_lookup_record IS RECORD
  3    ( lookup_id       NUMBER
  4    , lookup_type     VARCHAR2(30)
  5    , lookup_meaning VARCHAR2(255));
  6    TYPE plsql_table IS TABLE OF common_lookup_record
  7      INDEX BY PLS_INTEGER;
  8  END sample;
  9  /
```

Lines 2 through 5 hold the PL/SQL record data type. As discussed earlier in this chapter, this data type is most like a structure in C or C++.

The next change that's required is the removal of all object constructors because record types aren't objects. You'll have a different assignment pattern, too. The recast GET_PLSQL_TABLE function is shown here:

```
SQL> CREATE OR REPLACE FUNCTION get_plsql_table
  2  ( pv_table_name  VARCHAR2
  3  , pv_column_name VARCHAR2 )
  4  RETURN sample.plsql_table IS
  5    -- Define a dynamic cursor that takes two formal parameters.
  6    CURSOR c (table_name_in VARCHAR2, table_column_name_in VARCHAR2) IS
  7      SELECT   common_lookup_id AS lookup_id
  8      ,        common_lookup_type AS lookup_type
  9      ,        common_lookup_meaning AS lookup_meaning
 10      FROM     common_lookup
 11      WHERE    common_lookup_table = UPPER(table_name_in)
 12      AND      common_lookup_column = UPPER(table_column_name_in);
 13      -- Declare a counter variable.
 14    lv_counter INTEGER := 1;
 15      -- Declare a collection data type as a PL/SQL scope table return type.
 16    lv_list SAMPLE.PLSQL_TABLE;
 17  BEGIN
```

```
18     -- Assign the cursor return values to a record collection.
19     FOR i IN c(pv_table_name, pv_column_name) LOOP
20       lv_list(lv_counter) := i;
21       lv_counter := lv_counter + 1;
22     END LOOP;
23     -- Return the record collection.
24     RETURN lv_list;
25   END get_plsql_table;
26   /
```

Line 16 shows that the definition of the variable no longer has an assignment
constructor. Line 20 shows that you can assign the cursor's row return
directly to the element of the collection. This is possible because the cursor
row structure maps to a PL/SQL record structure.

Alternatively, you could manually assign each column value, as shown
here, but we'd advise against this:

```
lv_list(lv_counter).lookup_id := i.lookup_id;
lv_list(lv_counter).lookup_type := i.lookup_type;
lv_list(lv_counter).lookup_meaning := i.lookup_meaning;
```

Note that no change is required in the PRINT_COLLECTION function.
The reason for that is simple. You use the same semantics to call an element
of a nested table as you use for an associative array. The following
demonstrates how you manage the output:

```
SQL> CREATE OR REPLACE FUNCTION print_collection
  2  ( pv_composite_coll SAMPLE.PLSQL_TABLE )
  3  RETURN BOOLEAN IS
  4    lv_counter NUMBER := 0;
  5    lv_result  BOOLEAN := FALSE;
  6  BEGIN
  7    WHILE lv_counter < pv_composite_coll.COUNT LOOP
  8      lv_counter := lv_counter + 1;
  9      IF NOT lv_result THEN
 10        lv_result := TRUE;
 11      END IF;
 12      dbms_output.put_line(pv_composite_coll(lv_counter).lookup_meaning);
 13    END LOOP;
 14    RETURN lv_result;
 15  END;
 16  /
```

Line 12 holds the call to the element and nested member of the element.
Notice that the index reference is associated with the row, and then the
component select lets you reference a nested member of the structure.

The test program mirrors the one used earlier in the chapter in the nested table discussion, but it's small enough to repeat here to avoid having you flip back to it:

```
SQL> BEGIN
  2    IF NOT print_collection(get_plsql_table('ITEM','ITEM_TYPE')) THEN
  3      dbms_output.put_line('Not populated!');
  4    END IF;
  5  END;
  6  /
```

This, like the other program, would print the following:

```
DVD: Full Screen
DVD: Wide Screen
Nintendo GameCube
PlayStation2
VHS: Double Tape
VHS: Single Tape
XBOX
```

You can convert this output back to a SQL context by using a pipelined table function. Though, by now, you may wonder why pipelined table functions exist. We suggest that you move away from pipelined table functions in Oracle 11*g*.

Downloadable Code

The examples in this chapter are organized into two files:

- The `collection_basics.sql` script contains examples of varrays, nested tables, and associative arrays.

- The `collection_advanced.sql` script contains examples of collections of structures.

These programs should let you see the code in action. We think a download is friendlier then a cumbersome disc because the code doesn't take up a great deal of space.

Summary

This chapter has covered the basics of collection in Oracle server-side programming. You should be able to use this information as a foundation for working with collections in your role and especially in the balance of our examples.

You should also check the introduction for references to further your study of these topics.

Best Practice Review

■ You should use a *varray* only when you're certain the domain of possibilities won't change; otherwise, your code will require more frequent maintenance.

■ You should generally use a nested table data type for collections because it works in both SQL and PL/SQL contexts and it doesn't impose a fixed-size constraint.

■ You should use object types in lieu of record types because object types are formally defined inside the database catalog with meaningful names. PL/SQL record types and collection sets are qualified only after you implement a pipelined table function, and their names are system-generated gobbledygook.

Mastery Check

The mastery check is a series of true or false and multiple choice questions that let you confirm how well you understand the material in the chapter. You may check Appendix E for answers to these questions.

1. ☐ **True**   ☐ **False**   You can create collections with only numeric indexes.

2. ☐ **True**   ☐ **False**   You can create SQL collection with only scalar data types.

3. ☐ **True**   ☐ **False**   You can create a PL/SQL collection of varrays and nested tables.

4. ☐ **True** ☐ **False** You can create an associative array as a SQL collection.

5. ☐ **True** ☐ **False** You can create SQL collections of SQL object types.

6. ☐ **True** ☐ **False** You can create PL/SQL collections of PL/SQL record types.

7. ☐ **True** ☐ **False** All three collection types can access all of the methods in the Oracle Collection API.

8. ☐ **True** ☐ **False** Collections are always defined with densely populated indexes when they're defined in SQL.

9. ☐ **True** ☐ **False** Varray index values cannot have gaps in the index.

10. ☐ **True** ☐ **False** Nested table index values can have gaps when elements are deleted after the collection is created.

11. Which of the following Collection APIs work with varrays?

   A. A COUNT method

   B. A LIMIT method

   C. A LAST method

   D. All of the above

   E. Only A and C

12. Which of the following Collection APIs work with nested tables and associative arrays?

   A. The COUNT method

   B. The LIMIT method

   C. The LAST method

   D. All of the above

   E. Only B and C

13. You can define a nested table with which of the following base data types?

    A. A scalar data type, such as a date, number, or string

    B. A PL/SQL record type, such as a structure or single row table definition

    C. A SQL object type, such as a structure or single row table definition, except you populate it through a constructor call

    D. All of the above

    E. Only A and B

14. An associative array can be indexed by which of the following?

    A. A date

    B. An integer

    C. A string

    D. All of the above

    E. Only B and C

15. In a table function, not a pipelined table function, which data types can you return?

    A. A varray of any base scalar data type

    B. A nested table of any base scalar data type

    C. An associative array of any base scalar data type

    D. All of the above

    E. Only A and B

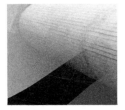

CHAPTER
8

Packages

ou can find PL/SQL in many Oracle products including PeopleSoft, Oracle Forms 11*g*, Oracle Database 11*g*, Oracle Application Server, Oracle Application Express, and Oracle E-Business Suite. For example, a typical database contains at least 300 thousand lines of PL/SQL. Furthermore, the E-Business Suite contains more than 20 million. What's more, Oracle built-in packages continue to increase with each major release of the database engine. PL/SQL is definitely not going away, and mastering package design and implementation is essential to your success as a DBA, data architect, or database developer.

This chapter shows you how to design and build packages that take full advantage of the Oracle PL/SQL feature set. We divide it into the following areas:

- Package architecture

- Package specifications

- Package bodies

- Modular programming

- Overloading

- Greater security

- Definer and invoker rights

We encourage your careful study of each section, as each contains important information and examples that are more complex than previous ones.

Package Architecture

PL/SQL packages are collections of Oracle objects and may contain scalar variables, data collections, data objects, system reference cursors, functions, and procedures. They normally have two parts: a package specification and a body.

The package specification contains public objects. This means that external programs can call and modify them. Moreover, package specifications can exist independent of package bodies. We call these types of specifications *bodiless* packages. They are helpful in publishing standard and frequently used data types, variables, and cursors. When used appropriately, they can considerably reduce package body size.

Package bodies cannot exist without their specifications. They contain private types, variables, cursors, and procedural code. They commonly represent the bulk of a package's size. Programming in packages provides the following benefits:

- Greater organization

- Program persistence

- Memory residency

- Larger program size

We describe these benefits briefly in the following sections. Our intent is to summarize them, not to delve into technical implementation (which we do so later on in this chapter).

Greater Organization

Most databases include thousands of functions and procedures. These programs can live in or out of packages, depending on the developers' and architects' perspectives. Imagine the workload associated with documentation and rights management in systems that do not employ packages.

To illustrate this idea, imagine 1,000 important documents, thrown on the floor in a large heap. These documents are vital to your everyday work, and hundreds of thousands of requests come in daily for access to the information contained therein.

You have no means of filing these packages because business requirements demand that you toss them back into the heap when you are finished with them. Your management of the pile would be mediocre at best, even if you had a small team of assistants to help you. In addition, team members would be irritated with each other because their activities would cause a constant state of chaos.

Now imagine those documents neatly stored in file cabinets, all of which are organized by application. In addition, a team of clerks know right where to go for each document. Finally, you can grant rights to the records by file cabinet instead of by individual files. Now ask yourself: How would you like your database organized, in a heap or within packages?

Program Persistence and Memory Residency

Another great benefit to package programming is Oracle's ability to pre-load your packages as a session starts, instead of instantiating objects as you call them. The overhead of object instantiation is a major factor in busy systems. What's more, the values contained in package objects persist throughout the calling session. For example, if you create a cursor in a package specification, you can call it many times throughout your session.

Larger Program Size

All PL/SQL programs are constrained to the programming limitations found in the Descriptive Intermediate Attribute Notion for ADA (DIANA). In addition, Oracle employs an Interface Description Language (IDL), which provides a virtual machine between source and executable code (m-code). Oracle created this method as a way to maximize interoperability between PL/SQL and the varying operating systems on which the Oracle Database runs. As a result, PL/SQL programs have a maximum size limit, dictated by DIANA parse trees.

Most standalone functions and procedures top out around 2,000 to 4,000 lines of code, depending on programming style; however, as of Oracle 7.2, the DIANA parse tree for package bodies is discarded. This means that programs existing within package bodies are limited only to the overall 256MB size limit. The following query illustrates this fact.

Example 8-1: Package Body Parsed Size Is 0

```
-- This is found in ex08-01.sql on the publisher's web site.
SQL> SELECT   name
  2        ,  type
  3        ,  source_size
  4        ,  parsed_size
  5        ,  code_size
  6     FROM  user_object_size
  7    WHERE  name IN ( 'DBL_AUDIT', 'TO_BASE' )
```

NAME	TYPE	SOURCE_SIZE	PARSED_SIZE	CODE_SIZE
TO_BASE	FUNCTION	521	297	1069
DBL_AUDIT	PACKAGE BODY	19977	0	16325
DBL_AUDIT	PACKAGE	1548	1703	1013

Best Practice
Always promote PL/SQL programs to production in packages. Add
functions and procedures to existing packages when possible.

Notice that the package specification has a PARSED_SIZE while the
body does not. It is OK for the specification to have a parse tree, because
procedural code does not exist there, and it is extremely difficult to create
code large enough to throw the PLS-00123 PROGRAM TOO LARGE error.

Package Specifications

The package specification is a menu or header for the package body.
Package specifications cannot hold procedural code. You can dramatically
reduce the size of package subprograms when you properly declare objects
within the specification. This allows procedural code to view and modify
objects defined in the specification. Here's an example.

Example 8-2: Declaring Variables and Cursors Within the Specification

```
-- This is found in ex08-02.sql on the publisher's web site.
SQL> CREATE OR REPLACE PACKAGE
  2     employee_benefits
  3     AUTHID CURRENT_USER
  4     AS
  8     ln_max_raise_percentage  CONSTANT NUMBER := .1;
  9     ln_employee_id           NUMBER;
 10     ln_department_id         NUMBER;
 11     ln_max_salary            NUMBER;
 12     ln_min_salary            NUMBER;
 13     ln_new_salary            NUMBER;
 14     lv_job_id                VARCHAR2(50);
 15     lv_full_name             VARCHAR2(100);
 19     CURSOR c_employees_by_eid IS
 20       SELECT  *
 21         FROM  hr.employees
 22        WHERE  employee_id = ln_employee_id;
 23
 24     CURSOR c_employees_by_dpt IS
 25       SELECT  *
```

```
26           FROM  hr.employees
27          WHERE  department_id = ln_department_id;
28
29      CURSOR c_jobs IS
30        SELECT  *
31          FROM  hr.jobs
32         WHERE  job_id = lv_job_id;
36      e_compensation_too_high    EXCEPTION;
40      PROCEDURE give_raise  ( pi_department_id       IN   NUMBER
41                            , pi_raise_percentage    IN   NUMBER
42                            , po_status              OUT  NUMBER
43                            , po_sqlerrm             OUT  VARCHAR2
44                            );
45    ------------------------------------------------------------
46    END employee_benefits;
47    /
```

Observe that one of our scalar variables, LN_MAX_RAISE_PERCENTAGE, is a constant. We cannot modify this value without recompiling the specification. This kind of variable is helpful when you want to enforce specific values. Also, note that the two cursors C_EMPLOYEES_BY_EID and C_EMPLOYEES_BY_DPT are dependent on the values LN_EMPLOYEE_ID and LN_DEPARTMENT_ID, respectively. The declaration of these two variables is required before cursor statements.

We create the employee cursors in the specification because we plan to use them throughout our EMPLOYEE_BENEFITS package. An added bonus is that we can reference the cursor at any time in the session, as shown next.

Example 8-3: Cursors in the Package Specification

```
-- This is found in ex08-03.sql on the publisher's web site.
SQL> BEGIN
  2     employee_benefits.ln_employee_id := 100;
  3
  4     FOR r_employees_by_eid IN employee_benefits.c_employees_by_eid LOOP
  5       employee_benefits.lv_full_name := r_employees_by_eid.first_name||' '||
  6                                         r_employees_by_eid.last_name;
  7
  8       DBMS_OUTPUT.PUT_LINE ( employee_benefits.lv_full_name );
  9     END LOOP;
 10  END;
 11  /

Steven King
```

Notice that we did not have to create variables or cursors in the preceding block. The LV_EMPLOYEE_ID scalar and C_EMPLOYEES_BY_EID cursor are referenced with their fully qualified name. In the following procedure named GIVE_RAISE, we continue to reference this package instead of declaring new variables and cursors. Subsequently, as the EMPLOYEE_BENEFITS package grows, we save ourselves at least 20 lines of code each time we reference them instead of declaring new objects within functions and procedures.

Example 8-4: Creating a Slimmed-Down GIVE_RAISE Procedure

```
-- This is found in ex08-04.sql on the publisher's web site.
SQL> CREATE OR REPLACE PACKAGE BODY
  2     employee_benefits
  3     AS
  4
  5     PROCEDURE give_raise   ( pi_department_id      IN   NUMBER
  6                            , pi_raise_percentage   IN   NUMBER
  7                            , po_status             OUT  NUMBER
  8                            , po_sqlerrm            OUT  VARCHAR2
  9                            )
 10     IS
 11     BEGIN
 12       FOR r_employees_by_dpt IN c_employees_by_dpt LOOP
 13         SELECT   min_salary
 14              ,   max_salary
 15           INTO   ln_min_salary
 16              ,   ln_max_salary
 17           FROM   hr.jobs
 18          WHERE   job_id = r_employees_by_dpt.job_id;
 19
 20         ln_new_salary :=   r_employees_by_dpt.salary +
 21                            r_employees_by_dpt.salary *
 22                            pi_raise_percentage;
 23
 24         IF  ln_new_salary < ln_max_salary
 25         AND ln_new_salary > ln_min_salary
 26         AND ln_new_salary < r_employees_by_dpt.salary +
 27                             r_employees_by_dpt.salary *
 28                             ln_max_raise_percentage
 29         THEN
 30           UPDATE  hr.employees
 31              SET  salary = ln_new_salary
```

> **Best Practice**
> Encourage reuse by placing your most commonly used package objects
> in the header of your package specification or body.

```
32              WHERE  employee_id = r_employees_by_dpt.employee_id;
33          ELSE
34            RAISE e_compensation_too_high;
35          END IF;
36        END LOOP;
37      END give_raise;
38  END;
39  /
```

Observe that we did not have to qualify the variables as we did in
Example 8-3. This is because Oracle ties the body to the specification,
eliminating the need to qualify object names. If private cursors and variables
are required, you can place them at the beginning of your package body.
They work identically to the public specification but will be available only
to the package.

Bodiless Packages

We use this type of package to instantiate most commonly used scalar
variables, constants, data objects, or cursors, such as the creation of
common obfuscation keys in an encryption package. Following is an
example.

Example 8-5: The Use of Package Specification
for Common Configurations

```
This is found in ex08-05.sql on the publisher's web site.
SQL> CREATE OR REPLACE PACKAGE encryption_conf
  2    AS
  3    PRAGMA SERIALLY_REUSABLE;
  4    lv_encryption_key#1a    CONSTANT  VARCHAR2(50) := 'NowIsTheTime';
  5    lv_encryption_key#1b              VARCHAR2(10);
  6  END encryption_conf;
  7  /
```

Note that we added the PRAGMA SERIALLY_REUSABLE keywords to this package. These keywords instruct the compiler to initialize the package in the System Global Area (SGA) instead of the User Global Area (UGA). Each time we call the package, the shared objects in the specification are set to null or their default value. As a cautionary step, we WRAP this package before compiling it. Appendix A demonstrates how you wrap code.

NOTE
You can use the PRAGMA SERIALLY_ REUSABLE keywords in packages with bodies; however, if you do so, you must specify them in both the body and the specification.

Package Bodies

Working code for all subprograms and cursors must reside in the package body. When you create objects in the package body without declaring them in the specification, you classify them as private, meaning that they are available only to subprograms within the package body. In addition, subprograms must match their declaration within the specification. This is because the PL/SQL compiler does a token-by-token comparison of the name and parameters in order to perform a match. If your subprograms do not match, you will receive a PLS-00323 error, as shown in the next example.

Example 8-6: Error Thrown when Subroutines Do Not Match   This example creates a package specification named VS_TRANSACTION in the VIDEO_STORE schema. We intend the VS_TRANSACTION.CHECK_OUT procedure to populate the VIDEO_STORE.TRANSACTION table:

```
-- This is found in ex08-06.sql on the publisher's web site.
SQL> CREATE OR REPLACE PACKAGE video_store.vs_transaction
  2    AS
  3    lv_account_number        varchar2(50);
  4    ln_payment_method        number;
 24    PROCEDURE check_out ( pi_created_by        IN NUMBER
 25                        , pi_last_updated_by   IN NUMBER
 26                        , pi_transaction_type  IN NUMBER
 27                        );
 28    END vs_transaction;
 29    /
```

In the package body, we modify the CHECK_OUT procedure slightly by changing the data type of PI_TRANSACTION_TYPE to VARCHAR2. Then we compile the package body.

```
SQL> CREATE OR REPLACE PACKAGE BODY video_store.vs_transaction
  2    AS
  3    PROCEDURE check_out ( pi_created_by        IN NUMBER
  4                        , pi_last_updated_by   IN NUMBER
  5                        , pi_transaction_type  IN VARCHAR2
  6                        )
  7    IS
     ... omitted for brevity ...
 39  END vs_transaction;
 40  /
Warning: Package Body created with compilation errors.

SQL> show err
Errors for PACKAGE BODY VIDEO_STORE.VS_TRANSACTION:
LINE/COL ERROR
-------- ------------------------------------------------------------------
24/13    PLS-00323: subprogram or cursor 'CHECK_OUT' is declared in a
         package specification and must be defined in the package body
```

Observe that the PL/SQL compiler does not recognize the CHECK_OUT procedure. It treats it as a private subprogram because the parameter data types do not match those in the specification.

Dependency Resolution

In large systems, maintenance of standalone functions and procedures is daunting. Main contributors to this are the dependencies formed between subprograms and other database objects such as tables and views. Because of these dependencies, changes in underlying objects can invalidate other program units. On the other hand, discrete use of standalone functions and procedures that incorporate and join packages is ideal.

Example 8-7: Subprograms Become Invalid   This block creates an employee suggestion table. We use it to illustrate subprogram interdependency.

```
-- This is found in ex08-07.sql on the publisher's web site.
SQL> CREATE TABLE employee_suggestions
  2  ( employee_id          NUMBER(25)
  3  , suggestion_id        NUMBER(25)
  4  , summary              VARCHAR2(100)
```

```
   5   , description             VARCHAR2(500)
   6   , approved_flag           CHAR
   7   , savings                 NUMBER(10,2)
   8   , bonus_paid              NUMBER(10,2)
   9   , bonus_paid_date         DATE
  10   )
```

The following block creates the standalone procedure GIVE_BONUS:

```
SQL> CREATE OR REPLACE PROCEDURE hr.give_bonus
   2    ( pi_employee_id         IN NUMBER
   3    , pi_savings             IN NUMBER
   4    , pi_bonus_paid          IN NUMBER
   5    , pi_bonus_paid_date     IN DATE
   6    )
   7    AS
   8      lv_termination_flag    CHAR := 'Y';
   9    BEGIN
  10      SELECT  termination_flag
  11        INTO  lv_termination_flag
  12        FROM  hr.employees
  13       WHERE  employee_id = pi_employee_id;
  14
  15
  16      IF  lv_termination_flag = 'N'
  17      AND pi_bonus_paid > 50
  18      AND pi_bonus_paid < pi_savings * .1
  19      THEN
  20        INSERT
  21          INTO  employee_suggestions
  22          VALUES  ( pi_employee_id
  23                  , es_suggestion_id_seq.nextval
          ... omitted for brevity ...
  46      END IF;
  47    END;
  48  /
```

Notice that the GIVE_BONUS procedure creates three dependencies on two tables and one sequence. It does so with the SELECT-INTO and INSERT statements on lines 12 and 21:

```
SQL> SELECT  owner
   2       ,  object_name
   3       ,  status
   4    FROM  all_objects
```

```
  5   WHERE   object_name = 'GIVE_BONUS'
  6   /

OWNER                              OBJECT_NAME                    STATUS
--------------------------------   -----------------------------  -------
HR                                 GIVE_BONUS                     VALID
```

Furthermore, the following query reveals two more dependencies aside from those mentioned earlier:

```
SQL> SELECT  name
  2       ,  type
  3       ,  referenced_owner as r_owner
  4       ,  referenced_name  as r_name
  5       ,  referenced_type  as r_type
  6       ,  dependency_type  as d_type
  7    FROM  user_dependencies
  8   WHERE  name = 'GIVE_BONUS'
  9   /

NAME          TYPE         R_OWNER R_NAME                         R_TYPE      D_TYPE
-----------   ----------   ------- ----------------------------   ----------  ------
GIVE_BONUS    PROCEDURE    SYS     STANDARD                       PACKAGE     HARD
GIVE_BONUS    PROCEDURE    SYS     SYS_STUB_FOR_PURITY_ANALYSIS   PACKAGE     HARD
GIVE_BONUS    PROCEDURE    HR      EMPLOYEES                      TABLE       HARD
GIVE_BONUS    PROCEDURE    HR      EMPLOYEE_SUGGESTIONS           TABLE       HARD
GIVE_BONUS    PROCEDURE    HR      ES_SUGGESTION_ID_SEQ           SEQUENCE    HARD
```

Notice the dependency on the SYS.STANDARD and SYS.SYS_STUB_FOR_PURITY_ANALYSIS packages. Oracle uses the SYS.STANDARD package to instantiate a plethora of objects needed for normal PL/SQL operation. Furthermore, it uses the SYS.SYS_STUB_FOR_PURITY_ANALYSIS package to assert the consistent state of stored functions and procedures:

```
SQL> ALTER TABLE hr.employees
  2    MODIFY ( termination_flag CHAR )
  3   /

SQL> SELECT  owner
  2       ,  object_name
  3       ,  status
  4    FROM  all_objects
  5   WHERE  object_name = 'GIVE_BONUS'
  6      OR  object_name = 'DO_IT'
  7   /
```

> **Best Practice**
> Cease dependence of subprograms to each other via package encapsulation.

```
OWNER                          OBJECT_NAME                    STATUS
------------------------------ ------------------------------ -------
HR                             DO_IT                          INVALID
HR                             GIVE_BONUS                     INVALID
```

Note that if we modify the underlying objects, standalone subprograms go invalid. The DO_IT procedure calls HR.GIVE_RAISE and becomes invalid. If your database includes hundreds or thousands of standalone subprograms, you force Oracle to recompile all of them whenever parent objects are changed. This is not the case when package bodies become invalid.

%TYPE and %ROWTYPE

Another method of reducing dependencies is the use of the %TYPE and %ROWTYPE keywords. With these keywords, Oracle determines the data type at runtime instead of creating a hard/static determination. This method is very handy in systems that change size allocation of a VARCHAR2 or NUMBER data size a lot.

The use of %TYPE and %ROWTYPE is not a good solution when parent objects are changed from one data type to another, like VARCHAR2 to DATE. This is because some data types provide no implicit casting between them. Your PL/SQL programs will experience cascading failure if you habitually anchor PL/SQL variables to their parent objects with %TYPE and %ROWTYPE, and then change parent object data types in this manner. This practice is only effective when you ensure that column data types will never change.

An example of anchoring follows in the next code sample. We modify the GIVE_BONUS procedure from our previous example to use data types anchored to the HR.EMPLOYEE_SUGGESTIONS.

Example 8-8: % TYPE Usage

```
-- This is found in ex08-08.sql on the publisher's web site.
SQL> CREATE OR REPLACE PACKAGE hr.employee_perks
  2     AUTHID
  3     CURRENT_USER
  4     AS
  5     PROCEDURE give_bonus
  6     ( pi_employee_id        IN hr.employee_suggestions.employee_id%TYPE
  7     , pi_savings            IN hr.employee_suggestions.savings%TYPE
  8     , pi_bonus_paid         IN hr.employee_suggestions.bonus_paid%TYPE
  9     , pi_bonus_paid_date    IN hr.employee_suggestions.bonus_paid_date%TYPE
 10     );
 11  END employee_perks;
 12  /
```

This block creates the HR.EMPLOYEE_PERKS package, which contains our GIVE_RAISE procedure as defined in Example 8-7. Instead of using statically defined data types, we use the dynamic COLUMN_NAME%TYPE keywords for all parameters. We also use this method for the LV_TERMINATION_FLAG variable in the body, like so:

```
SQL> CREATE OR REPLACE PACKAGE BODY hr.employee_perks
  2     AS
  3     PROCEDURE give_bonus
  4     ( pi_employee_id        IN hr.employee_suggestions.employee_id%TYPE
  5     , pi_savings            IN hr.employee_suggestions.savings%TYPE
  6     , pi_bonus_paid         IN hr.employee_suggestions.bonus_paid%TYPE
  7     , pi_bonus_paid_date    IN hr.employee_suggestions.bonus_paid_date%TYPE
  8     )
  9     IS
 10       lv_termination_flag   hr.employees.termination_flag%TYPE := 'Y';
...
```

The great thing about dynamic data type assignment is that Oracle automatically changes %TYPE variables and parameters to match their parent objects at runtime. This is true with record types as well; here's an example:

```
SQL> CREATE OR REPLACE PACKAGE hr.employee_perks
  2     AUTHID
  3     CURRENT_USER
  4     AS
  5     PROCEDURE give_bonus
  6     ( pi_employee_id        IN hr.employee_suggestions.employee_id%TYPE
  7     , pi_savings            IN hr.employee_suggestions.savings%TYPE
  8     , pi_bonus_paid         IN hr.employee_suggestions.bonus_paid%TYPE
  9     , pi_bonus_paid_date    IN hr.employee_suggestions.bonus_paid_date%TYPE
 10     );
 11     PROCEDURE give_raise   ( pi_employee_record     IN hr.employees%ROWTYPE );
 12  END employee_perks;
 13  /
```

There is no way to affect the same solution with object types. For this reason, you should be careful when you deploy %TYPE or %ROWTYPE anchoring. The best practice for collections is to use SQL data types, which include object types in lieu of a record structure. Object type collections let you avoid pipelined table functions because you can directly query them through SQL with the TABLE function. You should flip back to Chapter 7 for more detail on that approach, or back to Chapter 5 for a comparative example.

Our newly added GIVE_RAISE procedure accepts an entire row from the HR.EMPLOYEES table as its parameter in value. If you change the HR.EMPLOYEES table, the parameter automatically changes to match.

Modular Programming

Novice PL/SQL programmers tend to write very long functions and procedures. They do so in an attempt to fix everything in one massive code block. This practice has both maintenance and performance consequences. For example, larger programs naturally take longer to execute than smaller ones. In addition, large custom programs inherently contain redundant code, found within your database system. This redundancy needlessly multiplies the amount of code you must maintain.

Modularization is a practice that can speed up user response time, reduce maintenance overhead, and lighten administrative costs. You create modular programs by breaking down tasks into smaller, generic chunks that represent logical units of work. Then you write subroutines that fulfill those tasks. Finally, you enclose those modules in appropriate packages.

NOTE
To encourage reuse, create packages that can be decoupled and reused. If you build packages that are tightly interrelated and dependent, you will only succeed in creating rigid systems that are difficult to maintain.

Modularization relates to your Java solution space, even when you deploy it in a product like Hibernate. PL/SQL modularity that creates coupling is bad. An example of that bad practice would be creating a bunch of standalone functions and procedures.

Modularity that decreases coupling and builds reusable artifacts is good. Packages should become cohesive units. They should organize standalone components. This is the good form of PL/SQL modularization. Packages are powerful object-oriented components because they create cohesion in database-centric application development.

The following is an example of constructive modularization.

Example 8-9: Reuse via Modularization

```
-- This is found in ex08-09.sql on the publisher's web site.
SQL> CREATE OR REPLACE PACKAGE
  2      error_handling
  3      AS
  4      -----------------------------------------------------------------
  5      gn_status               number;
  6      gn_sqlerrm              varchar2(500);
  7      gd_timestamp            timestamp := systimestamp;
  8      gf_file                 utl_file.file_type;
  9      -----------------------------------------------------------------
 10      PROCEDURE printf ( pi_program_name   IN VARCHAR2
 11                       , pi_directory      IN VARCHAR2
 12                       , pi_file           IN VARCHAR2
 13                       , pi_log_level      IN VARCHAR2
 14                       , pi_status         IN NUMBER
 15                       , pi_error_message  IN VARCHAR2
 16                       );
 17
 18      PROCEDURE prints ( pi_program_name   IN VARCHAR2
 19                       , pi_log_level      IN VARCHAR2
 20                       , pi_status         IN NUMBER
 21                       , pi_error_message  IN VARCHAR2
 22                       );
 23      -----------------------------------------------------------------
 24  END error_handling;
 25  /
```

NOTE
The use of UTL_FILE is very handy; however, its use comes with some caveats. You must take care to secure the directories this package writes to, as it does so via the Oracle system user. Moreover, this user must have read/write privileges assigned to UTL_FILE directories.

The preceding block creates a specification for the ERROR_HANDLING package. It has two programs that are broken down into specific tasks, mainly print-to-file and print-to-screen. We list the body of this package in the following block:

```
SQL> CREATE OR REPLACE PACKAGE BODY
  2    error_handling
  3    AS
  4    -----------------------------------------------------------------
  5    PROCEDURE printf  ( pi_program_name    IN VARCHAR2
  6                      , pi_directory       IN VARCHAR2
  7                      , pi_file            IN VARCHAR2
  8                      , pi_log_level       IN VARCHAR2
  9                      , pi_status          IN NUMBER
 10                      , pi_error_message   IN VARCHAR2
 11                      )
 12    IS
 13    BEGIN
 14      gf_file := UTL_FILE.FOPEN
 15        ( pi_directory
 16        , pi_file
 17        , 'a' -- appends to the file.
 18        );
 19
 20      UTL_FILE.PUT_LINE
 21        ( gf_file
 22        , TO_CHAR( gd_timestamp,'HH:MM:SS.FF MON DD, YYYY' ) ||' ['||
 23          pi_log_level ||'] '||
 24          pi_program_name ||' '||
 25          pi_error_message
 26        );
 27
 28      UTL_FILE.FCLOSE( gf_file );
 29    END printf;
 30    -----------------------------------------------------------------
 31    PROCEDURE prints  ( pi_program_name    IN VARCHAR2
 32                      , pi_log_level       IN VARCHAR2
 33                      , pi_status          IN NUMBER
 34                      , pi_error_message   IN VARCHAR2
 35                      )
 36    IS
 37    BEGIN
 38      DBMS_OUTPUT.PUT_LINE
 39        ( TO_CHAR( gd_timestamp,'HH:MM:SS.FF MON DD, YYYY' ) ||' ['||
 40          pi_log_level ||'] '||
 41          pi_program_name ||' '||
```

```
42              pi_error_message
43          );
44    END prints;
45    -------------------------------------------------------------------------
46    END error_handling;
47    /
```

Notice that we do not have to specify the GF_FILE and GD_TIMESTAMP variables in the package body. This is because they are already instantiated in the package specification. Also, observe that we kept the PRINTF and PRINTS procedures brief. Furthermore, the name of their enclosing package is basic but descriptive. Its simplicity creates a package ready for use anywhere in our system. Finally, take note that each procedure does work directly related to a single purpose. For example, PRINTS does not write to a file or table; it only prints to screen.

Creating modular systems saves countless hours of programming and maintenance. Over time, modular systems grow in richness. They are agile because only small blocks of code need modification at any one time. Yet they are also practical because they are developed with a grander vision in mind.

Our final note on modular design has to do with the monetary benefits behind intelligent system design. Architectural oversight is essential in the development of systems that are designed to perform. In contrast, we cannot throw a few tables together with a little PL/SQL code and expect their design to perform and persist. It is only through the reuse of code that it becomes valuable. In Figure 8-1, observe the line that represents occasional refactoring. It eventually overcomes initial costs and begins to be more valuable to the business; however, the constant refactoring line loses money over time.

Best Practice
Design your packages and subroutines for general use throughout your database system(s). Remember to *write once, use many times.*

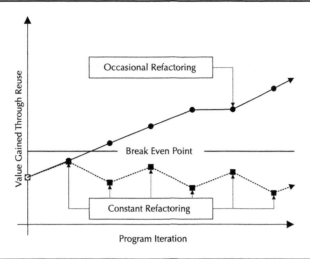

Figure 8-1.   *Value gained through code reuse*

Overloading

Overloading is the ability of PL/SQL to compile functions or procedures that have the same name and exist within the same package. To do this, subroutines need to differ only in their input or output parameters. This ability is very helpful when constructing programs that must function differently, based on their input data type.

The following example creates two functions named TRANSLATED. The first function transforms numeric data into binary format, or base-2. The second function returns numeric data in base-10 format.

Example 8-10: Creation of Two Overloaded Functions

```
-- This is found in ex08-10.sql on the publisher's web site.
SQL> CREATE OR REPLACE PACKAGE
  2     number_converter
  3     AS
  4     FUNCTION translated ( pi_number_value IN VARCHAR2 )
  5     RETURN VARCHAR2;
  6
  7     FUNCTION translated ( pi_number_value IN NUMBER )
```

```
  8    RETURN VARCHAR2;
  9  END number_converter;
 10  /
```

Did you spot the subtle change? The functions are identical with the exception of the data type of the parameter PI_NUMBER_VALUE. One is of NUMBER and the other is of VARCHAR2 data type.

```
SQL> CREATE OR REPLACE PACKAGE BODY
  2    number_converter
  3    AS
  4    --------------------------------------------------------------------
  5    FUNCTION translated ( pi_number_value IN VARCHAR2 )
  6    RETURN VARCHAR2
  7    IS
  8      lv_string       VARCHAR2(250);
  9      ln_number       NUMBER;
 10      lv_hex          VARCHAR2(50) := '0123456789ABCDEFGHIJKLMNOPQRSTUVWXYZ';
 11    BEGIN
 12      IF pi_number_value < 0
 13      OR pi_number_value IS NULL
 14      THEN
 15        RAISE PROGRAM_ERROR;
 16      END IF;
 17
 18      ln_number := pi_number_value;
 19
 20      WHILE ln_number > 0 LOOP
 21        lv_string := SUBSTR ( lv_hex, MOD ( ln_number, 2 ) + 1, 1 )||
 22                     lv_string;
 23        ln_number := TRUNC ( ln_number / 2 );
 24      END LOOP;
 25
 26      RETURN lv_string;
 27    END translated;
```

Overloaded functions and procedures can have entirely different semantics; however, for simplicity, our example differs only in parameter data type, and the divisor used to convert to base-2 or base-10:

```
 28    --------------------------------------------------------------------
 29    FUNCTION translated ( pi_number_value IN NUMBER )
 30    RETURN VARCHAR2
 31    IS
 32      lv_string       VARCHAR2(250);
 33      ln_number       NUMBER;
 34      lv_hex          VARCHAR2(50) := '0123456789ABCDEFGHIJKLMNOPQRSTUVWXYZ';
 35    BEGIN
 36      IF pi_number_value < 0
 37      OR pi_number_value IS NULL
```

```
38      THEN
39        RAISE PROGRAM_ERROR;
40      END IF;
41
42      ln_number := pi_number_value;
43
44      WHILE ln_number > 0 LOOP
45        lv_string := SUBSTR ( lv_hex, MOD ( ln_number, 10 ) + 1, 1 )||
46                      lv_string;
47        ln_number := TRUNC ( ln_number / 10 );
48      END LOOP;
49
50      RETURN lv_string;
51    END translated;
52  --------------------------------------------------------------------------
53  END number_converter;
54  /
```

The execution of each function returns the following:

```
SQL> SELECT   number_converter.translated ( '1234567890' ) base2
  2        ,  number_converter.translated (  1234567890  ) base10
  3    FROM  dual;


BASE2                                          BASE10
----------------------------------------       --------------------
1001001100101100000001011010010               1234567890
```

Overloaded functions and procedures may also differ in the number of parameters. For example, the NUMBER_CONVERTER package could have a third function named TRANSLATED, which might take multiple parameters as follows:

```
FUNCTION translated ( pi_number_value IN NUMBER
                    , pi_base          IN NUMBER
                    )
RETURN VARCHAR2
IS
...
```

Best Practice
Use overloading to create programs that function differently based on parameter data type. If you are using overloading merely to deal with disparate data types, we suggest the use of explicit data conversion or the ANYDATA data type.

Overloading is an extremely powerful tool that allows you to simplify the naming of subprograms. It also allows for the creation of distinct program units that have the same name.

Greater Security

As stated previously, package bodies are private. This means that external programs cannot see or modify scalar variables, data collections, data objects, and ref cursors created in the body. In addition, you are able to WRAP sensitive code in package bodies while leaving their specifications open for review.

For instance, credit card numbers are stored in many organizations, and database professionals are now required to encrypt them due to recent payment card laws and regulations. Wrapping the package body obscures its contents from would-be hackers and prevents users from viewing the logic behind our CC_ENCRYPT procedure. In our following example we

- Alter the VIDEO_STORE.MEMBER table, adding a CREDIT_CARD_LAST4 column

- Alter the CREDIT_CARD_NUMBER column to hold an encrypted value

- Create the VIDEO_STORE.ENCRYPTION package

- Wrap the ENCRYPTION.CC_ENCRYPT procedure

Example 8-11: Wrapping Package Bodies   This adds the column CREDIT_CARD_LAST4 to the MEMBER table:

```
-- This is found in ex08-11.sql on the publisher's web site.
SQL> ALTER TABLE video_store.member
  2    ADD    ( credit_card_last4 varchar2(20))
  3  /
```

This modifies the CREDIT_CARD_NUMBER column to accept a larger encrypted value:

```
SQL> ALTER TABLE video_store.member
  2    MODIFY ( credit_card_number varchar2(250) )
  3  /
```

This creates the `video_store.encryption` package specification:

```
SQL> CREATE OR REPLACE PACKAGE
  2     video_store.encryption
  3     AUTHID CURRENT_USER
  4     AS
  5
  6     PROCEDURE cc_encrypt  ( pi_key         in   varchar2
  7                          , pi_clear_txt   in   varchar2
  8                          , po_encrypted   out  varchar2
  9                          );
 10  END encryption;
 11  /
```

Our package specification is simple. It contains one procedure, CC_ENCRYPT. We want the specification to remain in clear text for your viewing convenience; however, we wrap the package body. We list its contents in the following block to illustrate the results of the Oracle WRAP utility:

```
SQL> CREATE OR REPLACE PACKAGE body video_store.encryption
  2    AS
  3    PROCEDURE cc_encrypt  ( pi_key        in   varchar2
  4                         , pi_clear_txt  in   varchar2
  5                         , po_encrypted  out  varchar2
  6                         )
  7    IS
  8      lv_data            varchar2(50);
  9    BEGIN
 10      lv_data :=  RPAD  ( pi_clear_txt
 11                        , ( TRUNC ( LENGTH ( pi_clear_txt ) / 8 ) + 1 ) * 8
 12                        ,   CHR(0) );
 13
 14      DBMS_OBFUSCATION_TOOLKIT.DESENCRYPT ( input_string     => lv_data
 15                                          , key_string       => pi_key
 16                                          , encrypted_string => po_encrypted
 17                                          );
 18    END cc_encrypt;
 19  END encryption;
 20  /
```

By wrapping the package body as follows, we obfuscate it, which prevents users from viewing its contents:

```
$> wrap iname=encryption.sql oname=encryption.plb
```

Now that we have a wrapped version of our package body, we save the
`ENCRYPTION.SQL` source code in a safe place. This is our master copy.
After compilation, users querying the `ALL_SOURCE` table see the following:

```
SQL> SELECT line
  2        , text
  3    FROM all_source
  4   WHERE name = 'ENCRYPTION'
  5     AND type = 'PACKAGE BODY'
  6  /
LINE TEXT
---------- -------------------------------------------------------------------
         1 PACKAGE body            encryption wrapped
           a000000
           b2
           abcd
           ... omitted for brevity ...
           kBYcoyAY+OJDX4mzQV/eJ+kf5mG3xd5TTc2FxF2J0e8Fi0ij3ggrnVvnRf+tZtnEaLXKMQzf
```

Finally, we compile the package, enabling the obfuscation of the
`CREDIT_CARD_NUMBER` column. We display its results in the following
query:

```
SQL> SELECT  member_id
  2        , credit_card_number
  3        , credit_card_last4
  4    FROM  video_store.member
  5  /
MEMBER_ID CREDIT_CARD_NUMBER                    CREDIT_CARD_LAST4
---------- ------------------------------------ -------------------------
      1001 ++éäñ7+c·=·æS++o?-?÷ç¯|(              ************4444
      1002 o¢n?|e |-r=S?·¢n~H+-?=+ç              ************5555
      1003 |«8óí ô-óÆ-?¥~?½é|Éh[s+·              ************6666
```

The ability to `WRAP` package bodies separate from their specification is
a great boon to DBAs and PL/SQL developers who want to secure source
code yet keep the specifications open to users. You should not assume that
you have to wrap all packages, however. We put together Appendix A to
help you get started on wrapping your code.

Best Practice
`WRAP` sensitive PL/SQL package specifications and bodies to protect
them from prying eyes.

Definer and Invoker Rights

Definer and invoker rights are easy to understand if you think of the definer as the owner and the invoker as the user executing the code. Applications inherit DEFINER rights by default when you create PL/SQL programs without the AUTHID CURRENT_USER keywords. This option is handy when you want to minimize the rights needed for data manipulation. Here's an example:

Example 8-12: Package Execution as Definer

```
-- This is found in ex08-12.sql on the publisher's web site.
SQL> CREATE OR REPLACE PACKAGE employee_benefits
  2    AUTHID DEFINER
  3    AS
  4    -----------------------------------------------------------------
  5    ln_max_raise_amount    CONSTANT NUMBER := .1;
  6    -----------------------------------------------------------------
  7    PROCEDURE give_raise  ( pi_employee_id        IN NUMBER
  8                          , pi_raise_percentage   IN NUMBER
  9                          );
 10    -----------------------------------------------------------------
 11  END employee_benefits;
 12  /
```

This block creates the GIVE_RAISE procedure within the HR.EMPLOYEE_BENEFITS package. We create the package with definer rights, meaning that users who execute it will do so as a surrogate to the HR user, not themselves. In the following block, we implement the GIVE_RAISE procedure and grant execute rights to the user JANE_DOE:

```
SQL> CREATE OR REPLACE PACKAGE BODY employee_benefits
  2    AS
  3    -----------------------------------------------------------------
  4    PROCEDURE give_raise  ( pi_employee_id        IN NUMBER
  5                          , pi_raise_percentage   IN NUMBER
  6                          )
  7    IS
  8    BEGIN
  9      IF  pi_raise_percentage <= ln_max_raise_amount
 10      AND pi_raise_percentage IS NOT NULL
 11      AND pi_employee_id IS NOT NULL
 12      THEN
```

```
13        UPDATE  hr.employees
14           SET  salary = salary + ( salary * pi_raise_percentage )
15         WHERE  employee_id = pi_employee_id;
16      END IF;
17    EXCEPTION
18      WHEN NO_DATA_FOUND THEN
19        DBMS_OUTPUT.PUT_LINE ('That employee does not exist.');
20    END give_raise;
21    -------------------------------------------------------------
22  END employee_benefits;
23  /
```

In the following block, we create the JANE_DOE user and GRANT EXECUTE rights on EMPLOYEE_BENEFITS to her:

```
SQL> CREATE USER jane_doe IDENTIFIED BY abc123;
```

Notice that we have DBA role privileges to make this grant, or we'd need to connect to account with the privilege to create a new user. After creating the user, you need to grant at least CONNECT privileges, which let the user sign on to the database. You grant the privilege, like this:

```
SQL> GRANT CONNECT TO jane_doe;
```

You can then grant the user EXECUTE permissions on the package. Here is the syntax for the command:

```
SQL> GRANT EXECUTE ON hr.employee_benefits TO jane_doe;
```

Observe that Jane is a new user with no more rights than CONNECT and EXECUTE on HR.EMPLOYEE_BENEFITS. We validate that the connected user is JANE_DOE with the SYS_CONTEXT function. Then we execute the GIVE_RAISE procedure for EMPLOYEE_ID 100:

```
SQL> SELECT SYS_CONTEXT ('USERENV','CURRENT_USER') who_am_i
  2    FROM dual;
WHO_AM_I
----------
JANE_DOE

SQL> CONNECT hr/hr;
SQL> SELECT  employee_id
  2       , first_name||' '||last_name full_name
  3       , salary
  4    FROM  hr.employees
  5   WHERE  employee_id = 100;
```

```
EMPLOYEE_ID FULL_NAME                                                   SALARY
----------- ------------------------------------------------- ----------
        100 Steven King                                                 24000

SQL> CONNECT jane_doe/abc123;
SQL> EXEC hr.employee_benefits.give_raise ( 100, .1 );
SQL> commit;

SQL> CONNECT hr/hr;
SQL> SELECT  employee_id
  2        ,  first_name||' '||last_name full_name
  3        ,  salary
  4     FROM  hr.employees
  5    WHERE  employee_id = 100;
EMPLOYEE_ID FULL_NAME                                                   SALARY
----------- ------------------------------------------------- ----------
        100 Steven King                                                 26400
```

Note that Jane's execution of GIVE_RAISE manipulated the salary of employee 100 without having SELECT, INSERT, UPDATE, or DELETE rights on the HR.EMPLOYEES table. With this method, you can create users that have few rights to speak of, but have the ability to execute via proxy-specific packages owned by an application account, such as HR. While this method is easy, it is also very risky. For example, if you grant Jane EXECUTE WITH GRANT OPTION, Jane can grant EXECUTE to other users who should not have the ability to change employee salaries. Furthermore, if you drop Jane's account, users who have been granted EXECUTE rights via Jane retain those privileges. We recreate the EMPLOYEE_BENEFITS with the AUTHID CURRENT_USER keywords as follows:

```
SQL> CREATE OR REPLACE PACKAGE hr.employee_benefits
  2     AUTHID CURRENT_USER
  3     AS
  4     ------------------------------------------------------------------
  5     ln_max_raise_amount    CONSTANT NUMBER := .1;
  6     ------------------------------------------------------------------
  7     PROCEDURE give_raise ( pi_employee_id      IN NUMBER
  8                          , pi_raise_percentage IN NUMBER
  9                          );
 10     ------------------------------------------------------------------
 11  END employee_benefits;
 12  /
```

> **Best Practice**
> Use invoker rights when you require additional security.

Afterward, Jane attempts to execute the same procedure with no additional rights:

```
SQL> EXEC hr.employee_benefits.give_raise ( 100, .1 );
BEGIN hr.employee_benefits.give_raise ( 100, .1 ); END;

*
ERROR at line 1:
ORA-00942: table or view does not exist
ORA-06512: at "HR.EMPLOYEE_BENEFITS", line 13
ORA-06512: at line 1
```

Notice that Jane's attempt to execute the GIVE_RAISE procedure returns an ORA-00942 error. This is because its execution inherits the rights of its invoker (due to the AUTHID CURRENT_USER keywords). Jane does not have rights to the HR.EMPLOYEES table; therefore, the package does not have rights either. This method is preferred because Oracle enforces integrity rules via specific rights granted to each user instead of to the rights of the package owner.

Using invoker rights allows you to create central packages that modify tables in multiple schemas and across database links, while maintaining strict rights management, per user.

Downloadable Code

The examples in this chapter are organized into 12 exercise files:

- ex08-01.sql demonstrates how to determine the source and parsed sizes.

- ex08-02.sql demonstrates how to declare shared package variables and cursors.

- ex08-03.sql demonstrates how to use shared package variables and cursors.

- `ex08-04.sql` demonstrates how to create a procedure in a package.

- `ex08-05.sql` demonstrates how to create a serially reusable configuration package.

- `ex08-06.sql` demonstrates why subroutines must match between package specification and body.

- `ex08-07.sql` demonstrates subprogram invalidation.

- `ex08-08.sql` demonstrates how to use `%TYPE` in programs.

- `ex08-09.sql` demonstrates how to modularize your programs.

- `ex08-10.sql` demonstrates how to create overloaded modules.

- `ex08-11.sql` demonstrates how wrap package bodies.

- `ex08-12.sql` demonstrates how to use definer rights programs.

These programs should let you see the code in action. We think a download is friendlier then a cumbersome disc because the code doesn't take a great deal of space.

Conclusion

Our story on files and file cabinets becomes increasingly valid when considering the confusion caused by organic/ad hoc design practices. We strongly caution you against pushing any standalone programs into your production environments. You may not see the initial harm in this in small systems; however, over time, maintenance skyrockets when standalone programs sprout up like weeds and take over your database system.

Best Practices Review

- Always promote PL/SQL programs to production in packages. Add functions and procedures to existing packages when possible.

- Encourage reuse by placing your most commonly used package objects in the header of your package specification or body.

- Cease dependence of subprograms to each other via package encapsulation.

- Design your packages and subroutines for general use throughout your database system(s). Remember to *write once, use many times.*

- Use overloading to create programs that function differently based on parameter data types. If you are using overloading merely to deal with disparate data types, we suggest the use of explicit data conversion or the ANYDATA data type.

- WRAP sensitive PL/SQL package specifications and bodies to protect them from prying eyes.

- Use invoker rights where you require additional security.

Mastery Check

The mastery check is a series of true or false and multiple choice questions that let you confirm how well you understand the material in the chapter. You may check Appendix E for answers to these questions.

1. ☐ **True**   ☐ **False**   You can increase the organization or cohesion of programs by putting them into packages.

2. ☐ **True**   ☐ **False**   Oracle uses an Interface Description Language (IDL) to maximize interoperability between stored programs.

3. ☐ **True**   ☐ **False**   Oracle's adoption of Descriptive Intermediate Attribute Notion for ADA (DIANA) doesn't limit the physical size of stored functions and procedures.

4. ☐ **True**   ☐ **False**   PRAGMA SERIALLY_REUSABLE tells the compiler to initialize a package in the UGA instead of the SGA.

5. ☐ **True**   ☐ **False**   Subprogram names and parameter signatures must match exactly between package specification and body.

6. ☐ **True** ☐ **False** Local functions and procedures in the package body are private to the other external program units.

7. ☐ **True** ☐ **False** The `SYS_STUB_FOR_PURITY_ANALYSIS` package lets you assert the consistent state of stored functions and procedures.

8. ☐ **True** ☐ **False** The `%TYPE` anchors a program variable to a column in a table.

9. ☐ **True** ☐ **False** You wrap a package to make the code source more readable.

10. ☐ **True** ☐ **False** Overloading a function or procedure requires that you change the names of variables.

11. What `PRAGMA` is restricted to packages only?

   A. The `PRAGMA EXCEPTION_INIT`

   B. The `PRAGMA AUTONOMOUS_TRANSACTION`

   C. The `SERIALLY_REUSABLE`

   D. All of the above

   E. Only A and B

12. You must do which of these steps when you convert a definer rights program to invoker rights program?

   A. Replicate all tables, views, and sequences to invoker scheme

   B. Add the `CURRENT_USER` clause to all packages

   C. Grant `EXECUTE` privilege on all packages to invoker scheme

   D. All of the above

   E. Only B and C

13. Which administrative views help you troubleshoot dependencies?

   A. The `USER_OBJECTS` view

   B. The `USER_CODE` view

C. The USER_DEPENDENCIES view

D. All of the above

E. Only A and C

14. Which permissions do external scheme require to work with definer rights packages?

A. They require EXECUTION privileges

B. They require SELECT privileges

C. They require SELECT, INSERT, UPDATE, and DELETE privileges

D. All of the above

E. Only A and C

15. Which of these describes a bodiless package?

A. A package without a header

B. A package without shared cursors

C. A package without a package body

D. All of the above

E. Only A and C

CHAPTER
9

Triggers

riggers are an excellent part of the Oracle Database feature set. They allow you to automate processes around the enforcement of security rules, maintain data integrity in distributed systems, audit database usage, create historical data trails, prevent harmful data transactions, and generate derived column values. Unfortunately, we see their use in scenarios that they were never intended to fulfill. For example, some database professionals use triggers to perform check constraints. While they are able to do so, *Oracle Database PL/SQL Language Reference 11*g specifically states that users should "not define triggers that duplicate database features."

This chapter will discuss the following methodologies on trigger design and implementation:

- Trigger architecture

- Trigger firing order

- Trigger types

- Oracle Fine Grained Auditing (FGA)

- Distributed data integrity

We are aware that there are many strong opinions about where developers should code business logic. In addition, many debates center on proper trigger usage. The purpose of this chapter is not to define where business logic should exist; however, we do want to educate you on trigger possibilities, thereby allowing you to make informed decisions on system-level design.

Trigger Architecture

The structure of triggers is very similar to that of functions and procedures. Triggers contain declarative, body, exception, and end sections. Unlike procedures and functions, the DECLARE keywords can be used in the header (with the exception of compound triggers). It is easier to understand triggers if you think of them as subprograms that can be directly associated to system events and schema objects.

You can create triggers that fire once per event or multiple times for each row affected. Furthermore, you can stipulate that they should fire before, after, or instead of the actions that cause them to start. For example, you

may want to audit modification of credit card entries in the
VIDEO_STORE.MEMBER table. Consider the following example.

Example 9-1: Use of Triggers for DML Auditing   This block creates the
VIDEO_STORE.CHANGE_HISTORY table. We use it to store a running
record of modifications within the VIDEO_STORE schema.

```
-- This is found in ex09-01.sql on the publisher's web site.
SQL> CREATE TABLE video_store.change_history
  2  ( dml_type            VARCHAR2(50)
  3  , table_name          VARCHAR2(30)
  4  , column_name         VARCHAR2(30)
  5  , db_user             VARCHAR2(50)
  6  , os_user             VARCHAR2(50)
  7  , os_host             VARCHAR2(100)
  8  , old_value           VARCHAR2(100)
  9  , new_value           VARCHAR2(100)
 10  , update_ts           TIMESTAMP
 11  )
 12  /
```

The following block creates a stored procedure that handles inserts into
the prior table. We create it to shorten overall trigger length and reuse
common code:

```
SQL> CREATE OR REPLACE PROCEDURE video_store.dml_log
  2  ( pi_dml_type        IN   VARCHAR2
  3  , pi_table_name      IN   VARCHAR2
  4  , pi_column_name     IN   VARCHAR2
  5  , pi_old_value       IN   VARCHAR2
  6  , pi_new_value       IN   VARCHAR2
  7  )
  8  IS
  9  BEGIN
 10     INSERT
 11       INTO  video_store.change_history
 12     VALUES ( pi_dml_type
 13            , pi_table_name
 14            , pi_column_name
 15            , SYS_CONTEXT ( 'USERENV', 'SESSION_USER' )
 16            , SYS_CONTEXT ( 'USERENV', 'OS_USER' )
 17            , SYS_CONTEXT ( 'USERENV', 'HOST' )||': '||
 18              SYS_CONTEXT ( 'USERENV', 'IP_ADDRESS' )
 19            , pi_old_value
 20            , pi_new_value
```

```
21                  , SYSTIMESTAMP
22                  );
23  END;
24  /
```

Notice that we dynamically assign the DB_USER, OS_USER, and OS_HOST column values via SYS_CONTEXT. This Oracle built-in function enables the database professional to collect a plethora of information about the database, session, and users who interact with it. Also, note that we place all of the code related to SYS_CONTEXT in the DML_LOG procedure. We do so to shorten trigger length and encourage code reuse.

The next block creates a simple INSERT/UPDATE trigger and associates it to the MEMBER table with the ON VIDEO_STORE.MEMBER phrase:

```
SQL> CREATE OR REPLACE TRIGGER video_store.member_change_history_trg
  2      BEFORE  INSERT
  3          OR  UPDATE
  4          ON  video_store.member
  5    REFERENCING OLD AS OLD NEW AS NEW
  6    FOR EACH ROW
  7    BEGIN
  8      IF INSERTING THEN
  9      video_store.dml_log ( 'INSERT'
 10                          , 'MEMBER'
 11                          , 'CREDIT_CARD_NUMBER'
 12                          , :NEW.credit_card_number
 13                          , :OLD.credit_card_number
 14                          );
 15      ELSIF UPDATING THEN
 16      video_store.dml_log ( 'UPDATE'
 17                          , 'MEMBER'
 18                          , 'CREDIT_CARD_NUMBER'
 19                          , :NEW.credit_card_number
 20                          , :OLD.credit_card_number
 21                          );
 22      END IF;
 23    END;
 24  /
```

Best Practice
Triggers should be concise. *Oracle Database PL/SQL Language Reference 11*g states that, if possible, triggers should not exceed 60 lines of code.

Observe that the trigger is aware of column NEW and OLD values. During data manipulation, insert statements contain only NEW data, delete statements contain only OLD data, and update statements contain both NEW and OLD data. Also, note that we stipulated that the trigger should fire FOR EACH ROW. In addition, we determine that the OLD and NEW variables should reference OLD and NEW values, respectively. The following query shows the results from our Data Manipulation Language (DML) audit trigger:

```
-- after inserting and updating two customers
SQL> SELECT   dml_type
  2        ,  db_user
  3        ,  os_user
  4        ,  os_host
  5        ,  old_value
  6        ,  new_value
  7        ,  update_ts
  8     FROM video_store.change_history
  9  /
```

DML_TYPE	DB_USER	OS_USER	OS_HOST
INSERT	SYS	HarperJM	HARPERJMCQVR: 192.168.1.4
INSERT	SYS	HarperJM	HARPERJMCQVR: 192.168.1.4
UPDATE	SYS	HarperJM	HARPERJMCQVR: 192.168.1.4
UPDATE	SYS	HarperJM	HARPERJMCQVR: 192.168.1.4

OLD_VALUE	NEW_VALUE	UPDATE_TS
(null)	6135 1659 8755 2691	6/20/2009 7:21:09 PM
(null)	3393 9209 2563 1409	6/20/2009 7:21:09 PM
6135 1659 8755 2691	2862 6046 3527 5584	6/20/2009 7:21:09 PM
3393 9209 2563 1409	3255 8814 2129 3834	6/20/2009 7:21:09 PM

Observe that the trigger catches both the database and OS usernames, along with the session user's machine name and IP address. This kind of auditing is very helpful in busy systems when you need to know which users modified specific data.

Security Auditing

Oracle recommends that you use Fine Grained Auditing (FGA) for security tests because users can invalidate triggers by making changes to underlying tables. We discuss FGA in detail later on in this chapter.

Trigger Firing Order

Oracle Database systems released prior to 11*g* gave developers very little control over trigger timing. Moreover, in busy systems, multiple triggers can be associated to a single event or object. This exacerbates timing problems associated with trigger firing order. In prior releases, the only mechanism for control consisted of the following default order:

- Before statement triggers

- Before row triggers

- After row triggers

- After statement triggers

If two before row triggers existed on a table, the developer could not guarantee which one would fire first. It was for this reason that Oracle introduced the FOLLOWS keyword in 11*g*. We show you how to use this in the following example.

Example 9-2: Using FOLLOWS to Determine Firing Order   This block creates three simple triggers on the VIDEO_STORE.CONTACT table:

```
-- This is found in ex09-02.sql on the publisher's web site.
SQL> CREATE OR REPLACE TRIGGER video_store.some_trigger1
  2    BEFORE INSERT ON video_store.contact
  3    FOR EACH ROW
  4  BEGIN
  5    DBMS_OUTPUT.PUT_LINE ( 'Whos on first' );
  6  END;
  7  /

SQL> CREATE OR REPLACE TRIGGER video_store.some_trigger2
  2    BEFORE INSERT on video_store.contact
  3    FOR EACH ROW
  4    FOLLOWS video_store.some_trigger1
  5  BEGIN
  6    DBMS_OUTPUT.PUT_LINE ( 'Whats on second' );
  7  END;
  8  /
```

```
SQL> CREATE OR REPLACE TRIGGER video_store.some_trigger3
  2    BEFORE INSERT on video_store.contact
  3    FOR EACH ROW
  4    FOLLOWS video_store.some_trigger2
  5  BEGIN
  6    DBMS_OUTPUT.PUT_LINE ( 'I dunnos on third' );
  7  END;
  8  /
```

An insert into the VIDEO_STORE.CONTACT table produces the following effect:

```
SQL> INSERT
  2    INTO  video_store.contact
  3  VALUES  ( 1008, 1001, 1003, 'Joe', 'B.', 'Schmoe', 2, sysdate
  4          , 2, sysdate )
  5  /

Whos on first
Whats on second
I dunnos on third
1 row created.
```

You should observe that subsequent triggers contain the FOLLOWS keyword and the name of its prior trigger. You must carefully construct triggers in this manner. Mixing trigger types that do and do not contain the FOLLOWS keyword greatly diminishes and supplants trigger timing control.

Best Practice
Carefully construct timed triggers with the FOLLOWING clause to stipulate firing order. Do not mix noncontrolled and controlled trigger types.

Trigger Types

Our preceding example illustrates how triggers aid database professionals in auditing DML activities. It is easy for new database programmers to fall into the trap of "automating everything." This attitude can ultimately lead to poor system performance or rigid system design. Both characteristics are typical of systems that are doomed for refactoring.

Best Practice
Do not create triggers just because you can, or in an attempt to automate everything, as doing so quickly reaches the point of diminishing returns.

Here are some possible trigger types:

- **Data Definition Language triggers**   These triggers fire when you modify database objects. You can use them to enforce standards in physical database design and programming.

- **Data Manipulation Language triggers**   These triggers fire when you modify data in a table. You can opt to fire them once or for each row affected.

- **Compound triggers**   These triggers are representative of blended DML triggers. They can fire at both statement and row level.

- **Instead of triggers**   These triggers intercept and replace DML entered by users. You typically create these kinds of triggers to provide a simplified view of your physical database to users and developers who do not care to understand the complexities behind physical database design.

- **System event triggers**   These triggers fire when predefined events occur within your database—for example, user logon, alter system, or password change events.

You can group triggers by DML, Data Definition Language (DDL), and system-level events. We illustrate this in the following sections.

DML Triggers

Earlier in this chapter, we demonstrated trigger-based DML auditing. In addition, we discussed some of the difficulties associated with trigger timing. In complex systems, trigger management becomes increasingly difficult because of interdependencies. For this reason, Oracle introduced the compound trigger type in 11*g*. In the next example, we demonstrate how a single trigger can fire both row-by-row and statement-level subroutines.

Example 9-3: Using Compound Triggers to Consolidate Multiple Trigger Types   This SQL query displays data about video store titles and their price structure:

```
-- This is found in ex09-03.sql on the publisher's web site.
SQL> SELECT  p.price_id
  2        ,  cl.common_lookup_type
  3        ,  i.item_title
  4        ,  p.amount
  5        ,  active_flag
  6     FROM  video_store.price p
  7        ,  video_store.common_lookup cl
  8        ,  video_store.item i
  9    WHERE  p.price_type = cl.common_lookup_id
 10      AND  p.item_id = i.item_id
 11      AND  p.active_flag = 'Y'
 12   /
```

Notice that we priced 1-Day rentals at $1.00. We create a trigger to monitor the modification of the AMOUNT column:

```
PRICE_ID COMMON_LOOKUP_TYPE ITEM_TITLE                AMOUNT  ACTIVE_FLAG
-------- ------------------ ------------------------- ------- ------------
1158     1-DAY RENTAL       Tomorrow Never Dies       1       Y
1159     1-DAY RENTAL       The World Is Not Enough   1       Y
...
```

The following block creates a table to hold invalid price modification attempts:

```
SQL> CREATE TABLE video_store.invalid_price_modification
  2  ( price_id              NUMBER
  3  , amount_old            NUMBER
  4  , amount_new            NUMBER
  5  , active_flag_old       CHAR
  6  , active_flag_new       CHAR
  7  , update_timestamp      TIMESTAMP
  8  )
  9  /
```

We create this trigger to trap modifications of the AMOUNT column. In particular, we are concerned with amounts below $1.00:

```
SQL> CREATE OR REPLACE TRIGGER video_store.invalid_price_trg
  2    FOR UPDATE ON video_store.price
  3    COMPOUND TRIGGER
  4      TYPE tt_invalid_price IS
  5        TABLE OF video_store.invalid_price_modification%ROWTYPE
  6        INDEX BY BINARY_INTEGER;
  7    lr_invalid_price  tt_invalid_price;
  8
  9    ln_index      BINARY_INTEGER := 0;
 10    lt_timestamp  TIMESTAMP := SYSTIMESTAMP;
 11
 12    PROCEDURE forall_flush IS
 13    BEGIN
 14      FORALL i IN 1 .. lr_invalid_price.COUNT
 15        INSERT
 16          INTO  video_store.invalid_price_modification
 17          VALUES  lr_invalid_price ( i );
 18      lr_invalid_price.delete;
 19      ln_index := 0;
 20    END;
 21   AFTER EACH ROW IS
 22     BEGIN
 23       IF :NEW.amount < 1 THEN
 24         ln_index := ln_index + 1;
 25         lr_invalid_price( ln_index ).price_id         := :NEW.price_id;
 26         lr_invalid_price( ln_index ).amount_old       := :OLD.amount;
 27         lr_invalid_price( ln_index ).amount_new       := :NEW.amount;
 28         lr_invalid_price( ln_index ).active_flag_old  := :OLD.active_flag;
 29         lr_invalid_price( ln_index ).active_flag_new  := :NEW.active_flag;
 30         lr_invalid_price( ln_index ).update_timestamp := lt_timestamp;
 31       END IF;
 32
 33       IF MOD ( ln_index, 50 ) = 0
 34       THEN forall_flush;
 35       ELSIF ln_index = lr_invalid_price.COUNT
 36       THEN forall_flush;
 37       END IF;
 38     END AFTER EACH ROW;
 39   AFTER STATEMENT IS
 40     BEGIN
 41       video_store.dml_log ( 'UPDATE'
 42                            , 'PRICE'
 43                            , 'AMOUNT'
 44                            , NULL
 45                            , NULL
 46                            );
 47     END AFTER STATEMENT;
 48   END invalid_price_trg;
 49   /
```

Observe that we create an inline procedure named `FORALL_FLUSH`. This is a private procedure that is attached directly to the trigger. Its purpose is to flush the arrays we populate in the `AFTER EACH ROW` section of our trigger. We use it for illustration purposes only, as you should encapsulate this kind of program in a package, instead of within the trigger.

Also note that we call the `FORALL_FLUSH` procedure whenever the `mod ( LN_INDEX, 50 ) = 0`. This tells the PL/SQL engine to chunk audit inserts into 50 row sets, thereby reducing memory and CPU overhead associated with the management of large updates.

The following block exercises our trigger by updating all active rental items:

```
SQL> UPDATE  video_store.price p
  2     SET  p.amount = p.amount - .5
  3   WHERE  p.active_flag = 'Y'
  4   /
SQL> COMMIT
```

See that the trigger appropriately audited all rental items below $1.00:

```
SQL> SELECT  *
  2     FROM  video_store.invalid_price_modification
  3   /
```

PRICE_ID	AMOUNT_OLD	AMOUNT_NEW	ACTIVE_FLAG_OLD
1094	1	0.5	Y
1095	1	0.5	Y
1096	1	0.5	Y

ACTIVE_FLAG_NEW	UPDATE_TIMESTAMP
Y	6/27/2009 3:04:35 PM
Y	6/27/2009 3:04:35 PM
Y	6/27/2009 3:04:35 PM
...	

The next query displays what the `AFTER STATEMENT` did with our update:

```
SQL> SELECT  *
  2     FROM  video_store.change_history
  3   WHERE  table_name = 'PRICE'
  4   /
```

```
DML_TYPE        TABLE_NAME      COLUMN_NAME      DB_USER      OS_USER
-----------     -------------   ---------------  ----------   ----------
UPDATE          PRICE           AMOUNT           JANE_DOE     doejane

OS_HOST
-----------------------------------
WORKGROUP\DOEJANE-PC: 192.168.1.4
```

Notice that the trigger logged evidence that Jane Doe issued the offending DML. This insert fired only once because it was part of the `AFTER STATEMENT` section of our compound trigger. The compound trigger enabled us to consolidate multiple triggers into one, showing that it is possible to condense trigger code and supply complex business logic in a single trigger.

Best Practice
Where possible, consolidate triggers into compound trigger types.

DDL Triggers

The only difference between DML and DDL triggers is the firing event. You use DDL triggers to enforce rules or audit the creation of database objects. For example, you may want to audit all `CREATE` statements issued in your database. The next example illustrates how this is accomplished.

Example 9-4: Using DDL Triggers to Enforce Coding Standards   We create a table named `AUDIT_CREATION`. Its intent is to store information about all objects created within the database. The following block creates this table:

```
SQL> CREATE TABLE video_store.audit_creation
  2  ( object_owner           varchar2(30)
  3  , object_name            varchar2(30)
  4  , created_by             varchar2(30)
  5  , created_date           date
  6  )
  7  /
```

This trigger tracks the creation of all objects, including which user issued the CREATE statement:

```
SQL> CREATE OR REPLACE TRIGGER video_store.audit_ddl
  2     BEFORE CREATE ON SCHEMA
  3   BEGIN
  4     INSERT
  5       INTO  video_store.audit_creation
  6     VALUES ( ORA_DICT_OBJ_OWNER
  7            , ORA_DICT_OBJ_NAME
  8            , SYS_CONTEXT ('USERENV', 'SESSION_USER')
  9            , SYSDATE
 10            );
 11   END;
 12   /
```

Note that we use the Oracle built-in ORA_DICT_OBJ_OWNER and ORA_DICT_OBJ_NAME attribute functions to populate the OBJECT_OWNER and OBJECT_NAME columns. Oracle created 27 event functions to enrich your DDL audit. The next block illustrates the results of our trigger:

```
SQL> select *
  2     from video_store.audit_creation
  3   /
OBJECT_OWNER     OBJECT_NAME      CREATED_BY      CREATED_DATE
---------------  ---------------  --------------  --------------------
  SDBJMH           XYX              SDBJMH          6/30/2009 7:15:32 PM
  VIDEO_STORE      XYZ              SDBJMH          6/30/2009 7:09:25 PM
```

System Event Triggers

One of the greatest reasons for triggers is to ease monitoring and maintenance tasks that DBAs perform. One such activity is the refreshing and preservation of test and development environments. Oracle introduced Flashback Database and Flashback Table in version 9*i* to simplify this effort.

With the flashback feature, the DBA is able to recover data and object manipulation to specific time points, System Change Numbers (SCN), or named events. The next example shows a simple trigger that creates a named restore point.

Example 9-5: Using Triggers to Aid in Flashback Recovery   This block creates the table HR.EMPLOYEES_FB. We use it to demonstrate Oracle flashback capabilities:

```
-- This is found in ex09-05.sql on the publisher's web site.
SQL> CREATE TABLE hr.employees_fb
  2  ( employee_id              NUMBER(10,0)
  3  , first_name               VARCHAR2(20)
  4  , last_name                VARCHAR2(25)
  5  , email                    VARCHAR2(25)
  6  , phone_number             VARCHAR2(20)
  7  , hire_date                DATE
  8  , job_id                   VARCHAR2(10)
  9  , salary                   NUMBER(10,2)
 10  , commission_pct           NUMBER(2,2)
 11  , manager_id               NUMBER(10,0)
 12  , department_id            NUMBER(5,0)
 13  , termination_flag         VARCHAR2(10)
 14  )
 15  /
```

The next block creates an audit table to hold login and flashback information:

```
SQL> CREATE TABLE sys.testbed_fb
  2  ( fb_name                  VARCHAR2(50)
  3  , session_user             VARCHAR2(30)
  4  , update_timestamp         TIMESTAMP
  5  )
  6  /
```

We create the SYS.SET_FLASHBACK_TESTBED procedure to shorten the trigger body:

```
SQL> CREATE OR REPLACE PROCEDURE sys.set_flashback_testbed
  2  AUTHID DEFINER
  3  AS
  4    lv_timestring            VARCHAR2(20);
  5  BEGIN
  6    lv_timestring := TO_CHAR ( SYSTIMESTAMP, 'MMDDYYYYSSFF');
  7    EXECUTE IMMEDIATE ' CREATE RESTORE POINT before_test'||lv_timestring;
  8
  9    INSERT
 10      INTO sys.testbed_fb
 11    VALUES ( 'BEFORE_TEST'||lv_timestring
 12           , SYS_CONTEXT ( 'USERENV', 'SESSION_USER' )
```

```
13                  ,   systimestamp
14                  );
15     COMMIT;
16  END;
17  /
```

Notice that the procedure creates a named restore point called
BEFORE_TEST. We suffix it with a timestamp. Typical test systems may
fire many tests simultaneously to simulate application load. By adding a
timestamp to the name of the restore point, we enable a more precise
method of rolling back changes made by developers and testers.

We create the trigger next. In this case, we choose to execute the trigger
after the HR user logs on:

```
SQL> CREATE OR REPLACE TRIGGER sys.logon_fb
  2      AFTER LOGON
  3          ON DATABASE
  4  BEGIN
  5    IF ora_login_user = 'HR' THEN
  6      set_flashback_testbed;
  7    END IF;
  8  END;
  9  /
```

The ORA_LOGIN_USER function on line 5 obtains the name of the user
attempting to log in. We call the SET_FLASHBACK_TESTBED procedure
only if the user is HR. We do so because we do not want this trigger to
create flashback points for every user who logs into our database. We
caution your use of this kind of trigger in production, however, because it
can block user login attempts if it becomes invalid.

This ALTER TABLE statement enables you to flashback tables to a
named SAVEPOINT:

```
SQL> ALTER TABLE hr.employees_fb
  2      ENABLE ROW MOVEMENT
  3  /
```

Best Practice
Construct system event triggers so that they do not block general user
activity.

This statement adds all of the rows from `HR.EMPLOYEES` to `HR.EMPLOYEES_FB`:

```
-- as hr
SQL> INSERT
  2    INTO hr.employees_fb
  3  SELECT *
  4    FROM hr.employees
  5  /

107 rows created.
```

When testers finish manipulating data, the DBA can issue a select statement on the `SYS.TESTBED_FB` table to discover the named restore point:

```
-- as sys
SQL> select * from sys.testbed_fb;
/
FB_NAME                            SESSION_USER      UPDATE_TIMESTAMP
-----------------------------      ---------------   --------------------
BEFORE_TEST0620200949947000000     HR                6/20/2009 11:54:49 PM
```

The DBA issues the following command to flashback all of the changes made by testers to the restore point:

```
SQL> FLASHBACK TABLE hr.employees_fb TO
  2  RESTORE POINT BEFORE_TEST0620200949947000000;
Flashback complete.
```

Finally, the tester attempts to query the `HR.EMPLOYEES_FB` table and discovers that it has been restored to its original, empty state:

```
-- as hr
SQL> SELECT  employee_id
  2        , first_name||' '||last_name full_name
  3    FROM  hr.employees_fb
  4   WHERE  rownum <= 3
  5  /
no rows selected
```

Our example does not completely illustrate the power this kind of trigger wields. For example, typical, enterprise-class, development, and test databases require many hours of data manipulation/recovery between test iterations.

> ### Best Practice
> Create system triggers that aid your efforts to maintain test beds that maximize tester and developer uptime.

In some cases, this effort can last days or weeks. The implementation of this trigger could save you countless hours maintaining test beds.

Security and Oracle Fine Grained Auditing

One drawback to trigger-based auditing is that users can invalidate triggers by changing underlying objects. It is possible to disable triggers completely and prevent their execution. In some cases, would-be hackers may attempt to disable trigger-based auditing before manipulating data, to cover their tracks.

Oracle introduced FGA in version 9*i*. We recommend that you use triggers to enforce security rules and coding standards and allow FGA to perform necessary audits.

Setting up FGA is easy. To do so, you must use the Oracle built-in procedure DBMS_FGA to create audit policies. Once policies are created, Oracle takes care of the auditing logic for you by logging the event, DML statements, bind variables, and user information. The following example demonstrates how this is done.

Example 9-6: Using FGA to Audit Events   This block executes the DBMS_FGA.ADD_POLICY procedure:

```
-- This is found in ex09-06.sql on the publisher's web site.
SQL> BEGIN
  2     DBMS_FGA.ADD_POLICY ( object_schema    =>  'VIDEO_STORE'
  3                         , object_name      =>  'PRICE'
```

> ### Best Practice
> Use Oracle FGA to perform security audits.

```
 4                    , policy_name       => 'AUDIT_PRICE_MODXML'
 5                    , audit_condition   => 'VIDEO_STORE.PRICE.AMOUNT < 1'
 6                    , audit_column      => 'AMOUNT'
 7                    , handler_schema    => NULL
 8                    , handler_module    => NULL
 9                    , enable            => TRUE
10                    , statement_types   => 'INSERT, UPDATE'
11                    , audit_trail       => DBMS_FGA.XML + DBMS_FGA.EXTENDED
12                    , audit_column_opts => DBMS_FGA.ANY_COLUMNS
13                    );
14   END;
15   /
```

Notice that some of the parameters are NULL. We leave them NULL because we want Oracle to put the audit information in its default location. If you substitute a NULL value in the AUDIT_CONDITION parameter, it acts as an always-on switch. You can also use subqueries; sequences; user-defined functions; or LEVEL, PRIOR, or ROWNUM values. However, the AUDIT_CONDITION parameter must always evaluate to TRUE or FALSE.

Observe that we create the policy with an enabled status. Moreover, we stipulate that the audit writes to XML files with the DBMS_FGA.XML + DBMS_FGA.EXTENDED parameter. Finally, we tell the AUDIT_COLUMN_OPTS to fire if any of its audit columns are affected. If you set the AUDIT_COLUMN_OPTS parameter to DBMS_FGA.ALL_COLUMNS, the audit condition will not execute unless all stipulated columns are affected.

The following update statement triggers our audit policy:

```
SQL> UPDATE   video_store.price
  2      SET   amount = .25
  3    WHERE   active_flag = 'Y'
  4      AND   rownum <= 5
  5   /
5 rows updated.
The update is recorded even if you issue a rollback:
SQL> ROLLBACK
  2   /
Rollback complete.
```

If you issue the following query, using an account with rights to the V$XML_AUDIT_TRAIL view, you can see the results of our audit:

```
SQL> SELECT os_user
  2        , os_host
  3        , object_schema
  4        , object_name
  5        , policy_name
```

```
  6          , sql_bind
  7          , sql_text
  8     FROM V$XML_AUDIT_TRAIL
  9   /

OS_USER     OS_HOST                 OBJECT_SCHEMA      OBJECT_NAME
---------   ---------------------   ---------------    --------------
harperjm    WORKGROUP\HARPERJM-PC   VIDEO_STORE        PRICE

POLICY_NAME          SQL_BIND      SQL_TEXT
------------------   -----------   ----------------------------------------------
AUDIT_PRICE_MODXML   (null)        UPDATE video_store.price SET amount = .25 ...
```

Notice that the audit policy captures user information and the SQL statement that violated our audit condition. Also, observe that only one row is inserted, instead of many rows for each record affected.

Our final sections on FGA demonstrate how you can obtain/view audit results outside the Oracle instance. You must first discover where the XML file is stored. You do this by querying the V$PARAMETER view or by issuing the show parameter command at a SQL*Plus prompt:

```
SQL> show parameter audit_file
NAME                                TYPE          VALUE
----------------------------------  -----------   ------------------------------
audit_file_dest                     string        /u01/app/oracle/product/11107/
                                                  db_01/admin/t001/adump
```

In our case, the AUDIT_FILE_DEST resides in our $ORACLE_HOME/DB_01 /ADMIN/T001/ADUMP directory. Upon investigation of this directory, we discover that an ORA_8126.XML file exists:

```
cd /u01/app/oracle/product/11107/db_01/admin/t001/adump
oracleldsslcll21:/u01/app/oracle/product/11107/db_01/admin/t001/adump> ls *.xml
ora_8126.xml
```

We shorten the output of this file; however, it still illustrates the depth of Oracle audit capabilities:

```
<?xml version="1.0" encoding="UTF-8"?>
  <Audit xmlns="http://xmlns.oracle.com/oracleas/schema/dbserver_audittrail-10_2.xsd"
   xmlns:xsi="http://www.w3.org/2001/XMLSchema-instance"
   xsi:schemaLocation="http://xmlns.oracle.com/oracleas/schema/dbserver_audittrail
10_2.xsd">
   <Version>10.2</Version>
<AuditRecord>
  ...
  <DB_User>SDBJMH</DB_User>
```

```
<OS_User>harperjm</OS_User>
<Userhost>WORKGROUP\HARPERJM-PC</Userhost>
<Object_Schema>VIDEO_STORE</Object_Schema>
<Object_Name>PRICE</Object_Name>
<Policy_Name>AUDIT_PRICE_MODXML</Policy_Name>
...
<Sql_Text>
UPDATE video_store.price
   SET amount = .25
 WHERE active_flag = 'Y'
   AND rownum <= 10
</Sql_Text>
</AuditRecord>
```

There are many benefits to this type of logging. For one, you can protect the XML file by placing it in a file system that has limited access. In addition, the XML files continue to be available even if the database instance is down.

Distributed Data Integrity

Few Enterprise Information Management (EIM) departments have the luxury of storing their data assets in one database system. Quite the opposite, many of them deal with hundreds of instances and multiple database vendors, spanning locations across the globe. In addition, connectivity between database systems is often limited. For these reasons, they opt to create intricate sets of materialized views and triggers to offline remote transactions.

In our final example on triggers, we illustrate how to create distributed DML transaction triggers. Actual implementations are much more complex. To set the stage for this example, imagine that our video store schema exists in a franchise environment. In this setting, EIM engineers connect remote video stores to a corporate database, over low-speed wide area networks (WANs).

Example 9-7: Distributed Transaction Triggers   The following block alters the VIDEO_STORE.ITEM table by adding a CUSTOMER_SCORE column:

```
-- This is found in ex09-07.sql on the publisher's web site.
SQL> ALTER TABLE video_store.item
  2    ADD ( customer_score  number CHECK ( customer_score BETWEEN 1 AND 5 ))
  3  /
```

On the remote database, we create a link to the corporate database:

```
SQL> CREATE DATABASE LINK test_link
  2      CONNECT TO video_store
  3      IDENTIFIED BY abc123
  4      USING 'T001A'
  5  /
```

In this block, engineers create a materialized view named ITEM_CORPORATE. They set it to be refreshed every morning at 12:00 with the START with and NEXT phrases:

```
SQL> CREATE MATERIALIZED VIEW item_corporate
  2      REFRESH FORCE
  3      START WITH TRUNC ( SYSDATE )
  4      NEXT TRUNC ( SYSDATE ) + 1
  5      AS
  6      SELECT  item_id
  7            , item_barcode
  8            , item_type
  9            , item_title
 10            , item_subtitle
 11            , item_rating
 12            , customer_score
 13            , last_updated_by
 14            , last_update_date
 15        FROM  video_store.itemtest_link
 16  /
```

We replace the local VIDEO_STORE.ITEM view with a view of the snapshot. We do so to facilitate the creation of instead of triggers:

```
SQL> CREATE VIEW item
  2      AS
  3      SELECT * FROM item_corporate
  4  /
```

The following block creates a failover table named ITEM_RATING_CACHE to store updates if the WAN link is down:

```
SQL> CREATE TABLE item_rating_cache
  2  ( item_id            NUMBER
  3  , customer_score     NUMBER
  4  , distributed_error  VARCHAR2(500)
  5  )
  6  /
```

This block creates a standalone procedure named
UPDATE_CUSTOMER_SCORE to handle the possibility of link interruptions:

```
CREATE OR REPLACE PROCEDURE distributed_dml
( pi_item_id          NUMBER
, pi_customer_score   NUMBER
)
AS
  ln_userid           NUMBER;
  lv_sqlerrm          VARCHAR2(500);
BEGIN
  UPDATE   video_store.itemtest_link
     SET   customer_score = pi_customer_score
   WHERE   item_id = pi_item_id;
EXCEPTION
  WHEN OTHERS THEN
    lv_sqlerrm := SUBSTR ( SQLERRM,1,500 );
    INSERT
      INTO   item_rating_cache
    VALUES   ( pi_item_id
             , pi_customer_score
             , lv_sqlerrm
             );
END;
/
```

Finally, we create an INSTEAD OF trigger to intercept updates and send
them in an autonomous manner to the corporate item table:

```
SQL> CREATE OR REPLACE TRIGGER item_corporate_trg
  2     INSTEAD OF UPDATE
  3     ON item
  4     FOR EACH ROW
  5   BEGIN
  6     distributed_dml ( :NEW.item_id
  7                     , :NEW.customer_score
  8                     );
  9   END;
 10   /
```

We update the item view with this DML statement:

```
SQL> UPDATE   item
  2     SET   customer_score = 3.0
  3   WHERE   item_id = 1040
  4   /
```

It is necessary to refresh the materialized view before viewing the changes. We do so with this anonymous block:

```
SQL> BEGIN
  2     DBMS_MVIEW.REFRESH ( 'ITEM_CORPORATE' );
  3  END;
  4  /
```

We display the results in the following block:

```
SQL> SELECT   ITEM_ID
  2        ,  CUSTOMER_SCORE
  3     FROM  item
  4    WHERE  item_id = 1040
  5  /

ITEM_ID CUSTOMER_SCORE
------- --------------
   1040              3
```

Observe that if the update fails, the procedure inserts affected records in the ITEM_RATING_CACHE table, where they await processing at another time. This activity prevents users from having to wait for the remote database and preserves the transaction.

Downloadable Code

The examples in this chapter are organized into seven exercise files:

- ex09-01.sql demonstrates how you use triggers for DML auditing.

- ex09-02.sql demonstrates how you use the FOLLOWS command to sequence trigger firing order.

- ex09-03.sql demonstrates how you use compound triggers to consolidate multiple triggers into one unit.

- ex09-04.sql demonstrates how you use DDL triggers to enforce coding standards.

- `ex09-05.sql` demonstrates how you use triggers for flashback recovery.

- `ex09-06.sql` demonstrates how you Fine Grain Auditing (FGA) to audit database events.

- `ex09-07.sql` demonstrates how you use distributed transaction triggers.

These programs should let you see the code in action. We think a download is friendlier then a cumbersome disc because the code doesn't take a great deal of space.

Conclusion

We stated that triggers are an excellent part of the Oracle feature set; however, it is our experience that engineers either do not take enough advantage of triggers or overdo them. Often times, they do so because they have lost sight of business needs related to trigger implementation.

Innovation for innovation's sake is never a good idea. A good rule of thumb in keeping your perspective clear is to ensure that you know exactly what the business needs are and how much "real" value your feature adds. Even if the idea is a great one, if it does not adequately support business need or add to the bottom line, it is not worth implementing.

Best Practices Introduced

- Triggers should be concise. *Oracle Database PL/SQL Language Reference 11*g states that, if possible, triggers should not exceed 60 lines of code.

- Carefully construct timed triggers with the `FOLLOWING` clause to stipulate firing order. Do not mix noncontrolled and controlled trigger types.

- Do not create triggers just because you can, or in an attempt to automate everything, as doing so quickly reaches the point of diminishing returns.

- Where possible, consolidate triggers into compound trigger types.

- Construct system event triggers so that they do not block general user activity.

- Create system triggers that aid your efforts to maintain test beds that maximize tester and developer uptime.

- Use Oracle Fine Grained Auditing to perform security audits.

Mastery Check

The mastery check is a series of true or false and multiple choice questions that let you confirm how well you understand the material in the chapter. You may check Appendix E for answers to these questions.

1. ☐ **True**   ☐ **False**   You can sequence event triggers with the Oracle 11*g* release.

2. ☐ **True**   ☐ **False**   You can define a DML trigger to run once per statement or row.

3. ☐ **True**   ☐ **False**   You can put a variable declaration in trigger bodies without using the DECLARE keyword.

4. ☐ **True**   ☐ **False**   There is no default firing order for triggers because they execute randomly.

5. ☐ **True**   ☐ **False**   In Oracle 11*g*, the FOLLOWS keyword indicates which trigger fires next.

6. ☐ **True**   ☐ **False**   DDL triggers fire when you change data.

7. ☐ **True**   ☐ **False**   System event triggers can help DBAs perform monitoring and maintenance tasks.

8. ☐ **True**   ☐ **False**   Hackers exploit triggers and hope they're deployed in databases.

9. ☐ **True**   ☐ **False**   Distributed transaction triggers can leverage instead of triggers when something interrupts network communication.

10. ☐ **True**   ☐ **False**   Triggers may use external functions and procedures, but large triggers are more cohesive and perform better.

11. What event(s) can a data manipulation trigger capture?

    A. INSERT

    B. UPDATE

    C. TRUNCATE

    D. All of the above

    E. Only A and B

12. Which type of trigger lets you intercept and replace OLD or NEW column values?

    A. STATEMENT level triggers

    B. COMPOUND triggers

    C. ROW level triggers

    D. All of the above

    E. Only B and C

13. What is the correct order for data manipulation triggers?

    A. Before row, before statement, after statement, after row

    B. Before statement, before row, after row, after statement

    C. Before row, after row, before statement, after statement

    D. Before statement, after statement, before row, after row

    E. None of the above

14. Which triggers work with views?

   A. A data definition trigger

   B. A data manipulation trigger

   C. A compound trigger

   D. A system event trigger

   E. None of the above

15. What are two examples of attribute functions that you can use in data definition triggers?

   A. ORA_DICT_OBJ_OWNER

   B. ORA_DICT_OBJ_SCHEMA

   C. ORA_DICT_OBJ_TABLE

   D. All of the above

   E. Only A and C

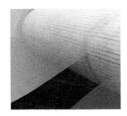

CHAPTER
10

Objects

few years ago, Oracle looked at objects and said, "Only 5 to 8 percent of customers are using these; therefore, they're not important." If you've looked at the XML Developer Kit (XDK) components or spatial data objects recently, you've probably seen how limited that view has become. Objects are here to stay in Oracle, and they present unique opportunities for hiding logic, organizing code, and achieving reuse.

Historic hindrances that impede PL/SQL object adoptions are threefold. Examples were sparse until the Oracle 11*g* documentation and principally limited to the *Expert Oracle PL/SQL* book. Java programmers who best understand the nature of objects write objects in open-source Hibernate because they don't understand enough about the strengths of PL/SQL database development. Lastly, the concept of how to use objects is poorly understood by a generation of PL/SQL developers who see themselves as procedural or database programmers.

This chapter aims to make using object types straightforward and convenient. We cover objects in the following order:

- Basic declaration, implementation, and use

- Comparing objects

- Inheritance and polymorphism

- Object collections

You may ask yourself, What's the biggest difference between objects and packages? We've thought about that long and hard. The biggest difference, we believe, is that those objects have two states. One is like a normal serialized package, and the other consists of a memory-resident data type with self-contained functions and procedures.

You define objects as you do packages. The actual differences between defining one or the other are small. While you define a specification and body for a package, you define a type and a body for an object. A package specification and object type both define the published operations. Those operations are available only through their respective programming container.

There is a bit of a twist here with the comparison, because you can define an object type without defining an object body when there aren't any object methods. You're able to treat that type of object type like a SQL structure when you don't implement an object body. This lets you use the default object body. However, you need to wrap it in a collection and then access it through the TABLE function in a query.

This type of object type mimics the behavior of a PL/SQL record type returned through a pipelined table function. Chapter 5 offered one example of this behavior of an object type as an alternative to a pipelined table. Chapter 11 discusses the limitations of this type of collection with system reference cursors.

Another key difference between a package specification and object type is how you access and use their internal variables. You can't see package variables when you describe them, but you can see attributes of object types. You can access package variables, provided your user has execute privileges on the package. An object's functions and procedures are the only ways you can access object type attributes without wrapping them in a collection. We'll show you how with *getters* and *setters* later in this chapter.

Package and object bodies provide the implementation of published operations. They may also define and implement local functions and procedures. Local functions and procedures aren't available outside of the package or object body because they're not published.

Objects also include specialized functions known as *constructors*. You use constructors to create object instances, which are often called objects. The default constructor has a signature that includes all object type attributes in the same order as they're defined by the object type. There's no limit on how many other constructors you provide for object types. Constructors act like overloaded functions or procedures in packages, but they're called *overriding* constructors because they alter how object instances are created in memory.

While packages have one type of public functions and procedures, objects have two types of public subroutines. They're known as *static* or *member* functions and procedures. Static functions and procedures are available without your needing to create an instance of an object type; they can also fill the role of constructors when they return a copy of the object type. Member functions and procedures are available only after you construct an instance of an object type.

Functions and procedures inside the object type let you manipulate the data into, inside, and out of the object instance. Static subroutines can access database components, but only member subroutines can access instance data.

This chapter discusses how you can create, use, and deploy objects in your application code. Where relevant to the examples, we've squeezed in as much as possible. Objects involve object-oriented analysis and design (OOAD), which also involves design patterns, which are basically a collection of best practices.

Basic Declaration, Implementation, and Use

This section shows you how to define and implement object types, how to define and implement getters and setters, and how to implement static methods. Along the way, we show you how to use these in SQL and PL/SQL.

Define and Implement Object Types

We borrowed a couple illustrative concepts from *Oracle Database 11g PL/SQL Programming*. These examples show you how to define an object specification and object body. The following illustration shows you how to define an object specification. Notice that the name of the object type is also the name of each constructor function. If you try to use something else as a constructor name, a PLS-00658 error is raised.

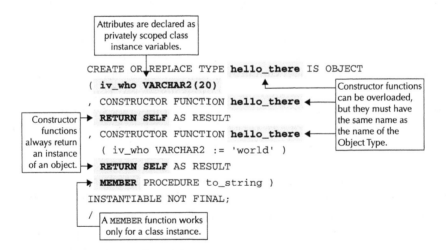

You can use instance variable names only inside constructor functions. If you try to use something else, a PLS-00307 error is raised at compile time. This appears to be related to the default constructor, which supersedes any other constructor that has the same positional signature. A matching position signature shares the same sequential list of data types. Oracle disallows constructor functions when their signatures are duplicates of the default.

Aside from the constructor functions, the hello_world object type includes a to_string member function. The function returns the contents of an object instance as a variable length string. A function is more flexible than a procedure because you can use it in either a SQL or a PL/SQL context.

Those of you familiar with object-oriented languages such as Java should note that Oracle PL/SQL objects return a copy of `SELF`. This differs from the `this` in Java. Don't waste a moment thinking that Oracle may change this, because too much is dependent on it now. Just learn to use the `SELF` as you would the `this` keyword in Java, because they're really the same thing.

NOTE
Object types without a return data type of
SELF may be used as SQL object tables.

After defining an object type, you create an object body. The basic rules mirror those of package bodies. The signature of subroutines must match between the object type and body. That matching process also includes any default values for formal parameters.

You implement the `hello_there` object type as shown in the following illustration. Two constructors are used in this object type because we want to show you how to create a default constructor and an override constructor. Default constructors generally don't have any formal parameters, and they generally call the overriding constructor with default values.

```
CREATE OR REPLACE TYPE BODY hello_there IS
  CONSTRUCTOR FUNCTION hello_there  -- Default constructor.
  RETURN SELF AS RESULT IS
    lv_hello HELLO_THERE := hello_there('Generic Object');
  BEGIN
    self := lv_hello;
    RETURN;
  END hello_there;
  CONSTRUCTOR FUNCTION hello_there  -- Overriding constructor.
  (iv_who VARCHAR2) RETURN SELF AS RESULT IS
  BEGIN
    self.iv_who := iv_who;
    RETURN;
  END hello_there;
  MEMBER PROCEDURE to_string IS
  BEGIN
    dbms_output.put_line('Hello '||self.iv_who||'.');
  END to_string;
END hello_there;
/
```

Construct a class instance by calling the overriding constructor with an actual parameter.

Assign the local class instance to the internal SELF instance.

Assign the actual parameter to the class instance variable.

Read the class instance variable.

Best Practice

Always implement a default constructor when you use an overriding constructor. The default constructor should always call any overriding constructor with default value(s). This should ensure that you don't trigger null parameter-driven exceptions.

The default constructor creates an instance of itself with a default value in the declaration section. This clearly demonstrates the dependency of an object body on its type. We couldn't declare a variable of the object type before defining it in the database catalog. Likewise, we can't construct an instance without a definition of the constructor functions in the catalog.

The default constructor shown in the foregoing illustration is an OOAD pattern, not the default constructor implemented by Oracle. Oracle treats the default constructor the same way it does a table or updateable view, which is the positional order of columns in the data dictionary.

The assignment inside the default constructor is simple—at least we think it's simple, because it mirrors how you assigning a row from a cursor to a record type variable. The difference is that the target variable isn't a local variable, but it's the instance, known as SELF; and the assignment variable is a local variable holding a constructed class variable.

The override constructor is different, because it assigns a call parameter to a variable of the instance before returning a copy of the hello_there object type. The RETURN statement differs from what we're accustomed to in PL/SQL. It simply returns a copy with the keyword RETURN, which *returns* the current memory reference for the object instance.

You can call the instance into existence in SQL or PL/SQL scope. The easiest way to demonstrate this behavior is with SQL. This shows you how to call an instance method of an object with the default constructor:

```
SQL> SELECT hello_there().to_string() FROM dual;
```

It prints this default message:

```
Hello Generic Object.
```

You call the overriding constructor like this:

```
SQL> SELECT HELLO_THERE('Object World!').to_string() FROM dual;
```

It prints this override message:

```
Hello Object World!
```

These object instances are created and discarded at runtime, so it's not surprising that they're known as *transient* objects. While defined in the database catalog, they exist only at runtime. You also have *persistent* objects, which are defined as data types in tables or other stored programs. They're called *standalone* persistent objects when they're deployed in tables and *embedded* persistent objects when they're deployed in other programs.

Deciding how to deploy object instances is very important. A transient deployment strategy means that you won't have a migration cost during upgrades. Persistent deployment is another story. You need to migrate all data from persistent objects to a temporary location during an upgrade. Oracle may provide a mechanism in the future, but until then, you should choose a deployment path carefully.

Calling a transient object into existence is easy, as shown in the preceding example. Calling a persistent object into existence is trickier, so we offer a little example. You create a table with a single column that uses the `hello_there` object type as a data type, like this:

```
SQL> CREATE TABLE sample_object
  2  ( persistent HELLO_THERE );
```

We insert both default and override constructor instances, because we want to see them in their natural state. You create the inserts with a call to the constructors:

```
SQL> INSERT INTO sample_object VALUES (hello_there());
SQL> INSERT INTO sample_object VALUES (hello_there('Object World!'));
```

You can query to see what's been inserted, and you may be surprised to find that you see the constructor that you inserted. This is a *flattened* object, and it doesn't exist in memory when it's stored in a table.

```
SQL> SELECT * FROM sample_object;
```

The query returns a column name with a formal parameter list, unless you override it with a column alias of your choice.

```
PERSISTENT(IV_WHO)
---------------------------------
HELLO_THERE('Generic Object.')
HELLO_THERE('Object World!')
```

You must call it from the table like so:

```
SQL> SELECT TREAT(persistent AS HELLO_THERE).to_string() AS contents
  2  FROM   sample_object;
```

The `TREAT` function takes a column name, the `AS` keyword, and an object type from the database catalog, and it instantiates the object into memory. It returns the following:

```
CONTENTS
--------------------
Hello Generic Object.
Hello Object World!
```

We've covered how you define, implement, and use object types in two of their three contexts. Next we examine how you implement getters and setters.

Implement Getters and Setters

A *getter* is a method that reaches into an object and grabs something. A *setter* is a method that sends a message into an object to set an instance variable. You typically implement a getter as a member function and a setter as a member procedure. Getters and setters work only on instance variables.

The following example extends the `hello_there` object type from the preceding section. It adds a `get_who` getter and `set_who` setter to the existing object type.

The object type is defined as follows:

```
SQL> CREATE OR REPLACE TYPE hello_there IS OBJECT
  2  ( iv_who VARCHAR2(20)
  3  , CONSTRUCTOR FUNCTION hello_there
  4    RETURN SELF AS RESULT
  5  , CONSTRUCTOR FUNCTION hello_there
  6    ( iv_who VARCHAR2 )
  7    RETURN SELF AS RESULT
  8  , MEMBER FUNCTION get_who RETURN VARCHAR2
  9  , MEMBER PROCEDURE set_who (pv_who VARCHAR2)
 10  , MEMBER FUNCTION to_string RETURN VARCHAR2)
 11  INSTANTIABLE NOT FINAL;
 12  /
```

Best Practice
Always prepend get_ and set_ to getter and setter method names, because they clarify purpose and ensure proper method use.

There's a slight departure from our naming convention here, because the formal parameter to the overriding constructor is iv_who, not pv_who. The reason for the change is that object type constructor parameters must match the attributes of the object type. If they don't, an ORA-00307 error is raised.

The implementation of the definition is in this object body:

```
SQL> CREATE OR REPLACE TYPE BODY hello_there IS
  2
  3    CONSTRUCTOR FUNCTION hello_there
  4    RETURN SELF AS RESULT IS
  5      hello HELLO_THERE := hello_there('Generic Object.');
  6    BEGIN
  7      self := hello;
  8      RETURN;
  9    END hello_there;
 10
 11    CONSTRUCTOR FUNCTION hello_there (iv_who VARCHAR2)
 12    RETURN SELF AS RESULT IS
 13    BEGIN
 14      self.iv_who := iv_who;
 15      RETURN;
 16    END hello_there;
 17
 18    MEMBER FUNCTION get_who RETURN VARCHAR2 IS
 19    BEGIN
 20      RETURN self.iv_who;
 21    END get_who;
 22
 23    MEMBER PROCEDURE set_who (pv_who VARCHAR2) IS
 24    BEGIN
 25      self.iv_who := pv_who;
 26    END set_who;
 27
 28    MEMBER FUNCTION to_string RETURN VARCHAR2 IS
 29    BEGIN
 30      RETURN 'Hello '||self.iv_who;
 31    END to_string;
 32
 33  END;
 34  /
```

Line 25 assigns the input parameter to the instance variable, thereby replacing whatever the value was. Line 20 returns an unformatted value for the `iv_who` instance variable. This differs slightly from the formatted string returned on line 30.

The following anonymous block shows how to call the getter and setter:

```
SQL> DECLARE
  2    lv_object HELLO_THERE := hello_there('Object World!');
  3  BEGIN
  4    dbms_output.put_line(lv_object.to_string());
  5    dbms_output.put_line(lv_object.get_who());   -- Call the getter.
  6    lv_object.set_who('Batman!');                -- Call the setter.
  7    dbms_output.put_line(lv_object.to_string());
  8  END;
  9  /
```

Line 5 calls the `get_who` function that gets the current copy of the instance variable. Line 6 calls the `set_who` procedure, which assigns a new value to the instance variable.

Implement Static Methods

Static methods let you use an object type like a standard package. You can use static functions and procedures to print constant values and messages, but you can't use them to access instance variables. That said, you can create a static function to return an instantiated class.

This is a new example that leverages the video store model to return a video title, subtitle, and MPAA rating. The beauty of this approach is that the construction exercise is hidden, or in object-oriented (OO) parlance *encapsulated*, from developers who use your object type.

We're going to expand this example more than we need to, to illustrate something that you will see more clearly later in the "Object Collections" section. The following is an object type without a constructor, much like the one shown in Chapter 7. This actually has an unpublished default constructor as does a table or updateable view, and it is the signature of the object. A signature is the positional order by data type of the object type attributes. It creates a SQL data type that we can use in collections:

```
SQL> CREATE OR REPLACE TYPE item_struct IS OBJECT
  2  ( item_title    VARCHAR2(60)
  3  , item_subtitle VARCHAR2(60)
  4  , item_rating   VARCHAR2(14));
  5  /
```

This object type structure is the return type of a getter function in the `item_object` type. You also have a static function in the `item_object` type. It lets you create and return an instance of the class without calling the formal constructor.

Here's the definition of the `item_object` type:

```
SQL> CREATE OR REPLACE TYPE item_object IS OBJECT
  2  ( item_title    VARCHAR2(60)
  3  , item_subtitle VARCHAR2(60)
  4  , item_rating   VARCHAR2(14)
  5  , CONSTRUCTOR FUNCTION item_object
  6    RETURN SELF AS RESULT
  7  , CONSTRUCTOR FUNCTION item_object
  8    (item_title VARCHAR2, item_subtitle VARCHAR2, item_rating VARCHAR2)
  9    RETURN SELF AS RESULT
 10  , STATIC FUNCTION get_item_object (item_id NUMBER) RETURN ITEM_OBJECT
 11  , MEMBER FUNCTION get_title_and_rating RETURN ITEM_STRUCT
 12  , MEMBER FUNCTION to_string RETURN VARCHAR2 )
 13  INSTANTIABLE NOT FINAL;
 14  /
```

Line 10 contains the definition for a static function that returns an instance of the `item_object` type. Line 11 demonstrates how you return a record structure that can be leveraged in SQL and PL/SQL contexts.

Here's the implementation of this object type:

```
SQL> CREATE OR REPLACE TYPE BODY item_object IS
  2
  3    CONSTRUCTOR FUNCTION item_object RETURN SELF AS RESULT IS
  4      lv_item ITEM_OBJECT := item_object('Generic Title'
  5                                        ,'Generic Subtitle'
  6                                        ,'Generic Rating');
  7    BEGIN
  8      self := lv_item;
  9      RETURN;
 10    END item_object;
 11
 12    CONSTRUCTOR FUNCTION item_object
 13    ( item_title    VARCHAR2
 14    , item_subtitle VARCHAR2
 15    , item_rating   VARCHAR2 )
 16    RETURN SELF AS RESULT IS
 17    BEGIN
 18      self.item_title := item_title;
 19      self.item_subtitle := item_subtitle;
 20      self.item_rating := item_rating;
 21      RETURN;
 22    END item_object;
 23
 24    STATIC FUNCTION get_item_object (item_id NUMBER) RETURN ITEM_OBJECT IS
 25      lv_item ITEM_OBJECT;
 26      CURSOR c (item_id_in NUMBER) IS
```

```
27          SELECT    item_title
28          ,         item_subtitle
29          ,         item_rating_agency||': '||item_rating AS item_rating
30          FROM      item
31          WHERE     item_id = item_id_in;
32        BEGIN
33          FOR i IN c (item_id) LOOP
34            lv_item := item_object(i.item_title,i.item_subtitle,i.item_rating);
35          END LOOP;
36          RETURN lv_item;
37        END get_item_object;
38
39        MEMBER FUNCTION get_title_and_rating RETURN ITEM_STRUCT IS
40          lv_record ITEM_STRUCT;
41        BEGIN
42          lv_record := item_struct(item_title,item_subtitle,item_rating);
43          RETURN lv_record;
44        END get_title_and_rating;
45
46        MEMBER FUNCTION to_string RETURN VARCHAR2 IS
47        BEGIN
48          RETURN '['||self.item_title||'] ['||item_rating||']';
49        END to_string;
50
51      END;
52      /
```

Lines 24 through 37 implement a static function that returns an object instance. It takes a primary key value as a parameter and queries the database for values to instantiate an object instance. Then it returns the instantiated instance. However, a better solution would be to rewrite the function as an overriding constructor.

Lines 39 through 44 implement a getter. The getter function constructs an instance of the structure by using instance variables.

You can query results by doing the following:

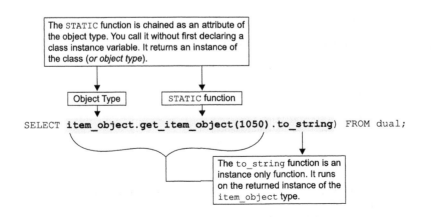

This shows how you call the static function to create a transient object. Once instantiated, you use the component selector (the dot, or period) to call the `to_string` instance function. It would return the following:

```
[Pirates of the Caribbean - Dead Man's Chest] [MPAA: PG-13]
```

NOTE
If you call the `to_string()` function without parentheses, an `ORA-00904` error is raised for an invalid identifier. This occurs because object member methods require parentheses, while other schema and package functions and procedures don't.

The following anonymous block shows you how to access the object structure returned by the getter function. This type of call doesn't work in a SQL context, but we do cover an alternative that extends coverage in Chapter 7.

```
DECLARE
   lv_struct ITEM_STRUCT;
BEGIN
   lv_struct := item_object.get_item_object(1055).get_title_and_rating();
   dbms_output.put_line(lv_struct.item_title||' - '||lv_struct.item_rating);
END;
/
```

It prints this:

```
Indiana Jones and the Raiders of the Lost Ark - MPAA: PG
```

If you attempt to call this structure from SQL, like this,

```
SELECT item_object.get_item_object(item_id).get_title_and_rating() AS struct
FROM    item
WHERE   item_id = 1018;
```

it prints the collapsed structure, known as a *flatten* object. The alias triggers an undocumented SQL*Plus column title that uses the alias as the object type preceding the attribute list.

```
STRUCT(ITEM_TITLE, ITEM_SUBTITLE, ITEM_RATING)
-------------------------------------------------
ITEM_STRUCT('Scrooge', NULL, 'MPAA: G')
```

What we'd like to do is return the data by the columns of the object type, or structure. As of Oracle 11*g*, that's not possible for a structure by itself. A workaround is required to return the data as a collection of the object type.

Here's the definition for a collection of the object type:

```
CREATE OR REPLACE TYPE list_elements IS TABLE OF item_struct;
/
```

You can now create a function that returns the collection of an object type, like this:

```
SQL> CREATE OR REPLACE FUNCTION get_elements
  2  ( pv_range_low  NUMBER
  3  , pv_range_high NUMBER ) RETURN list_elements IS
  4    lv_list LIST_ELEMENTS := list_elements();
  5    CURSOR c (cv_low NUMBER, cv_high NUMBER) IS
  6      SELECT item_object.get_item_object(item_id).get_title_and_rating()
  7      FROM    item
  8      WHERE   item_id BETWEEN cv_low AND cv_high;
  9  BEGIN
 10    OPEN c (pv_range_low, pv_range_high);
 11    FETCH c BULK COLLECT INTO lv_list;
 12    CLOSE c;
 13    RETURN lv_list;
 14  END;
 15  /
```

There's a magic trick here. You created the mechanism to get at the elements of your collection when you defined it based on your object type. This same thing happens when you create a pipelined function to return a varray, nested table, or associative array of a PL/SQL record structure.

You can now query the results of the object attributes through a normal query. This sample statement also uses SQL*Plus to format the output:

```
SQL> COLUMN item_title    FORMAT A30
SQL> COLUMN item_subtitle FORMAT A16
SQL> COLUMN item_rating   FORMAT A12
SQL>
SQL> SELECT       DISTINCT *
  2  FROM         TABLE(get_elements(1011,1016))
  3  ORDER BY 1;
```

The DISTINCT operator eliminates any duplicates from the return set. When you run this against the sample database, you see the following:

```
ITEM_TITLE                       ITEM_SUBTITLE     ITEM_RATING
-------------------------------- ----------------- ------------
Brave Heart                                        MPAA: R
Camelot                                            MPAA: G
Christmas Carol                                    MPAA: NR
The World Is Not Enough                            MPAA: PG-13
Tomorrow Never Dies              Special Edition   MPAA: PG-13
```

In the "Object Collections" section later in this chapter, we transfer the collection logic from the external function into the object type. It provides a nice cohesiveness to PL/SQL programming.

Comparing Objects

While we compare variables of numbers or variable length strings, we don't have equivalent operations for object types. That's why we must write them.

Oracle object types support two methods: the MAP and ORDER functions. The MAP function doesn't take a formal parameter and can return only a scalar type of CHAR, DATE, NUMBER, and VARCHAR2. The ORDER function performs more like what you'd want to do to compare objects in Java, and it is the preferred solution.

A MAP function compares object types when they have a single scalar attribute. They're more complex when an object has two or more attributes. The COMPARE function compares object types when they're defined with nonscalar attributes or multiple scalar attributes. The COMPARE function also lets the object type encapsulate the comparison logic.

Best Practice
Implement the ORDER function as the comparison method in all object types.

TIP
Subclasses can't override the MAP *and* ORDER
functions found in parent classes.

The following sections show you how the MAP and ORDER functions are used to compare object instances. You can assess which fits your needs from the examples provided.

MAP Function Comparison

There's no implicit casting of objects beyond normal casting of scalar data types. The following defines a MAP_COMP object type:

```
SQL> CREATE OR REPLACE TYPE map_comp IS OBJECT
  2  ( who VARCHAR2(30)
  3  , CONSTRUCTOR FUNCTION map_comp (who VARCHAR2) RETURN SELF AS RESULT
  4  , MAP MEMBER FUNCTION equals RETURN VARCHAR2 )
  5  INSTANTIABLE NOT FINAL;
  6  /
```

The implementation of this object type is very straightforward, because there's only one attribute. If there were two or more attributes, it would be more complex. You'd need to create a hash or concatenated value from the attributes to perform comparison with the MAP function.

```
SQL> CREATE OR REPLACE TYPE BODY map_comp IS
  2    CONSTRUCTOR FUNCTION map_comp (who VARCHAR2) RETURN SELF AS RESULT IS
  3    BEGIN
  4      self.who := who;
  5      RETURN;
  6    END map_comp;
  7    MAP MEMBER FUNCTION equals RETURN VARCHAR2 IS
  8    BEGIN
  9      RETURN self.who;
 10    END equals;
 11  END;
 12  /
```

Line 4 constructs the instance, while line 9 returns the instance for comparison. The test program creates a table for these objects. It also creates a local swap procedure to sort object instances in alphabetical order. The execution block implements a simple bubble sort algorithm.

```
SQL> DECLARE
  2    TYPE object_list IS TABLE OF MAP_COMP; -- Define a collection
  3
  4    -- Initialize object instances in jumbled order.
```

```
 5     lv_object1 MAP_COMP := map_comp('Ron Weasley');
 6     lv_object2 MAP_COMP := map_comp('Harry Potter');
 7     lv_object3 MAP_COMP := map_comp('Luna Lovegood');
 8     lv_object4 MAP_COMP := map_comp('Ginny Weasley');
 9     lv_object5 MAP_COMP := map_comp('Hermione Granger');
10
11     -- Declare a collection.
12     lv_objects OBJECT_LIST := object_list(lv_object1, lv_object2
13                                          ,lv_object3, lv_object4
14                                          ,lv_object5);
15
16     -- Swaps A and B by reference.
17     PROCEDURE swap (pv_a IN OUT MAP_COMP, pv_b IN OUT MAP_COMP) IS
18       lv_c MAP_COMP;
19     BEGIN
20       lv_c := pv_b;
21       pv_b := pv_a;
22       pv_a := lv_c;
23     END swap;
24
25   BEGIN
26     FOR i IN 1..lv_objects.COUNT LOOP      -- Bubble sort
27       FOR j IN 1..lv_objects.COUNT LOOP
28         IF lv_objects(i).equals =
29          LEAST(lv_objects(i).equals,lv_objects(j).equals) THEN
30           swap(lv_objects(i),lv_objects(j));
31         END IF;
32       END LOOP;
33     END LOOP;
34
35     FOR i IN 1..lv_objects.COUNT LOOP      -- Print reordered set.
36       dbms_output.put_line(lv_objects(i).equals);
37     END LOOP;
38   END;
39   /
```

Lines 28 to 31 manage the comparison and swap operations. A LEAST function provides an ascending sort, while the GREATEST function would provide a descending sort.

It prints the reordered names in alphabetical order starting with first name. It would be more work to sort by last and then first name because you'd have to parse the string.

```
Harry Potter
Hermione Granger
Luna Lovegood
Ron Weasley
```

The `MAP` function is most useful when you work with persistent objects, provided they've got a single attribute. For example, this type of query sorts persistent objects:

```
SQL> SELECT    persistent_object_id AS primary_key
  2  ,          TREAT(mapping_object AS map_comp).equals() AS fellowship
  3  FROM       persistent_object
  4  WHERE      mapping_object IS OF (map_comp)
  5  ORDER BY 2;
```

We've shown you how to implement a `MAP` function for comparison purposes. We hope you notice the amount of work done outside the object. The `ORDER` function takes the logic from the anonymous block by hiding it inside the object.

ORDER Function Comparison

The `ORDER` function lets you define any data type as a formal parameter. You can mimic how Java compares objects by defining the formal parameter as the same object type. This lets you pass a copy of another object into an object. You can then compare the two and see if they're a like.

The following defines an object type that will let you sort by last name before first name—because it supports two attributes in its definition.

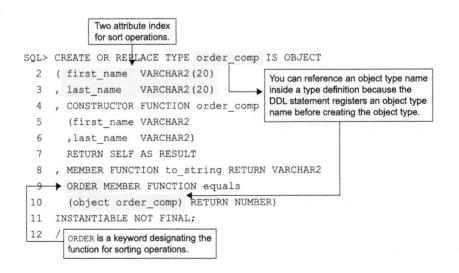

```
                    Two attribute index
                    for sort operations.

SQL> CREATE OR REPLACE TYPE order_comp IS OBJECT
  2  ( first_name    VARCHAR2(20)
  3  , last_name     VARCHAR2(20)
  4  , CONSTRUCTOR FUNCTION order_comp
  5    (first_name VARCHAR2
  6    ,last_name  VARCHAR2)
  7    RETURN SELF AS RESULT
  8  , MEMBER FUNCTION to_string RETURN VARCHAR2
  9    ORDER MEMBER FUNCTION equals
 10    (object order_comp) RETURN NUMBER)
 11  INSTANTIABLE NOT FINAL;
 12  /
```

You can reference an object type name inside a type definition because the DDL statement registers an object type name before creating the object type.

`ORDER` is a keyword designating the function for sorting operations.

Truth or Not

When languages don't support a Boolean type, 0 (zero) is assigned false and any other number is true. That being said, the number 1 is typically returned for truth. Oracle does the same with most built-in functions, because, that way, they can be used inside SQL and PL/SQL contexts.

The implementation is also straightforward. The comparison method is more complex. Inside the ORDER function, the comparison addresses both attributes. The object type hides the prioritization of one attribute over another. Those calling the comparison would only have documentation to tell them whether it's an ascending or descending sort. It returns a 1 when the current instance comes alphabetically first and a 0 when it doesn't.

Here's the implementation:

```
SQL> CREATE OR REPLACE TYPE BODY order_comp IS
  2
  3      CONSTRUCTOR FUNCTION order_comp
  4      (first_name VARCHAR2, last_name VARCHAR2) RETURN SELF AS RESULT IS
  5      BEGIN
  6        self.first_name := first_name;
  7        self.last_name := last_name;
  8        RETURN;
  9      END order_comp;
 10
 11      MEMBER FUNCTION to_string RETURN VARCHAR2 IS
 12      BEGIN
 13        RETURN '['||self.last_name||'], ['||self.first_name||']';
 14      END to_string;
 15
 16      ORDER MEMBER FUNCTION equals (object order_comp) RETURN NUMBER IS
 17      BEGIN
 18        IF self.last_name < object.last_name THEN
 19          RETURN 1;
 20        ELSIF self.last_name = object.last_name AND
 21              self.first_name < object.first_name THEN
 22          RETURN 1;
 23        ELSE
 24          RETURN 0;
 25        END IF;
 26      END equals;
 27
 28  END;
 29  /
```

The `equals` comparison checks for different last names first. Then it checks for equal last names and different first names. When you want an ascending sort, you evaluate for truth or a number 1. Evaluating for a 0 return from the function yields a descending sort.

```
SQL> DECLARE
  2    TYPE object_list IS TABLE OF ORDER_COMP; -- Define collection.
  3
  4    -- Initialize objects in mixed order.
  5    lv_object1 ORDER_COMP := order_comp('Ron','Weasley');
  6    lv_object2 ORDER_COMP := order_comp('James','Potter');
  7    lv_object3 ORDER_COMP := order_comp('Luna','Lovegood');
  8    lv_object4 ORDER_COMP := order_comp('Fred','Weasley');
  9    lv_object5 ORDER_COMP := order_comp('Hermione','Granger');
 10    lv_object6 ORDER_COMP := order_comp('Harry','Potter');
 11    lv_object7 ORDER_COMP := order_comp('Cedric','Diggory');
 12    lv_object8 ORDER_COMP := order_comp('Severus','Snape');
 13    lv_object9 ORDER_COMP := order_comp('Ginny','Weasley');
 14
 15    -- Declare a collection.
 16    lv_objects OBJECT_LIST := object_list(lv_object1, lv_object2
 17                                         ,lv_object3, lv_object4
 18                                         ,lv_object5, lv_object6
 19                                         ,lv_object7, lv_object8
 20                                         ,lv_object9);
 21
 22    -- Swaps A and B by reference.
 23    PROCEDURE swap (pv_a IN OUT ORDER_COMP, pv_b IN OUT ORDER_COMP) IS
 24      lv_c ORDER_COMP;
 25    BEGIN
 26      lv_c := pv_b;
 27      pv_b := pv_a;
 28      pv_a := lv_c;
 29    END swap;
 30
 31  BEGIN
 32    FOR i IN 1..lv_objects.COUNT LOOP      -- Bubble sort.
 33      FOR j IN 1..lv_objects.COUNT LOOP
 34        IF lv_objects(i).equals(lv_objects(j)) = 1 THEN
 35          swap(lv_objects(i),lv_objects(j));
 36        END IF;
 37      END LOOP;
 38    END LOOP;
 39
 40    FOR i IN 1..lv_objects.COUNT LOOP      -- Print reordered records.
 41      dbms_output.put_line(lv_objects(i).to_string);
 42    END LOOP;
 43  END;
 44  /
```

Lines 34 to 36 contain the evaluation of truth, which means you get an ascending output from the sort. It prints this:

```
[Diggory, Cedric]
[Granger, Hermione]
[Lovegood, Luna]
[Potter, Harry]
[Potter, James]
[Snape, Severus]
[Weasley, Fred]
[Weasley, Ginny]
[Weasley, Ron]
```

We hope you agree with our conclusion that the ORDER function is more effective than the MAP function.

Inheritance and Polymorphism

An *object type* definition sets a basis or starting point. When we find ways to extend the behavior of the starting point, we call those extensions *specializations*. They're actually subclasses. The presence of subclasses promotes the base object type to a generalization, which is also known as a *super class.*

Some basic rules come with inheritance in Oracle object types. These are important points that you should consider when implementing object types:

- Attributes in an object type aren't listed in a subtype because they're inherited.

- Subtype construction assigns variables to super class attributes.

- Subtypes have access to super class constructor functions.

- Subtypes can't override super class constructor functions.

- The MAP and ORDER functions of an object type can't be overridden by the object's subtypes.

- The TREAT function should always reference the object type, not the object subtype, for persistent object columns.

- Object type evolution means that you can't change an object with dependents.

In this section, we build upon the `order_comp` object type. You should know that Oracle 11*g* introduced generalized object invocation, which we demonstrate in this section.

The definition for the new object type is shown here:

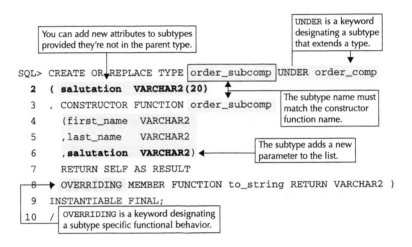

Line 2 adds a `salutation` to the `order_subcomp` class. The `order_subcomp` class inherits the `first_name` and `last_name` attributes from the `order_comp` class. The subclass provides a new constructor that provides values to all three class attributes.

Here's the body for this class:

```
SQL> CREATE OR REPLACE TYPE BODY order_subcomp IS
  2
  3    CONSTRUCTOR FUNCTION order_subcomp
  4    (first_name   VARCHAR2
  5    ,last_name    VARCHAR2
  6    ,salutation   VARCHAR2)
  7    RETURN SELF AS RESULT IS
  8    BEGIN
  9      self.first_name := first_name;
 10      self.last_name := last_name;
 11      self.salutation := salutation;
 12      RETURN;
 13    END order_subcomp;
 14
 15    OVERRIDING MEMBER FUNCTION to_string RETURN VARCHAR2 IS
 16    BEGIN
```

```
17       RETURN (self as order_comp).to_string||', '||self.salutation;
18     END to_string;
19
20   END;
21   /
```

The overriding function `to_string` returns the salutation from the subclass and the name from the parent class on line 17. You may notice that we didn't have to call the super class to access its `to_string` method. We simply cast ourselves as the super class, and use the component selector to access a parent class method.

```
SQL> DECLARE
  2      TYPE object_list IS TABLE OF ORDER_COMP; -- Define collection.
  3
  4      -- Initialize one subtype.
  5      lv_object1 ORDER_SUBCOMP :=
  6        order_subcomp('Severus','Snape','Professor');
  7
  8      -- Initialize objects in mixed order.
  9      lv_object2 ORDER_COMP := order_comp('Ron','Weasley');
 10      lv_object3 ORDER_COMP := order_comp('James','Potter');
 11      lv_object4 ORDER_COMP := order_comp('Luna','Lovegood');
 12      lv_object5 ORDER_COMP := order_comp('Fred','Weasley');
 13      lv_object6 ORDER_COMP := order_comp('Hermione','Granger');
 14      lv_object7 ORDER_COMP := order_comp('Harry','Potter');
 15      lv_object8 ORDER_COMP := order_comp('Cedric','Diggory');
 16      lv_object9 ORDER_COMP := order_comp('Ginny','Weasley');
 17
 18      -- Declare a collection.
 19      lv_objects OBJECT_LIST := object_list(lv_object1, lv_object2
 20                                         ,lv_object3, lv_object4
 21                                         ,lv_object5, lv_object6
 22                                         ,lv_object7, lv_object8
 23                                         ,lv_object9);
 24
 25      -- Swaps A and B by reference.
 26      PROCEDURE swap (pv_a IN OUT ORDER_COMP, pv_b IN OUT ORDER_COMP) IS
 27        lv_c ORDER_COMP;
 28      BEGIN
 29        lv_c := pv_b;
 30        pv_b := pv_a;
 31        pv_a := lv_c;
 32      END swap;
 33
 34   BEGIN
 35     FOR i IN 1..lv_objects.COUNT LOOP          -- Bubble sort.
 36       FOR j IN 1..lv_objects.COUNT LOOP
 37         IF lv_objects(i).equals(lv_objects(j)) = 1 THEN
 38           swap(lv_objects(i),lv_objects(j));
 39         END IF;
```

```
40      END LOOP;
41    END LOOP;
42
43    FOR i IN 1..lv_objects.COUNT LOOP          -- Print reordered records.
44      dbms_output.put_line(lv_objects(i).to_string);
45    END LOOP;
46  END;
47  /
```

This tests the generalized object invocation, and prints this:

```
[Diggory, Cedric]
[Granger, Hermione]
[Lovegood, Luna]
[Potter, Harry]
[Potter, James]
[Snape, Severus], Professor
[Weasley, Fred]
[Weasley, Ginny]
[Weasley, Ron]
```

This demonstrates that the sorting algorithm in the `equals` function works for generalized and specialized objects. It also shows that the overriding `to_string` function is called only when the object type is a subclass. The general `to_string` method from the super class is called for all object instances initialized as that data type.

Object Collections

The only difference between an object type and a collection object type is that the object holds a single object type, while a collection holds a varray or nested table of an object type. That object type can be instantiable or not. Since noninstantiable types act as SQL record structures, our example shows you how to use that type of collection. The book *Expert Oracle PL/SQL* (McGraw-Hill/Professional, 2005) contains compound objects and demonstrates how you handle calls between object collections and nested instantiable object types.

The example depends on an object type, or SQL record structure, used in the "Implement Static Methods" section earlier in the chapter. Rather than asking you to flip back a few pages, here's the definition of that type:

```
SQL> CREATE OR REPLACE TYPE item_struct IS OBJECT
  2  ( item_title    VARCHAR2(60)
  3  , item_subtitle VARCHAR2(60)
  4  , item_rating   VARCHAR2(14));
  5  /
```

The following defines an object type the `item_struct` collection as an attribute:

```
SQL> CREATE OR REPLACE TYPE items_object IS OBJECT
  2  ( items_table        ITEM_TABLE
  3  , CONSTRUCTOR FUNCTION items_object
  4    (items_table ITEM_TABLE) RETURN SELF AS RESULT
  5  , CONSTRUCTOR FUNCTION items_object
  6    RETURN SELF AS RESULT
  7  , MEMBER FUNCTION get_size RETURN NUMBER
  8  , MEMBER FUNCTION get_table RETURN ITEM_TABLE
  9  , STATIC FUNCTION get_items_table
 10    ( pv_range_low  NUMBER
 11    , pv_range_high NUMBER ) RETURN ITEM_TABLE)
 12  INSTANTIABLE NOT FINAL;
 13  /
```

Lines 9 though 11 contain the definition for a function that can construct a collection of variable size. As we develop the example, this static function's purpose becomes more clear, but it's a critical element to making our collection object effective.

Here's the object body for this:

```
SQL> CREATE OR REPLACE TYPE BODY items_object IS
  2
  3    CONSTRUCTOR FUNCTION items_object
  4    (items_table ITEM_TABLE) RETURN SELF AS RESULT IS
  5    BEGIN
  6      self.items_table := items_table;
  7      RETURN;
  8    END items_object;
  9
 10    CONSTRUCTOR FUNCTION items_object
 11    RETURN SELF AS RESULT IS
 12      c            NUMBER := 1; -- Counter for table index.
 13      item         ITEM_STRUCT;
 14      CURSOR cv IS
 15        SELECT item_title, item_subtitle, item_rating FROM item;
 16    BEGIN
 17      FOR i IN cv LOOP
 18        item := item_STRUCT(i.item_title,i.item_subtitle,i.item_rating);
 19        items_table.EXTEND;
 20        self.items_table(c) := item;
 21        c := c + 1;
 22      END LOOP;
 23      RETURN;
 24    END items_object;
 25
```

```
26    MEMBER FUNCTION get_size RETURN NUMBER IS
27    BEGIN
28      RETURN self.items_table.COUNT;
29    END get_size;
30
31    MEMBER FUNCTION get_table RETURN ITEM_TABLE IS
32    BEGIN
33      RETURN self.items_table;
34    END get_table;
35
36    STATIC FUNCTION get_items_table
37    ( pv_range_low  NUMBER
38    , pv_range_high NUMBER) RETURN ITEM_TABLE IS
39      c            NUMBER := 1; -- Counter for table index.
40      item         ITEM_STRUCT;
41      items_table ITEM_TABLE := item_table();
42      CURSOR cv (cv_low NUMBER, cv_high NUMBER) IS
43        SELECT item_title, item_subtitle, item_rating
44        FROM   item
45        WHERE  item_id BETWEEN cv_low AND cv_high;
46    BEGIN
47      FOR i IN cv(pv_range_low, pv_range_high) LOOP
48        item := item_struct(i.item_title,i.item_subtitle,i.item_rating);
49        items_table.EXTEND;
50        items_table(c) := item;
51        c := c + 1;
52      END LOOP;
53      RETURN items_table;
54    END get_items_table;
55
56  END;
57  /
```

Lines 3 through 8 implement a constructor that takes a formal parameter of a collection. The problem with that approach is that we need to know how to construct the table from outside of the object type. That type of design on its own would mean that structural coupling between the code builds the table and the object type. Rather than do that, we've included a static function on lines 36 to 54. The static function contains the logic to create the table for the constructor function. This makes the object type cohesive. It also means you can call it with standard inputs, as you would other stored functions or procedures.

Best Practice
You should opt for noninstantiable object types, because they're interchangeable through the Oracle Call Interface (OCI) or Java Database Connectivity (JDBC) with external programming languages.

You can now construct and query this collection object type in SQL or PL/SQL. The easiest example is in SQL. Here it is:

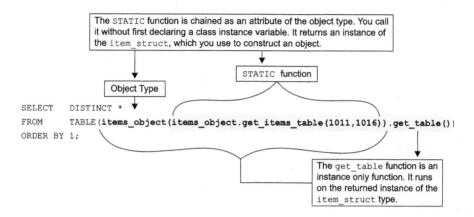

It returns the following distinct set from the object:

```
ITEM_TITLE                      ITEM_SUBTITLE     ITEM_RATING
------------------------------- ----------------- -----------
Brave Heart                                       R
Camelot                                           G
Christmas Carol                                   NR
The World Is Not Enough                           PG-13
Tomorrow Never Dies             Special Edition   PG-13
```

This section has shown you how to leverage collections inside object types. You can likewise embed object types with methods in lieu of the noninstantiable object type we've shown you. The benefit of the approach we've demonstrated is that you can use it to control and pass collections back and forth between Java, PHP, or other external programming languages.

Downloadable Code

The examples in this chapter are organized into four files:

- The `create_hellothere_objects.sql` script shows you how to create the basic object type examples.

- The `create_item_object.sql` script contains the `item_object` examples.

- The `map_comp.sql` script contains the MAP function comparison scripts.

- The `order_comp.sql` script contains the ORDER function comparison scripts.

These programs should let you see the code in action. We think a download is friendlier then a cumbersome disc because the code doesn't take a great deal of space.

Summary

This chapter has covered the basics of user-defined object types in Oracle server-side programming. You should be able to use this information as a foundation for working with objects in your role and especially in the balance of our examples.

You should also check the introduction for references to further your study of these topics.

Best Practice Review

- Always implement a default constructor when you use an overriding constructor. The default constructor should always call any overriding constructor with default value(s). This should ensure that you don't trigger null parameter driven exceptions.

- Always prepend `get_` and `set_` to getter and setter method names, because they clarify purpose and ensure proper method use.

- Implement the ORDER function as the comparison method in all object types.

- You should opt for noninstantiable object types because they're interchangeable through the OCI or JDBC with external programming languages.

Mastery Check

The mastery check is a series of true or false and multiple choice questions that let you confirm how well you understand the material in the chapter. You may check Appendix E for answers to these questions.

1. ☐ **True** ☐ **False** You can use and access an object type without an object body.

2. ☐ **True** ☐ **False** Outside of a collection, getter functions are the only way you can access internal attributes.

3. ☐ **True** ☐ **False** You can't create a constructor function that has the same signature as the default constructor for an object type.

4. ☐ **True** ☐ **False** Oracle object types return a copy of themselves by using the same this keyword found in the Java programming language.

5. ☐ **True** ☐ **False** You can create an instance of an object type in SQL.

6. ☐ **True** ☐ **False** You can call an object type's static functions in PL/SQL.

7. ☐ **True** ☐ **False** You can call any object type's member functions or procedures from a SQL query.

8. ☐ **True** ☐ **False** You can compare objects by passing a copy of the other object as a call parameter to the MAP function.

9. ☐ **True** ☐ **False** You can override a MAP or ORDER function of the parent class in a subclass.

10. ☐ **True** ☐ **False** The TREAT function applies only to placing subclasses in memory.

11. How you deploy object types leads to how you define them. What are the two types of deployments?

    A. Embedded

    B. Transient

    C. Standalone

    D. All of the above

    E. Only A and C

12. When you deploy object types in the database catalog, they may be called what?

    A. Embedded

    B. Transient

    C. Persistent

    D. All of the above

    E. Only A and C

13. You can't define a MAP function to return which data type(s)?

    A. CHAR

    B. BOOLEAN

    C. DATE

    D. NUMBER

    E. None of the above

14. You can define which type of function and procedure in an object type?

    A. MEMBER

    B. CONSTRUCTOR

    C. COMPARISON

    D. All of the above

    E. Only A and B

15. What keyword lets you change the behavior of a parent class in a subclass?

    A. An OVERRIDE keyword

    B. A SUBTYPE keyword

    C. An OVERRIDING keyword

    D. All of the above

    E. Only A and C

PART
III

PL/SQL Advanced
Programming

CHAPTER
11

Dynamic SQL

ative Dynamic SQL (NDS) began replacing the DBMS_SQL package in Oracle 9*i*. As of Oracle 11*g*, NDS has replaced all but one type of dynamic statement. Clearly, NDS is the future of dynamic SQL in the Oracle database.

While Oracle's product management would prefer we discuss current release technology, we understand that some firms delay upgrades for some time. We also know that a lot of older DBMS_SQL code is deployed. Therefore, we focus here on NDS and cover some of the features of the DBMS_SQL package.

This chapter provides working examples of dynamic statements without bind variables and dynamic statements with bind variables for both NDS and the DBMS_SQL package.

Dynamic SQL allows you to make your programs flexible. It lets you create templates for Data Definition Language (DDL) and Data Manipulation Language (DML) commands. The templates act like *lambda-style functions* with an unknown number of input and output parameters. These parameters aren't quite as tidy as functions or procedures, or, for that matter, object types, because they act as *placeholders* in a statement. Oracle jargon and documentation more frequently call these placeholders *bind variables,* but the terms are interchangeable.

As you can imagine, there needs to be a clear process to make something this flexible practical. The process involves two to four steps, depending on which type of dynamic statement you're using. First, all statements are parsed at runtime. Second, statements have local variables bound into them when they contain placeholders; this works much the same for external programming languages, too. Third, statements are executed. And, finally, values are returned to the calling statement. These values can be returned in several contexts, as we discuss in this chapter.

Native Dynamic SQL

NDS is the newest, easiest, and most recommended approach to dynamic SQL. We strongly recommend you use it first, and default to DBMS_SQL only when there's no other way to accomplish it. While Oracle hasn't announced the deprecation of DBMS_SQL, it will someday go away. You should begin the migration now, because later it may be an exodus with the accompanying risk of data loss or damage.

Best Practice
Where possible, always use NDS for dynamic statements rather than
DBMS_SQL statements.

Dynamic statements happen one of two ways: You can glue them together,
which is the fancy way for saying concatenating strings. Concatenation is a risky
behavior; we might say that it is practicing unsafe computing because it's
subject to SQL injection attacks. Oracle 11*g* provides the DBMS_ASSERT
package to help mitigate risks, but binding variables, the second way, is much
safer.

We borrowed the sidebar "SQL Injection Attacks" from *Oracle Database
11g PL/SQL Programming*. We think it qualifies the problem and also
explains DBMS_ASSERT.

You should use bind variables because SQL injection strings can't be
assigned to string data types unless they're prequalified as strings. This lets
you sanitize your input values before using them. Likewise, DBMS_ASSERT
does the same thing. Use it when you feel compelled to concatenate
fragments into dynamic statements, or you require a dynamic table name.

SQL Injection Attacks
SQL injection attacks are attempts to fake entry by using unbalanced
quotes in SQL statements. Dynamic SQL is a place where hackers try to
exploit your code.

Oracle now has the DBMS_ASSERT package to help you prevent
SQL injection attacks. DBMS_ASSERT has the following functions:

- The ENQUOTE_LITERAL function takes a string input and adds
  a leading and trailing single quote to the output string.

- The ENQUORE_NAME function takes a string input and promotes
  it to uppercase before adding a leading and trailing double
  quote to the output string. There's an optional parameter
  Boolean parameter that lets you disable capitalization when
  you set it to false.

(continued)

■ The NOOP function takes a string input and returns the same value as an output without any validation. The NOOP function is overloaded and can manage a VARCHAR2 or CLOB data type.

■ The QUALIFIED_SQL_NAME function validates the input string as a valid schema-object name. This function lets you validate your functions, procedure, packages, and user-defined objects. The actual parameter evaluates in lowercase, mixed case, or uppercase.

■ The SCHEMA_NAME function takes a string input and validates whether it is a valid schema name. The actual parameter needs to be uppercase for this to work properly. So, you should pass the actual parameter inside a call to the UPPER function.

■ The SIMPLE_SQL_NAME function validates the input string as a valid schema-object name. This function lets you validate your functions, procedure, packages, and user-defined objects.

■ The SQL_OBJECT_NAME function validates the input string as a valid schema-object name. This function lets you validate your functions, procedures, and packages. At the time of writing it raised an ORA-44002 error when checking a user-defined object type.

You can find more about the DBMS_ASSERT package in the *Oracle Database PL/SQL Packages and Types Reference*. Oracle NDS is immune to SQL injection attacks when you use bind variables as opposed to gluing things together.

We cover NDS statements in two sections: The first section creates statements without bind variables. The second section creates statements with bind variables.

Dynamic Statements Without Bind Variables

Static strings are the simplest example of dynamic statements. Demonstrating them is also easy because the Oracle database doesn't support a conditional "drop if exists" syntax. A major use of static strings as NDS statements involves dropping objects when they exist before trying to re-create them.

The following anonymous block checks the database catalog to see if a TRANSACTION table exists before attempting to drop it. It uses a static shell string for the command, but executes it only if the cursor returns a row.

```
SQL> BEGIN
  2    FOR i IN (SELECT null
  3                FROM   user_objects
  4                WHERE  object_name = 'TRANSACTION') LOOP
  5      EXECUTE IMMEDIATE 'DROP TABLE transaction CASCADE CONSTRAINTS';
  6    END LOOP;
  7  END;
  8  /
```

Line 5 contains an NDS call to a static command. The natural problem with this type of statement is maintenance. We'd need to replace the transaction table name in both the query and NDS statement.

NOTE
These techniques let us perform DDL inside NDS statements, but as a rule they should be used only in upgrade scripts.

A better alternative would leverage the cursor to return the name of the table to drop. Since we also have a sequence named TRANSACTION_S1, the statement could handle both with slight modification and dynamic substitution.

The following shows how you can do this:

```
SQL> BEGIN
  2    FOR i IN (SELECT object_name
  3                   ,      object_type
  4                FROM   user_objects
  5                WHERE  REGEXP_LIKE(object_name,'TRANSACTION.')) LOOP
  6      IF i.object_type = 'SEQUENCE' THEN
  7        EXECUTE IMMEDIATE 'DROP SEQUENCE '||i.object_name;
  8      ELSIF i.object_type = 'TABLE' THEN
  9        EXECUTE IMMEDIATE
 10          'DROP TABLE '||i.object_name||' CASCADE CONSTRAINTS';
 11      END IF;
 12    END LOOP;
 13  END;
 14  /
```

Lines 6 and 8 evaluate the return value for OBJECT_TYPE, and lines 7 through 10 dynamically glue the values from the OBJECT_NAME into statements. We could also rewrite the statement to use the object type dynamically from the cursor, but we'd still have to manage appending the CASCADE CONSTRAINTS clause. That's why we didn't bother.

You might ask, "Why not also bind the table name?" We didn't do this because it's not supported. It raises an ORA-00903 error if you attempt to bind a table name in an NDS DDL. Naturally, without the WHERE clause in the cursor, the anonymous block would remove all tables and sequences found in a schema. It's an important note, because deferred processing can have big consequences if they're done wrong.

The DBMS_ASSERT isn't useful when we're querying the data dictionary, but it becomes useful when we write a procedure that takes inputs from an external source. The next example creates a stored procedure that uses the DBMS_ASSERT package to sanitize inputs:

```
SQL> CREATE OR REPLACE PROCEDURE insert_lookup
  2  ( table_name      VARCHAR2
  3  , lookup_table    VARCHAR2
  4  , lookup_column   VARCHAR2
  5  , lookup_type     VARCHAR2
  6  , lookup_code     VARCHAR2 := ''
  7  , lookup_meaning VARCHAR2 ) IS
  8
  9    stmt VARCHAR2(2000);
 10
 11  BEGIN
 12    stmt := 'INSERT INTO '||dbms_assert.simple_sql_name(table_name)
 13          || ' VALUES '
 14          || '( common_lookup_s1.nextval '
 15          || ','||dbms_assert.enquote_literal(lookup_table)
 16          || ','||dbms_assert.enquote_literal(lookup_column)
 17          || ','||dbms_assert.enquote_literal(lookup_type)
 18          || ','||dbms_assert.enquote_literal(lookup_code)
 19          || ','||dbms_assert.enquote_literal(lookup_meaning)
 20          || ', 3, SYSDATE, 3, SYSDATE)';
 21
 22    EXECUTE IMMEDIATE stmt;
 23
 24  END insert_lookup;
 25  /
```

Line 12 still uses concatenation—and, no, it isn't an error. The one thing you can't bind into a statement is a table name, which must be glued into the statement. The SIMPLE_SQL_NAME function validates that the runtime

table name is a valid schema-object name. Lines 15 through 19 use the
ENQUOTE_LITERAL function, which puts leading and trailing quotes
around any input parameter.

You would call the INSERT_LOOKUP procedure like this:

```
SQL> BEGIN
  2      insert_lookup(table_name => 'COMMON_LOOKUP'
  3                   ,lookup_table => 'CATALOG'
  4                   ,lookup_column => 'CATALOG_TYPE'
  5                   ,lookup_type => 'CROSS_REFERENCE'
  6                   ,lookup_meaning => 'Cross Reference');
  7  END;
  8  /
```

Note that the call to the INSERT_LOOKUP procedure excludes the
LOOKUP_CODE parameter found on line 6 of the procedure. We can do that
because the parameter has a default value and is an *optional* parameter.
Named notation allows us to work exclusively with the mandatory columns
in the procedure's signature.

This is about all you can do without bind variables. The next section
shows you how to use bind variables in a number of ways.

Dynamic Statements with Bind Variables

As we mentioned earlier in the chapter, bind variables are placeholders in
strings that become dynamic statements. While they're interspersed inside
the statement, they occur in positional order. NDS statements require that
you call these in positional order. The positional order starts from the
beginning of the statement and continues as if it were a single stream until
the end of statement.

The following is a generic NDS statement:

```
EXECUTE IMMEDIATE statement USING local_variable1, local_variable2, …
```

You place your call parameters in the USING subclause. Call parameters
can be local variables or literals—either strings or numbers. At least that's
true when you're using IN mode parameters. IN OUT or OUT mode
variables must be local variables. A compile-time error would be thrown if
you used a literal value.

NOTE
Date literals aren't really dates. They're strings that meet a default format mask for implicit casting to a DATE data type.

Following are some key recommendations from the Oracle 11*g* documentation governing the use of placeholder variables:

- If a dynamic SQL SELECT statement returns at most one row, you should return the value through an INTO clause. This requires that you either (a) open the statement as a reference cursor, or (b) enclose the SQL statement inside an anonymous block. The former does not use an IN OUT or OUT mode parameter in the USING clause, while the latter requires it.

- If a dynamic SQL SELECT statement returns more than one row, you should return the value through a BULK COLLECT INTO clause. Like the INTO clause, the bulk collection requires that you either (a) open the statement as a reference cursor, or (b) enclose the SQL statement inside an anonymous block. The former does not use an IN OUT or OUT mode parameter in the USING clause, while the latter requires it.

- If a dynamic SQL statement is a DML with input only placeholders, you should put them in the USING clause.

- If a dynamic SQL statement is a DML and uses a RETURNING INTO clause, you should put the input values in the USING clause and the output values in the NDS RETURNING INTO clause.

- If the dynamic SQL statement is a PL/SQL anonymous block or CALL statement, you should put both input and output parameters in the USING clause. All parameters listed in the USING clause are IN mode only. You must override the default and designate them as IN OUT or OUT.

We cover all the approaches to placeholders in examples, but we'd like to make a recommendation. As a rule of thumb, *don't enclose dynamic statements in PL/SQL anonymous blocks*. You should use the RETURNING INTO subclause, because that's what the design calls for. If you opt for the enclosing block, remember that this behavior could get deprecated.

Best Practice
Don't enclose dynamic statements in anonymous PL/SQL blocks; always use the RETURNING INTO subclause.

The following example rewrites the INSERT_LOOKUP procedure from the preceding section. This one uses placeholders (or bind variables). You should note two things about the placeholder call parameters: They're locally scoped variables and they are IN mode parameters.

```
SQL> CREATE OR REPLACE PROCEDURE insert_lookup
  2  ( table_name      VARCHAR2
  3  , lookup_table    VARCHAR2
  4  , lookup_column   VARCHAR2
  5  , lookup_type     VARCHAR2
  6  , lookup_code     VARCHAR2 := ''
  7  , lookup_meaning  VARCHAR2 ) IS
  8
  9    stmt VARCHAR2(2000);
 10
 11  BEGIN
 12    stmt := 'INSERT INTO '||dbms_assert.simple_sql_name(table_name)
 13           ||  ' VALUES '
 14           ||  '( common_lookup_s1.nextval '
 15           ||  ',:lookup_table '
 16           ||  ',:lookup_column '
 17           ||  ',:lookup_type '
 18           ||  ',:lookup_code '
 19           ||  ',:lookup_meaning '
 20           ||  ', 3, SYSDATE, 3, SYSDATE)';
 21
 22    EXECUTE IMMEDIATE stmt USING lookup_table, lookup_column, lookup_type,
 23                                  lookup_code, lookup_meaning;
 24
 25  END insert_lookup;
 26  /
```

Line 12 still glues the table in, because that's unavoidable. Lines 15 to 19 contain placeholder variables. You can always spot placeholders because they're preceded by a colon. The formal parameter list contains local variables in the USING subclause.

TIP
You must glue a CHR(58) into the statement when you want to add a colon as an ordinary string component.

Best Practice
Where possible, try to keep things supportable, such as naming placeholders and formal parameters the same. Naturally, the placeholder has a colon while the local variable doesn't.

It is only for convenience that the :LOOKUP_TYPE placeholder and LOOKUP_TYPE local variable are the same string. They don't have to be the same, but it makes your code much more readable and supportable.

You could use the same anonymous block to call this procedure; here's virtually the same calling block again. We included the optional LOOKUP_CODE parameter this time with a string value to override the default null value.

```
SQL> BEGIN
  2    insert_lookup(table_name => 'COMMON_LOOKUP'
  3                 ,lookup_table => 'CATALOG'
  4                 ,lookup_column => 'CATALOG_TYPE'
  5                 ,lookup_code => 'XREF'
  6                 ,lookup_type => 'CROSS_REFERENCE'
  7                 ,lookup_meaning => 'Cross Reference');
  8  END;
  9  /
```

The alternative call with a value on line 5 to the optional parameter works. This type of signature can cause problems when you use a position-specific call signature, however.

The preceding dynamic statements have used only placeholders as inputs. The next program demonstrates an input placeholder while returning the result set as a weakly typed reference cursor.

Unlike the collection examples used previously, the next example uses a PL/SQL record type. This is, unfortunately, a requirement when you return a reference cursor. There is no way to assign the row contents of a reference cursor to an object type. It's probably the only remaining place where pipelined table functions serve a purpose.

TIP
You can get a function to compile by doing a
BULK COLLECT into a table of an object type,
but it'll fail at runtime with an ORA-00932
error.

Before we take you down the complex row of dynamic cursor return sets, we'll show you how it works. The anonymous block shows you how to return a dynamic result set. As you'll probably notice, you must know the internals of the record structure to work with this approach.

```
SQL> DECLARE
  2    TYPE lookup_record IS RECORD        -- Record structure
  3    ( lookup_type      VARCHAR2(30)
  4    , lookup_code      VARCHAR2(5)
  5    , lookup_meaning   VARCHAR2(255));
  6
  7    lookup_cursor      SYS_REFCURSOR;
  8    lookup_row         LOOKUP_RECORD;
  9    stmt               VARCHAR2(2000);
 10  BEGIN
 11    stmt := 'SELECT   common_lookup_type '
 12          || ',       common_lookup_code '
 13          || ',       common_lookup_meaning '
 14          || 'FROM    common_lookup '
 15          || 'WHERE   REGEXP_LIKE(common_lookup_type,:input)';
 16
 17    OPEN lookup_cursor FOR stmt USING '(CR|D)E(D|B)IT';
 18    LOOP
 19      FETCH lookup_cursor INTO lookup_row;
 20      EXIT WHEN lookup_cursor%NOTFOUND;
 21      dbms_output.put_line(
 22        '['||lookup_row.lookup_type||'] ['||lookup_row.lookup_code||']');
 23    END LOOP;
 24    CLOSE lookup_cursor;
 25  END;
 26  /
```

Lines 2 through 5 contain the definition of a local PL/SQL record type. Line 17 shows passing in a regular expression, which is then resolved inside the dynamic statement. Line 19 demonstrates that you call the system reference cursor into a variable of the record type.

NOTE
You can't assign a cursor variable to an object type because there's no syntax to support its constructor. An attempt raises an ORA-00308 error. This means you must assign the variable to a PL/SQL record type.

It's important to note that NDS doesn't limit you to row-by-row processing. You can alter this anonymous block to perform a bulk operation. Bulk operations require that you define some package components first.

The record type needs to be defined in a package specification, which makes the record data type available to other PL/SQL programs. Record types can be used only by other PL/SQL programs in an exclusively PL/SQL context. We also need to define two collection types in the same package and develop both a procedure and a function. While we could put the logic of the procedure in the function, it wouldn't let us demonstrate some important variations.

You define data types inside package specifications when you want them to be reused by other PL/SQL programming units. This defines a `LIB` package specification. There is no requirement for the implementation of a package when a package defines only data types.

```
SQL> CREATE OR REPLACE PACKAGE lib IS
  2     -- This defines a PL/SQL record structure.
  3     TYPE lookup_record IS RECORD
  4     ( lookup_type      VARCHAR2(30)
  5     , lookup_code      VARCHAR2(5)
  6     , lookup_meaning   VARCHAR2(255));
  7     -- These defines an associative array and nested table collection.
  8     TYPE lookup_assoc_table IS TABLE OF lookup_record
  9     INDEX BY BINARY_INTEGER;
 10     TYPE lookup_table IS TABLE OF lookup_record;
 11  END lib;
 12  /
```

PL/SQL only data types are an opportunity to anchor types, but remember that anchoring fails in other contexts. We'd remind you to anchor only when it's advantageous, not always, and certainly *not* as a best practice. If you'd like to anchor in this case, the `LIB` package would look like the following:

```
SQL> CREATE OR REPLACE PACKAGE lib IS
  2     TYPE lookup_record IS RECORD
  3     ( lookup_type      common_lookup.common_lookup_type%TYPE
  4     , lookup_code      common_lookup.common_lookup_code%TYPE
  5     , lookup_meaning   common_lookup.common_lookup_meaning%TYPE);
  6     -- This defines a PL/SQL record structure.
  7     TYPE lookup_assoc_table IS TABLE OF lookup_record
  8     INDEX BY BINARY_INTEGER;
  9     -- These defines an associative array and nested table collection.
 10     TYPE lookup_table IS TABLE OF lookup_record;
 11
 12  END lib;
 13  /
```

The next step requires the definition of a pass-by-reference procedure. The procedure takes an input, dynamically builds a statement, and executes the statement. A weakly typed reference cursor is the target of the opened statement, which you then assign to a PL/SQL record type. As qualified earlier, there's no way to substitute a nested table that would support a pipelined table function design.

The procedure takes the first formal parameter in the procedure as a pass-by-value, while the second is a pass-by-reference. The second parameter acts as the output from the procedure.

Here's the SET_DYNAMIC_TABLE procedure:

```
SQL> CREATE OR REPLACE PROCEDURE set_dynamic_table
  2  ( pv_lookup_type  IN       VARCHAR2
  3  , pv_lookup_table IN OUT lib.LOOKUP_ASSOC_TABLE ) IS
  4    lv_counter              NUMBER := 1;
  5    lv_lookup_cursor        SYS_REFCURSOR;
  6    lv_lookup_row           lib.LOOKUP_RECORD;
  7    lv_stmt                 VARCHAR2(2000);
  8  BEGIN
  9    lv_stmt := 'SELECT   common_lookup_type '
 10            || ',       common_lookup_code '
 11            || ',       common_lookup_meaning '
 12            || 'FROM    common_lookup '
 13            || 'WHERE   REGEXP_LIKE(common_lookup_type,:input)';
 14
 15    OPEN lv_lookup_cursor FOR lv_stmt USING pv_lookup_type;
 16    LOOP
 17      FETCH lv_lookup_cursor INTO lv_lookup_row;
 18      EXIT WHEN lv_lookup_cursor%NOTFOUND;
 19      pv_lookup_table(lv_counter) := lv_lookup_row;
 20      lv_counter := lv_counter + 1;
 21    END LOOP;
 22    CLOSE lv_lookup_cursor;
 23  END set_dynamic_table;
 24  /
```

Lines 9 through 13 contain the definition of the dynamic query. Line 13 has a single placeholder in the statement. Line 15 opens a reference cursor variable (an exclusively PL/SQL data type) for the statement by using the PV_LOOKUP_TYPE as a call parameter. The call parameter is also an exclusively PL/SQL record data type. Line 19 assigns the record to an associative array of records, again an exclusively PL/SQL record type.

The preceding procedure handled row-by-row processing. You can simplify the procedure by performing a bulk collection into the table. The following procedure replaces the row-by-row model:

```
SQL> CREATE OR REPLACE PROCEDURE set_dynamic_table
  2  ( pv_lookup_type   IN        VARCHAR2
  3  , pv_lookup_table IN OUT lib.LOOKUP_ASSOC_TABLE ) IS
  4    lv_lookup_cursor      SYS_REFCURSOR;
  5    lv_stmt               VARCHAR2(2000);
  6  BEGIN
  7    lv_stmt := 'SELECT   common_lookup_type '
  8            || ',       common_lookup_code '
  9            || ',       common_lookup_meaning '
 10            || 'FROM    common_lookup '
 11            || 'WHERE   REGEXP_LIKE(common_lookup_type,:input)';
 12
 13    OPEN lv_lookup_cursor FOR lv_stmt USING pv_lookup_type;
 14    FETCH lv_lookup_cursor BULK COLLECT INTO pv_lookup_table;
 15    CLOSE lv_lookup_cursor;
 16  END set_dynamic_table;
 17  /
```

Lines 13 and 14 show the simplicity of this approach, and line 13 changes the assignment target from a record structure to a collection of a record structure. This eliminates the loop structure. Line 14 provides the call semantic to load the cursor return values into the collection.

The next part of the solution is a wrapper to the procedure. It would work with either of the SET_DYNAMIC_TABLE procedures.

The following is a pipelined table function, which may return a PL/SQL varray or a nested table collection type. The wrapper takes the original input, redirects it to the procedure, and then consumes the returned associative array. *Consumes* may seem like an odd word to you, but it is appropriate because the wrapper takes that return value and converts its contents to a nested table. The nested table is then returned through a pipelined function.

```
SQL> CREATE OR REPLACE FUNCTION get_dynamic_table
  2  ( pv_lookup_type VARCHAR2 ) RETURN lib.lookup_table
  3  PIPELINED IS
  4    lv_lookup_cursor      SYS_REFCURSOR;
  5    lv_lookup_row         lib.LOOKUP_RECORD;
  6    lv_lookup_assoc       lib.LOOKUP_ASSOC_TABLE;
```

```
 7    lv_lookup_table        lib.LOOKUP_TABLE := lib.lookup_table();
 8    lv_stmt                VARCHAR2(2000);
 9  BEGIN
10    set_dynamic_table(pv_lookup_type, lv_lookup_assoc);
11    FOR i IN 1..lv_lookup_assoc.COUNT LOOP
12      lv_lookup_table.EXTEND;
13      lv_lookup_table(i) := lv_lookup_assoc(i);
14      PIPE ROW(lv_lookup_table(i));
15    END LOOP;
16    RETURN;
17  END get_dynamic_table;
18  /
```

Line 10 has the wrapped call to the SET_DYNAMIC_TABLE procedure, which returns a populated associative array. Lines 12 and 13 show how you can increase space in the collection before assigning a value to the nested table. The nested table is then piped into an aggregate table that is accessible in SQL. (See Chapter 5 for more on pipelined table functions.)

You can then call the pipelined GET_DYNAMIC_TABLE function with a regular expression inside SQL, like this:

```
SQL> COLUMN lookup_type     FORMAT A12
SQL> COLUMN lookup_code     FORMAT A12
SQL> COLUMN lookup_meaning FORMAT A14
SQL> SELECT *
  2  FROM TABLE(get_dynamic_table('(CR|D)E(D|B)IT'));
```

This returns the credits or debits values in the table:

```
LOOKUP_TYPE    LOOKUP_CODE    LOOKUP_MEANING
------------   ------------   --------------
DEBIT          D              Debit
CREDIT         C              Credit
```

The next type of NDS statement involves the RETURNING INTO clause. It's a critical skill when you're working with CLOB and BLOB data types because of how Oracle implements the DBMS_LOB package.

Given that our little video store supports only one table with a CLOB column, we've opted to borrow a couple examples from *Oracle Database 11g PL/SQL Programming*. These examples are nice and tight and show you how these NDS approaches work. We changed as little as possible, but we wanted them to work with our base data set.

A large object (LOB) locator is a reference to your Private Global Area (PGA). It lets you read and write a LOB from or into the database. The example uses an UPDATE statement to grab a reference to the LOB and the RETURNING INTO clause to return that reference. You could use an INSERT statement with a RETURNING INTO, but our data model requires an EMPTY_CLOB() call for each row because it's a mandatory column.

```
SQL> DECLARE
  2    -- Define explicit record structure.
  3    lv_target  CLOB;
  4    lv_source  VARCHAR2(2000) := 'Harry Potter struggles against ...';
  5    lv_movie   VARCHAR2(60) := 'Phoenix';
  6    lv_stmt    VARCHAR2(2000);
  7  BEGIN
  8    -- Set statement.
  9    lv_stmt := 'UPDATE   item '
 10            || 'SET      item_desc = empty_clob() '
 11            || 'WHERE    item_id = '
 12            || '              (SELECT item_id '
 13            || '               FROM   item '
 14            || '               WHERE  REGEXP_LIKE(item_title,:input)) '
 15            || 'RETURNING item_desc INTO :descriptor';
 16    EXECUTE IMMEDIATE lv_stmt USING lv_movie RETURNING INTO lv_target;
 17    dbms_lob.writeappend(lv_target,LENGTH(lv_source),lv_source);
 18    COMMIT;
 19  END;
 20  /
```

Line 15 contains a RETURNING INTO clause that returns the :DESCRIPTOR placeholder to the external local variable context. Line 16 calls the statement. It uses LV_MOVIE as a local pass-by-value call parameter and LV_TARGET as a local pass-by-reference call parameter. It effectively writes our trivial LV_SOURCE string to the CLOB.

Yes, that's a lot of work for no tangible gain, other than showing you how the technology works. But it will prove to be an invaluable tool as you work with large objects.

NOTE
An ORA-22275 error will result from the DBMS_LOB package if the row isn't found. This error number should help you build the proper exception handler.

This next section has a caveat: Just because you can doesn't mean you should! There are ways to call stored procedures with NDS: you nest the calls inside a PL/SQL anonymous block.

We'll write the last program as a procedure, like this:

```
SQL> CREATE OR REPLACE PROCEDURE get_clob
  2  ( item_title_in  VARCHAR2, item_desc_out IN OUT CLOB ) IS
  3  BEGIN
  4    UPDATE   item
  5    SET      item_desc = empty_clob()
  6    WHERE    item_id =
  7               (SELECT item_id
  8                FROM   item
  9                WHERE  REGEXP_LIKE(item_title,:input))
 10               RETURNING item_desc INTO item_desc_out;
 11  END get_clob;
 12  /
```

Line 2 defines the second formal parameter as an IN OUT mode variable, or a pass-by-reference variable. Line 10 returns the CLOB descriptor to the IN OUT mode parameter variable.

We show you how to create an NDS statement with an anonymous block that calls the previous GET_CLOB procedure. Note that the placeholder in the statement is the second call parameter.

```
SQL> DECLARE
  2    -- Define explicit record structure.
  3    target  CLOB;
  4    source  VARCHAR2(2000) := 'Harry Potter struggles against ...';
  5    movie   VARCHAR2(60) := 'Phoenix';
  6    stmt    VARCHAR2(2000);
  7  BEGIN
  8    -- Set statement
  9    stmt := 'BEGIN '
 10           || '  get_clob(:input,:output); '
 11           || 'END;';
 12    EXECUTE IMMEDIATE stmt USING movie, IN OUT target;
 13    dbms_lob.writeappend(target,LENGTH(source),source);
 14    COMMIT;
 15  END;
 16  /
```

Line 10 shows that the second call parameter is an IN OUT mode variable. Line 12 shows that the statement uses the second call parameter as an IN OUT mode variable, and there is no RETURNING INTO clause.

This concludes our coverage of NDS. Now let's review the older DBMS_SQL package.

DBMS_SQL Package

Oracle 7 introduced the DBMS_SQL package. It gave us a way to store dynamic object code in the database against potential runtime events. This innovation lets us define things before they exist in the database catalog.

Best Practice
Use the DBMS_SQL package only when the method isn't supported by NDS.

Four methods are used in DBMS_SQL. They're basically static DDL or DML statements, dynamic statements with bind variables, and dynamic variables that return something like a LOB descriptor. The full depth of the DBMS_SQL package is covered in *Oracle Database 11g PL/SQL Programming*.

While we maintained our standards on variable naming generally, this section uses the traditional names assigned to DBMS_SQL variables. We're not certain why everyone seems disposed to these variable names, but we can't change the world. We also know those new to SQL may need the consistency to dive in quickly and work with legacy DBMS_SQL code.

Here we cover two core aspects: how to run DDL and DML statements with DBMS_SQL, and how to mix DBMS_SQL with NDS in Oracle 11*g*.

Dynamic Statements Without Bind Variables

Creating statements using the older style is a bit longer, because we have to define some additional variables. These variables are unnecessary or managed internally for us. More or less, they're managed for us, behind the scenes, in NDS.

The following anonymous block lets us define and execute a dynamic query based on static information. In this case, it simply checks whether a database constraint exists before dropping it.

```
SQL> DECLARE
  2    -- Define local DBMS_SQL variables, and open cursor.
  3    c     INTEGER := dbms_sql.open_cursor;
  4    fdbk  INTEGER;
  5    stmt  VARCHAR2(2000);
  6  BEGIN
  7    -- Use a loop to check whether to drop a sequence.
```

```
 8    FOR i IN (SELECT null
 9              FROM    user_objects
10              WHERE   object_name = 'COMMON_LOOKUP_UNIQUE_SET'
11              AND     object_type = 'CONSTRAINT') LOOP
12      -- Build, parse, and execute SQL statement, then close cursor.
13      stmt := 'DROP CONSTRAINT sample_constraint';
14      dbms_sql.parse(c,stmt,DBMS_SQL.NATIVE);
15      fdbk := dbms_sql.execute(c);
16      dbms_sql.close_cursor(c);
17      dbms_output.put_line('Dropped Constraint [SAMPLE_CONSTRAINT].');
18    END LOOP;
19  END;
20  /
```

Lines 3 and 4 create a reference for an open cursor and a feedback variable (fdbk, a convention a lot of folks copied) that's critical when we execute the cursor. Line 14 parses the statement, line 15 executes the statement, and line 16 closes the cursor. All of that is done with a single line in NDS.

Dynamic Statements with Bind Variables

We examine two situations in this section. The first shows you how to use bind variables in an insert statement. The second shows you how to use bind variables for input and output variables with a query.

DML Statement with Bind Variables

The dynamic DML statement is enclosed in the INSERT_LOOKUP procedure. We used the same concept from the NDS section so that you can compare the two more easily.

```
SQL> CREATE OR REPLACE PROCEDURE insert_lookup
 2  ( table_name     VARCHAR2
 3  , lookup_table   VARCHAR2
 4  , lookup_column  VARCHAR2
 5  , lookup_type    VARCHAR2
 6  , lookup_code    VARCHAR2 := ''
 7  , lookup_meaning VARCHAR2 ) IS
 8
 9    -- Required variables for DBMS_SQL execution.
10    c    INTEGER := dbms_sql.open_cursor;
11    fdbk INTEGER;
12    stmt VARCHAR2(2000);
13
```

```
14   BEGIN
15     stmt := 'INSERT INTO '||dbms_assert.simple_sql_name(table_name)
16            || ' VALUES '
17            || '( common_lookup_s1.nextval '
18            || ',:lookup_table '
19            || ',:lookup_column '
20            || ',:lookup_type '
21            || ',:lookup_code '
22            || ',:lookup_meaning '
23            || ', 3, SYSDATE, 3, SYSDATE)';
24
25     -- Parse the statement and assign it to a cursor.
26     dbms_sql.parse(c,stmt,dbms_sql.native);
27
28     -- Bind local scope variables to placeholders in the statement.
29     dbms_sql.bind_variable(c,'lookup_table',lookup_table);
30     dbms_sql.bind_variable(c,'lookup_column',lookup_column);
31     dbms_sql.bind_variable(c,'lookup_type',lookup_type);
32     dbms_sql.bind_variable(c,'lookup_code',lookup_code);
33     dbms_sql.bind_variable(c,'lookup_meaning',lookup_meaning);
34
35     -- Execute and close the cursor.
36     fdbk := dbms_sql.execute(c);
37     dbms_sql.close_cursor(c);
38
39     -- Conditionally commit the record.
40     IF fdbk = 1 THEN
41       COMMIT;
42     END IF;
43   END insert_lookup;
44   /
```

Line 10 begins the process of differences, where it calls the OPEN_CURSOR function to get a cursor number from the database. Throughout the program until we close it, that is the reference to our dynamic statement. Line 26 parses the statement. You can parse with any of three constants, but generally you should see DBMS_SQL.NATIVE in the code. Anything else, while legal, should be changed to DBMS_SQL.NATIVE in any Oracle 8 or greater database.

TIP
If you forget that placeholders have a type and don't require delimiting single quotes, an ORA-01006 error will be raised when you add enclosing quotes to a statement.

Lines 29 through 33 bind local variables to placeholders. These statements don't use positional notation like NDS. They use named notation, which requires that you map the name of the placeholder to the local variable. Their ordering is arbitrary—in whatever order you prefer.

Line 36 executes the cursor, or our `INSERT` statement. It assigns a value of 1 when successful and 0 when not. After attempting the statement, be sure you always close the cursor.

Data Query Language (DQL) Statement with Bind Variables

The next statement demonstrates that you can query with placeholders to filter data, and you can simultaneously retrieve the column values from a query. This is a bit awkward, but possible. As this type of statement was used infrequently, it's been replaced by the reference cursor, as shown in an example earlier in the chapter.

```
SQL> DECLARE
  2      -- The traditional DBMS_SQL variables.
  3      c            INTEGER := dbms_sql.open_cursor;
  4      fdbk         INTEGER;
  5      stmt         VARCHAR2(2000);
  6
  7      -- Local variables.
  8      lv_lookup_id     NUMBER;
  9      lv_lookup_type   VARCHAR2(30) := 'DEBIT';
 10      lv_lookup_code   VARCHAR2(30);
 11
 12  BEGIN
 13      -- Create dynamic statement with placeholder.
 14      stmt := 'SELECT common_lookup_id '
 15          || ',       common_lookup_code '
 16          || 'FROM    common_lookup '
 17          || 'WHERE   common_lookup_type = :lookup_type';
 18
 19      -- Parse the statement.
 20      dbms_sql.parse(c,stmt,dbms_sql.native);
 21
 22      -- Define query return columns.
 23      dbms_sql.define_column(c,1,lv_lookup_id);
 24      dbms_sql.define_column(c,2,lv_lookup_code,5);
 25
 26      -- Bind a local variable to a placeholder.
 27      dbms_sql.bind_variable(c,'lookup_type',lv_lookup_type);
 28
 29      -- Assign output values when execute and fetch works.
```

```
30      IF dbms_sql.execute_and_fetch(c) = 1 THEN
31        dbms_sql.column_value(c,1,lv_lookup_id);
32        dbms_sql.column_value(c,2,lv_lookup_code);
33      END IF;
34
36      -- Close open cursor.
37      dbms_sql.close_cursor(c);
38
39      -- Print the output retrieved.
40      dbms_output.put_line('['||lv_lookup_id||']['||lv_lookup_code||']');
41    END;
42    /
```

Lines 23 and 24 contain calls to the DEFINE_COLUMN procedure, which maps the select columns to local variables. Line 30 calls the EXECUTE_AND_FETCH function, which works when you have a single fetch operation. Lines 31 and 32 assign the column values returned to the designated local variables.

There's a bit of a difference when you fetch more than once. You need to do that in a looping structure, like this:

```
IF dbms_sql.execute(c) = 1 THEN
  LOOP
    EXIT WHEN dbms_sql.fetch_rows(c) = 0;
    dbms_sql.column_value(c,1,lv_lookup_id);
    dbms_sql.column_value(c,2,lv_lookup_type);
    dbms_output.put
  END LOOP;
END IF;
```

You could place this snippet of code into lines the region occupied by lines 30 to 33 in the preceding program. The FETCH_ROWS function returns 0 when all rows are read. It would let you manage multiple row returns from the dynamic query.

Mixing and Matching NDS and DBMS_SQL

Sometimes you need to support an unknown number of inputs when you create a NDS template. This type of statement dynamically builds or adds clauses to a SQL statement before executing it.

We leverage this example to demonstrate the combination of NDS with the older DBMS_SQL package. This is possible only in Oracle 11*g* because

the TO_REFCURSOR and TO_CURSOR_NUMBER functions were added in the
DBMS_SQL package.

```
SQL> DECLARE
  2    -- Declare explicit record structure and table of structure.
  3    TYPE title_record IS RECORD
  4    ( item_title      VARCHAR2(60)
  5    , item_subtitle  VARCHAR2(60));
  6    TYPE title_table IS TABLE OF title_record;
  7    -- Declare dynamic variables.
  8    title_cursor  SYS_REFCURSOR;
  9    title_rows    TITLE_TABLE;
 10    -- Declare DBMS_SQL variables.
 11    c             INTEGER := dbms_sql.open_cursor;
 12    fdbk          INTEGER;
 13    -- Declare local variables.
 14    counter       NUMBER := 1;
 15    column_names  DBMS_SQL.VARCHAR2_TABLE;
 16    item_ids      DBMS_SQL.NUMBER_TABLE;
 17    stmt          VARCHAR2(2000);
 18    substmt       VARCHAR2(2000) := '';
 19  BEGIN
 20    -- Find the rows that meet the criteria.
 21    FOR i IN (SELECT 'item_ids' AS column_names
 22                 ,        item_id
 23              FROM    item
 24              WHERE   REGEXP_LIKE(item_title,'^Harry Potter')) LOOP
 25      column_names(counter) := counter;
 26      item_ids(counter) := i.item_id;
 27      counter := counter + 1;
 28    END LOOP;
 29    -- Dynamically create substatement.
 30    IF item_ids.COUNT = 1 THEN
 31      substmt := 'WHERE item_id IN (:item_ids)';
 32    ELSE
 33      substmt := 'WHERE item_id IN (';
 34      FOR i IN 1..item_ids.COUNT LOOP
 35        IF i = 1 THEN
 36          substmt := substmt ||':'||i;
 37        ELSE
 38          substmt := substmt ||',:'||i;
 39        END IF;
 40      END LOOP;
 41      substmt := substmt || ')';
 42    END IF;
 43    -- Set statement.
 44    stmt := 'SELECT  item_title, item_subtitle '
 45         || 'FROM    item '
 46         || substmt;
 47    -- Parse the statement with DBMS_SQL.
 48    dbms_sql.parse(c,stmt,dbms_sql.native);
 49    -- Bind the bind variable name and value.
 50    FOR i IN 1..item_ids.COUNT LOOP
```

```
51        dbms_sql.bind_variable(c,column_names(i),item_ids(i));
52      END LOOP;
53      -- Execute using DBMS_SQL.
54      fdbk := dbms_sql.execute(c);
55      -- Convert the cursor to NDS.
56      title_cursor := dbms_sql.to_refcursor(c);
57      -- Open and read dynamic curosr, then close it.
58      FETCH title_cursor BULK COLLECT INTO title_rows;
59      FOR i IN 1..title_rows.COUNT LOOP
60        dbms_output.put_line(
61        '['||title_rows(i).item_title||']['||title_rows(i).item_subtitle||']');
62      END LOOP;
63      -- Close the System Reference Cursor.
64      CLOSE title_cursor;
65    END;
66    /
```

Lines 44 through 46 shows the concatenating of the base statement with a dynamically built subordinate statement. After executing the query, line 56 converts the DBMS_SQL result to an NDS system reference cursor.

Mixing and matching NDS with DBMS_SQL is the only way to solve problems when you face unknown output from the program. The balance of the code works similar to our earlier NDS examples.

Best Practice
When you need to solve a problem with an unknown list of outputs, you should start in DBMS_SQL and convert the cursor to a SQL cursor before returning it as a reference cursor.

Downloadable Code

The examples in this chapter are organized into five files:

- The nds_static_dml.sql script shows you how to glue strings with variables to create NDS DML statements.

- The nds_dynamic_dml.sql script shows you how to use placeholders in NDS DML statements.

- The nds_dynamic_types.sql script shows you how use reference cursors, record types, and collections with NDS statements.

- The `dbms_sql_dml.sql` script shows you how to work with basic dynamic statements with the `DBMS_SQL` package.

- The `dbms_sql_query.sql` script shows you how to work with basic `DBMS_SQL` dynamic queries, which require special handling of the `SELECT` list return variables.

These programs should let you see the code in action. We think a download is friendlier then a cumbersome disc because the code doesn't take a great deal of space.

Summary

This chapter has covered the basics of NDS and the `DBMS_SQL` package. You should be able to use this information as a foundation for working with dynamic runtime SQL statements in your role. We hope you can leverage our examples.

You should also check the introduction for references to further your study of these topics.

Best Practice Review

- Where possible, always use NDS for dynamic statements over `DBMS_SQL` statements.

- Don't enclose dynamic statements in anonymous PL/SQL blocks; always use the `RETURNING INTO` subclause.

- Where possible, keep things supportable, such as naming placeholder and formal parameters the same. Naturally, the placeholder has a colon while the local variable doesn't.

- Use the `DBMS_SQL` package only when the process isn't supported by NDS.

- When you need to solve a problem with an unknown list of outputs, you should start in `DBMS_SQL` and convert the cursor to an SQL cursor before returning it as a reference cursor.

Mastery Check

The mastery check is a series of true or false and multiple choice questions that let you confirm how well you understand the material in the chapter. You may check Appendix E for answers to these questions.

1. ☐ **True** ☐ **False** You can use static or dynamic SQL statements with NDS.

2. ☐ **True** ☐ **False** You can glue strings into statement strings anywhere you like.

3. ☐ **True** ☐ **False** You can use the DBMS_ASSERT package to sanitize inputs and eliminate SQL injection attacks.

4. ☐ **True** ☐ **False** You can use SQL_NAME to verify whether a string is a valid schema object in the database catalog.

5. ☐ **True** ☐ **False** The terms *bind variable* and *placeholder* are synonymous.

6. ☐ **True** ☐ **False** You don't have to provide call parameters in positional order to NDS statements.

7. ☐ **True** ☐ **False** The USING clause supports IN, IN OUT, and OUT modes of operation.

8. ☐ **True** ☐ **False** It isn't a good practice to use the RETURNING INTO clause and avoid returning values through an IN OUT or OUT mode.

9. ☐ **True** ☐ **False** You can't have a colon in an NDS statement unless you define it as an ASCII character value.

10. ☐ **True** ☐ **False** You can assign an NDS statement output to a reference cursor and return the reference cursor into an object type.

11. What types of statements are supported by NDS?

    A. DDL statement without binding

    B. DDL statements with object name binding

    C. DML statements with object name binding

    D. All of the above

    E. Only A and C

12. What does the **:** (colon) in front of a name indicate inside an NDS statement?

    A. The colon signifies a session-level variable

    B. The colon represents a formal parameter of the statement

    C. The colon represents a placeholder variable

    D. All of the above

    E. Only B and C

13. Which function in the `DBMS_ASSERT` package validates a table name?

    A. The `QUALIFIED_SQL_NAME` function

    B. The `SIMPLE_SQL_NAME` clause

    C. The `SQL_OBJECT_NAME` clause

    D. All of the above

    E. Only A and C

14. An NDS statement can return a system reference cursor into which data type(s)?

    A. A SQL object type

    B. A PL/SQL record type

    C. A PL/SQL collection of an object type

    D. All of the above

    E. Only A and C

15. You can get an outbound parameter from an NDS statement by doing which of the following?

A. Define an IN OUT mode variable in the USING clause for a SQL statement.

B. Define an IN OUT mode variable in the USING clause for a PL/SQL block.

C. Define an outbound variable in the RETURNING INTO clause.

D. All of the above

E. Only B and C

CHAPTER
12

External Files

xternal files are typically sources for import or targets for export. They can be proprietary formats, such as those generated by Oracle Data Pump. More often, they are comma-separated value (CSV), position-specific, or tab-separated value (TSV) files. They're important tools for Extract Transform and Load (ETL) processes.

Not too long ago, we'd read these files with the UTL_FILE package. It was and is a very effective tool. Since the advent of external tables, however, UTL_FILE seems more work than external tables. Character Large Objects (CLOBs) are another story. They use DBMS_LOB and are covered at the end of the chapter.

This chapter shows you how to use external tables; we see them as part of the future direction for Oracle and ETL processing. XML data files are another issue. We recommend that you convert XML data files into CSV files before loading them into the database or do so through XML and the XML Developer's Kit (XDK).

This chapter works through these topics in this order:

- External table architecture

  - CSV files

  - Position-specific files

  - Tab-separated value (TSV) files

  - Convert XML to CSV files

  - Clean up files with Java stored libraries

- Importing CLOBs

Although there are also other approaches to loading data, we've opted not to cover these because of their required space. One way is to use the UTL_FILE package, another is to use Java, and a third is to use C. You can learn how to configure Java and external procedures in Chapter 13 of *Oracle Database 11g PL/SQL Programming*. That coverage demonstrates how to use C to write external files and how to use Java to read them.

We recommend external tables as the best platform-independent import sources, but you need a process to remove the data after you've imported it into your transactional or data warehouse model. Too often, developers and DBAs leave these unencrypted files in the file system, where it's much easier to compromise data. An import architecture is covered in the last section of this chapter, and it shows you how to manage these import files to minimize the risk of compromising the data.

External Table Architecture

External tables have their source in an external file. These files are most frequently CSV, position-specific, or TSV files. You can generate these files from Microsoft Excel spreadsheets, other programs, or simply a text editor.

These data structures are unique, at the time of writing, to Oracle databases. They're extremely advantageous for push-pull imports. The push comes from an external source to a designated location on the file system with a predetermined filename. The pull looks for the file, reads it, audits it, transforms it (where necessary), and loads it into the database. This is a typical ETL process used by many data warehouses.

Before you define an external table, you need to know where you're going to put the external file and what you're going to name it. You should also know where you'd like to write any error messages. The simplest solution is simply to put the source files in the same location as your log files. We'd strongly encourage you not to take the simplest approach, however. You should typically put your log files in a different physical directory from the source file.

The instructions show you how to define and maintain an upload directory. It should contain two subdirectories: one should contain the source data files and the other the bad, discard, and log files. This architecture lets you grant the minimum permissions to each of these external directories. It also lets you restrict the database from writing to your source files, which ensures that they're read as delivered.

Best Practice
Always separate the source and log files by directory. Allow read-only rights to the source directory and read-write to the log directory.

The first thing you need to do is create the physical directories. The examples use Windows but the only difference is mapping the logical drive C:\ to a mount point, and switching the \ (backslash) to a / (forward slash). In Windows, the files are accessible by the administrator account that installed the Oracle software, but not by other administrator accounts. Also, Linux or UNIX file directories must have read or read-write permission on the directory granted to the Oracle (or dba group typically) user.

TIP
You don't want these directories in the $ORACLE_HOME, and you generally want to provide the directory with only group or other privileges for the Oracle user.

The instructions assume the following file structure:

```
C:\upload\source
C:\upload\log
```

You use the SYSTEM user to create virtual directories and grant permissions to these directories. Based on the directories provided, you should issue the following commands to create virtual directories:

```
SQL> CREATE DIRECTORY upload_source AS 'C:\upload\source';
SQL> CREATE DIRECTORY upload_log AS 'C:\upload\log';
```

After creating the directories, you should grant appropriate privileges on these to your user. We use a plsql user name, which shouldn't be a surprise by now.

```
SQL> GRANT READ ON DIRECTORY upload_source TO plsql;
SQL> GRANT READ, WRITE ON DIRECTORY upload_log TO plsql;
```

That's all the setup required. Now you can create the tables as the plsql user.

CSV Files

The first step requires that you understand the syntax used to create external tables. There's a natural temptation to cover the options in detail, but this is a workbook, so we focus on the best way to define an external table.

You use a hybrid *create* statement to build external tables. All columns must be optional or null allowed because you can't constrain external table columns. A NOT NULL constraint on any of the columns of an external table would raise an ORA-30657 error because it's a disallowed syntax.

The best nonproprietary external file process uses SQL*Loader, which is the oracle_loader type. An alternative type is Oracle Data Pump (with a designation of oracle_datapump), but it's used to export and import data from the database. Files generated from a Data Pump export are proprietary files; likewise, those proprietary files are required to import the data back into the database.

The following statement works with a nonproprietary CSV file and is the one of the simplest ways to import data into an Oracle database. It defines a three column table using Oracle SQL*Loader. The SQL*Loader designation in the table definition is oracle_loader on line 6 of the following statement:

```
SQL> CREATE TABLE item_load
  2  ( item_title     VARCHAR2(60)
  3  , item_subtitle VARCHAR2(60)
  4  , release_date  DATE)
  5    ORGANIZATION EXTERNAL
  6    ( TYPE oracle_loader
  7      DEFAULT DIRECTORY UPLOAD_SOURCE
  8      ACCESS PARAMETERS
  9      ( RECORDS DELIMITED BY NEWLINE CHARACTERSET US7ASCII
 10        BADFILE      'UPLOAD_LOG':'item_load.bad'
 11        DISCARDFILE 'UPLOAD_LOG':'item_load.dis'
 12        LOGFILE      'UPLOAD_LOG':'item_load.log'
 13        FIELDS TERMINATED BY ','
 14        OPTIONALLY ENCLOSED BY "'"
 15        MISSING FIELD VALUES ARE NULL )
 16        LOCATION ('item_load.csv'))
 17    REJECT LIMIT UNLIMITED;
```

Line 7 designates the virtual directory where the file should be located. Line 16 provides the filename. Lines 10 through 12 designate the virtual directory where log files should be written and designates their filenames. Line 16 designates the location as the physical filename, which is case-sensitive on Linux, UNIX, or Mac OS X.

Another key access parameter is READSIZE. It sets the maximum length of any record or row in the external file. It has a default value of 512KB. You must set it to a larger value if your rows are longer than that default.

When you have a header row that you'd like to ignore, you can specify the following access parameter:

```
SKIP 1
```

You can also filter out rows that aren't of interest or don't meet data qualifications by using equality or nonequality comparisons. The AND and OR operators are also allowed, but you can't use the LIKE operator or other nested functions.

```
LOAD WHEN (item_title != 'Harry Potter and the Order of the Phoenix')
```

You can also use something other than the double quote to enclose data. A set of parentheses could be used, as follows:

```
OPTIONALLY ENCLOSED BY "(" AND ")"
```

This is handy syntax for a string with both single and double quotes in it. You can also use a single quote instead of the double provided in this example.

We haven't covered the additional access parameters, but you can find them in Chapter 13 of the Oracle Database Utilities 11*g* manual. They offer, more or less, some interesting tidbits, but we'd suggest you filter the data after it's loaded in a PL/SQL function or procedure.

You can now select from the table provided a file exists in the file system. When there is no file in the designated location, it throws the following error stack:

```
SELECT * FROM item_load
       *
ERROR at line 1:
ORA-29913: error in executing ODCIEXTTABLEOPEN callout
ORA-29400: data cartridge error
KUP-04040: file character.csv in UPLOAD_SOURCE not found
```

This error actually has three triggers. The first and simplest is that the physical file isn't where it should be. We show you how to fix that with a wrapping function later in this section. The other two triggering events are operating system configuration decisions.

You trigger the first configuration error when you don't have read permissions to the file or read/write permission to the log directory. The file must be in a directory where the operating system owner of Oracle has read permission. Likewise, the same operating system user needs read/write permission to the log directory. Actually, we would suggest that these be

Best Practice

Always put upload source files in non–Oracle owned directories to protect the security of your database.

deployed in a directory not owned by the Oracle user. Group permissions are adequate and you really don't want to grant upload permission to Oracle owned directories because it's a security risk.

The second configuration error is typically Windows port–specific. If you have two administrator accounts on the machine, the administrator that installed Oracle should always start Oracle to avoid this error. In addition, the Windows domain of the user must match the domain of your Oracle 11*g* installation.

You can avoid raising the exception for a nonexisting file by encapsulating the table in a function. This type of function requires that you create a user-defined type. The type should mimic an external table structure. As explained in Chapter 7, you also need a collection as a container of that object type. Flip back there if you need more detail.

The object type would look like this:

```
SQL> CREATE OR REPLACE TYPE item_load_obj IS OBJECT
  2  ( item_title      VARCHAR2(60)
  3  , item_subtitle   VARCHAR2(60)
  4  , release_date    DATE );
  5  /
```

Here's the object collection that wraps it:

```
SQL> CREATE OR REPLACE TYPE item_load_obj_table IS TABLE OF item_load_obj;
  2  /
```

We can now wrap the table and prevent it from publishing that there isn't an external file. This prevents extra handling in programs such as ETL code. It also ensures that the upload process details are hidden from developers who don't need to know about it.

The function takes no formal parameters and returns a set of values when data is found. It would be defined like this:

```
SQL> CREATE OR REPLACE FUNCTION item_source_file
  2  RETURN item_load_obj_table IS
  3    lv_c            NUMBER;
```

```
 4     lv_collection ITEM_LOAD_OBJ_TABLE := item_load_obj_table();
 5  BEGIN
 6    FOR i IN (SELECT * FROM item_load) LOOP
 7      lv_collection.EXTEND;
 8      lv_collection(lv_c) := item_load_obj( i.item_title
 9                                          , i.item_subtitle
10                                          , i.release_date);
11      lv_c := lv_c + 1;
12    END LOOP;
13    RETURN lv_collection;
14  EXCEPTION
15    WHEN OTHERS THEN
16      RETURN lv_collection;
17  END;
18  /
```

The trick here is simple. The only error relates to the absence of a file or permissions to work with a file. We return the collection of values on line 13 when there's no problem and an empty collection on line 16 when there is a problem. This encapsulates the issue by suppressing the error.

Naturally, you can insert an e-mail routine in this function to alert the appropriate party that the file failed to arrive. It would go between lines 15 and 16 in the code sample. This is the best way to manage a push paradigm, which is typically why we use external files.

Position-Specific Files

While we'd like to forget those pesky position-specific files, they exist. They'll probably still be in business solutions when our kids retire from their careers.

A different syntax is used when you define an external table for position-specific files. You must drop the lines TERMINATED BY and OPTIONALLY ENCLOSED BY from your script. They're replaced with character allocation with the CHAR data type.

Best Practice
Always put an escalation or notification action in the exception handler that wraps the push-paradigm upload protocol.

Here is our external table modified to work as a position-specific file:

```
SQL> CREATE TABLE item_load
  2  ( item_title    VARCHAR2(60)
  3  , item_subtitle VARCHAR2(60)
  4  , release_date  DATE)
  5    ORGANIZATION EXTERNAL
  6    ( TYPE oracle_loader
  7      DEFAULT DIRECTORY UPLOAD_SOURCE
  8      ACCESS PARAMETERS
  9      ( RECORDS DELIMITED BY NEWLINE CHARACTERSET US7ASCII
 10        BADFILE      'UPLOAD_LOG':'item_load.bad'
 11        DISCARDFILE  'UPLOAD_LOG':'item_load.dis'
 12        LOGFILE      'UPLOAD_LOG':'item_load.log'
 13        FIELDS
 14        MISSING FIELD VALUES ARE NULL
 15        ( item_title    CHAR(60)
 16        , item_subtitle CHAR(60)
 17        , release_date  CHAR(9))
 16        LOCATION ('item_load.csv'))
 17    REJECT LIMIT UNLIMITED;
```

You should note that the type, virtual directories, and filename have remained the same as those in the CSV file. Lines 15 through 17 are new in this Data Definition Language (DDL) statement. They allocate the first 60 characters to an item title, the next 60 to an item subtitle, and the last 9 to a date. That means the fields in the position specific file are 1–60, 61–120, and 121–129. That's a one-based numbering system, which is the rule with most position-specific files.

You must use position-specific files when you want to use date format masks. This is the only way to implement date formats that differ from the NLS_DATE format. Let's say, for example, that you need to convert a RELEASE_DATE value that wasn't in a default format mask layout. You could do it by modifying line 17. You would provide an instruction to SQL*Loader on how to convert it to a valid date, like this:

```
 17        , release_date  CHAR(10) date_format DATE mask "yyyy/mm/dd")
```

The singular advantage of position-specific external files is important to note because without it, all nonconforming date values would be rejected. You will find this and other details in Chapter 13 of the Oracle Database Utilities 11g manual.

We'd like to make a politically incorrect statement: *Avoid these types of files unless you have nonconforming date formats!* That having been said, when they can't be avoided, you now know how to implement them.

TSV Files

There's only one difference between a TSV and a CSV file: the designation of the tab over the comma. The problem with tabs as delimiters is that they have varying implementations across platforms. Commas and position-specific files are generic across platforms, which is why we'd recommend you use them before tab-delimited files.

The following shows you how to create a TSV external file:

```
SQL> CREATE TABLE item_load
  2  ( item_title    VARCHAR2(60)
  3  , item_subtitle VARCHAR2(60)
  4  , release_date  DATE)
  5    ORGANIZATION EXTERNAL
  6    ( TYPE oracle_loader
  7      DEFAULT DIRECTORY UPLOAD_SOURCE
  8      ACCESS PARAMETERS
  9      ( RECORDS DELIMITED BY NEWLINE CHARACTERSET US7ASCII
 10        BADFILE     'UPLOAD_LOG':'item_load.bad'
 11        DISCARDFILE 'UPLOAD_LOG':'item_load.dis'
 12        LOGFILE     'UPLOAD_LOG':'item_load.log'
 13        FIELDS TERMINATED BY 0x'09'
 14        MISSING FIELD VALUES ARE NULL)
 15        LOCATION ('item_load.tsv'))
 16    REJECT LIMIT UNLIMITED;
```

Line 13 shows you how to implement the most common tab, which is an ASCII 9. You should notice that tabs do eliminate the alternative quoting mechanism provided by the OPTIONALLY ENCLOSED BY clause option.

The ASCII 9 works with files exported from Microsoft Excel as tab-delimited. These files have two natural file extensions: .txt (text) and .tsv (tab separated values). Since we don't always control our data sources, it's nice to know how to work around them by seeing the different delimiters.

Convert XML to CSV Files

Most frequently, external table development falls to a database developer or DBA. Sometimes, they're not experts at writing Java to parse and manage XML files. We thought it would be handy to include a section that shows you how to convert XML to a CSV. The examples use Java, but only through a command-line call. It's a minimalist approach, because a lot of other work is already required to support external tables.

The process requires that you've installed the Java Software Development Kit (JDK) on the server. While Oracle installs a copy for itself, this process requires a separate copy. It supports your Java needs outside of the database. Our example assumes Windows, because generally Linux or UNIX users already know where to put things, even when the instructions are for Windows. They also use open source software where possible.

After you've installed the JDK, you need to download and install a Java-based XML parser. We've chosen Apache Xalan. You can view an overview of the Apache Xalan software at http://xml.apache.org/xalan-j/overview.html.

You can download the software from the same site. Once you've installed it on your system, you should probably create a shell script or a Windows batch file. The file sets five environment variables. This will make running the parser easier when you want to use it.

The five files must be in the Java %CLASSPATH% (or Linux, Mac OS X, or UNIX $CLASSPATH) to run the parser. The following Windows batch file assumes that you installed Apache Xalan in the topmost directory of the C:\ logical drive:

```
set CLASSPATH=%CLASSPATH%;C:\xalan-j_2_7_1\xalan.jar;.
set CLASSPATH=%CLASSPATH%;C:\xalan-j_2_7_1\serializer.jar
set CLASSPATH=%CLASSPATH%;C:\xalan-j_2_7_1\xercesImpl.jar
set CLASSPATH=%CLASSPATH%;C:\xalan-j_2_7_1\xml-apis.jar
set CLASSPATH=%CLASSPATH%;C:\xalan-j_2_7_1\xsltc.jar
```

For our example, we have a small XML file like this:

```
<?xml version="1.0" encoding="ISO-8859-1"?>
<item_load>
  <item>
    <title>Harry Potter and the Order of the Phoenix</title>
    <subtitle>Special Edition</subtitle>
    <release>11-DEC-2007</release>
  </item>
  <item>
    <title>Indiana Jones and the Kingdom of the Crystal Skull</title>
    <subtitle>Two-disc</subtitle>
    <release>14-Oct-2008</release>
  </item>
</item_load>
```

That was the easy part. Now we'll work through the complex part, which is XSLT.

NOTE
We recommend XSLT, 2nd Edition, *by Doug Tidwell (O'Reilly, 2008) if you're interested in learning more beyond editing this program to meet your particular needs. XSLT scripts are powerful but would require more space than we have to explain it in detail.*

```
<?xml version="1.0" encoding="ISO-8859-1"?>
<xsl:stylesheet version="1.0" xmlns:xsl="http://www.w3.org/1999/XSL/Transform">
<xsl:template match="/">
  <!-- This loops through the branch when a sibling meets a condition. -->
  <xsl:for-each select="item_load/item">
  <!-- Sorts based on the value in the "title" element. -->
  <xsl:sort select="title" />
    <!-- An apostrophe before and after with a line return. -->
    <xsl:text>&#39;</xsl:text>
    <xsl:value-of select="title"/>
      <!-- An apostrophe followed by a comma -->
      <xsl:text>&#39;&#44;</xsl:text>
      <xsl:text>&#39;</xsl:text>
    <xsl:value-of select="subtitle"/>
      <xsl:text>&#39;&#44;</xsl:text>
      <xsl:text>&#39;</xsl:text>
    <xsl:value-of select="release"/>
      <!-- An apostrophe followed by a line return -->
      <xsl:text>&#39;&#10;</xsl:text>
  </xsl:for-each>
</xsl:template>
</xsl:stylesheet>
```

You use the Xalan libraries to translate the XML file to a CSV file. The translator is the preceding XSLT script. The example assumes your XML source file is `item.xml`, your XSLT file is `change.xsl`, and your target text file is `item_load.csv`.

While it's a long line that probably wraps, this call transforms your XML to a CSV file:

```
C:\> java org.apache.xalan.xslt.Process -IN item.xml -XSL
change.xsl -TEXT > item_load.csv
```

The `org.apache.xalan.xslt.Process` calls a static Java method, which lets you treat the Apache Xalan like a traditional library. This will produce your CSV file, like this:

```
'Harry Potter and the Order of the Phoenix','Special Edition','11-DEC-2007'
'Indiana Jones and the Kingdom of the Crystal Skull','Two-disc','14-OCT-2007'
```

This section has launched you into the XML space. If it seems like a "gravity-free zone," that may be true for a while as you catch up with the technology.

Clean Up Files with Java Stored Libraries

This section shows you how to remove external files after your programs have read them into the database. Any application data left in a file is less secure than when it is safely tucked away in the database. External files should be removed after they're consumed, provided they are error-free. Unfortunately, there's not enough space to cover exception processing here, too.

The best design is a complete import mechanism. The samples that provide import management include Java, which lets you reach outside the database and delete the source file. It was tempting to start at the big picture and fill in the pieces, but we think it makes more sense to build the pieces one at a time, and then integrate them at the end.

This puts the smallest piece first, which is a target or destination table for the imported data. The `ITEM_TARGET` table is our destination. It mirrors our external table definition.

```
SQL> CREATE TABLE item_target
  2  ( item_title    VARCHAR2(60)
  3  , item_subtitle VARCHAR2(60)
  4  , release_date  DATE);
```

A function lets us manage the insert into this table. We've defined it with a single formal parameter, which is a collection like that returned from the `ITEM_SOURCE_FILE` function. The function returns a Boolean variable. This means we plan to deploy it in the PL/SQL context only. It's defined as follows:

```
SQL> CREATE OR REPLACE FUNCTION insert_items
  2  ( pv_item_list ITEM_LOAD_OBJ_TABLE ) RETURN BOOLEAN IS
  3    lv_return_value BOOLEAN := FALSE;
```

```
 4  BEGIN
 5    FOR i IN 1..pv_item_list.COUNT LOOP
 6      INSERT INTO item_target VALUES
 7      ( pv_item_list(i).item_title
 8      , pv_item_list(i).item_subtitle
 9      , pv_item_list(i).release_date );
10    END LOOP;
11    IF SQL%ROWCOUNT > 0 THEN
12      lv_return_value := TRUE;
13    END IF;
14    RETURN lv_return_value;
15  END;
16  /
```

Lines 5 and 11–13 contain a trick. Line 5 guards entry to the loop by checking for any rows in the collection. As qualified in the "CSV Files" section earlier in the chapter, the ITEM_SOURCE_FILE function returns an empty collection when the external file is missing. We plan to use the result form that function as the call parameter to the INSERT_ITEMS function. That means it's possible that no rows are inserted. Lines 11–13 contain a conditional evaluation that checks whether or not rows were inserted by calling the anonymous SQL%ROWCOUNT. It returns a zero value when nothing has been inserted.

The next step requires us to write a Java program that deletes the external file after reading its contents. We've written it so that you can run it from SQL*Plus prompt because we believe it's simpler. When we run Java programs from the SQL*Plus prompt, they require that we disable substitution variables. That means we treat the ampersand as an ordinary text character. We do this because two ampersands represent a logical AND operator in Java. You disable the ampersand's special property by setting the following at the SQL*Plus environment variable:

```
SQL> SET DEFINE OFF
```

Now you can create, replace, and compile Java from the SQL*Plus command line. The following creates a stored Java library that we use to delete the external file from the file system. You should note that earlier we did not grant write permission on the virtual directory for importing files. That won't change, but we grant read, write, and delete privileges to Java programs to accomplish this deletion. That grant requires that we are the SYS user, and we'll show you how to do this shortly.

Here's the Java code:

```
SQL> CREATE OR REPLACE AND COMPILE JAVA SOURCE NAMED "DeleteFile" AS
  2    // Java import statements
  3    import java.io.File;
  4    import java.security.AccessControlException;
  5
  6    // Class definition.
  7    public class DeleteFile {
  8
  9      // Define variable(s).
 10      private static File file;
 11
 12      // Define copyTextFile() method.
 13      public static void deleteFile(String fileName)
 14        throws AccessControlException {
 15
 16        // Create files from canonical file names.
 17        file = new File(fileName);
 18
 19        // Delete file(s).
 20        if (file.isFile() && file.delete()) {}}}
 21   /
```

Line 20 checks if the file exists and then deletes it from the file system. The deletion isn't recoverable through the trash or recycle bin: the file is completely gone.

The Java library lets you reach beyond the database to delete the external file. You can't access stored Java libraries directly. You must create PL/SQL wrappers to access Java libraries. The following creates a wrapper to our newly added library:

```
SQL> CREATE OR REPLACE PROCEDURE delete_file (dfile VARCHAR2) IS
  2  LANGUAGE JAVA
  3  NAME 'DeleteFile.deleteFile(java.lang.String)';
  4  /
```

At this point, you need to open another session as the SYS user. You want to connect as SYSDBA. If you haven't done this before, here's the syntax:

```
C:\Data>sqlplus sys as sysdba
SQL*Plus: Release 11.1.0.7.0 - Production on Sat Jul 11 23:04:30 2009
Copyright (c) 1982, 2008, Oracle.  All rights reserved.
Enter password:
```

```
Connected to:
Oracle Database 11g Enterprise Edition Release 11.1.0.7.0 - 64bit Production
With the Partitioning, OLAP, Data Mining and Real Application Testing options
SQL> show user
USER is "SYS"
```

You can run the following anonymous block to grant permissions to the Java program run by the `PLSQL` user. You should note that these permissions are limited to Java programs run by the `PLSQL` user. They don't change other previously or subsequently set access permissions on the virtual directory.

```
SQL> BEGIN
  2    DBMS_JAVA.GRANT_PERMISSION('PLSQL'
  3                              ,'SYS:java.io.FilePermission'
  4                              ,'C:\Upload\Source'
  5                              ,'read,write,delete');
  6  END;
  7  /
```

Don't sign out right away. Your `PLSQL` user needs some other privileges. You need to grant `SELECT` privileges on two catalog objects to the `SYSTEM` user. While the `SYSTEM` user can see these because privileges are granted *by default* through a role, you can't reference them inside a PL/SQL block without granting them as a direct privilege.

```
SQL> GRANT SELECT ON v_$database TO SYSTEM;
SQL> GRANT SELECT ON dba_directories TO SYSTEM;
```

We can sign off as the `SYS` user. After granting the privileges, we sign on as the `SYSTEM` user to perform the next steps. We're going to supplement Oracle's catalog with some new functions. The first function lets us determine whether we're on a Linux/UNIX or a Windows system. It returns a forward slash for Linux/UNIX operating systems and backslash for Windows operating systems.

The function is defined as follows:

```
SQL> CREATE OR REPLACE FUNCTION get_file_delimiter RETURN VARCHAR2 IS
  2    lv_return_value VARCHAR2(1);
  3  BEGIN
  4    SELECT CASE
  5             WHEN REGEXP_LIKE(platform_name,'.(W|w)indows.')
  6             THEN '\'
  7             ELSE '/'
```

```
 8            END AS delimiter
 9    INTO   lv_return_value
10    FROM   sys.v_$database;
11    RETURN lv_return_value;
12  END;
13  /
```

Line 5 uses a regular expression comparison to determine whether the platform name contains a Windows phrase. If so, we get the backslash. Otherwise, we get the forward slash.

The next function lets us translate the virtual directory name to a fully qualified file path, which is also known as the *canonical* file path. This function lets us peel back the information hiding and make our code more dynamic:

```
SQL> CREATE OR REPLACE FUNCTION get_absolute_path
  2  (lv_virtual_name   VARCHAR2) RETURN VARCHAR2 IS
  3    lv_return_value VARCHAR2(4000);
  4  BEGIN
  5    SELECT directory_path
  6    INTO   lv_return_value
  7    FROM   sys.dba_directories
  8    WHERE  directory_name = lv_virtual_name;
  9    RETURN lv_return_value;
 10  END;
 11  /
```

Since the query always returns a single row, we use the SELECT-INTO syntax, but it's more for clarity than a best practice. After creating these, we need to grant execute privilege on them to the PLSQL user. The grants would be as follows:

```
SQL> GRANT EXECUTE ON get_file_delimiter TO plsql;
SQL> GRANT EXECUTE ON get_absolute_path TO plsql;
```

At this point, we can sign off as the SYSTEM user. The balance of what we need to do for this process will be done as the PLSQL user.

The whole management process can now be wrapped in to a MANAGE_IMPORT function. You should note that it's only 23 lines long, but packed with leverage. It takes the external table name as the only input value because all the other information can be gathered by the other coding components. As with a couple other earlier functions, this one returns a Boolean data type. That means we plan to use it in an exclusively PL/SQL operating context.

Here's the final function for managing the import process:

```
SQL> CREATE OR REPLACE FUNCTION manage_import
  2  ( pv_external_table VARCHAR2 ) RETURN BOOLEAN IS
  3    lv_absolute_path  VARCHAR2(4000);
  4    lv_delimiter      VARCHAR2(1);
  5    lv_return_value BOOLEAN := FALSE;
  6    CURSOR cv_file_name ( pv_virtual_name VARCHAR2 ) IS
  7      SELECT   location
  8      ,        directory_name
  9      FROM     user_external_locations
 10      WHERE    table_name = cv_virtual_name;
 11  BEGIN
 12    IF insert_items(item_source_file) THEN
 13      FOR i IN cv_file_name(pv_external_table) LOOP
 14        lv_absolute_path := get_absolute_path(i.directory_name);
 15        lv_delimiter := get_file_delimiter;
 16        delete_file(lv_absolute_path||lv_delimiter||i.location);
 17      END LOOP;
 18      lv_return_value := TRUE;
 19    END IF;
 20    RETURN lv_return_value;
 21  END;
 22  /
```

Lines 12–21 hold the core logic. The conditional evaluation of whether we were able to insert records into the target table determines whether a true or false is returned. If the insertion was successful, we open the cursor for a specific external table, build a fully qualified path, and delete the external file source.

We wouldn't use the LV_ABSOLUTE_PATH or LV_DELIMITER variables in real code. They are there only to increase novice readability

Best Practice

Always use natural expressions as call parameters rather than assigning them to variables before the call to a pass-by-value function. Naturally, they can't be used when the formal parameters are pass-by-reference variables.

and to stay within our allotted 80-character length per line in this book. The function calls should be expressions and call parameters to the DELETE_FILES function. It's simply a better coding practice.

This concludes our coverage of external tables. The next section covers importing CLOBs. We recommend you include only a virtual directory and filename in your external tables because this is simply the *most scalable approach* to large object imports.

Importing CLOBs

SQL*Loader was designed prior to the existence of large objects in the database. It isn't really suitable for loading large objects. You should use the DBMS_LOB package to manage the upload of large objects. This section explains how to do that.

We'd recommend that you use external tables to import a virtual directory and filename for each large object stored in a row of data. Only large objects less than 4000 bytes are stored inline. Large objects bigger than that are stored *out-of-line*, which means that the row of data points to another location in the same tablespace.

You can use the DBMS_METADATA.GET_DDL function to see how a table and its large objects are stored. Two things are important when you define Binary Large Object (BLOB) or CLOB columns. The first is that you should provide a storage name; otherwise, they're assigned slightly different system-generated segment names. System-generated names for large objects start with SYS_LOB, while large object indexes start with SYS_IL. This makes them hard to match without regular expressions.

The following SQL*Plus formatting and query lets you perform that matching trick for a table and schema of your choice:

```
SQL> COL owner         FORMAT A5  HEADING "Owner"
SQL> COL table_name    FORMAT A5  HEADING "Table|Name"
SQL> COL column_name   FORMAT A10 HEADING "Column|Name"
SQL> COL segment_name  FORMAT A26 HEADING "Segment Name"
SQL> COL segment_type  FORMAT A10 HEADING "Segment|Type"
SQL> COL bytes                    HEADING "Segment|Bytes"
SQL> SELECT    l.owner
  2  ,         l.table_name
  3  ,         l.column_name
  4  ,         s.segment_name
  5  ,         s.segment_type
  6  ,         s.bytes
```

```
 7  FROM      dba_lobs l
 8  ,         dba_segments s
 9  WHERE     REGEXP_SUBSTR(l.segment_name,'([[:alnum:]]|[[:punct:]])+'
10            , CASE
11               WHEN REGEXP_INSTR(s.segment_name,'[[:digit:]]',1) > 0
12               THEN REGEXP_INSTR(s.segment_name,'[[:digit:]]',1)
13               ELSE 1
14              END) =
15            REGEXP_SUBSTR(s.segment_name,'([[:alnum:]]|[[:punct:]])+'
16              , CASE
17                 WHEN REGEXP_INSTR(s.segment_name,'[[:digit:]]',1) > 0
18                 THEN REGEXP_INSTR(s.segment_name,'[[:digit:]]',1)
19                 ELSE 1
20                END)
21  AND       l.table_name = UPPER('&table_name')
22  AND       l.owner = UPPER('&owner')
23  ORDER BY l.column_name, s.segment_name;
```

Lines 9–20 provide the way to match named and system-generated matches. This type of query is an important tool when you want to discover and align large object sizing. The best way to avoid having this level of complexity is to define things right when you create your data model.

The following DDL makes sure that you have named LOB segments:

```
SQL> CREATE TABLE item
  2  ( item_id              NUMBER        CONSTRAINT pk_item     PRIMARY KEY
  3  , item_barcode         VARCHAR2(20)  CONSTRAINT nn_item_1   NOT NULL
  4  , item_type            NUMBER        CONSTRAINT nn_item_2   NOT NULL
  5  , item_title           VARCHAR2(60)  CONSTRAINT nn_item_3   NOT NULL
  6  , item_subtitle        VARCHAR2(60)
  7  , item_desc            CLOB          CONSTRAINT nn_item_4   NOT NULL
  8  , item_blob            BLOB
  9  , item_photo           BFILE
 10  , item_rating          VARCHAR2(8)   CONSTRAINT nn_item_5   NOT NULL
 11  , item_rating_agency   VARCHAR2(4)   CONSTRAINT nn_item_6   NOT NULL
 12  , item_release_date    DATE          CONSTRAINT nn_item_7   NOT NULL
 13  , created_by           NUMBER        CONSTRAINT nn_item_8   NOT NULL
 14  , creation_date        DATE          CONSTRAINT nn_item_9   NOT NULL
 15  , last_updated_by      NUMBER        CONSTRAINT nn_item_10  NOT NULL
 16  , last_update_date     DATE          CONSTRAINT nn_item_11  NOT NULL
 17  , CONSTRAINT fk_item_1                FOREIGN KEY(item_type)
 18    REFERENCES common_lookup(common_lookup_id)
 19  , CONSTRAINT fk_item_2                FOREIGN KEY(created_by)
 20    REFERENCES system_user(system_user_id)
 21  , CONSTRAINT fk_item_3                FOREIGN KEY(last_updated_by)
 22    REFERENCES system_user(system_user_id))
```

```
23    LOB (item_desc) STORE AS BASICFILE item_desc
24    (TABLESPACE users ENABLE STORAGE IN ROW CHUNK 32768
25     PCTVERSION 10 NOCACHE LOGGING
26     STORAGE (INITIAL 1048576
27            NEXT 1048576
28            MINEXTENTS 1
29            MAXEXTENTS 2147483645))
30    , LOB (item_blob) STORE AS item_blob
31    (TABLESPACE users ENABLE STORAGE IN ROW CHUNK 32768
32     PCTVERSION 10 NOCACHE LOGGING
33     STORAGE (INITIAL 1048576
34            NEXT 1048576
35            MINEXTENTS 1
36            MAXEXTENTS 2147483645));
```

Lines 23 and 30 name the LOB segment the same as their respective column names. If you do this consistently, the regular expression to resolve system-generated names can be eliminated. Lines 24 and 31 use the maximum chunk value of 32K. This value minimizes the number of rows required to store a large object.

You can fix your code, but remember that you can't fix everything. Oracle seeds some LOB columns without explicit segment names. If you've inherited a system without segment names, you can't redefine them without dropping them and re-creating them. Any attempt to modify a LOB column's storage raises an ORA-22859, which is an invalid modification of a column.

TIP
You can't alter a column to add a segment name. The original column contents must be migrated, the column dropped, and then re-created.

Best Practice
Always assign storage names when defining LOB columns; otherwise, you have to use regular expressions to match the objects with their indexes.

The following `ALTER` statement demonstrates adding a new column to the `ITEM` table in the video store example:

```
ALTER TABLE item ADD (another CLOB)
LOB (another) STORE AS BASICFILE item_clob
(TABLESPACE users ENABLE STORAGE IN ROW CHUNK 32768
 PCTVERSION 10 NOCACHE LOGGING
 STORAGE (INITIAL 1048576
          NEXT 1048576
          MINEXTENTS 1
          MAXEXTENTS 2147483645));
```

Assuming you've mastered the basics of adding LOB columns, we now examine how to import text files into `CLOB` columns. The next example works with a `GENERIC` virtual directory. You need to create that directory before trying to run this procedure.

The following schema-level procedure lets you import `CLOB` files into the database:

```
SQL> CREATE OR REPLACE PROCEDURE load_clob_from_file
  2  ( src_file_name      IN VARCHAR2
  3  , table_name         IN VARCHAR2
  4  , column_name        IN VARCHAR2
  5  , primary_key_name   IN VARCHAR2
  6  , primary_key_value  IN VARCHAR2 ) IS
  7
  8     -- Define local variables for DBMS_LOB.LOADCLOBFROMFILE procedure.
  9     des_clob   CLOB;
 10     src_clob   BFILE := BFILENAME('GENERIC',src_file_name);
 11     des_offset NUMBER := 1;
 12     src_offset NUMBER := 1;
 13     ctx_lang   NUMBER := dbms_lob.default_lang_ctx;
 14     warning    NUMBER;
 15
 16     -- Define a pre-reading size.
 17     src_clob_size NUMBER;
 18
 19     -- Define local variable for Native Dynamic SQL.
 20     stmt VARCHAR2(2000);
 21
 22  BEGIN
 23
 24     -- Opening source file is a mandatory operation.
 25     IF dbms_lob.fileexists(src_clob) = 1 AND NOT
 26        dbms_lob.isopen(src_clob) = 1 THEN
 27       src_clob_size := dbms_lob.getlength(src_clob);
 28       dbms_lob.open(src_clob,DBMS_LOB.LOB_READONLY);
 29     END IF;
 30
```

```
31    -- Assign dynamic string to statement.
32    stmt := 'UPDATE '||table_name||' '
33       || 'SET    '||column_name||' = empty_clob() '
34       || 'WHERE  '||primary_key_name||' = '||''''||primary_key_value||''''
35       || 'RETURNING '||column_name||' INTO :locator';
36
37    -- Run dynamic statement.
38    EXECUTE IMMEDIATE stmt USING OUT des_clob;
39
40    -- Read and write file to CLOB, close source file and commit.
41    dbms_lob.loadclobfromfile( dest_lob     => des_clob
42                             , src_bfile    => src_clob
43                             , amount       => dbms_lob.getlength(src_clob)
44                             , dest_offset  => des_offset
45                             , src_offset   => src_offset
46                             , bfile_csid   => dbms_lob.default_csid
47                             , lang_context => ctx_lang
48                             , warning      => warning );
49
50    -- Close open source file.
51    dbms_lob.close(src_clob);
52
53    -- Commit write and conditionally acknowledge it.
54    IF src_clob_size = dbms_lob.getlength(des_clob) THEN
55      $IF $$DEBUG = 1 $THEN
56        dbms_output.put_line('Success!');
57      $END
58      COMMIT;
59    ELSE
60      $IF $$DEBUG = 1 $THEN
61        dbms_output.put_line('Failure.');
62      $END
63      RAISE dbms_lob.operation_failed;
64    END IF;
65
66  END load_clob_from_file;
67  /
```

The LOAD_CLOB_FROM_FILE procedure is very flexible because you can run it for any table that has a single-column primary key and a CLOB column. Lines 32–35 make this possible because they build a dynamic statement that returns a large object descriptor. We use the descriptor to read or write data into a CLOB column. This special handling occurs because CLOB or BLOB data types are actually objects, and we can access them only through the methods that Oracle provides. The DBMS_LOB package wraps those methods.

The debugging portion of the code can be enabled in Oracle 11*g* by altering the session, like this:

```
ALTER SESSION SET PLSQL_CCFLAGS = 'debug:1';
```

You would call this procedure with code like the following:

```
SQL> BEGIN
  2    FOR i IN
  3      (SELECT item_id
  4       FROM    item
  5       WHERE   item_title = 'The Lord of the Rings - Fellowship of the Ring'
  6       AND     item_type IN
  7        (SELECT common_lookup_id
  8         FROM    common_lookup
  9         WHERE   common_lookup_table = 'ITEM'
 10         AND     common_lookup_column = 'ITEM_TYPE'
 11         AND     REGEXP_LIKE(common_lookup_type,'^(dvd|vhs)*','i'))) LOOP
 12      -- Call procedure for matching rows.
 13      load_clob_from_file( src_file_name      => 'LOTRFellowship.txt'
 14                         , table_name         => 'ITEM'
 15                         , column_name        => 'ITEM_DESC'
 16                         , primary_key_name   => 'ITEM_ID'
 17                         , primary_key_value  => TO_CHAR(i.item_id) );
 18    END LOOP;
 19  END;
 20  /
```

Lines 13–17 contain the call to the LOAD_CLOB_FROM_FILE procedure. The only problem with this call is its dependency on the existence of the file. The absence of the file in the designated location or missing permissions yields an error:

```
BEGIN
*
ERROR at line 1:
ORA-22288: file or LOB operation GETLENGTH failed
The system cannot find the file specified.
ORA-06512: at "SYS.DBMS_LOB", line 678
ORA-06512: at "PLSQL.LOAD_CLOB_FROM_FILE", line 40
ORA-06512: at line 11
```

We can fix this, as we deleted the external file after consuming the data. We simply put some Java in the database to read the directory contents to ensure the file exists before we attempt to read it.

The first step to implement this type of Java solution requires that we create a collection for the list of files. The following creates such a collection:

```
SQL> CREATE OR REPLACE TYPE file_list AS TABLE OF VARCHAR2(255);
  2  /
```

Then we create and compile a Java library. This library performs most like a normal query for two reasons: It returns rows when they're found and a "no rows found" message when there aren't any files.

```
SQL> CREATE OR REPLACE AND COMPILE JAVA SOURCE NAMED "ListVirtualDirectory" AS
  2
  3    // Import required classes.
  4    import java.io.*;
  5    import java.security.AccessControlException;
  6    import java.sql.*;
  7    import java.util.Arrays;
  8    import oracle.sql.driver.*;
  9    import oracle.sql.ArrayDescriptor;
 10    import oracle.sql.ARRAY;
 11
 12    // Define the class.
 13    public class ListVirtualDirectory {
 14
 15      // Define the method.
 16      public static ARRAY getList(String path) throws SQLException {
 17
 18        // Declare variable as a null, required because of try-catch block.
 19        ARRAY listed = null;
 20
 21        // Define a connection (this is for Oracle 11g).
 22        Connection conn =
 23          DriverManager.getConnection("jdbc:default:connection:");
 24
 25        // Use a try-catch block to ignore errors.
 26        try {
 27          // Declare a class with the file list.
 28          File directory = new File(path);
 29
 30          // Declare a mapping to the schema-level SQL collection type.
 31          ArrayDescriptor arrayDescriptor =
 32            new ArrayDescriptor("FILE_LIST",conn);
 33
 34          // Translate the Java String[] to the Oracle SQL collection type.
 35          listed =
 36            new ARRAY(arrayDescriptor,conn,((Object[]) directory.list()));}
 37        catch (AccessControlException e) {}
 38      return listed; }}
 39  /
```

After creating the Java library, we need to create a PL/SQL wrapper function and grant the Java PLSQL user permissions to the file through Java. We may encounter an ORA-29549 error when rerunning a script with embedded Java. We simply run it once more to alter the state, and it should run without throwing an error.

The PL/SQL wrapper for this library follows:

```
SQL> CREATE OR REPLACE FUNCTION list_files(path VARCHAR2) RETURN FILE_LIST IS
  2  LANGUAGE JAVA NAME
  3  'ListVirtualDirectory.getList(java.lang.String) return oracle.sql.ARRAY';
  4  /
```

We connect as the SYS user to run the following anonymous block:

```
BEGIN
  DBMS_JAVA.GRANT_PERMISSION('PLSQL'
                            ,'SYS:java.io.FilePermission'
                            ,'C:\TEMP'
                            ,'read');
END;
/
```

We can confirm our access with the following query:

```
SQL> SELECT column_value
  2  FROM   TABLE(list_files(get_absolute_path('GENERIC')));
```

We need to prepare our video store model to support a more failsafe approach. The first thing we need to do is add two new columns: One provides the virtual directory name and the other, the filename. We can do this with the following ALTER statement:

```
SQL> ALTER TABLE item
  2  ADD (file_dir   VARCHAR2(255))
  3  ADD (file_name  VARCHAR2(255));
```

We populate the data with values that support our model. This means setting the virtual directory to GENERIC and the filename to LOTRFellowship.txt. The UPDATE statement manages that for us:

```
SQL> UPDATE item
  2  SET    file_dir = 'GENERIC'
  3  ,      file_name = 'LOTRFellowship.txt'
  4  WHERE  item_title = 'The Lord of the Rings - Fellowship of the Ring'
  5  AND    item_type IN
  6         (SELECT common_lookup_id
  7          FROM   common_lookup
  8          WHERE  common_lookup_table = 'ITEM'
  9          AND    common_lookup_column = 'ITEM_TYPE'
 10          AND    REGEXP_LIKE(common_lookup_type,'^(dvd|vhs)*','i'));
```

The last step lets us replace our anonymous block call to the LOAD_CLOB_FROM_FILE procedure. It now validates against the contents of the directory. There's no attempt to load the file when it's not found in the virtual directory or the user lacks read permissions on the directory.

Here's the anonymous block:

```
SQL> BEGIN
  2    FOR i IN (SELECT item_id
  3                   ,         file_dir
  4                   ,         file_name
  5              FROM    item
  6              WHERE   file_dir IS NOT NULL
  7              AND     file_name IS NOT NULL) LOOP
  8      FOR j IN (SELECT m.file_name
  9                FROM   (SELECT column_value AS file_name
 10                        FROM    TABLE(list_files(
 11                                      get_absolute_path(i.file_dir)))) m
 12                WHERE  m.file_name = i.file_name) LOOP
 13
 14      -- Call procedure for matching rows.
 15      load_clob_from_file( src_file_name      => j.file_name
 16                         , table_name         => 'ITEM'
 17                         , column_name        => 'ITEM_DESC'
 18                         , primary_key_name   => 'ITEM_ID'
 19                         , primary_key_value  => TO_CHAR(i.item_id));
 20      END LOOP;
 21    END LOOP;
 22  END;
 23  /
```

This section has shown you how to read source text files into CLOB columns. You've seen that the key to the architecture leverages Java as it did for cleaning up external files.

Throughout this chapter, you've seen how a technology can be exploited when we blend skills. It has shown you how to use external tables. More importantly, it has shown you how to architect a solution and exposed you to the complexity and power of Oracle 11*g*.

Downloadable Code

The examples in this chapter are organized into five files. You should run an external_sys.sql setup script first as the SYS privileged user. An external_system.sql setup script should then be run as the SYSTEM privileged user. Then you've three permutations on theme:

■ The external_csv_plsql.sql tests everything with a CSV file.

- The `external_pos_plsql.sql` tests everything with a position-specific file.

- The `external_tsv_plsql.sql` tests the concepts with a TSV file.

You also have the `load_clob_from_file.sql` script, which allows you to load any number of files into CLOB columns. As recommended in the "Importing CLOBs" section, you should first import the filename and virtual directory. During your transformation of source data, you call an embedded Java program to verify the presence of files before loading them with `LOAD_CLOB_FROM_FILE` procedure. Three files support testing the CLOB loading procedure:

- `clob_import_sys.sql` sets Java source permissions.

- `clob_import_system.sql` sets permissions for the model.

- `clob_import_plsql.sql` tests the concepts.

These programs should let you see the code in action. We think a download is friendlier then a cumbersome disc because the code doesn't take a great deal of space.

Summary

This chapter has covered external tables and architecting solutions with some of the components presented in the book. We hope you can leverage our examples.

You should also check the introduction for references to further your study of these topics.

Best Practice Review

- Always separate the source and log files by directory. Allow read-only rights to the source directory and read-write to the log directory.

- When you're allowed to choose import delimiters, always choose the comma because it is the safest and easiest to implement.

- Always put upload source files in non–Oracle owned directories to protect the security of your database.

- Always put an escalation or notification action in the exception handle that wraps the push-paradigm upload protocol.

- Always separate the source and log files by directory, and allow read-only rights to the source, and read-write to the log directories.

- Always use natural expressions as call parameters rather than assigning them to variables before the call to a pass-by-value function. Naturally, they can't be used when the formal parameters are pass-by-reference variables.

- Always assign storage names when defining LOB columns; otherwise, you have to use regular expressions to match the objects with their indexes.

Mastery Check

The mastery check is a series of true or false and multiple choice questions that let you confirm how well you understand the material in the chapter. You may check Appendix E for answers to these questions.

1. ☐ **True** ☐ **False** You can import comma-separated value files directly into Oracle tables.

2. ☐ **True** ☐ **False** You can import dates without regard to default date formats with TSV files.

3. ☐ **True** ☐ **False** You can use CSV external files when you want to use overriding date format masks.

4. ☐ **True** ☐ **False** You can use position-specific external files when you import dates in any format with a format mask.

5. ☐ **True** ☐ **False** You can't filter data during the load with the LIKE comparison operator.

6. ☐ **True** ☐ **False** Header rows must be stripped before they're made available to an external table because you can't ignore the header line when you load the data.

7. ☐ **True** ☐ **False** There's no way to suppress a query from raising a missing file error, KUP-04040.

8. ☐ **True** ☐ **False** Converting XML files to CSV files is possible with XSLT.

9. ☐ **True** ☐ **False** It is important to clean up source files after loading the data to the database.

10. ☐ **True** ☐ **False** Tab-delimited files are the most portable because tabs are consistent across operating systems.

11. Which of the following access parameter(s) let you filter data before loading it?

   A. LOAD WHEN (column = 'string')

   B. LOAD WHEN (column IN 'string')

   C. LOAD WHEN (column = 'string' AND column = 'string')

   D. All of the above

   E. Only A and C

12. Which of the following access parameters work with CSV or TSV files?

   A. The TERMINATED BY clause

   B. The OPTIONALLY ENCLOSED BY clause

   C. The MISSING FIELD

   D. All of the above

   E. Only A and B

13. Which of the following access parameters work with a position-specific file?

   A. The TERMINATED BY clause

   B. The MISSING FIELD clause

    C. The `OPTIONALLY ENCLOSED BY` clause

    D. All of the above

    E. Only A and C

14. Which of the following is the most generic value for a tab that works in Oracle?

    A. `'0X09'`

    B. `'0X0A'`

    C. `0X'09'`

    D. All of the above

    E. Only A and C

15. Which of the following would work in a CSV?

    A. `OPTIONALLY ENCLOSED BY "(" AND ")"`

    B. `OPTIONALLY ENCLOSED BY "'"`

    C. `OPTIONALLY ENCLOSED BY '(' AND ')'`

    D. All of the above

    E. Only A and C

PART
IV

Appendixes

APPENDIX
A

Wrapping PL/SQL

racle 11*g* lets you wrap or obfuscate your PL/SQL stored programs. Wrapping your code makes the business logic of your applications encapsulated from prying eyes by hiding the source code. It converts the clear text in the database to an unreadable stream of data. You can obfuscate the clear text by using the command line `wrap` utility or by calling the `CREATE_WRAPPED` procedure or `WRAP` function found in the `DBMS_DDL` package.

You should wrap only the implementation details. This means you should wrap only functions, procedures, package bodies, and type bodies. You enable developers to use your code by leaving the package specification and type specification. They won't know how it performs the task, but they'll know what actual parameters they can submit and expect back from functions or type methods. You should ensure that you comment the specification with any helpful information to take advantage of wrapped code units, especially procedures, because they don't define a direct return type like functions.

This appendix includes the following topics:

- Limitations of wrapping PL/SQL

- Using the `wrap` command line utility

- Using `DBMS_DDL` package to wrap PL/SQL

  - `WRAP` function

  - `CREATE_WRAPPED` procedure

The limitations imposed by wrapping are qualified first, then you'll learn how to wrap using the command line, and then you'll see the built-in procedure and functions of the `DBMS_DDL` package.

Limitations of Wrapping PL/SQL

There are three limitations of generically wrapping PL/SQL code in the database:

- You cannot wrap the source code of a database trigger, but you can reduce the logic to a single call to a wrapped stored function or procedure.

- Wrapping does not detect syntax or semantic errors, such as missing tables or views, which differs from normal compilation. Wrapped code units manifest runtime errors for missing tables or views, such as a Native Dynamic SQL (NDS) statement.

- Wrapped code is forward compatible only for import into the database. This means that you can import a wrapped module built by an Oracle 10*g* database into an 11*g* database, but you can't do the opposite.

While it can be difficult to decipher passwords in wrapped code, it isn't impossible. Oracle recommends that you don't embed passwords in wrapped program units.

Specific errors are generated by the method that you choose to wrap your code. Limitations are covered in the next two subsections.

Limitations of the PL/SQL wrap Utility

The wrap utility is parsed by the PL/SQL compiler, not by the SQL*Plus compiler. This means that you cannot include a SQL*Plus DEFINE notation inside wrapped program units. In addition, most comments are removed when wrapped.

Limitations of the DBMS_DDL.WRAP Function

When you invoke DBMS_SQL.PARSE with a data type that is a VARCHAR2A or VARCHAR2S and the text exceeds 32,767 bytes, you must set the LFFLG parameter to false. If you fail to do so, the DBMS_SQL.PARSE adds newline characters to the wrapped unit and corrupts it.

Using the wrap Command Line Utility

The wrap command line utility works with files. This is a critical distinction because it wraps everything in the file. When you use the wrap utility, package specifications and type definitions should be in different physical files from their respective package bodies and type bodies. As discussed earlier, you should wrap only the implementation details, not the published specifications.

The prototype for the wrap utility is:

```
wrap iname=input_file[{.sql |.ext}] [oname=output_file[{.plb |.ext}]
```

You can qualify the input and output files as relative or canonical filenames. Canonical filenames start at the root mount point in Linux or UNIX and from a logical file system reference in Microsoft Windows. The default file extension for input files is .sql, and it's .plb for output files. You do not need to provide either extension if you are prepared to accept the default values, but you must provide overriding values when they differ.

The next example works when the `wrap` command runs from the same directory as the input and output files:

```
wrap iname=input_file.sql oname=output_file.plb
```

After you wrap the files, you can run them into the database. The compilation process will not raise exceptions when there are missing table or view dependencies because there is no syntax, semantic, or dependency checking during compilation of wrapped program units. They compile because the SQL Data Definition Language (DDL) commands to `CREATE` (or `REPLACE`) functions, procedures, package specifications and bodies, and type definitions and bodies are scrambled into a form understood by the PL/SQL compiler.

The `CREATE (or REPLACE) TRIGGER` statement and anonymous block `DECLARE`, `BEGIN`, and `END` keywords are not obfuscated. Comments inside the header declaration and C-style multiple line comments, delimited by /* and */, are also not obfuscated.

Using the DBMS_DDL Command Line Utility

The `DBMS_DDL` package contains an overloaded `WRAP` function and overloaded `CREATE_WRAPPED` procedure. You can use either to create a wrapped stored programming unit. We cover both.

WRAP Function

The `WRAP` function is an overloaded function that accepts a DDL statement as a single variable length string of 32,767 or less, a table of strings 256 bytes in length, or a table of strings 32,767 bytes in length. You supply a lower and upper bound for the table of strings when the actual parameter is a table of strings. The lower bound is always *1*, and the upper bound is the maximum number of rows in the collection of strings.

The first prototype supports using a single input parameter:

```
DBMS_DDL.WRAP(ddl VARCHAR2) RETURN VARCHAR2
DBMS_DDL.WRAP(ddl DBMS_SQL.VARCHAR2S) RETURN VARCHAR2S
DBMS_DDL.WRAP(ddl DBMS_SQL.VARCHAR2A) RETURN VARCHAR2A
```

You can use this function to wrap a stored program unit as follows:

```
DECLARE
  source VARCHAR2(32767);
  result VARCHAR2(32767);
BEGIN
  source := 'CREATE FUNCTION one RETURN NUMBER IS BEGIN RETURN 1; END;';
  result := DBMS_DDL.WRAP(ddl => source);
  EXECUTE IMMEDIATE result;
END;
/
```

The program defines a DDL string, obfuscates it into the result variable, and then uses NDS to create the obfuscated function in the database. You can see the function specification by using the SQL*Plus DESCRIBE command:

```
SQL> DESCRIBE one
FUNCTION one RETURNS NUMBER
```

Any attempt to inspect its detailed operations will yield an obfuscated result. You can test this by querying stored function implementation in the TEXT column of the USER_SOURCE table, such as the following:

```
SQL> COLUMN text FORMAT A80 HEADING "Source Text"
SQL> SET PAGESIZE 49999
SQL> SELECT text FROM user_source WHERE name = 'ONE';
```

The following output is returned:

```
FUNCTION one wrapped
a000000
369
abcd
...
```

The function can be rewritten to use a table of strings, as follows:

```
DECLARE
  source DBMS_SQL.VARCHAR2S;
  result DBMS_SQL.VARCHAR2S;
BEGIN
  source(1) := 'CREATE FUNCTION two RETURN NUMBER IS ';
  source(2) := '  BEGIN RETURN 2;';
  source(3) := '  END;';
  result := DBMS_DDL.WRAP(ddl => source, lb => 1, ub => source.COUNT);
  FOR i IN 1..result.COUNT LOOP
    stmt := stmt || result(i);
  END LOOP;
  EXECUTE IMMEDIATE stmt;
END;
/
```

The actual table input and return value must be either the DBMS_SQL.VARCHAR2S or the DBMS_SQL.VARCHAR2A data type. The former holds strings up to 256 bytes, while the latter holds strings up to 32,767 bytes. Any other data type raises a PLS-00306 exception because the actual parameter doesn't match the data type of the formal parameter.

The statement is built by concatenating the strings from the table. It then calls the obfuscated SQL DDL statement and creates the two function. You can see the function specification by using the SQL*Plus DESCRIBE command:

```
SQL> DESCRIBE two
FUNCTION two RETURNS NUMBER
```

CREATE_WRAPPED Procedure

The CREATE_WRAPPED function is an overloaded function that accepts a DDL statement as a single variable length string of 32,767 or less, a table of strings 256 bytes in length, or a table of strings 32,767 bytes in length. You supply a lower and upper bound for the table of strings when the actual parameter is a table of strings. The lower bound is always *1*, and the upper bound is the maximum number of rows in the collection of strings.

The prototypes support using a single input parameter or table of strings:

```
DBMS_DDL.CREATE_WRAPPED(ddl VARCHAR2) RETURN VARCHAR2
DBMS_DDL.CREATE_WRAPPED(ddl DBMS_SQL.VARCHAR2S) RETURN VARCHAR2S
DBMS_DDL.CREATE_WRAPPED(ddl DBMS_SQL.VARCHAR2A) RETURN VARCHAR2A
```

You can use this anonymous block to test the wrapping procedure:

```
BEGIN
  dbms_ddl.create_wrapped(
    'CREATE OR REPLACE FUNCTION hello_world RETURN STRING AS '
    ||'BEGIN '
    ||'  RETURN ''Hello World!''; '
    ||'END;');
END;
/
```

After creating the function, you can query it by using the following SQL*Plus column formatting and query:

```
SQL> COLUMN message FORMAT A20 HEADING "Message"
SQL> SELECT hello_world AS message FROM dual;

Message
--------------------
Hello World!
```

You can describe the function to inspect its signature and return type:

```
SQL> DESCRIBE hello_world
FUNCTION hello_world RETURNS VARCHAR2
```

Any attempt to inspect its detailed operations will yield an obfuscated result. You can test this by querying stored function implementation in the TEXT column of the USER_SOURCE table, such as the following:

```
SQL> COLUMN text FORMAT A80 HEADING "Source Text"
SQL> SET PAGESIZE 49999
SQL> SELECT text FROM user_source WHERE name = 'HELLO_WORLD';
```

The following output is returned:

```
FUNCTION hello_world wrapped
a000000
369
abcd
...
```

The procedure can be rewritten to use a table of strings, as follows:

```
DECLARE
   source DBMS_SQL.VARCHAR2S;
   stmt      VARCHAR2(4000);
BEGIN
   source(1) := 'CREATE FUNCTION hello_world2 RETURN VARCHAR2 IS ';
   source(2) := '  BEGIN RETURN 2;';
   source(3) := '  END;';
   DBMS_DDL.CREATE_WRAPPED(ddl => source, lb => 1, ub => source.COUNT);
END;
/
```

You don't have to use NDS to build the function when you call the CREATE_WRAPPED procedure. This is because the CREATE_WRAPPED procedure builds the stored program for you, unlike the WRAP function that only returns the wrapped string or table of strings.

Summary

This appendix has shown you how to hide the implementation details of your PL/SQL stored programming units. You've seen how to use the command line wrap utility and the built-in CREATE_WRAPPED procedure and WRAP function from the DBMS_DDL package. You should remember to hide only the implementation details, not the package specifications and object type definitions.

APPENDIX

B

PL/SQL Hierarchical Profiler

racle 11*g* introduced the PL/SQL hierarchical profiler, which lets you capture the dynamic execution performance of your PL/SQL programs. It divides PL/SQL execution times into two parts: SQL statement and PL/SQL program unit execution times.

A hierarchical profiler provides you with more insight than a nonhierarchical profiler. A nonhierarchical profiler reports only how much time a module consumed. A hierarchical profile tells you which program called what subroutine, and how many times the subroutine was called. The PL/SQL hierarchical profiler stores results in a set of hierarchical profiler tables. It divides the data by subprogram units, including the relationship between calling and called subroutines, and it further subdivides execution time by the SQL statement versus PL/SQL execution segments.

This appendix describes the PL/SQL hierarchical profiler and demonstrates how to configure and use it. Coverage of the profiler is organized into the following topics:

- Configuring the schema

- Collecting profile data

- Understanding profiler output

- Using the `plshprof` command line utility

The topics are organized in this order, but you can jump directly to the information required provided the schema is configured.

Configuring the Schema

The first step to configure the PL/SQL hierarchical profiler is building the tables in the `SYS` schema. You do this by connecting to the database as the privileged user. You connect from the command line:

```
# sqlplus sqlplus '/ as sysdba'
```

As the privileged user, you can now build the supplemental data catalog tables required to support the PL/SQL hierarchical profiler. The following runs the `dbmshptab.sql` script:

```
SQL> @?/rdbms/admin/dbmshptab.sql
```

The script hopefully raises some exceptions for missing tables, which you can ignore. The PL/SQL hierarchical profiler uses the DBMS_HPROF package, which is invalid until you create the tables. Figure B-1 depicts the tables and their relationships, but you should remember that they're owned by SYS unless you grant SELECT permissions to development schemas or you rerun the dbmshptab.sql against the target plsql schema.

If you don't rerun the script against the target plsql schema, you won't be able to analyze your output. Therefore, you should connect to the plsql schema and rerun this command:

```
SQL> ?/rdbms/admin/dbmshptab.sql
```

The "Understanding Profiler Data" section a bit later in this appendix has more detail on the three tables that support the profiler, which are necessary if you want to build your own analytical modeling capability.

After creating the tables, you grant execute permission on the package to your target schema, create a profiler virtual directory, and grant read and

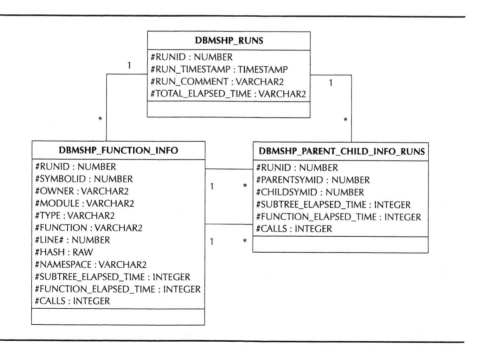

FIGURE B-1. *PL/SQL hierarchical profiler tables*

write permissions on the directory to your target schema. You execute these commands as SYSDBA:

```
GRANT EXECUTE ON dbms_hprof TO plsql;
CREATE OR REPLACE DIRECTORY profiler_dir AS '/tmp/';
GRANT READ, WRITE ON DIRECTORY profiler_dir TO plsql;
```

You do not need to create a synonym because the Oracle 11*g* database seeds a public synonym for the DBMS_HPROF package. This is also true for the DBMSHP_RUNNUMBER sequence created when you build the PL/SQL hierarchical profiler repository. Verify that you can see the package by connecting as the plsql user and describing the package:

```
SQL> DESCRIBE dbms_hprof
FUNCTION ANALYZE RETURNS NUMBER
 Argument Name                  Type                         In/Out Default?
 ------------------------------ ---------------------------- ------ --------
 LOCATION                       VARCHAR2                     IN
 FILENAME                       VARCHAR2                     IN
 SUMMARY_MODE                   BOOLEAN                      IN     DEFAULT
 TRACE                          VARCHAR2                     IN     DEFAULT
 SKIP                           BINARY_INTEGER               IN     DEFAULT
 COLLECT                        BINARY_INTEGER               IN     DEFAULT
 RUN_COMMENT                    VARCHAR2                     IN     DEFAULT
PROCEDURE START_PROFILING
 Argument Name                  Type                         In/Out Default?
 ------------------------------ ---------------------------- ------ --------
 LOCATION                       VARCHAR2                     IN     DEFAULT
 FILENAME                       VARCHAR2                     IN     DEFAULT
 MAX_DEPTH                      BINARY_INTEGER               IN     DEFAULT
PROCEDURE STOP_PROFILING
```

The DBMS_HPROF package has two procedures for starting and stopping data collection, and one function for gathering and analyzing data. The next section explains how to use these methods.

Collecting Profiler Data

Collecting data from the PL/SQL hierarchical profiler requires that you configure the database, as covered in the preceding section. Then, you must start the profiler, run your test, and stop the profiler. You stop it because running it constantly consumes unnecessary database resources.

To collect data from the profiler, you'll need to build a test case. This test case requires that you've run the video store code scripts found in the introduction of this book. The test_profiler.sql script creates the code components, starts the profiler, runs the test, and stops the profiler. It will also verify that you got all the configuration steps correct, because it will fail if it can't call the package methods or write a file to your /tmp directory.

The first step in this test requires that you build a glue_string function that will be called for every row of a cursor statement. The function definition follows:

```
-- This is found in test_profiler.sql on the publisher's web site.
CREATE OR REPLACE FUNCTION glue_strings
(string1 VARCHAR2, string2 VARCHAR2) RETURN VARCHAR2(2000) IS
  new_string VARCHAR2(2000);
BEGIN
  IF string1 IS NOT NULL THEN
    IF string2 IS NOT NULL THEN
      new_string := string1 || ': ' || string2;
    ELSE
      new_string := string1;
    END IF;
  ELSE
    IF string2 IS NOT NULL THEN
      new_string := string2;
    END IF;
  END IF;
  RETURN new_string;
END glue_strings;
/
```

The function is designed to take two strings and concatenate them, provided one or the other isn't a null value. When one is a null value, the not null value is returned. Naturally, a null is returned when both inputs are null, because the new_string variable is declared not defined, and all declared scalar variables are initialized with a null value by default.

The next component for the test is a quantity_onhand procedure. It takes two formal parameters by value and two by reference. Both IN OUT mode parameters are nested table collections (see Chapter 7 for details on collections).

The collections require you to define two user-defined SQL data types, like this:

```
CREATE OR REPLACE TYPE varchar2_table IS TABLE OF VARCHAR2(2000);
/
CREATE OR REPLACE TYPE number_table IS TABLE OF NUMBER;
/
```

TIP
Oracle 11g rumored to allocate 1999 bytes when you declare a VARCHAR2 variable of 1999 bytes, regardless of the physical size of your data. But this is not true. Large variable length strings sizes are dynamically allocated.

Here's the procedure:

```
-- This is found in test_profiler.sql on the publisher's web site.
CREATE OR REPLACE PROCEDURE quantity_onhand
( item_title          IN      VARCHAR2
, item_rating_agency IN      VARCHAR2
, item_titles         IN OUT VARCHAR2_TABLE
, quantities          IN OUT NUMBER_TABLE) IS
  -- Define counter variable.
  counter             NUMBER := 1;
  -- Define dynamic cursor.
  CURSOR c
  ( item_title_in          VARCHAR2
  , item_rating_agency_in VARCHAR2) IS
    SELECT   glue_strings(item_title,item_subtitle) AS full_title
    ,        COUNT(*) AS quantity_onhand
    FROM     item
    WHERE    REGEXP_LIKE(item_title,item_title_in)
    AND      item_rating_agency = item_rating_agency_in
    GROUP BY glue_strings(item_title,item_subtitle)
    ,        item_rating_agency;
BEGIN
  -- Read cursor and assign column values to parallel arrays.
  FOR i IN c (item_title,item_rating_agency) LOOP
    item_titles.EXTEND;
    item_titles(counter) := i.full_title;
    quantities.EXTEND;
```

```
      quantities(counter) := i.quantity_onhand;
      counter := counter + 1;
    END LOOP;
END;
/
```

You assign *row-by-row* values to the nested table collections, but production systems would use a BULK COLLECT (as qualified in Chapter 2). The counter variable indexes the nested table collections because the FOR loop i variable is a pointer referencing the rows returned by the cursor.

Another alternative would involve using a system reference cursor, which you'd explicitly open inside the procedure. While examples of this are not presented in this book, you can find a system reference cursor example on the publisher's web site, named test_profiler_with_cursor.sql.

NOTE
When a system reference cursor replaces a set of parallel collection, the IN OUT mode SYS_ REFCURSOR is passed back to the calling program as a pointer to the internal cursor work area.

As mentioned, the glue_strings function runs for all returned rows. The anonymous-block program starts the profiler as the first action in the execution block, and it stops the profiler as the last action.

The following testing program runs the quantity_onhand procedure once:

```
-- This is found in test_profiler.sql on the publisher's web site.
DECLARE
  -- Input values.
  item_title          VARCHAR2(30) := 'Harry Potter';
  item_rating_agency  VARCHAR2(4)  := 'MPAA';
  -- Output values.
  full_title          VARCHAR2_TABLE := varchar2_table();
  rating_agency       NUMBER_TABLE := number_table();
BEGIN
  -- Start PL/SQL hierarchical profiler.
  dbms_hprof.start_profiling('PROFILER_DIR','harry.txt');
```

```
  -- Call reference cursor.
  quantity_onhand(item_title,item_rating_agency,full_title,rating_agency);

  -- Loop through parallel collections until all records are read.
  FOR i IN 1..full_title.COUNT LOOP
    dbms_output.put(full_title(i));
    dbms_output.put(rating_agency(i));
  END LOOP;

  -- Stop PL/SQL hierarchical profiler.
  dbms_hprof.stop_profiling;
END;
/
```

If everything is configured correctly, you will now find a `harry.txt` file in your `/tmp` directory. The file should have 235 lines in it.

You can simply call a stored procedure or function between the `START_PROFILING` and `STOP_PROFILING` procedures, as an alternative to testing anonymous-block programs such as the example. At this point, all the data is external to the database and in the raw analyze file.

The next section will demonstrate how you interpret the profiler's output.

Understanding Profiler Data

You can interpret the PL/SQL profiler output in three ways: You can review the raw output file, analyze the data in the analysis tables, or create hierarchical queries of the analytical data. The next three subsections explore these data analysis tools.

Reading the Raw Output

The raw output is really designed to be read by the analyzer component of the PL/SQL hierarchical profiler. However, you can derive some information before you analyze it by leveraging the indicator codes from Table B-1, which follows. Here's a small snapshot from the raw `harry.txt` file:

```
P#X 1
P#R
P#C SQL."".""."__sql_fetch_line17" #17
P#X 27
P#R
```

```
P#C PLSQL."SYS"."DBMS_OUTPUT"::11."PUT"#5892e4d73b579470 #77
P#X 1
P#R
P#C PLSQL."SYS"."DBMS_OUTPUT"::11."PUT"#5892e4d73b579470 #77
P#X 1
P#R
P#C PLSQL."SYS"."DBMS_OUTPUT"::11."PUT_LINE"#5892e4d73b579470 #109
P#X 1
P#R
P#C SQL.""."".".__sql_fetch_line17" #17
P#X 23
P#R
```

While you can discern what the lines do when you know the indicator codes, it is more difficult to draw out the relationship and statistical information from the raw data than from the analyzed data.

The PL/SQL hierarchical profiler tracks several operations as if they were functions with names and namespaces, as shown in Table B-2. (The list of tracked operations doesn't appear comprehensive as of this writing. It is likely that other tracked operations may later be added by Oracle.)

NOTE
This conclusion is drawn from testing, which has produced gaps between parent and child keys in the DBMSHP_PARENT_CHILD_INFO_ RUNS table.

Indicator	Description
P#C	Indicates a call to a subprogram; known as a call event
P#R	Indicates a return from a subprogram to a calling program; known as a return event
P#X	Indicates the elapsed time between the preceding and following events
P#!	Indicates a comment in the analyzed file

TABLE B-1.   *Raw PL/SQL Hierarchical Profiler Data*

Function Name	Tracked Operation	Namespace
`__anonymous_block`	Anonymous block PL/SQL execution	PL/SQL
`__dyn_sql_exec_line`*line#*	Dynamic SQL statement call made at a specific line number in a program	SQL
`__pkg_init`	Initialization code from a package specification or body	PL/SQL
`__plsql_vm`	PL/SQL Virtual Machine (VM) call	PL/SQL
`__sql_fetch_line`*line#*	SQL FETCH statement occurring at a designated line number in a program	SQL
`__static_sql_exec_line`*line#*	SQL statement occurring at a specific line number in a program	SQL

TABLE B-2. *Operations Tracked by the PL/SQL Hierarchical Profiler*

The tracked operations show up as functions in your raw and filtered output, and they often bridge like a parent between a grandparent and grandchild.

Defining the PL/SQL Profiler Tables

The PL/SQL hierarchical profiler tables are created when you run the dbmshptab.sql script, which is found in the $ORACLE_HOME/rdbms/admin directory. It must be run against the SYS schema and any user schema where you want to collect profiler data. This is required because the DBMS_HPROF package uses invoker rights. (You can read more about invoker rights in Chapter 3.)

Name	Data Type	Description
RUNID	NUMBER	A surrogate primary key generated from the DBMSHP_PROFILER sequence
RUN_TIMESTAMP	TIMESTAMP	Timestamp set when you run the DBMS_HPROF.ANALYZE function
RUN_COMMENT	VARCHAR2(2047)	User comment that you provide when calling the DBMS_HPROF.ANALYZE function
TOTAL_ELAPSED_TIME	INTEGER	The elapsed time for the analysis process called by the DBMS_HPROF.ANALYZE function

TABLE B-3. *DBMSHP_RUNS Table Description*

Figure B-1 showed the Unified Modeling Language (UML) depiction of these tables and their relationships. Tables B-3, B-4, and B-5 list the columns, data types, and column descriptions for the analysis tables.

The DBMSHP_RUNS table contains information only about the execution of the DBMS_HPROF.ANALYZE function. The DBMSHP_FUNCTION_INFO table contains information about executed functions, and the DBMSHP_PARENT_CHILD_INFO table has the hierarchical relationship between executed functions.

The RUNID maps straight across to the DBMSHP_PARENT_CHILD_INFO table as the same column name. The SYMBOLID column maps to both the PARENTSYMID and CHILDSYMID columns. When you recursively join these structures, you should ensure that you join the tables on the SYMBOLID and PARENTSYMID columns. The "Querying the Analyzed Data" section a bit later contains an example of this type of join.

Name	Data Type	Description
RUNID	NUMBER	A foreign key from the DBMSHP_RUNS table; it is part of a composite primary key. The RUNID and SYMBOLID columns define the primary key for the table.
SYMBOLID	NUMBER	The execution sequence ID value. Unique when combined with the RUNID column value, and together they define a composite primary key for this table.
OWNER	VARCHAR2(32)	Owner of the module called.
MODULE	VARCHAR2(2047)	The module name contains a subprogram, such as a package name; for example DBMS_LOB, DBMS_SQL, or a user-defined package.
TYPE	VARCHAR2(32)	The module type defines the source of the module. Some examples are package, procedure, or function.
FUNCTION	VARCHAR2(4000)	A subprogram name or operation (such as those in Table B-1) tracked by the PL/SQL hierarchical profiler.
LINE#	NUMBER	The line number where the function is defined in the schema owner module.
HASH	RAW(32)	Hash code for the subprogram signature, which is unique for any run of the DBMS_HPROF.ANALYZE function.
NAMESPACE	VARCHAR2(32)	Namespace of subprogram, which can be either SQL or PL/SQL.
SUBTREE_ELAPSED_TIME	INTEGER	Elapsed time, in microseconds, for subprogram, excluding time spent in descendant subprograms.
FUNCTION_ELAPSED_TIME	INTEGER	Elapsed time, in microseconds, for a subprogram, excluding time spent in descendant subprograms.
CALLS	INTEGER	The number of calls to a subprogram.

TABLE B-4. *DBMSHP_FUNCTION_INFO Table Columns*

Name	Data Type	Description
RUNID	NUMBER	A surrogate primary key generated from the DBMSHP_PROFILER sequence.
PARENTSYMID	NUMBER	The execution sequence ID value. The PARENTSYMID is unique when combined with the RUNID column value, and together they define a composite foreign key that maps to the DBMSHP_FUNCTION_INFO table RUNID and SYMBOLID columns.
CHILDSYMID	NUMBER	The execution sequence ID value. The CHILDSYMID is unique when combined with the RUNID column value, and together they define a composite foreign key that maps to the DBMSHP_FUNCTION_INFO table RUNID and SYMBOLID columns.
SUBTREE_ELAPSED_TIME	INTEGER	Elapsed time, in microseconds, for a subprogram, excluding time spent in descendant subprograms.
FUNCTION_ELAPSED_TIME	INTEGER	Elapsed time, in microseconds, for a subprogram, excluding time spent in descendant subprograms.
CALLS	INTEGER	The number of calls to a child row that is identified by a composite key of RUNID and CHILDSYMID columns.

TABLE B-5. *DBMSHP_PARENT_CHILD_INFO Table Columns*

Querying the Analyzed Data

A recursive query is the best way to get meaningful results. The following query captures the nesting of method names and uses SQL*Plus column formatting to organize the output:

```
-- This is found in query_profiler.sql on the publisher's web site.
COL method_name          FORMAT A30
COL function_name        FORMAT A24
```

```
COL subtree_elapsed_time  FORMAT 99.90 HEADING "Subtree|Elapsed|Time"
COL function_elapsed_time FORMAT 99.90 HEADING "Function|Elapsed|Time"
COL calls                 FORMAT 99    HEADING "Calls"

SELECT   RPAD(' ',level*2,' ')||dfi.owner||'.'||dfi.module AS method_name
,        dfi.function AS function_name
,        (dpci.subtree_elapsed_time/1000) AS subtree_elapsed_time
,        (dpci.function_elapsed_time/1000) AS function_elapsed_time
,        dpci.calls
FROM     dbmshp_parent_child_info dpci
,        dbmshp_function_info dfi
WHERE    dpci.runid = dfi.runid
AND      dpci.parentsymid = dfi.symbolid
AND      dpci.runid = 4
CONNECT
BY PRIOR dpci.childsymid = dpci.parentsymid  -- Child always connects on left.
START
WITH     dpci.parentsymid = 1;
```

This yields the following output:

```
-- This is output from the query_profiler.sql script
                                                  Subtree Function
                                                  Elapsed Elapsed
METHOD_NAME                   FUNCTION_NAME           Time    Time Calls
----------------------------- ----------------------- ------- -------- -----
      .                       __plsql_vm                 .04     .04    11
  PLSQL.GLUE_STRINGS          GLUE_STRINGS               .00     .00     0
    PLSQL.QUANTITY_ONHAND     QUANTITY_ONHAND            .29     .05     1
      PLSQL.QUANTITY_ONHAND   QUANTITY_ONHAND.C          .24     .24     1
    PLSQL.QUANTITY_ONHAND     QUANTITY_ONHAND            .12     .03    11
      SYS.DBMS_OUTPUT         PUT_LINE                   .02     .02    11
      SYS.DBMS_OUTPUT         PUT_LINE                   .06     .05    11
        SYS.DBMS_OUTPUT       PUT                        .02     .02     1
    PLSQL.QUANTITY_ONHAND     QUANTITY_ONHAND           3.27    3.19     1

9 rows selected.
```

We've now demonstrated an approach to querying the PL/SQL profiler table data and introduced you the details of leveraging recursive SQL queries in Oracle 11*g*. You've learned how to interpret the PL/SQL profiler output, review the raw output file, and analyze data. The analysis discussion showed you how to create hierarchical queries of that profile the analytical data.

The next section demonstrates how to generate a web page report equivalent.

Using the plshprof Command Line Utility

The `plshprof` command line utility lets you generate simple HTML reports. You can generate a report from one or two sets of analyzed data. You'll find the `plshprof` utility in the `$ORACLE_HOME/bin/` directory.

The `plshprof` utility has several command options that let you generate different report types, as shown in Table B-6.

You can generate an output report by using the following syntax:

```
$ plshprof -output /tmp/magic /tmp/harry.txt
```

It echoes the following to the console when generating the file:

```
PLSHPROF: Oracle Database 11g Enterprise Edition Release 11.1.0.6.0
[8 symbols processed]
[Report written to '/tmp/magic.html']
```

Option	Description	Default
`-collect count`	Collects the information for `count` calls. You should use this in combination only with the `-trace symbol` option.	`1`
`-output filename`	Sets the output filename. Don't include an extension because you could end up with a strange filename, such as `magic.htm.html`.	`filename.html` or `tracefile.html`
`-skip count`	Skips the first `count` calls. You should use this only in combination with the `-trace symbol` option.	`0`
`-summary`	Prints only the elapsed time.	None
`-trace symbol`	Specifies the function name of the tree root.	Not applicable

TABLE B-6.   `plshprof` Command Line Options

This generates an index web page, `magic.html`. You use this page to navigate to the other generated Web reports.

```
magic_2c.html   magic.html      magic_nsc.html   magic_tc.html
magic_2f.html   magic_md.html   magic_nsf.html   magic_td.html
magic_2n.html   magic_mf.html   magic_nsp.html   magic_tf.html
magic_fn.html   magic_ms.html   magic_pc.html    magic_ts.html
```

The `magic.html` page shown in Figure B-2 demonstrates the list of reports produced by the `plshprof` utility. You can write a wrapper to read and store these into Character Large Object (CLOB) columns in the database or as external files accessible to your web server. Alternatively, you can simply generate them to the `/tmp` directory, browse them individually, and then remove them from the file system.

The `plshprof` command line utility generates a set of effective analysis tools that you should examine before attempting to write your own.

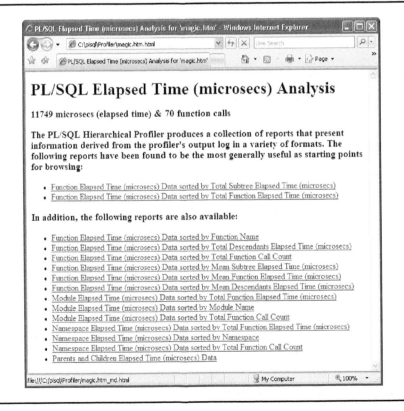

FIGURE B-2. *Sample* `plshprof` *index web page*

APPENDIX
C

PL/Scope

ew to Oracle 11*g*, PL/Scope is a compiler-driven tool. It collects and organizes data about user-defined identifiers from PL/SQL source code. Identifiers can be reserved words, predefined identifiers, quoted identifiers, user-defined variables, subroutines, user-defined data types, or stored program names. Chapter 3 in *Oracle Database 11g PL/SQL Programming* covers identifiers in PL/SQL thoroughly.

The PL/Scope data is stored in static data dictionary views that contain declaration, definition, reference, call, and assignment of identifiers. They also provide the location of each usage in the source code.

This appendix covers the following topics:

- Configuring PL/Scope data collection

- Viewing PL/Scope collected data

You should also note that Oracle SQL*Developer can access PL/Scope data.

Configuring PL/Scope Data Collection

The default behavior of PL/Scope is disabled. You enable PL/Scope by setting the PLSCOPE_SETTINGS parameter to the 'IDENTIFIERS:ALL' value. This parameter can be set at the database and session level. Only identifiers set while this parameter is enabled are captured by PL/Scope routines. Here's the syntax:

```
ALTER SESSION SET PLSCOPE_SETTINGS = 'IDENTIFIERS:ALL'
```

Once you enable PL/Scope, it runs until the session ends or the database is altered back to the default. It is intended only for development databases; Oracle doesn't recommend enabling it for production databases.

Next, you should monitor its impact on the SYSAUX tablespace. You can query the space consumed by using the following:

```
SELECT space_usage_kbytes
FROM   v$sysaux_occupants
WHERE  occupant_name = 'PL/SCOPE'
```

NOTE
PL/Scope works only in an Oracle 11g database, but you can activate it during upgrade by running the utlirplscope.sql *script in* UPGRADE *mode.*

Viewing PL/Scope Collected Data

PL/Scope collected data is available by three methods: You can query static data dictionary views, use the PL/SQL Web Application demonstration tool, or write your own web-based application to profile the data.

PL/Scope captures identifiers only when the PLSCOPE_SETTINGS parameter is set to the 'IDENTIFIERS:ALL' value. You can enable it from any SQL Developer session. It stores identifiers by the signature of individual store programming units, and overloaded signatures are treated as unique identifier contexts.

NOTE
PL/Scope does not collect identifiers for wrapped program units.

You can query the ALL_IDENTIFIERS, DBA_IDENTIFIERS, or USER_IDENTIFIERS views. The definition of the ALL_* and DBA_* views include the owner, while the USER_* view doesn't. Here's the definition of these views:

```
Name                             Null?    Type
-------------------------------- -------- ---------------------------
OWNER                            NOT NULL VARCHAR2(30)
NAME                                      VARCHAR2(30)
SIGNATURE                                 VARCHAR2(32)
TYPE                                      VARCHAR2(18)
OBJECT_NAME                      NOT NULL VARCHAR2(30)
OBJECT_TYPE                               VARCHAR2(13)
USAGE                                     VARCHAR2(11)
USAGE_ID                                  NUMBER
LINE                                      NUMBER
COL                                       NUMBER
USAGE_CONTEXT_ID                          NUMBER
```

The predelivered HTML-based demonstration tool runs using the PL/SQL Web Toolkit. You'll find it as the `$ORACLE_HOME/plsql/demo/plscopedemo.sql` script. This script requires you to build a wrapper web page or configure the Oracle HTTP Server (OHS), which is covered in Chapter 16.

SQL*Developer lets you enable PL/Scope by right-clicking the connection name in the Connections navigator display. Then select Toggle PL/Scope Identifier Collection. This sets the session `PLSCOPE_SETTINGS` parameter to the `'IDENTIFIERS:ALL'` value. Viewing the data still requires a manual query or implementing your own web page. PL/Scope collects the following identifiers:

ASSOCIATIVE_ARRAY	FORMAL OUT	RECORD
BFILE	FUNCTION	REFCURSOR
BLOB	INTERVAL	SUBTYPE
BOOLEAN	ITERATOR	SYNONYM
CHARACTER	LABEL	TIME
CLOB	LIBRARY	TIMESTAMP
CONSTANT	NESTED TABLE	TRIGGER
CURSOR	NUMBER	UROWID
DATE	OBJECT	VARRAY
EXCEPTION	OPAQUE	VARIABLE
FORMAL IN	PACKAGE	
FORMAL IN OUT	PROCEDURE	

The supported data types are base types defined by the STANDARD package. Labels have their unique context in PL/Scope, while iterators are available only when they are the index of a FOR loop. The ANYDATA and XMLType data types are examples of the OPAQUE type. PL/Scope treats object attributes, local variables, package variables (defined in the package specification), and record structures as VARIABLE data types. Also, PL/Scope does not resolve base object names for synonyms, which leaves you to query the *_SYNONYMS view.

APPENDIX
D

PL/SQL Built-in
Packages and Types

racle's PL/SQL built-in packages and types are some of the most underutilized features in the Oracle database management system. Moreover, they represent a treasure trove of premade programs for your use. We could fill volumes with examples on how to take advantage of this rich feature set. We encourage you to study the *Oracle Database PL/SQL Packages and Types Reference*, as it can save you many hours attempting to create and maintain similar products.

Oracle updated or introduced 90 packages and 4 types in the 11*g* release of its RDBMS. In all, there are around 240 documented programs and data types in the *Oracle Database PL/SQL Packages and Types Reference*, and they do everything from managing HTTP cookies to parsing XML. This appendix merely outlines them.

We start with a general listing of the schema owners that hold built-in packages and types. Most of the commonly used packages exist in the SYS and SYSMAN schemas. Table D-1 represents the packages and types in our sample database. Your database may include more or fewer packages than this.

Owner	Packages	Types	Technology
CTXSYS	70	31	Oracle Intermedia text (analytics)
DBSNMP	3	8	SNMP management
EXFSYS	18	28	Expression filters
MDSYS	69	139	Spatial Geo rasterizing
OLAPSYS	45	7	OLAP catalogs and packages
ORDSYS	27	448	OLAP
SYS	592	1174	Owner/administrator of the DB
SYSMAN	187	640	Oracle Enterprise Manager
SYSTEM	1	1	DB administration utility packages
WKSYS	22	25	UltraSearch packages: WebCrawler search packages
WMSYS	22	14	Workspace Manager
XDB	30	97	XML database

TABLE D-1. *Package Owners and Their Associated Technologies*

Notice that our sample database contains 1086 packages and 2612 types. Instead of boring you with the details of 3698 objects, we list only those packages that are documented in the *Oracle Database PL/SQL Packages and Types Reference*.

The following tables contain four columns defining the name of the object, technology affected, and whether the object has been newly introduced or updated in 11*g*. The first set of built-in objects, in Table D-2, has to do with data warehousing. You may have already used them if your job requires you to work with materialized views, extract transform load, and data mining.

Package/Type	Technology	New	UPD
DBMS_ADVANCED_REWRITE	Query rewrite		
DBMS_DATA_MINING	Data mining/warehousing		X
DBMS_DATA_MINING_TRANSFORM	Data mining/warehousing trasformation		X
DBMS_DIMENSION	Validation of data dimensional relationships		
DBMS_LOGMNR...	LogMiner packages		
DBMS_MVIEW	Management of materialized views		X
DBMS_PREDICTIVE_ANALYTICS	Data mining prediction		X
DBMS_TRANSFORM	Interface to the message format transformation		
DBMS_AW_STATS	OLAP statistics generation	X	
DBMS_CUBE	OLAP cube creation/ management	X	
DBMS_CUBE_ADVISE	OLAP cube performance	X	

TABLE D-2.   *Data Warehousing Packages and Types*

Package/Type	Technology	New	UPD
DBMS_DEBUG	PL/SQL Debugger		
DBMS_ERRLOG	Provides error logging for DML operations		
DBMS_HPROF	PL/SQL profiling	X	
DBMS_OUTPUT	Print output to screen		
DBMS_PIPE	Push messages to other sessions		
DBMS_PREPROCESSOR	Print/retreive source of Pl/Sql units		
DBMS_WARNING	PL/SQL error stack manipulation		
DEBUG_EXTPROC	Debug of external procedures		
UTL_LMS	Format of error messages in different languages		

TABLE D-3. *Debug Related Packages and Types*

PL/SQL developers use the set of objects in Table D-3 to aid them in debugging, profiling, and error stack formatting. Commonly used packages are DBMS_OUPUT and DBMS_PIPE.

Oracle built the packages shown in Table D-4 to manage job control. You should be very familiar with them if your job includes database administration.

We discussed DBMS_ASSERT and DBMS_FGA in Chapters 8 and 9. You should know and use DBMS_ASSERT to validate input passed into procedures and functions. Hackers write FUZZING programs to determine

Package/Type	Technology	New	UPD
DBMS_AUTO_TASK_ADMIN	Autotask controls	X	
DBMS_JOB	Job management		
DBMS_SCHEDULER	Job management		X

TABLE D-4. *Job Management Packages and Types*

Package/Type	Technology	New	UPD
DBMS_ASSERT	Parameter input validation		
DBMS_DISTRIBUTED_TRUST_ADMIN	Management of trusted server lists		
DBMS_FGA	Fine Grained Auditing		

TABLE D-5.   *Security Related Packages and Types*

which procedures and functions are vulnerable to SQL injection. In addition, you can greatly streamline your auditing efforts with DBMS_FGA (see Table D-5).

   Database professionals use Oracle Streams for data replication and warehouse loading. This feature set is similar to other third-party extract transform load tools; with the exception that Oracle built *Streams* (shown in Table D-6) to interface directly with its RDBMS, which affords it extra performance benefits like hot mining of redo logs to reduce latency.

Package/Type	Technology	New	UPD
DBMS_APPLY_ADM	Oracle Streams		X
DBMS_AQ...	Oracle Streams advance queuing		X
DBMS_CAPTURE_ADM	Oracle Streams capture processes		X
DBMS_FILE_GROUP	Management of file groups/versions		
DBMS_PROPAGATION_ADM	Management of Streams propagation		X
DBMS_STREAMS...	Management of Streams interfaces	X	X
UTL_SPADV	Oracle Streams statistical analysis	X	X

TABLE D-6.   *Streams Related Packages and Types*

The packages shown in Table D-7 help you diagnose performance problems with your SQL and PL/SQL code.

Table D-8 lists all of the utility objects that Oracle documents in the *Oracle Database PL/SQL Packages and Types Reference*. It is the largest grouping by far; however, a general understanding of these packages is essential.

Package/Type	Technology	New	UPD
DBMS_ADVISOR	Performance diagnostics		X
DBMS_IOT	Management of index organized tables		
DBMS_MONITOR	Tracing and Statistics gathering		
DBMS_OUTLN...	Management of stored outlines		X
DBMS_PCLXUTIL	Creation of partition aware indexes		
DBMS_PROFILER	Profile interface for PL/SQL programs		
DBMS_RESOURCE_MANAGER...	Consumer group resource planning		X
DBMS_SPM	SQL plan management	X	
DBMS_SQLDIAG	SQL diagnostics		
DBMS_SQLPA	SQL Performance Analyzer		
DBMS_SQLTUNE	SQL tuning interface		X
DBMS_STATS...	View and manage performance statistics		X
DBMS_WORKLOAD...	Gathering of workload statistics	X	X

TABLE D-7. *Performance Related Packages and Types*

Package/Type	Technology	New	UPD
DMBS_ALERT	Programatic notification of database events		
DBMS_APPLICATION_INFO	Code instrumentation and tracing		
DBMS_CQ_NOTIFICATION	Provides alerts to clients on DML or DDL modification		X
DBMS_DG	Oracle Data Guard event notification	X	
APEX_CUSTOM_AUTH	Apex authenticaion	X	
APEX_APPLICATION	Apex application support	X	
DBMS_COMPARISON	Comparison and convergence of data objects	X	
DBMS_CRYPTO	Encryption		
DBMS_OBFUSCATION_TOOLKIT	Encryption		
DBMS_EPG	PL/SQL execution via HTTP		
DBMS_AQIN	Secure access to Oracle JMS		
DBMS_JAVA	Database functionality to Java		
DBMS_OFFLINE_OG	Advanced replication		
CTX_	Oracle text analytics		
DBMS_ADDM	Automatic diagnostic monitor	X	
DBMS_CDC_	Change data capture		X
DBMS_CONNECTION_POOL	Management of database resident connection pools	X	
DBMS_DATAPUMP	Moving all/part of a database		X
DBMS_DB_VERSION	Determines RDBMS release		

TABLE D-8.   *Utility Packages and Types*

Package/Type	Technology	New	UPD
DBMS_DDL	Returns DDL information about stored procedures		
DBMS_DESCRIBE	Returns information about stored procedures		
DBMS_DEFER...	Defers remote transactions		
DBMS_FILE_TRANSFER	Moving binary files between DBs		
DBMS_FLASHBACK	Rolls back DML/DDL		X
DBMS_HM	Database health check	X	
DBMS_HS_PARALLEL	Hetrogeneous parallel processing	X	
DBMS_HS_PASSTHROUGH	Passthrough processing to non-Oracle systems		X
DBMS_LDAP...	LDAP query		
DBMS_LIBCACHE	Remote extraction of PL/SQL and SQL		
DBMS_LOB	Management of LOBS		X
DBMS_LOCK	Management of locks		
DBMS_METADATA	Data dictionary to XML metadata or creation		
DBMS_MGD_ID_UTL	Sets/gets: loging level, proxy, metadata	X	
DBMS_MGW...	Oracle Messaging Gateway Services		X
DBMS_RANDOM	Random data generation		
DBMS_RECTIFIER_DIFF	Detect and rectify data differences among replicated sites		
DBMS_REFRESH	Management of materialized view refresh groups		

TABLE D-8. *Utility Packages and Types (continued)*

Package/Type	Technology	New	UPD
DBMS_REPAIR	Detect and repair corrupt data blocks		
DBMS_REPCAT	Management of symmetric replication users/templates		
DBMS_REPUTIL	Management of shadow tables		
DBMS_RESULT_CACHE	Partial management of shared pool cache	X	
DBMS_RESUMABLE	Suspend/time-out large running programs		
DBMS_RLMGR	Rules Manager API		X
DBMS_RLS	Fine Grained Access Control for virtual private databases		
DBMS_ROWID	Management of ROWID, including creation and retrieval		
DBMS_RULE_	Rules Manager API		X
DBMS_SERVER_ALERT	Alerts the DBA when thresholds of DB Server are met		X
DBMS_SERVICE	Management of DB services		
DBMS_SESSION	Alter session programmatically		X
DBMS_SHARED_POOL	Management of the shared pool memory space		
DBMS_SPACE...	Analysis of segment growth		X
DBMS_SQL	Dynamic PL/SQL and types		X
DBMS_STORAGE_MAP	Communication with FMON		
DBMS_TDB	RMAN transportable diagnostics for moving DBs		

TABLE D-8. *Utility Packages and Types (continued)*

Package/Type	Technology	New	UPD
DBMS_TRACE	Tracing and statistics gathering		X
DBMS_TRANSACTION	Management interface to SQL transactions		
DBMS_TTS	Transportable tablespace management		
DBMS_TYPES	Built-in constants and types		
DBMS_UTILITY	Various utilities		X
DBMS_WM	Interface to the Database Workspace Manager		
DBMS_XA	Interface to the XA/Open interface	X	
HTF	Hypertext functions and procedures		
HTP	Hypertext functions and procedures		
ORD...	Management of medical digital imaging and communications		
OWA...	PL/SQL web applications		
SDO...	Spatial/mapping	X	
SEM...	Resource description framework and Web Ontology Language interface	X	
UTL_COLL	Determines whether collection items are locators or not		
UTL_COMPRESS	Data compression		
UTL_DBWS	Database Web Services		

TABLE D-8. *Utility Packages and Types (continued)*

Package/Type	Technology	New	UPD
UTL_ENCODE	Conversion of RAW to standard data		
UTL_FILE	Writing to OS files		
UTL_HTTP	Access to the Internet within PL/SQL		
UTL_I18N	Globalization support within PL/SQL		
UTL_INADDR	Internet addressing utilities		X
UTL_MAIL	E-mail utility		
UTL_NLA	Statistical analysis within VARRAYs		
UTL_RAW	Raw data type manipulation		
UTL_RECOMP	Recompilation of invalid DB objects		X
UTL_REF	Support of reference-based operations/generic type methods		
UTL_SMTP	E-mail utility		X
UTL_TCP	TCP/IP utilities		X
UTL_URL	URL address character management		
WPG_DOCLOAD	Interface for downloading BLOBs and BFILEs		
ANYDATA...	Management of the Oracle AnyData data type		

TABLE D-8. *Utility Packages and Types (continued)*

Package/Type	Technology	New	UPD
DBMS_CSX_ADMIN	Moving XML tablespaces	X	
DBMS_RESCONFIG	XML listener configuration	X	
DBMS_XDB...	XML access control list and user management	X	X
DBMS_XEVENT	XML event management	X	
DBMS_XML...	XML object management and manipulation	X	X

TABLE D-9. *XML Packages and Types*

Table D-9 represents Oracle efforts to support XML databases. The company is committed to providing XML functionality to its users.

In all, Oracle provides an extensive built-in library of code to support its users. These feature sets, along with SQL functions, enable you to accomplish more with less code, in comparison with products from other RDBMS vendors.

Examples of Package Usage

The following code snippets demonstrate a few of the packages outlined in the preceding tables. Our intent is to illustrate how the use of Oracle built-in packages streamlines and simplifies your coding experience:

- DBMS_COMPARISON
- DBMS_FGA
- DBMS_OBFUSCATION_TOOLKIT

Throughout the book, we intentionally added built-in packages to our examples to draw your attention to them.

DBMS_COMPARISON

The following example demonstrates the power of DBMS_COMPARISON
(a newly added package in 11*g*). Oracle wrote it with the intention of
synchronizing shared tables that exist in distributed database systems.

Example D-1: DBMS_COMPARISON   The following blocks create two
tables for demonstration purposes:

```
SQL> CREATE TABLE video_store.member#1
  2    AS
  3    SELECT * FROM video_store.member
  4  /
Table created.

SQL> CREATE TABLE video_store.member#2
  2    AS
  3    SELECT * FROM video_store.member
  4  /
Table created.
```

This statement alters the CREDIT_CARD_NUMBER column to accept our
update:

```
SQL> ALTER TABLE video_store.member#2
  2    MODIFY ( credit_card_number varchar2(25))
  3  /
Table altered.
```

We must create unique, NOT NULL indexes for DBMS_COMPARISON to
use during its evaluation of rows. In this case, we created a primary key on
the MEMBER_ID column of each table:

```
SQL> ALTER TABLE video_store.member#1
  2    ADD CONSTRAINT m1_pky
  3    PRIMARY KEY ( member_id )
  4  /
Table altered.

SQL> ALTER TABLE video_store.member#2
  2    ADD CONSTRAINT m2_pky
  3    PRIMARY KEY ( member_id )
  4  /
Table altered.
```

Our next block updates the `MEMBER#2` table and displays the results of that update:

```
SQL> UPDATE  video_store.member#2
  2      SET  credit_card_number = credit_card_number || '123'
  3  /
2 rows updated.

SQL> SELECT  m1.member_id
  2       ,  m1.credit_card_number
  3       ,  m2.credit_card_number
  4    FROM  video_store.member#1 m1
  5       ,  video_store.member#2 m2
  6   WHERE  m1.member_id = m2.member_id
  7  /
MEMBER_ID CREDIT_CARD_NUMBER  CREDIT_CARD_NUMBER
--------- ------------------- -------------------------
        1 2862 6046 3527 5584 2862 6046 3527 5584123
        2 3255 8814 2129 3834 3255 8814 2129 3834123
```

Notice that the `CREDIT_CARD_NUMBER` column values are different. In the following anonymous block, we create and execute a comparison named `MY_COMPARE_NAME`. It detects this difference and submits those differences to data dictionary tables:

```
SQL> DECLARE
  2    lr_compare_results         DBMS_COMPARISON.COMPARISON_TYPE;
  3    lb_diff                    BOOLEAN;
  4  BEGIN
  5    DBMS_COMPARISON.CREATE_COMPARISON ( comparison_name    =>
  6  'my_compare_name'
  7                                      , schema_name        => 'VIDEO_STORE'
  8                                      , object_name        => 'MEMBER#1'
  9                                      , dblink_name        => 'T001a'
 10                                      , remote_schema_name => 'VIDEO_STORE'
 11                                      , remote_object_name => 'MEMBER#2'
 12                                      );
 13    lb_diff :=
 14      DBMS_COMPARISON.COMPARE  ( 'my_compare_name'
 15                               , lr_compare_results
 16                               , NULL
 17                               , NULL
 18                               , TRUE
 19                               );
 20    IF   lb_diff = TRUE
 21    THEN DBMS_OUTPUT.PUT_LINE ( 'NONE FOUND' );
 22    ELSIF lb_diff = FALSE
 23    THEN DBMS_OUTPUT.PUT_LINE ( 'DIFF FOUND' );
```

```
24    END IF;
25  END;
26  /
DIFF FOUND
PL/SQL procedure successfully completed.
```

Observe that we assigned a different table name to the REMOTE_OBJECT_NAME parameter on line 11. Also, note that the DBMS_COMPARISON.COMPARE function returns a Boolean value on line 13. The following query returns some of the stored metadata about the differences detected by our table comparison:

```
SQL> SELECT  comparison_name
  2       ,  scan_id
  3       ,  status
  4    FROM  dba_comparison_row_dif
  5  /

COMPARISON_NAME                       SCAN_ID STA
----------------------------- ---------- ---
MY_COMPARE_NAME                            23 DIF
MY_COMPARE_NAME                            24 DIF
```

See that Oracle assigned a SCAN_ID for each row that is different. Further, observe that Oracle assigns a status of DIF in the STA column. Twelve data dictionary views display information about the changes:

- DBA_COMPARISON

- USER_COMPARISON

- DBA_COMPARISON_COLUMNS

- USER_COMPARISON_COLUMNS

- DBA_COMPARISON_SCAN

- USER_COMPARISON_SCAN

- DBA_COMPARISON_SCAN_SUMMARY

- USER_COMPARISON_SCAN_SUMMARYv

- DBA_COMPARISON_SCAN_VALUESv

- USER_COMPARISON_SCAN_VALUES

- DBA_COMPARISON_ROW_DIF

- USER_COMPARISON_ROW_DIF

We use the information from the view DBA_COMPARISON_ROW_DIF to drive the resynchronization of data between MEMBER#1 and MEMBER#2 in the following code block:

```
SQL> DECLARE
  2    lr_compare_results       DBMS_COMPARISON.COMPARISON_TYPE;
  3    lb_diff                  BOOLEAN;
  4    lv_message               VARCHAR2(10);
  5    ln_counter               NUMBER := 0;
  6
  7    CURSOR c_switch_back IS
  8      SELECT  comparison_name
  9           ,  scan_id
 10           ,  status
 11        FROM  dba_comparison_row_dif;
 12  BEGIN
 13    FOR r_switch_back IN c_switch_back LOOP
 14      DBMS_COMPARISON.CONVERGE   ( comparison_name      => 'my_compare_name'
 15                                 , scan_id              => r_switch_back.scan_id
 16                                 , scan_info            => lr_compare_results
 17                                 , converge_options     =>
 18  DBMS_COMPARISON.CMP_CONVERGE_LOCAL_WINS
 19                                 , perform_commit       => TRUE
 20                                 , local_converge_tag   => NULL
 21                                 , remote_converge_tag  => NULL
 22                                 );
 23
 24      lb_diff := DBMS_COMPARISON.RECHECK  ( 'my_compare_name'
 25                                          , r_switch_back.scan_id
 26                                          , true
 27                                          );
 28
 29      IF lb_diff = TRUE THEN
 30        DBMS_OUTPUT.PUT_LINE ( r_switch_back.scan_id||': is good.');
 31      ELSE
 32        DBMS_OUTPUT.PUT_LINE ( r_switch_back.scan_id||': is diff.');
 33        ln_counter := ln_counter + 1;
 34      END IF;
 35    END LOOP;
 36    IF ln_counter > 1 THEN
 37    DBMS_COMPARISON.PURGE_COMPARISON   ( 'my_compare_name' );
 38    DBMS_COMPARISON.DROP_COMPARISON    ( 'my_compare_name' );
 39    END IF;
 40  END;
 41  /
23: is good.
24: is good.

PL/SQL procedure successfully completed.
```

Notice that we check the value of LB_DIFF on line 29. If it is false, we bump up the LN_COUNTER variable by one. Once our code completes its FOR LOOP, we evaluate the counter value, purge the comparison results from our data dictionary views, and drop the comparison. Our final block displays the results of our synchronization:

```
SQL> SELECT  m1.member_id
  2       ,  m1.credit_card_number
  3       ,  m2.credit_card_number
  4    FROM  video_store.member#1 m1
  5       ,  video_store.member#2 m2
  6   WHERE  m1.member_id = m2.member_id
  7  /

MEMBER_ID CREDIT_CARD_NUMBER  CREDIT_CARD_NUMBER
--------- ------------------- ------------------------
        1 2862 6046 3527 5584 2862 6046 3527 5584
        2 3255 8814 2129 3834 3255 8814 2129 3834
```

The creation of this type of program, with the level of auditing and customizations, can span several hundred lines of code. Instead, our code spans 65. In addition, we do not have to figure out how to code the difference checker or maintain that code.

DBMS_FGA

Setting up Fine Grained Auditing (FGA) is one of the easier methods available in Oracle's built-in library. To do so, you use the Oracle built-in package DBMS_FGA to create audit policies. In the next example, we demonstrate this.

Example D-2: Using FGA to Audit Events   This block executes the DBMS_FGA.ADD_POLICY procedure:

```
SQL> BEGIN
  2    DBMS_FGA.ADD_POLICY ( object_schema    => 'VIDEO_STORE'
  3                        , object_name      => 'PRICE'
  4                        , policy_name      => 'AUDIT_PRICE_MODXML'
  5                        , audit_condition  => 'VIDEO_STORE.PRICE.AMOUNT < 1'
  6                        , audit_column     => 'AMOUNT'
  7                        , handler_schema   => NULL
  8                        , handler_module   => NULL
  9                        , enable           => TRUE
 10                        , statement_types  => 'INSERT, UPDATE'
```

```
11                    , audit_trail       => DBMS_FGA.XML + DBMS_FGA.EXTENDED
12                    , audit_column_opts => DBMS_FGA.ANY_COLUMNS
13                    );
14    END;
15    /
```

Observe that the entire setup spans only 15 lines of code. This is much easier than coding audit triggers. Oracle automatically logs an update of the VIDEO_STORE.PRICE table in the data dictionary:

```
SQL> UPDATE  video_store.price
  2      SET  amount = .25
  3    WHERE  active_flag = 'Y'
  4      AND  rownum <= 5
  5  /
5 rows updated.
The update is recorded even if you issue a rollback:
SQL> ROLLBACK
  2  /
Rollback complete.
```

If you issue the following query, using an account with rights to the V$XML_AUDIT_TRAIL view, you can see the results of our audit:

```
SQL> SELECT os_user
  2        , os_host
  3        , object_schema
  4        , object_name
  5        , policy_name
  6        , sql_bind
  7        , sql_text
  8     FROM V$XML_AUDIT_TRAIL
  9  /
```

OS_USER	OS_HOST	OBJECT_SCHEMA	OBJECT_NAME
harperjm	WORKGROUP\HARPERJM-PC	VIDEO_STORE	PRICE

POLICY_NAME	SQL_BIND	SQL_TEXT
AUDIT_PRICE_MODXML	(null)	UPDATE video_store.price SET amount = .25 ...

Notice that the audit policy captures user information and the SQL statement that violated our audit condition. Also, observe that we inserted only one row, instead of many rows for each record affected.

DBMS_OBFUSCATION_TOOLKIT

Correct implementation of encryption requires a balanced approach. For example, having no encryption will leave your database in a vulnerable state, while encrypting everything can bog it down, preventing scalability. It is absurd to think that either practice represents the best approach. If you are to succeed in securing your sensitive data, you must implement an executively backed data governance program that cognitively seeks balance between cost and feasibility.

Oracle provides the DBMS_OBFUSCATION_TOOLKIT, DBMS_CRYPTO, and tablespace encryption for your use in securing sensitive data. These methods can provide maximum protection to your data when implemented correctly.

The following example demonstrates all three encryption methods in the DBMS_OBFUSCATION_TOOLKIT package.

Example D-3: Overview of DBMS_OBFUSCATION_TOOLKIT   The U.S. government first introduced the Data Encryption Standard (DES) method in the early 1970s as a way to encrypt sensitive information; however, because of its age, hackers have had many years to work on cracking methods. For example, two German universities recently created a DES cracking machine (code named COPACOBANA) that can perform a brute-force attack in less than a week.

Obtaining/building a cracking machine like this is no small feat, and for some applications DES encryption is fine for discouraging hackers; however, the U.S. National Institutes of Standards and Technology (NIST) no longer recommends DES encryption. It is for this reason that you should choose modern Triple DES methods:

```
SQL> DECLARE
  2     lv_some_string          VARCHAR2(255);
  3     lv_some_key             VARCHAR2(255);
  4     lv_encrypted            VARCHAR2(255);
  5     lv_decrypted            VARCHAR2(255);
  6
  7     lr_encrypt_this         RAW(255);
  8     lr_seed_raw             RAW(255);
  9  BEGIN
 10     lv_some_string    := DBMS_RANDOM.STRING ( 'A',80);
 11     lr_seed_raw       := UTL_RAW.CAST_TO_RAW ( lv_some_string );
 12     lr_encrypt_this := UTL_RAW.CAST_TO_RAW ( 'TheQuickBrownFox' );
 13
 14     DBMS_OUTPUT.PUT_LINE ( RPAD ( 'Input String:', 18, ' ' )||'TheQuickBrownFox' )
```

```
15     ----------------------------------------------------------------------
16     -- DES Encryption
17     ----------------------------------------------------------------------
18     DBMS_OBFUSCATION_TOOLKIT.DESGETKEY ( seed  => lr_seed_raw
19                                        , key   => lv_some_key
20                                        );
21
22
23     DBMS_OBFUSCATION_TOOLKIT.DESENCRYPT ( input          => lr_encrypt_this
24                                         , key            => lv_some_key
25                                         , encrypted_data => lv_encrypted
26                                         );
27
28     DBMS_OBFUSCATION_TOOLKIT.DESDECRYPT ( input          => lv_encrypted
29                                         , key            => lv_some_key
30                                         , decrypted_data => lv_decrypted
31                                         );
32
33     lv_decrypted := UTL_RAW.CAST_TO_VARCHAR2 ( lv_decrypted );
34
35     DBMS_OUTPUT.PUT_LINE ( RPAD ( 'DES:', 18, ' ' )||lv_some_key );
36     DBMS_OUTPUT.PUT_LINE ( RPAD ( 'ENCRYPTED VALUE:', 18, ' ' )||lv_encrypted );
37     DBMS_OUTPUT.PUT_LINE ( RPAD ( 'DECRYPTED VALUE:', 18, ' ' )||lv_decrypted );
```

Oracle's Triple DES method increases key length from the 56 bits employed in standard DES to a potential of 128 bits in two-way and 192 bits in three-way encryption. If a hacker had a spare billion dollars lying around, and a team of cryptanalysts, he could crack this, too, providing that you *never* change your encryption key and provide no IV vector block to prepend your encrypted data.

The following block illustrates how we accomplish two-way Triple DES encryption with the DBMS_OBFUSCATION_TOOLKIT:

```
38     ----------------------------------------------------------------------
39     -- 2-way DES3 Encryption
40     ----------------------------------------------------------------------
41     DBMS_OBFUSCATION_TOOLKIT.DES3GETKEY ( which => 0
42                                         , seed  => lr_seed_raw
43                                         , key   => lv_some_key
44                                         );
45
46
47
48     DBMS_OBFUSCATION_TOOLKIT.DES3ENCRYPT ( input          => lr_encrypt_this
49                                          , key            => lv_some_key
50                                          , encrypted_data => lv_encrypted
51                                          , which          => 0
52                                          , iv             => NULL
53                                          );
54
55     DBMS_OBFUSCATION_TOOLKIT.DES3DECRYPT ( input          => lv_encrypted
56                                          , key            => lv_some_key
```

```
57                                     , decrypted_data  => lv_decrypted
58                                     , which           => 0
59                                     , iv              => NULL
60                                     );
61
62     lv_decrypted := UTL_RAW.CAST_TO_VARCHAR2 ( lv_decrypted );
63
64     DBMS_OUTPUT.PUT_LINE ( RPAD ( 'DES3GETKEY-2Way:', 18, ' ' )||lv_some_key );
65     DBMS_OUTPUT.PUT_LINE ( RPAD ( 'ENCRYPTED VALUE:', 18, ' ' )||lv_encrypted );
66     DBMS_OUTPUT.PUT_LINE ( RPAD ( 'DECRYPTED VALUE:', 18, ' ' )||lv_decrypted );
```

This block demonstrates three-way Triple DES:

```
67     -----------------------------------------------------------------------------
68     -- 3-way DES3 Encryption
69     -----------------------------------------------------------------------------
70     DBMS_OBFUSCATION_TOOLKIT.DES3GETKEY ( which => 1
71                                         , seed  => lr_seed_raw
72                                         , key   => lv_some_key
73                                         );
74
75     DBMS_OBFUSCATION_TOOLKIT.DES3ENCRYPT ( input           => lr_encrypt_this
76                                          , key             => lv_some_key
77                                          , encrypted_data  => lv_encrypted
78                                          , which           => 1
79                                          , iv              => NULL
80                                          );
81
82     DBMS_OBFUSCATION_TOOLKIT.DES3DECRYPT ( input           => lv_encrypted
83                                          , key             => lv_some_key
84                                          , decrypted_data  => lv_decrypted
85                                          , which           => 1
86                                          , iv              => NULL
87                                          );
88
89     lv_decrypted := UTL_RAW.CAST_TO_VARCHAR2 ( lv_decrypted );
90
91     DBMS_OUTPUT.PUT_LINE ( RPAD ( 'DES3GETKEY-3Way:', 18, ' ' )||lv_some_key );
92     DBMS_OUTPUT.PUT_LINE ( RPAD ( 'ENCRYPTED VALUE:', 18, ' ' )||lv_encrypted );
93     DBMS_OUTPUT.PUT_LINE ( RPAD ( 'DECRYPTED VALUE:', 18, ' ' )||lv_decrypted );
94     END;
95     /
```

Our anonymous block produces the following results:

```
Input String:       TheQuickBrownFox
DES:                2F43F881B336FC30
ENCRYPTED VALUE:    1F98C4444A8ECC54EEB0E68E800370C2
DECRYPTED VALUE:    TheQuickBrownFox
DES3GETKEY-2Way:    6141D71B08826C1DD974BD4ABFE4CE9A
ENCRYPTED VALUE:    8F66F8315A07456DCD92D85ADFE98F2B
DECRYPTED VALUE:    TheQuickBrownFox
```

```
DES3GETKEY-3Way:  A9605F4198EEBDE9D174F372B7F0F769093EA1846DD88C5C
ENCRYPTED VALUE:  ACBB314321390BF65E6F5A04EE2B2302
DECRYPTED VALUE:  TheQuickBrownFox

PL/SQL procedure successfully completed.
```

Observe that switching from two-way to three-way encryption required that the WHICH parameter be changed from 0 to 1. Also, note that we used an encryption key length of 80 characters, the minimum for both methods. You should adjust your key length as needed. Best practices include the following:

- Use a key that is of adequate length.

- Change that key periodically.

- Use an IV vector to make each message unique.

While we created this example to demonstrate all three encryption procedures in the DBMS_OBFUSCATION_TOOLKIT package, it is academic in nature. The next example illustrates how we use the DESENCRYPT package in a more realistic manner.

Example D-4: DBMS_OBFUSCATION_TOOLKIT.DESENCRYPT   This ALTER TABLE command modifies the CREDIT_CARD_NUMBER column in the VIDEO_STORE.MEMBER table to accept a larger encrypted value:

```
SQL> ALTER TABLE video_store.member
  2    MODIFY ( credit_card_number varchar2(250) )
  3  /
```

This ALTER TABLE command adds the column CREDIT_CARD_LAST4 to the MEMBER table:

```
SQL> ALTER TABLE video_store.member
  2    ADD     ( credit_card_last4 varchar2(20))
  3  /
```

The following package specification contains only one procedure:

```
SQL> CREATE OR REPLACE PACKAGE
  2    video_store.encryption
  3    AUTHID CURRENT_USER
  4    AS
  5
```

```
 6      PROCEDURE cc_encrypt  ( pi_key          in  varchar2
 7                            , pi_clear_txt    in  varchar2
 8                            , po_encrypted    out varchar2
 9                            );
10  END encryption;
11  /
```

Our package body is short because most of the procedural code exists in the DBMS_OBFUSCATION_TOOLKIT package. As a result, the package specification and body total 30 lines of code:

```
SQL> CREATE OR REPLACE PACKAGE body video_store.encryption
  2     AS
  3     PROCEDURE cc_encrypt  ( pi_key          in  varchar2
  4                           , pi_clear_txt    in  varchar2
  5                           , po_encrypted    out varchar2
  6                           )
  7     IS
  8       lv_data            varchar2(50);
  9     BEGIN
 10       lv_data :=  RPAD  ( pi_clear_txt
 11                         , ( TRUNC ( LENGTH ( pi_clear_txt ) / 8 ) + 1 ) * 8
 12                         ,   CHR(0) );
 13
 14       DBMS_OBFUSCATION_TOOLKIT.DESENCRYPT ( input_string      => lv_data
 15                                           , key_string        => pi_key
 16                                           , encrypted_string  => po_encrypted
 17                                           );
 18     END cc_encrypt;
 19  END encryption;
 20  /
```

We display the results of our package in the following query:

```
SQL> SELECT   member_id
  2         ,  credit_card_number
  3         ,  credit_card_last4
  4      FROM  video_store.member
  5  /
MEMBER_ID CREDIT_CARD_NUMBER                   CREDIT_CARD_LAST4
--------- ----------------------------------   -----------------------------
     1001 ++éàñ7+c·=·æS++o?-?÷ç¯ (              ************4444
     1002 o¢n?  e   -r=S?·¢n~H+-?=+ç            ************5555
     1003 8     - ˜-?¥~?‰Øƒ h[s+•               ************6666
```

Your implementation of DESENCRYPT may be more complex, because, in a production environment, you need to manage encryption keys and segregation of duties between key owners.

We encourage you to study the *Oracle Database PL/SQL Packages and Types Reference*. This guide should be the first place you look when asked to implement a particular feature.

APPENDIX
E

Mastery Check
Answers

his appendix contains the answer key to mastery check questions from the chapters in the book. Brief explanations and code examples also appear for the problems. It is organized by chapter.

Chapter 1

Here are the questions and answers for Chapter 1:

1. ■ **True** ☐ **False**   You use DDL statements to create tables.

    The answer is **True**. You use the CREATE statement to create tables, and it is a DDL statement.

2. ■ **True** ☐ **False**   You use DML statements to manipulate data.

    The answer is **True**. You use INSERT, UPDATE, DELETE, and SELECT statements to manipulate data, and they change data or query it.

3. ■ **True** ☐ **False**   You use DCL statements to grant or revoke privileges.

    The answer is **True**. You use a GRANT or REVOKE statement to grant or revoke privileges.

4. ☐ **True** ■ **False**   You use TCL statements to control timestamps.

    The answer is **False**. You use TCL statements to control transactions; they include SAVEPOINT, COMMIT, and ROLLBACK.

5. ☐ **True** ■ **False**   A SELECT statement is a DQL statement, not a DML statement, in all cases.

    The answer is **False**. You use should consider the SELECT statement as a DML statement for Oracle certification purposes. However, one school of thought believes the SELECT should be a DQL statement, not a DML statement.

6. ☐ **True** ■ **False**   The PL/SQL version numbers have always been synchronized with the Oracle Database release numbers.

The answer is **False**. Check Figure 1-1, which shows that PL/SQL
was version 1 in Oracle 6, version 2 in Oracle 7, and finally
synchronized with the database release with Oracle Database 8 in
1997.

7. ☐ **True**   ■ **False**   You can't connect without a network alias.

The answer is **False**. You can connect without a network alias. You
can connect as local if you're the user who installed the product or
with a fully qualified Oracle TNS string.

8. ☐ **True**   ■ **False**   You must have a local copy of a `tnsnames.ora`
file when you use Oracle Client software.

The answer is **False**. You should have a `tnsnames.ora` file, but
you don't need one if you provide the fully qualified Oracle TNS
string.

9. ■ **True**   ☐ **False**   Oracle, unlike MySQL, includes its listener
service as a separate process from its database
server-side daemon.

The answer is **True**. You have a listener process that is separate from
the database in the Oracle product. This is a departure from
competing database management systems, and it allows Oracle to
use a single listener and port to support multiple databases.

10. ☐ **True**   ■ **False**   You can spool individual script files without
interfering with a session spool file.

The answer is **False**. You can't spool individual script files inside a
spool sequence. The second spool kills the first one. Not even a
partial log file is written because the file is never closed.

11. Which are valid two-tier communication types?

    A. Oracle standalone communication

    B. Oracle client communication

    C. JDBC communication

    D. All of the above

    E. Only B and C

The answer is **D**. They're all valid data two-tier communication types.

12. Which of the following is a valid JDBC driver for Oracle 11g?

   A. The `ojdbc6_g.jar` file

   B. The `ojdbc6.jar` file

   C. The `ojdbc5.jar` file

   D. All of the above

   E. Only A and B

   The answer is **D**. They're all valid JDBC drivers for Oracle 11g.

13. Which of the following does Oracle deploy with each release of the database server?

   A. The Oracle Client software

   B. The JDBC driver files

   C. The ODBC driver files

   D. All of the above

   E. Only A and B

   The answer is **D**. Oracle ships the server with the client software installed, and the current ODBC and JDBC driver files.

14. Where does the state-aware connection exist in a three-tier model?

   A. Between the JServlet middle-tier and the database

   B. Between the client and the database

   C. Between the Apache server and the database

   D. All of the above

   E. Only B and C

The answer is **B**. A JServlet would contain a multithreaded connection class, which is generally implemented following the Singleton OOAD pattern. The client in a three-tier solution communicates to middle-tier and generally is a stateless connection. The Apache Server hands off the connection to an Apache module (Apache mod), which is where the connection pool and state-aware connection would be maintained.

15. Which tier can create pooled connections to share?

    A. The client

    B. The server

    C. The middle-tier

    D. None of the above

    E. Only A and B

    The answer is **C**. Only the middle-tier qualifies. The client typically shares nothing other than a connection spawned by a middle-tier component. The server supports pooled connections but only when you configure the `listener.ora` file to support them. The server doesn't create the pooled connections; that's the responsibility of external software.

Chapter 2

Here are the questions and answers for Chapter 2:

1. ☐ **True**   ■ **False**   You can define a block without a statement in it.

    The answer is **False**. You must have at least a `NULL;` statement in a block or you raise a compile time exception.

2. ☐ **True**   ■ **False**   You can use the `ELSE IF` block in an `IF` block.

    The answer is **False**. You can do an `ELSE IF` in an `IF` block but the syntax is `ELSIF` in PL/SQL.

3. ■ **True** ☐ **False** You can define and use a RECORD structure in PL/SQL.

The answer is **True**. You can and must define a RECORD structure in PL/SQL because it is an exclusively PL/SQL context variable.

4. ■ **True** ☐ **False** You can define an OBJECT type in SQL or PL/SQL.

The answer is **True**. When you define an OBJECT type in PL/SQL, you narrow its scope to PL/SQL only. Inside a package specification, you can use it in other external programs. Inside a package body, OBJECT type, or anonymous block program, you can use it on in that scope. In SQL, it becomes globally available within the schema, and globally within the database with a public synonym and appropriate grant.

5. ■ **True** ☐ **False** You can use a *for* loop when you know the exit condition in advanced and you're guarding exit not entrance to the loop.

The answer is **True**. You must know the upward bound of a range *for* loop, and the number of rows returned by a cursor sets the upward bound of a cursor *for* loop.

6. ■ **True** ☐ **False** A *while* loop guards on entry.

The answer is **True**. A *while* loop guards on entry, which means a condition must be met before you can enter the iterative structure.

7. ☐ **True** ■ **False** A simple loop must work with a cursor.

The answer is **False**. You can and often do work with a cursor in a simple loop, but that's not a requirement. All you must do is know why you are looping and when to exit when a condition is met.

8. ☐ **True** ■ **False** You use the CONTINUE statement to exit a loop.

The answer is **False**. You can use the CONTINUE statement to stop the process in a loop, but it doesn't exit the loop. It simply returns execution to the top of the loop for the next iteration.

9. ☐ **True** ■ **False**   Like Java, PL/SQL makes the GOTO a keyword, but doesn't let you use it.

The answer is **False**. You can actually use the GOTO a keyword, which means you can write lousy code. We've found that the GOTO statement is typically a poor solution for loop control and an indicator of potential problems.

10. ■ **True** ☐ **False**   The BULK COLLECT INTO lets you select a complete cursor or a range of rows from a cursor into a collection of a record structure.

The answer is **True**. You can use a BULK COLLECT INTO statement for a complete cursor or a range of rows from a cursor into a collection of a record structure. You limit it to a set of rows with the LIMIT keyword.

11. Which are valid PL/SQL data types?

   A. BOOLEAN

   B. PLS_INTEGER

   C. BINARY_DOUBLE

   D. All of the above

   E. Only A and B

The answer is **D**. They're all valid data types in Oracle 11*g*.

12. Which of the following are valid cursor attributes?

   A. %FOUND

   B. %ISOPEN

   C. %COUNT

   D. All of the above

   E. Only A and B

The answer is **E**. %FOUND and %ISOPEN are valid cursor attributes, and so is %ROWCOUNT and %NOTFOUND. However, %COUNT is invalid.

13. Which of the following are label delimiters?

A. <>

B. <<>>

C. {}

D. All of the above

E. Only A and B

The answer is **B**. Those symbols are called *guillemets,* also known as angle brackets, and they're used for labels only in PL/SQL.

14. Which is the correct way to descend through a range of numbers in a FOR loop?

A. FOR i IN 10..1 LOOP

B. FOR i IN 1..10 REVERSE LOOP

C. FOR i IN REVERSE 1..10 LOOP

D. All of the above

E. Only B and C

The answer is **B**. The first digit must be lower than the second when connected by the .. range operator, and the REVERSE keyword must follow the range. It can't precede the range values.

15. Which syntax ends a FORALL statement?

A. END FORALL;

B. END LOOP;

C. END FORALL LOOP;

D. None of the above

E. Only A and B

The answer is **D**. You put a FORALL inside a loop, but it doesn't have a closing block statement; it's an exception to the blocking rules of the language.

Chapter 3

Here are the questions and answers for Chapter 3:

1. ■ **True** ☐ **False** The acronym ACID represents a standard for transaction processing in relational databases.

The answer is **True**. This is the definition, and without it we can't have multiuser database products.

2. ■ **True** ☐ **False** Atomicity means all or no part of a transaction is written to permanent storage.

The answer is **True**. This is the definition, and without it we can't have multiuser database products.

3. ■ **True** ☐ **False** Consistency means that all transactions in a concurrent, multiuser system are granted even amounts of time to the server's CPU and memory.

The answer is **True**. This is the definition, and without it we can't have multiuser database products.

4. ■ **True** ☐ **False** Isolation means that no part of a transaction can be seen until all of it is completed and committed to the database.

The answer is **True**. This is the definition, and without it we can't have multiuser database products.

5. ■ **True** ☐ **False** Durability means that transactions are written to redundant disk arrays after the transaction is complete.

The answer is **True**. This is the definition, and without it we can't have multiuser database products.

6. ■ **True** ☐ **False** A SAVEPOINT lets you set a marker that lets you undo transactions that occur after the SAVEPOINT without undoing the transactions before the SAVEPOINT.

The answer is **True**. The SAVEPOINT sets a marker, which lets you undo it, or you may ignore it and undo everything since the last COMMIT or the start of a session.

7. ■ **True**   □ **False**   A rollback lets you undo everything in the session since you signed on, and can ignore SAVEPOINT markers that you've set.

The answer is **True**. The rollback can undo to a SAVEPOINT, the last COMMIT, or the start of a session.

8. □ **True**   ■ **False**   A rollback lets you undo everything in the session since you set a SAVEPOINT.

The answer is **False**. Not quite right, because it can do more. The rollback can undo to a SAVEPOINT, the last COMMIT, or the start of a session.

9. □ **True**   ■ **False**   A COMMIT is always automatic with each DML statement.

The answer is **False**. You can enable auto commit, but generally a COMMIT is required explicitly. For reference, the Oracle Application Express product ships with auto commit enabled.

10. □ **True**   ■ **False**   The NOWAIT option of a COMMIT ensures that you validate all writes to the redo and archive log files.

The answer is **False**. The NOWAIT does the opposite: it doesn't validate the writing of changes to the redo and archive log files.

11. Which are valid sequencing patterns for a transaction?

    A. A SAVEPOINT, COMMIT, and ROLLBACK

    B. A SAVEPOINT, ROLLBACK, and COMMIT

    C. A SAVEPOINT and COMMIT

    D. All of the above

    E. Only B and C

The answer is **E**. you can set a SAVEPOINT, and then ROLLBACK to it before a COMMIT, or you can set a SAVEPOINT, not ROLLBACK, and simply COMMIT the work.

12. Which of the following is not part of the ACID acronym?

    A. Acid

    B. Concurrency

    C. Isolation

    D. Durability

    E. None of the above

    The answer is **B**. While concurrency is an aim, *consistency* is the keyword of the acronym.

13. The acronym MVCC represents Oracle's attempt to achieve what?

    A. A multiuser voice communication concurrency protocol

    B. A multiversioned concurrency control for database consistency

    C. A multidatabase virtual community concurrency protocol

    D. All of the above

    E. None of the above

    The answer is **B**. the MVCC acronym represents multiversioned concurrency control and supports Oracle's ability to keep consistent snapshots.

14. Which of these parameters let you extend or shorten how long the database retains transaction history?

    A. An UNDO_WAIT parameter

    B. An UNDO_LOCK parameter

    C. An UNDO_RETENTION parameter

    D. All of the above

    E. Only A and B

    The answer is **C**. The UNDO_RETENTION parameter sets the length of time that a statement runs in memory.

15. Which of these are valid lock modes in an Oracle database?

    A. A `ROW SHARE` parameter

    B. A `SHARE` parameter

    C. A `ROW EXCLUSIVE` parameter

    D. All of the above

    E. Only A and C

The answer is **D**. All of these are valid lock modes. The missing two are `SHARE ROW EXCLUSIVE` and `EXCLUSIVE`.

Chapter 4

Here are the questions and answers for Chapter 4:

1. ☐ **True** ■ **False**   Semantic errors occur at compile time.

The answer is **False**. *Semantic errors* are another phrase for *runtime errors*.

2. ■ **True** ☐ **False**   You should always filter in-bound web parameters with the `DBMS_ASSERT` package.

The answer is **True**. The `DBMS_ASSERT` package allows you to validate input parameters and should always validate input parameters according to Open Web Application Security Project (owasp.org).

3. ■ **True** ☐ **False**   Compile-time errors happen when you use improper syntax or keywords.

The answer is **True**. *Compile-time errors* happen when you use improper identifiers, identifiers can be keywords, symbols, or operators.

4. ☐ **True** ■ **False**   `DRG-` errors are related to the `DBVERIFY` utility.

The answer is **False**. `DRG-` errors are related to Oracle Text problems.

5. ■ **True**   ☐ **False**   `PLS-` errors are related to PL/SQL.

The answer is **True**. `PLS-` errors are PL/SQL errors.

6. ■ **True**   ☐ **False**   `ORA-` errors are related to general database errors and SQL.

The answer is **True**. `ORA-` errors are related to general database errors and SQL.

7. ☐ **True**   ■ **False**   `LPX-` errors are related to InterMedia.

The answer is **False**. `LPX-` errors are related to XML.

8. ☐ **True**   ■ **False**   The `RAISE_APPLICATION_ERROR` lets you throw a custom exception and is equivalent to the `RAISE` statement.

The answer is **False**. The `RAISE_APPLICATION_ERROR` lets you throw a custom exception, but isn't equivalent to the `RAISE` statement. The `RAISE` statement lets you through a predefined `EXCEPTION` variable that you have in your declaration block.

9. ☐ **True**   ■ **False**   The `EXCEPTION_INIT` is a `PRAGMA` that lets you use default exceptions in your PL/SQL block.

The answer is **False**. It's not quite correct that the `EXCEPTION_INIT` is a `PRAGMA` that lets you use default exceptions in your PL/SQL block. `EXCEPTION_INIT` lets you map a default error number to a user-defined variable, which you can then throw with the `RAISE` statement.

10. ■ **True**   ☐ **False**   The SQLCODE returns the error code number for a thrown error in your PL/SQL block.

The answer is **True**. SQLCODE returns the error code number for a thrown error in your PL/SQL block.

11. Which of the following error code prefixes might you see working with the import utility?

   A. `EXP-`

   B. `IMP-`

C. KUP-

D. All of the above

E. Only A and C

The answer is **B**. IMP- prefixes the import utility errors.

12. Which of the following error code prefixes might you see working with the export utility?

   A. IMP-

   B. EXP-

   C. KUP-

   D. All of the above

   E. Only B and C

   The answer is **B**. EXP- prefixes the export utility errors.

13. Which of the following error code prefixes might you see working with external tables?

   A. IMP-

   B. EMP-

   C. KUP-

   D. All of the above

   E. None of the above

   The answer is **C**. KUP- prefixes the external table errors with both SQL*Loader and Oracle Data Pump.

14. You use a PRAGMA EXCEPTION_INIT to do what?

   A. Declare a user-defined exception.

   B. Enable a user-defined exception.

   C. Create an exception name that maps to an Oracle error code number.

D. All of the above.

E. Only A and C.

The answer is **C**. `PRAGMA EXCEPTION_INIT` maps a known Oracle error number to a user-defined exception variable.

15. What must you do to throw the call `RAISE_APPLICATION_ERROR` function?

A. You first set the `PRAGMA EXCEPTION_INIT` in the program block.

B. You use a range of error numbers between -20,000 and -20,999.

C. You must declare a variable of the `EXCEPTION` type.

D. All of the above.

E. Only B and C.

The answer is **B**. The `RAISE_APPLICATION_ERROR` stands more or less independent from the other tools. It lets you raise a custom user-defined error and message text anywhere in your PL/SQL programs.

Chapter 5

Here are the questions and answers for Chapter 5:

1. ■ **True**   □ **False**   You can use positional call notation when passing only mandatory parameters, provided all optional parameters are at the end of the signature.

The answer is **True**. You can use positional call notation when passing only mandatory parameters when all optional parameters follow them in sequence. You can also use it by passing optional parameters as null values if they're interspersed in the parameter list.

2. □ **True**   ■ **False**   You can use positional references after named references when using a mixed call notation.

The answer is **False**. You can't use positional references after named references. You can use positional references only before any named references.

3. ■ **True** □ **False** You define a deterministic function when you can guarantee that it works the same way all the time.

The answer is **True**. You define deterministic functions only when you can guarantee that they work the same way all the time.

4. ■ **True** □ **False** The PARALLEL_ENABLE clause tells the optimizer that a function is safe to parallelize.

The answer is **True**. You use the PARALLEL_ENABLE clause to advertise that a function is safe to parallelize. If you forget to use the clause, the cost optimizer checks anyway.

5. □ **True** ■ **False** Pipelined table functions are indispensable tools that let you manage collections of object types.

The answer is **False**. You can't use a pipelined table function with a collection of object types. They are indispensable tools when you want to leverage an associative array of PL/SQL record types in a SQL context.

6. □ **True** ■ **False** You can define RESULT_CACHE functions to work with any type of SQL collection data type.

The answer is **False**. You use a RESULT_CACHE function to work with any type of a *scalar* SQL collection type. A collection type of an object type isn't supported by the current Oracle Database 11*g* version of result caching.

7. ■ **True** □ **False** The RELIES_ON clause creates a dependency between the cached function results and a table, which discards the function results when the table data changes.

The answer is **True**. You use the RELIES_ON clause anchor a result set to the current state of a table or view.

8. □ **True** ■ **False** You can put DML statements inside functions that are callable from queries.

The answer is **False**. You can't put a DML statement inside a function when you plan to call it from inside a query. That is an unsupported behavior.

9. ■ **True**   □ **False**   You can define recursive functions in PL/SQL.

The answer is **True**. You can define recursive functions in PL/SQL.

10. ■ **True**   □ **False**   The default mode of formal parameter operation in PL/SQL supports a pass-by-value function type.

The answer is **True**. You never have to enter IN mode when that's all you want, because it is the default. IN mode means a pass-by-value model. In some cases, Oracle provides a reference to the external variable, but you can't change the contents inside a called execution scope.

11. What are the valid clauses that describe functions in PL/SQL?

A. A RESULT_CACHE clause

B. A RELIES_ON clause

C. A PIPELINED clause

D. All of the above

E. Only A and C

The answer is **E**. RESULT_CACHE and PIPELINED are function clauses, while RELIES_ON is a subclause of a RESULT_CACHE function.

12. What mode(s) of operation supports a pass-by-reference parameter?

A. The IN mode

B. The IN OUT mode

C. The OUT mode

D. All of the above

E. Only B and C

The answer is **E**. The IN mode is the only pass-by-value semantic in PL/SQL. The others are pass-by-reference. IN OUT takes a reference in with a value and returns a reference to potentially a different value. OUT takes a reference in without a value and returns a reference to a different value.

13. A pipelined table function typically returns what type of variable?

  A. A SQL collection of an object data type

  B. A PL/SQL collection of a record data type

  C. A PL/SQL record data type

  D. All of the above

  E. Only B and C

The answer is **B**. That's the purpose of a pipelined table function. It converts a PL/SQL collection to a SQL aggregate table or a normal SQL return result set.

14. What type of function would you use in a materialized view?

  A. A deterministic function

  B. A parallel-enabled function

  C. A pipelined table function

  D. All of the above

  E. Only A and B

The answer is **E**. While deterministic functions always work in materialized views, sometimes deterministic functions can be parallel-enabled.

15. What makes a pipelined function necessary?

  A. Calling the function with a collection data type in the parameter list

  B. Calling the function inside a SQL context

  C. Calling the function inside a PL/SQL context

  D. All of the above

  E. Only B and C

The answer is **B**. Pipelined functions convert PL/SQL collections to SQL aggregate tables.

Chapter 6

Here are the questions and answers for Chapter 6:

1. ☐ **True** ■ **False** You can use a procedure as a right operand in another PL/SQL block.

    The answer is **False**. You can't use a procedure as a right operand, because unlike a function that returns a data type, it returns none.

2. ☐ **True** ■ **False** You can use session-level bind variables inside procedure definitions.

    The answer is **False**. You can't use a session level bind variable inside a procedure. Functions and procedures accept parameters through their respective formal parameter lists. Only anonymous block programs have external access to calling scope variables, and then only when they don't override the variable name.

3. ☐ **True** ■ **False** You should declare variables by assigning them static or dynamic call parameter values inside the procedure's declaration block.

    The answer is **False**. You can assign call parameter values to local variables inside the declaration block, but you shouldn't. Any assignment that fails in the declaration block can't be captured by a local exception handler. The exception is thrown to the calling scope program unit.

4. ■ **True** ☐ **False** You can call a procedure without a parameter list when all parameters have default values.

    The answer is **True**. You can call a procedure with only its name when all of its parameters are optional, which means that they have default values.

5. ☐ **True** ■ **False** You can exclude open and closed parentheses when no call parameters are included.

    The answer is **False**. You can exclude open and closed parentheses when no formal parameters are defined for a function or procedure. You can't exclude them when the function or procedure has only optional parameters. Calling a function with only optional parameters returns an "X" from a query and raises an ORA-06576 from a statement like this:

```
CALL function_name INTO :bind_variable;
```

6. ■ **True**　□ **False**　Procedures are best suited to managing a transaction inside another PL/SQL block's execution scope.

The answer is **True**. You should as a rule use procedures when you want to perform some activity inside the scope of another function. Naturally, the rules for defining procedures as activities are (1) isolate the logic, and (2) implement a reusable component.

7. □ **True**　■ **False**　Procedures should always include a COMMIT unless they're called as autonomous program units.

The answer is **False**. You should use a COMMIT only inside a procedure when it performs as an autonomous program unit. If you put a COMMIT inside a procedure and call the procedure inside an all-or-nothing transaction scope, the internal COMMIT saves part of the transaction before the whole transaction is complete. This can cause a problem with your transactional management.

8. □ **True**　■ **False**　There is no practical alternative to procedures that use cursors to check for records before deciding to insert a new row or update an existing role.

The answer is **False**. You can use a function as an alternative. We'd recommend that you use a function when the activity is a standalone process, which means its an autonomous execution scope. This is true for database transaction models and models called from web applications.

9. □ **True**　■ **False**　Insert statements inside a procedure can call local functions defined in the procedure.

The answer is **False**. You can't call local functions or procedures from inside SQL statements because they're not available inside the database catalog. You can call schema-level, published package, and object type static functions and procedures from SQL because they're defined in the database catalog.

10. ☐ **True**   ■ **False**   Autonomous transaction procedures should always use default IN mode formal parameters.

The answer is **False**. You can use an autonomous transaction procedure with an IN-only, IN OUT, or OUT-only parameter mode. You should generally use an IN OUT or OUT-only parameter mode on at least one of the parameters because the return value may advise your calling scope program about whether the procedure completed or failed.

11. Which are valid clauses in a PL/SQL procedure?

A. A RESULT_CACHE clause

B. A RELIES_ON clause

C. A PIPELINED clause

D. None of the above

E. Only A and C

The answer is **D**. Procedures don't support these function clauses.

12. What mode(s) of operation supports a pass-by-value parameter?

A. The IN mode

B. The IN OUT mode

C. The OUT mode

D. All of the above

E. Only B and C

The answer is **A**. The IN mode alone passes a copy of a value, though it may be a reference to a value that is treated as a copy. An IN mode variable can't be an assignment target.

13. What PRAGMA lets you create an autonomous procedure?

A. An AUTONOMOUS_FUNCTION

B. An AUTONOMOUS_PROCEDURE

    C. An `AUTONOMOUS_TRANSACTION`

    D. All of the above

    E. Only B and C

The answer is **C**. The others don't exist; they're provided to trick you like a certification question.

14. What mode of operation should a pass-by-reference procedure use?

    A. An `IN` mode

    B. An `IN OUT` mode

    C. An `OUT` mode

    D. All of the above

    E. Only B and C

The answer is **E**. `IN OUT` and `OUT` are parameter references. The `OUT` mode presents a problem when the variable doesn't have a correct size in the calling scope block.

15. What is the biggest problem with using pass-by-value procedures in web-based applications?

    A. It is difficult to prepare a JDBC statement for a procedure.

    B. It is difficult to prepare a PHP statement for a procedure.

    C. There is no way to confirm processing without a subsequent query.

    D. All of the above

    E. Only A and B

The answer is **C**. A pass-by-value procedure can't signal its success or failure unless you raise an exception. Prepared statements in external programming languages are difficult to write.

Chapter 7

Here are the questions and answers for Chapter 7:

1. □ **True**   ■ **False**   You can create collections only with numeric indexes.

   The answer is **True**. You can create varray and nested tables only with numeric indexes, but associative arrays can be created with numeric or string indexes.

2. □ **True**   ■ **False**   You can create a SQL collection with only scalar data types.

   The answer is **False**. You can create collections of scalar, SQL object types (structures with constructors), and PL/SQL record types. Varrays and nested tables can create only collections of scalar and SQL object types. Associative arrays can use all of the potential base data types.

3. ■ **True**   □ **False**   You can create a PL/SQL collection of varrays and nested tables.

   The answer is **True**. You can create any type of collection in a PL/SQL scope.

4. □ **True**   ■ **False**   You can create an associative array as a SQL collection.

   The answer is **False**. You can create associative array only in a PL/SQL scope. While you can define them to work inside functions, they fail at runtime.

5. ■ **True**   □ **False**   You can create SQL collections of SQL object types.

   The answer is **True**. You can create varrays and nested tables of SQL object types. The only caveat is that you must use a constructor to populate each element in the collection.

6. ■ **True** □ **False** You can create PL/SQL collections of PL/SQL record types.

The answer is **True**. You can create varrays, nested table, and associative arrays that use a PL/SQL record type as their base data type. You must call them in an exclusively PL/SQL scope.

7. □ **True** ■ **False** All three collection types can access all of the methods in the Oracle Collection API.

The answer is **False**. You can't use the LIMIT function with anything but the varray. You also can't use the EXTEND method with an associative array.

8. □ **True** ■ **False** Collections are always defined with densely populated indexes when they're defined in SQL.

The answer is **False**. You define collections without indexes. Indexes are declared at runtime, unless you declare an index as a constant inside a PL/SQL declaration block.

9. ■ **True** □ **False** Varray index values cannot have gaps in the index.

The answer is **True**. You can't delete elements from the middle of a varray. You must remove the last or highest element first.

10. ■ **True** □ **False** Nested table index values can have gaps when elements are deleted after the collection is created.

The answer is **True**. You can delete elements from the middle of a nested table. While they must be declared initially with a densely populated index, it is possible to delete an element from the middle of a collection. Checking for a gap is a good coding practice, since you could receive one that isn't densely populated from a function. That precaution avoids an ugly SQL error.

11. Which of the following Collection APIs work with varrays?

  A. A COUNT method

  B. A LIMIT method

C. A LAST method

D. All of the above

E. Only A and C

The answer is **D**. All of these work with a varray. The LIMIT method works only with a varray data type.

12. Which of the following Collection APIs work with nested tables and associative arrays?

   A. The COUNT method

   B. The LIMIT method

   C. The LAST method

   D. All of the above

   E. Only A and C

   The answer is **E**. Only the COUNT and LAST methods work with an associative array. The LIMIT method works only with a varray data type.

13. You can define a nested table with which of the following base data types?

   A. A scalar data type, such as a date, number, or string

   B. A PL/SQL record type, such as a structure or single row table definition

   C. A SQL object type, such as a structure or single row table definition, except you populate it through a constructor call

   D. All of the above

   E. Only A and B

   The answer is **D**. All of these work with a nested table. The PL/SQL record type works only when you restrict the nested table to a PL/SQL scope.

14. An associative array can be indexed by which of the following?

   A. A date

   B. An integer

   C. A string

   D. All of the above

   E. Only B and C

   The answer is **E**. Only an integer or string work as an index.

15. In a table function, not a pipelined table function, which data types can you return?

   A. A varray of any base scalar data type

   B. A nested table of any base scalar data type

   C. An associative array of any base scalar data type

   D. All of the above

   E. Only A and B

   The answer is **E**. Only the SQL data types work in SQL. This means that only a varray and nested table work in SQL, provided they're defined in SQL as schema-level collections.

Chapter 8

Here are the questions and answers for Chapter 8:

   1. ■ **True**   ☐ **False**   You can increase the organization or cohesion of
                                     programs by putting them into packages.

   The answer is **True**. You generally increase the cohesion of programs by colocating them in the same package.

   2. ■ **True**   ☐ **False**   Oracle uses an Interface Description Language
                                     (IDL) to maximize interoperability between
                                     stored programs.

The answer is **True**. The use of IDL has improved the consistency of interoperability and support for development of functions and procedures in other languages. You can find an example of this interoperability in the Java libraries of Chapter 12, or you can refer to Chapter 15 in *Oracle Database 11g PL/SQL Programming*.

3. ☐ **True**   ■ **False**   Oracle's adoption of Descriptive Intermediate Attribute Notion for ADA (DIANA) doesn't limit the physical size of stored functions and procedures.

The answer is **False**. *DIANA* physically limits the size of standalone functions and procedures but doesn't limit the physical size of packages.

4. ☐ **True**   ■ **False**   `PRAGMA SERIALLY_REUSABLE` tells the compiler to initialize a package in the UGA instead of the SGA.

The answer is **False**. Not quite right: the opposite is true. It instantiates the package in the SGA, not the UGA, which once caused problems because cursors weren't exclusive in their execution. It appears that was fixed in Oracle 10g Release 2, but we couldn't find an official statement in the documentation.

5. ■ **True**   ☐ **False**   Subprogram names and parameter signatures must match exactly between package specification and body.

The answer is **True**. The match is absolute. The list of parameters must be unique. Default parameters must also agree between package specifications and bodies, which was introduced in Oracle 9*i*.

6. ■ **True**   ☐ **False**   Local functions and procedures in the package body are private to the other external program units.

The answer is **True**. Any local functions and procedures are private to the PL/SQL block where they are defined. In a package body, functions and procedures defined in the header are available throughout the package, and this access level is package-level, not local.

7. ■ **True** ☐ **False** The SYS_STUB_FOR_PURITY_ANALYSIS package lets you assert the consistent state of stored functions and procedures.

The answer is **True**. The question states exactly what the Oracle database PL/SQL compilation process states. It checks for consistent state of stored functions and procedures, but it also performs what's known as a lazy compile. At call time, a function or procedure is validated when previously invalid provided the invalidating condition was repaired.

8. ■ **True** ☐ **False** The %TYPE anchors a program variable to a column in a table.

The answer is **True**. The %TYPE anchors a program variable to a column, specifically the column data type, in a table. The %ROWTYPE anchors a program composite variable to a table or view structure in the database catalog.

9. ☐ **True** ■ **False** You wrap a package to make the code source more readable.

The answer is **False**. You wrap a package to hide the code source to prevent disclosure of proprietary methods.

10. ☐ **True** ■ **False** Overloading a function or procedure requires that you change the names of variables.

The answer is **False**. You needn't worry about the names because they're irrelevant. You must change the positional order of the data types to have an overloaded signature.

11. What PRAGMA is restricted to packages only?

A. The PRAGMA EXCEPTION_INIT

B. The PRAGMA AUTONOMOUS_TRANSACTION

C. The SERIALLY_REUSABLE

D. All of the above

E. Only A and B

The answer is **C**. SERIALLY_REUSABLE is the only one restricted to packages.

12. You must do which of these steps when you convert a definer rights program to an invoker rights program?

   A. Replicate all tables, views, and sequences to invoker scheme

   B. Add the CURRENT_USER clause to all packages

   C. Grant EXECUTE privilege on all packages to invoker scheme

   D. All of the above

   E. Only B and C

   The answer is **D**. You must do all those steps, and you should do them in this order: add the CURRENT_USER clause to all packages, grant EXECUTE privileges, and replicate the tables, views, and sequences to the consuming scheme.

13. Which administrative views help you troubleshoot dependencies?

   A. The USER_OBJECTS view

   B. The USER_CODE view

   C. The USER_DEPENDENCIES view

   D. All of the above

   E. Only A and C

   The answer is **E**. The IUSER_OBJECTS and USER_DEPENDENCIES views are critical, but there is no USER_CODE view. The source code is in the USER_SOURCE view. You also have broader views, starting the ALL_ and DBA_ for each of these views.

14. Which permissions do external schemes require to work with definer rights packages?

   A. They require EXECUTION privileges

   B. They require SELECT privileges

   C. They require SELECT, INSERT, UPDATE, and DELETE privileges

   D. All of the above

   E. Only A and C

The answer is **E**. You need only the EXECUTE permission because packages inherit the natural privileges of the *definer*, which means they automatically have SELECT, INSERT, UPDATE, and DELETE privileges.

15. Which of these describes a bodiless package?

   A. A package without a header

   B. A package without shared cursors

   C. A package without a package body

   D. All of the above

   E. Only A and C

   The answer is **C**. You create a package specification when you want to create PL/SQL only variables or data types. A package body provides the implementation of functions and procedures. You don't need a package body when you opt not to include any functions or procedures in the specification. That makes it a bodiless package.

Chapter 9

Here are the questions and answers for Chapter 9:

1. ■ **True** □ **False**   You can sequence event triggers with the Oracle 11*g* release.

   The answer is **True**. You can now sequence triggers by using the FOLLOWS clause. You define the trigger you want to fire first without a FOLLOWS clause, and then make sure all other triggers have FOLLOWS clauses that point to the trigger they should follow.

2. ■ **True** □ **False**   You can define a DML trigger to run once per statement or row.

   The answer is **True**. You can define a data manipulation language trigger to run at the statement or row level. The statement level means you can perform one event per insert, update, or delete.

3. ☐ **True**   ■ **False**   You can put a variable declaration in trigger
bodies without using the `DECLARE` keyword.

The answer is **False**. You must use the `DECLARE` keyword in a trigger
body unless you're defining a compound trigger. An `ORA-04079`
compile time error results when you forget the `DECLARE` keyword.
The compound trigger raises a `PLS-00103` compile time error when
you attempt to include the `DECLARE` keyword.

4. ■ **True**   ☐ **False**   There is no default firing order for triggers
because they execute randomly.

The answer is **True**. There is no defined sequencing for database
triggers. They execute randomly except for this order: before
statement, before row, after row, after statement. You can create
order by using the `FOLLOWS` keyword.

5. ☐ **True**   ■ **False**   In Oracle 11*g*, the `FOLLOWS` keyword indicates
which trigger fires next.

The answer is **False**. You can use the keyword `FOLLOWS`, but not to
define the next trigger. It defines the preceding trigger. The trigger
without a `FOLLOWS` clause fires first, when all the others use the
`FOLLOWS` clause.

6. ☐ **True**   ■ **False**   DDL triggers fire when you change data.

The answer is **False**. You define data definition triggers to fire when
you change structure, not data.

7. ■ **True**   ☐ **False**   System event triggers can help DBAs perform
monitoring and maintenance tasks.

The answer is **True**. You can use system event triggers to support
DBA job functions that monitor or maintain the database.

8. ☐ **True**   ■ **False**   Hackers exploit triggers and hope they're
deployed in databases.

The answer is **False**. Your triggers are the first thing that a hacker
wants to disable because they may track the hacker's actions.

9. ■ **True** ☐ **False** Distributed transaction triggers can leverage instead of triggers when something interrupts network communication.

The answer is **True**. You can use distributed transaction triggers instead of triggers to store information in an alternative location when a network link fails to resolve.

10. ☐ **True** ■ **False** Triggers may use external functions and procedures, but large triggers are more cohesive and perform better.

The answer is **False**. You should always write small triggers, and they should be concise because they should run fast. Logic supporting triggers should be in external functions and procedures. These supporting functions and procedures should be wrapped to prevent inadvertent disclosure of your auditing rules.

11. What event(s) can a data manipulation trigger capture?

   A. INSERT

   B. UPDATE

   C. TRUNCATE

   D. All of the above

   E. Only A and B

The answer is **E**. the INSERT and UPDATE statements are data manipulation commands. The TRUNCATE removes data, resets the high water mark, and changes structure. That makes TRUNCATE a DDL command.

12. Which type of trigger lets you intercept and replace OLD or NEW column values?

   A. STATEMENT level triggers

   B. COMPOUND triggers

   C. ROW level triggers

   D. All of the above

   E. Only B and C

The answer is **E**. The COMPOUND and ROW level triggers let you capture and change the OLD and NEW column values. STATEMENT level triggers fire once per statement. They have no context to row events.

13. What is the correct order for data manipulation triggers?

   A. Before row, before statement, after statement, after row

   B. Before statement, before row, after row, after statement

   C. Before row, after row, before statement, after statement

   D. Before statement, after statement, before row, after row

   E. None of the above

The answer is **B**. The before statement comes first and after statement is last; in between those are the before row and after row level events. Naturally, the before precedes the after events.

14. Which triggers work with views?

   A. A data definition trigger

   B. A data manipulation trigger

   C. A compound trigger

   D. A system event trigger

   E. None of the above

The answer is **E**. The instead of trigger works with views, and it's missing from the list of choices.

15. What are two examples of attribute functions that you can use in DDL triggers?

   A. ORA_DICT_OBJ_OWNER

   B. ORA_DICT_OBJ_SCHEMA

   C. ORA_DICT_OBJ_TABLE

   D. All of the above

   E. Only A and C

The answer is **A**. The others are made up values, and, yes, you would have to look them up in the documentation or in Chapter 10 of *Oracle Database 11g PL/SQL Programming*.

Chapter 10

Here are the questions and answers for Chapter 10:

1. ■ **True** ☐ **False**   You can use and access an object type without an object body.

   The answer is **True**. You can define an object type without an object body. These are used like SQL record types. They've got some restrictions, however: You can't access them directly but you can deploy them inside a collection and access them with the TABLE function, like a pipelined table function result set. You also can't assign the results of a system reference cursor to a collection of object types, because the assignment must be through a constructor.

2. ☐ **True** ■ **False**   Outside of a collection, getter functions are the only way you can access internal attributes.

   The answer is **False**. You can also access internal attributes from inside a collection. You do this through the TABLE function in a SQL statement.

3. ☐ **True** ■ **False**   You can't create a constructor function that has the same signature as the default constructor for an object type.

   The answer is **False**. You can create a constructor function that has the same signature as the default constructor but don't need to as it is automatically provided when you define the object type. This behavior mirrors the automatic signature of tables defined by their data catalog definitions.

4. ☐ **True** ■ **False**   Oracle object types return a copy of themselves by using the same this keyword found in the Java programming language.

   The answer is **False**. You must use the SELF keyword, because that's how Oracle implemented it.

5. ■ **True**   □ **False**   You can create an instance of an object type in SQL.

The answer is **True**. You can create an instance of an object type by using the `TREAT` function in a SQL statement.

6. ■ **True**   □ **False**   You can call an object type's static functions in PL/SQL.

The answer is **True**. You can call an object type's static function in PL/SQL or in SQL. The only time you can't do it in SQL is when the parameter data type is a PL/SQL-only data type.

7. □ **True**   ■ **False**   You can call any object type's member functions or procedures from a SQL query.

The answer is **False**. You can't call any, or all, member functions from a SQL query because some of them may use a PL/SQL-only data type. You can't call a procedure from a query at all. You must only use functions and define the formal parameter list with SQL-only data types when you want to call it from SQL.

8. □ **True**   ■ **False**   You can compare objects by passing a copy of the other object as a call parameter to the `MAP` function.

The answer is **False**. You can't call the `MAP` function with any parameters because it takes none.

9. ■ **True**   □ **False**   You can't override a `MAP` or `ORDER` function of the parent class in subclasses.

The answer is **True**. You cannot override the `MAP` or `ORDER` function of a parent class, which makes a lot of sense if you think about it for a moment. A comparison that includes subtype attributes makes little sense, because the object types could compare different subtypes or the generalized type. In these cases, only the comparison of the similar, or generalized, attributes and behaviors makes sense.

10. ☐ **True**   ■ **False**   The TREAT function applies only to placing subclasses in memory.

The answer is **False**. You can call the TREAT function to put any standalone object type into your PGA memory. You need to designate whether you want to use a generalized or specialized object type only when the object type may be a subclass.

11. Object types defined inside PL/SQL block are hidden and called what?

A. Embedded

B. Transient

C. Standalone

D. All of the above

E. Only A and C

The answer is **B**. There are two types of deployment. One is inside PL/SQL blocks and the other is inside the catalog as some form of data type reference. You implement transient object types inside PL/SQL blocks. Persistent object types may be implemented in two ways. One way lets you embed them as formal parameter types or function return data types. The other lets you use them as column data types.

12. When you deploy object types in the database catalog, they may be called what?

A. Embedded

B. Transient

C. Persistent

D. All of the above

E. Only A and C

The answer is **E**. The transient deployments are for transient object types. Transient objects exist inside the body of PL/SQL blocks. *Persistent* deployment involves putting the object type in a column, a formal parameter, or a function return data type. A column implementation is a standalone object type. An implementation as a formal parameter or as the return type of a function is an *embedded* object type. Therefore, persistent, or a subtype of persistent, and embedded are the correct answers.

13. You can't define a MAP function to return which data type(s)?

    A. CHAR

    B. BOOLEAN

    C. DATE

    D. NUMBER

    E. None of the above

    The answer is **B**. The MAP function doesn't support a BOOLEAN data type. It does support the CHAR, DATE, NUMBER, and VARCHAR2 data types.

14. You can define which type of function and procedure in an object type?

    A. MEMBER

    B. CONSTRUCTOR

    C. COMPARISON

    D. All of the above

    E. Only A and B

    The answer is **E**. The correct keywords are COMPARE, CONSTRUCTOR, MAP, MEMBER, and STATIC.

15. What keyword lets you change the behavior of a parent class in a subclass?

    A. An OVERRIDE keyword

    B. A SUBTYPE keyword

    C. An `OVERRIDING` keyword

    D. All of the above

    E. Only A and C

The answer is **C.** There's no magic to this; `OVERRIDING` is simply the right keyword. The others aren't keywords.

Chapter 11

Here are the questions and answers for Chapter 11:

    1. ■ **True** ☐ **False**   You can use static or dynamic SQL statements with NDS.

The answer is **True.** You can create a static string and run it through NDS or a dynamic string and run it through NDS. A dynamic string is a bunch of characters or sets of characters that you glue together or a statement into which you bind values.

    2. ■ **True** ☐ **False**   You can glue strings into statement strings anywhere you like.

The answer is **True.** You can glue strings together into statements without restrictions. You should consider limiting this to table names and use the `DBMS_ASSERT` package to sanitize data types. This makes your program less susceptible to SQL injection attacks.

    3. ■ **True** ☐ **False**   You can use the `DBMS_ASSERT` package to sanitize inputs and eliminate SQL injection attacks.

The answer is **True.** You can and should, where possible, use the `DMBS_ASSERT` package to sanitize inputs and eliminate SQL injection attacks.

    4. ☐ **True** ■ **False**   You can use `SQL_NAME` to verify whether a string is a valid schema object in the database catalog.

The answer is **False**. You can't use SQL_NAME because it doesn't exist. You should use only QUALIFIED_SQL_NAME, SIMPLE_SQL_NAME, or SQL_OBJECT_NAME because they do check the catalog to validate a name.

5. ■ **True**   □ **False**   The terms *bind variable* and *placeholder* are synonymous.

The answer is **True**. The terms *bind variable* and *placeholder* are synonymous. Their use is frequent in multiple Oracle source documents.

6. □ **True**   ■ **False**   You don't have to provide call parameters in positional order to NDS statements.

The answer is **False**. You must provide all call parameters in the positional order in which the placeholders occur. While you can use named assignment with OCI8 library, positional syntax is more consistent across the Oracle product stack.

7. ■ **True**   □ **False**   The USING clause supports IN, IN OUT, and OUT modes of operation.

The answer is **True**. The USING clause support all three modes of operation, but with some restrictions. You must include the statement in an anonymous block if you want to pass IN OUT or OUT mode variables through the USING clause. However, you should note that outbound variables should be returned by the RETURNING INTO clause.

8. □ **True**   ■ **False**   It isn't a good practice to use the RETURNING INTO clause and avoid returning values through an IN OUT or OUT mode.

The answer is **False**. You should generally return outbound variables with the RETURNING INTO clause, not the USING clause. The alternative requires an anonymous block when you want to pass IN OUT or OUT mode variables through the USING clause.

9. ■ **True**   □ **False**   You can't have a colon in an NDS statement unless you define it as an ASCII character value.

The answer is **True**. The colon is a reserved character inside an NDS statement. If you need a colon to occur anywhere in a statement, you must include it as a CHR(58) value. The binding phase discovers colons before assigning local variables to placeholders. The execution of an NDS statement translates ASCII function calls to their string equivalents, which is why you can use a CHR(58) in an NDS statement. More or less, the same holds true from the DBMS_SQL package. The only difference is that the conversion occurs in the PARSE phase when you're using the DBMS_SQL package.

10. ☐ **True** ■ **False** You can assign an NDS statement output to a reference cursor and return the reference cursor into an object type.

The answer is **False**. You can't assign an NDS statement output to a reference cursor, and you can't assign the reference cursor to an object type. You must assign it to a PL/SQL record type or collection of a PL/SQL record type. The structure of the record type must match the list of returned variables from the cursor.

11. What types of statements are supported by NDS?

   A. DDL statements without binding

   B. DDL statements with object name binding

   C. DML statements with object name binding

   D. All of the above

   E. Only A and C

The answer is **A**. There are no supported object name bindings for DDL or DML statements. You must glue table names into the string, preferably with the DBMS_ASSET package functions.

12. What does the : (colon) in front of a name indicate inside an NDS statement?

   A. The colon signifies a session-level variable

   B. The colon represents a formal parameter of the statement

   C. The colon represents a placeholder variable

D. All of the above

E. Only B and C

The answer is **E**. Whether we call it a bind variable, formal parameter, or placeholder is insignificant because the terms are synonymous.

13. Which function in the DBMS_ASSERT package validates a table name?

A. The QUALIFIED_SQL_NAME function

B. The SIMPLE_SQL_NAME function

C. The SQL_OBJECT_NAME function

D. All of the above

E. Only A and C

The answer is **D**. All of these functions verify a table name before returning value.

14. An NDS statement can return a system reference cursor into which data type(s)?

A. A SQL object type

B. A PL/SQL record type

C. A PL/SQL collection of an object type

D. All of the above

E. Only A and C

The answer is **B**. You can return it into a record type or through a bulk operation into a collection of a record type. You can't use an object type or collection of an object type as a target of assignment because they require a constructor. For now, no syntax can be used to make the assignment from the system reference cursor into an object type constructor.

15. You can get an outbound parameter from an NDS statement by doing which of the following?

A. Define an IN OUT mode variable in the USING clause for a SQL statement.

B. Define an IN OUT mode variable in the USING clause for a PL/SQL block.

C. Define an outbound variable in the RETURNING INTO clause.

D. All of the above

E. Only B and C

The answer is **E**. You can use the USING clause for an anonymous PL/SQL block. You should use the RETURNING INTO clause routinely. That clause supports SQL and PL/SQL statements.

Chapter 12

Here are the questions and answers for Chapter 12:

1. ■ **True** ☐ **False** You can import comma-separated value files directly into Oracle tables.

The answer is **True**. You can import comma-separated value files directly into Oracle through Oracle external tables.

2. ☐ **True** ■ **False** You can import dates without regard to default date formats with TSV files.

The answer is **False**. You can't import dates when they're not in one of Oracle's default format masks without using a conversion filter. You typically use conversion filters in position-specific files.

3. ☐ **True** ■ **False** You can use CSV external files when you want to use overriding date format masks.

The answer is **False**. You can't use CSV external files when you want to use overriding date formats. You must use position specific external files because you can then use date format masks.

4. ■ True   □ False   You can use position-specific external files when you import dates in any format with a format mask.

The answer is **True**. You can and must use a position-specific external file when you import nonconforming date formats.

5. ■ True   □ False   You can't filter data during the load with the LIKE comparison operator.

The answer is **True**. You can't use the LIKE operator. You would have to use a series of comparisons with the logical AND operator.

6. □ True   ■ False   Header rows must be stripped before they're made available to an external table, because you can't ignore the header line when you load the data.

The answer is **False**. You can simply provide the SKIP 1 syntax when you define the external table. If headers take more than one line, you can simply change the integer to match the number of lines requires.

7. □ True   ■ False   There's no way to suppress a query from raising a missing file error, KUP-04040.

The answer is **False**. You can suppress it by wrapping it in a function, as shown in Chapter 12.

8. ■ True   □ False   Converting XML files to CSV files is possible with XSLT.

The answer is **True**. You can convert XML files to CSV files. It is a convenient approach unless you're importing to XML_TYPE columns. Unfortunately, we didn't have space to get to that.

9. ■ True   □ False   It is important to clean up source files after loading the data to the database.

The answer is **True**. You can and should clean up files as soon as you've read and processed the contents of the files. Java libraries let you accomplish that task, as shown in Chapter 12.

10. ☐ **True**　■ **False**　Tab-delimited files are the most portable because tabs are consistent across operating systems.

    The answer is **False**. You can use tab-delimited or separated values, but they're the least portable. It's a small step to opt for positional or comma-delimited data sets, but it's one that we recommend over tab-delimited files.

11. Which of the following access parameter(s) lets you filter data before loading it?

    A. `LOAD WHEN (column = 'string')`

    B. `LOAD WHEN (column IN 'string')`

    C. `LOAD WHEN (column = 'string' AND column = 'string')`

    D. All of the above

    E. Only A and C

    The answer is **E**. Equality comparisons and logical operators are supported by SQL*Loader.

12. Which of the following access parameters work with CSV or TSV files?

    A. The `TERMINATED BY` clause

    B. The `OPTIONALLY ENCLOSED BY` clause

    C. The `MISSING FIELD`

    D. All of the above

    E. Only A and B

    The answer is **D**. All may apply to the values separated by commas or tabs.

13. Which of the following access parameters work with a position-specific file?

    A. The `TERMINATED BY` clause

    B. The `MISSING FIELD` clause

C. The OPTIONALLY ENCLOSED BY clause

D. All of the above

E. Only A and C

The answer is **B**. Termination and enclosure don't matter in position-specific files; only the physical position of the characters is important.

14. Which of the following is the most generic value for a tab that works in Oracle?

    A. 'OX09'

    B. 'OX0A'

    C. OX'09'

    D. All of the above

    E. Only A and C

    The answer is **C**. It represents the hexadecimal value for a tab, known as ASCII 9.

15. Which of the following would work in a CSV?

    A. OPTIONALLY ENCLOSED BY "(" AND ")"

    B. OPTIONALLY ENCLOSED BY "'"

    C. OPTIONALLY ENCLOSED BY '(' AND ')'

    D. All of the above

    E. Only A and C

    The answer is **D**. The double quotes can delimit a special character that is used before and after a field, or you can use single quotes. The logical AND operator lets you use two different special characters, which have no physical ordering properties. This means you could enclose a name like this: (Samuel) or)Joseph(.

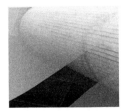

Index

C

D

F

GET YOUR FREE SUBSCRIPTION
TO *ORACLE MAGAZINE*

Oracle Magazine is essential gear for today's information technology professionals. Stay informed and increase your productivity with every issue of *Oracle Magazine*. Inside each free bimonthly issue you'll get:

- Up-to-date information on Oracle Database, Oracle Application Server, Web development, enterprise grid computing, database technology, and business trends
- Third-party news and announcements
- Technical articles on Oracle and partner products, technologies, and operating environments
- Development and administration tips
- Real-world customer stories

If there are other Oracle users at your location who would like to receive their own subscription to *Oracle Magazine*, please photocopy this form and pass it along.

Three easy ways to subscribe:

① Web
Visit our Web site at **oracle.com/oraclemagazine**
You'll find a subscription form there, plus much more

② Fax
Complete the questionnaire on the back of this card and fax the questionnaire side only to **+1.847.763.9638**

③ Mail
Complete the questionnaire on the back of this card and mail it to **P.O. Box 1263, Skokie, IL 60076-8263**

ORACLE®

Want your own FREE subscription?

To receive a free subscription to *Oracle Magazine*, you must fill out the entire card, sign it, and date it (incomplete cards cannot be processed or acknowledged). You can also fax your application to +1.847.763.9638. **Or subscribe at our Web site at oracle.com/oraclemagazine**

○ **Yes, please send me a FREE subscription** *Oracle Magazine*. ○ No.

○ From time to time, Oracle Publishing allows our partners exclusive access to our e-mail addresses for special promotions and announcements. To be included in this program, please check this circle. If you do not wish to be included, you will only receive notices about your subscription via e-mail.

○ Oracle Publishing allows sharing of our postal mailing list with selected third parties. If you prefer your mailing address not to be included in this program, please check this circle.

If at any time you would like to be removed from either mailing list, please contact Customer Service at +1.847.763.9635 or send an e-mail to oracle@halldata.com. If you opt in to the sharing of information, Oracle may also provide you with e-mail related to Oracle products, services, and events. If you want to completely unsubscribe from any e-mail communication from Oracle, please send an e-mail to: unsubscribe@oracle-mail.com with the following in the subject line: REMOVE [your e-mail address]. For complete information on Oracle Publishing's privacy practices, please visit oracle.com/html/privacy/html

X _____ _____
signature (required)   date

name   title

company   e-mail address

street/p.o. box

city/state/zip or postal code   telephone

country   fax

Would you like to receive your free subscription in digital format instead of print if it becomes available? ○ Yes ○ No

---

YOU MUST ANSWER ALL 10 QUESTIONS BELOW.

① WHAT IS THE PRIMARY BUSINESS ACTIVITY OF YOUR FIRM AT THIS LOCATION? (check one only)

- ☐ 01 Aerospace and Defense Manufacturing
- ☐ 02 Application Service Provider
- ☐ 03 Automotive Manufacturing
- ☐ 04 Chemicals
- ☐ 05 Media and Entertainment
- ☐ 06 Construction/Engineering
- ☐ 07 Consumer Sector/Consumer Packaged Goods
- ☐ 08 Education
- ☐ 09 Financial Services/Insurance
- ☐ 10 Health Care
- ☐ 11 High Technology Manufacturing, OEM
- ☐ 12 Industrial Manufacturing
- ☐ 13 Independent Software Vendor
- ☐ 14 Life Sciences (biotech, pharmaceuticals)
- ☐ 15 Natural Resources
- ☐ 16 Oil and Gas
- ☐ 17 Professional Services
- ☐ 18 Public Sector (government)
- ☐ 19 Research
- ☐ 20 Retail/Wholesale/Distribution
- ☐ 21 Systems Integrator, VAR/VAD
- ☐ 22 Telecommunications
- ☐ 23 Travel and Transportation
- ☐ 24 Utilities (electric, gas, sanitation, water)
- ☐ 98 Other Business and Services _____

② WHICH OF THE FOLLOWING BEST DESCRIBES YOUR PRIMARY JOB FUNCTION? (check one only)

CORPORATE MANAGEMENT/STAFF
- ☐ 01 Executive Management (President, Chair, CEO, CFO, Owner, Partner, Principal)
- ☐ 02 Finance/Administrative Management (VP/Director/ Manager/Controller, Purchasing, Administration)
- ☐ 03 Sales/Marketing Management (VP/Director/Manager)
- ☐ 04 Computer Systems/Operations Management (CIO/VP/Director/Manager MIS/IS/IT, Ops)

IS/IT STAFF
- ☐ 05 Application Development/Programming Management
- ☐ 06 Application Development/Programming Staff
- ☐ 07 Consulting
- ☐ 08 DBA/Systems Administrator
- ☐ 09 Education/Training
- ☐ 10 Technical Support Director/Manager
- ☐ 11 Other Technical Management/Staff
- ☐ 98 Other

③ WHAT IS YOUR CURRENT PRIMARY OPERATING PLATFORM (check all that apply)

- ☐ 01 Digital Equipment Corp UNIX/VAX/VMS
- ☐ 02 HP UNIX
- ☐ 03 IBM AIX
- ☐ 04 IBM UNIX
- ☐ 05 Linux (Red Hat)
- ☐ 06 Linux (SUSE)
- ☐ 07 Linux (Oracle Enterprise)
- ☐ 08 Linux (other)
- ☐ 09 Macintosh
- ☐ 10 MVS
- ☐ 11 Netware
- ☐ 12 Network Computing
- ☐ 13 SCO UNIX
- ☐ 14 Sun Solaris/SunOS
- ☐ 15 Windows
- ☐ 16 Other UNIX
- ☐ 98 Other
- 99 ☐ None of the Above

④ DO YOU EVALUATE, SPECIFY, RECOMMEND, OR AUTHORIZE THE PURCHASE OF ANY OF THE FOLLOWING? (check all that apply)

- ☐ 01 Hardware
- ☐ 02 Business Applications (ERP, CRM, etc.)
- ☐ 03 Application Development Tools
- ☐ 04 Database Products
- ☐ 05 Internet or Intranet Products
- ☐ 06 Other Software
- ☐ 07 Middleware Products
- 99 ☐ None of the Above

⑤ IN YOUR JOB, DO YOU USE OR PLAN TO PURCHASE ANY OF THE FOLLOWING PRODUCTS? (check all that apply)

SOFTWARE
- ☐ 01 CAD/CAE/CAM
- ☐ 02 Collaboration Software
- ☐ 03 Communications
- ☐ 04 Database Management
- ☐ 05 File Management
- ☐ 06 Finance
- ☐ 07 Java
- ☐ 08 Multimedia Authoring
- ☐ 09 Networking
- ☐ 10 Programming
- ☐ 11 Project Management
- ☐ 12 Scientific and Engineering
- ☐ 13 Systems Management
- ☐ 14 Workflow

HARDWARE
- ☐ 15 Macintosh
- ☐ 16 Mainframe
- ☐ 17 Massively Parallel Processing

- ☐ 18 Minicomputer
- ☐ 19 Intel x86(32)
- ☐ 20 Intel x86(64)
- ☐ 21 Network Computer
- ☐ 22 Symmetric Multiprocessing
- ☐ 23 Workstation Services

SERVICES
- ☐ 24 Consulting
- ☐ 25 Education/Training
- ☐ 26 Maintenance
- ☐ 27 Online Database
- ☐ 28 Support
- ☐ 29 Technology-Based Training
- ☐ 30 Other
- 99 ☐ None of the Above

⑥ WHAT IS YOUR COMPANY'S SIZE? (check one only)

- ☐ 01 More than 25,000 Employees
- ☐ 02 10,001 to 25,000 Employees
- ☐ 03 5,001 to 10,000 Employees
- ☐ 04 1,001 to 5,000 Employees
- ☐ 05 101 to 1,000 Employees
- ☐ 06 Fewer than 100 Employees

⑦ DURING THE NEXT 12 MONTHS, HOW MUCH DO YOU ANTICIPATE YOUR ORGANIZATION WILL SPEND ON COMPUTER HARDWARE, SOFTWARE, PERIPHERALS, AND SERVICES FOR YOUR LOCATION? (check one only)

- ☐ 01 Less than $10,000
- ☐ 02 $10,000 to $49,999
- ☐ 03 $50,000 to $99,999
- ☐ 04 $100,000 to $499,999
- ☐ 05 $500,000 to $999,999
- ☐ 06 $1,000,000 and Over

⑧ WHAT IS YOUR COMPANY'S YEARLY SALES REVENUE? (check one only)

- ☐ 01 $500, 000, 000 and above
- ☐ 02 $100, 000, 000 to $500, 000, 000
- ☐ 03 $50, 000, 000 to $100, 000, 000
- ☐ 04 $5, 000, 000 to $50, 000, 000
- ☐ 05 $1, 000, 000 to $5, 000, 000

⑨ WHAT LANGUAGES AND FRAMEWORKS DO YOU USE? (check all that apply)

- ☐ 01 Ajax
- ☐ 02 C
- ☐ 03 C++
- ☐ 04 C#
- ☐ 13 Python
- ☐ 14 Ruby/Rails
- ☐ 15 Spring
- ☐ 16 Struts
- ☐ 05 Hibernate
- ☐ 06 J++/J#
- ☐ 07 Java
- ☐ 08 JSP
- ☐ 09 .NET
- ☐ 10 Perl
- ☐ 11 PHP
- ☐ 12 PL/SQL
- ☐ 17 SQL
- ☐ 18 Visual Basic
- ☐ 98 Other

⑩ WHAT ORACLE PRODUCTS ARE IN USE AT YOUR SITE? (check all that apply)

ORACLE DATABASE
- ☐ 01 Oracle Database 11g
- ☐ 02 Oracle Database 10g
- ☐ 03 Oracle9i Database
- ☐ 04 Oracle Embedded Database (Oracle Lite, Times Ten, Berkeley DB)
- ☐ 05 Other Oracle Database Release

ORACLE FUSION MIDDLEWARE
- ☐ 06 Oracle Application Server
- ☐ 07 Oracle Portal
- ☐ 08 Oracle Enterprise Manager
- ☐ 09 Oracle BPEL Process Manager
- ☐ 10 Oracle Identity Management
- ☐ 11 Oracle SOA Suite
- ☐ 12 Oracle Data Hubs

ORACLE DEVELOPMENT TOOLS
- ☐ 13 Oracle JDeveloper
- ☐ 14 Oracle Forms
- ☐ 15 Oracle Reports
- ☐ 16 Oracle Designer
- ☐ 17 Oracle Discoverer
- ☐ 18 Oracle BI Beans
- ☐ 19 Oracle Warehouse Builder
- ☐ 20 Oracle WebCenter
- ☐ 21 Oracle Application Express

ORACLE APPLICATIONS
- ☐ 22 Oracle E-Business Suite
- ☐ 23 PeopleSoft Enterprise
- ☐ 24 JD Edwards EnterpriseOne
- ☐ 25 JD Edwards World
- ☐ 26 Oracle Fusion
- ☐ 27 Hyperion
- ☐ 28 Siebel CRM

ORACLE SERVICES
- ☐ 28 Oracle E-Business Suite On Demand
- ☐ 29 Oracle Technology On Demand
- ☐ 30 Siebel CRM On Demand
- ☐ 31 Oracle Consulting
- ☐ 32 Oracle Education
- ☐ 33 Oracle Support
- ☐ 98 Other
- 99 ☐ None of the Above